The Power of the Space Club

Why do nation-states choose to develop national space programs? How can they justify national efforts to acquire capabilities by arguing for membership of the space club? This book presents a unique and insightful perspective on the factors that drive states to indigenously develop world-class space technology in the past, present, and future of space exploration and technological development in world politics. Based on a rich and detailed analysis of a range of space programs in states that are not usually at the focus of world politics and its research, the author shows that joining the space club is a legitimate and rational decision. A country that sees itself as a power deserving of a seat at the table of world governance is expected to race for space. This book provides a different way of looking at international relations through a relatively understudied area of policy – the space club.

Deganit Paikowsky holds a Ph.D. in political science from Tel Aviv University. She is a senior researcher at the Yuval Neeman Workshop for Science, Technology and Security at Tel Aviv University as well as a non-resident scholar at the George Washington University Space Policy Institute.

The Power of the Space Club

Deganit Paikowsky
Tel Aviv University

CAMBRIDGE
UNIVERSITY PRESS

Shaftesbury Road, Cambridge CB2 8EA, United Kingdom

One Liberty Plaza, 20th Floor, New York, NY 10006, USA

477 Williamstown Road, Port Melbourne, VIC 3207, Australia

314–321, 3rd Floor, Plot 3, Splendor Forum, Jasola District Centre, New Delhi – 110025, India

103 Penang Road, #05-06/07, Visioncrest Commercial, Singapore 238467

Cambridge University Press is part of Cambridge University Press & Assessment, a department of the University of Cambridge.

We share the University's mission to contribute to society through the pursuit of education, learning and research at the highest international levels of excellence.

www.cambridge.org
Information on this title: www.cambridge.org/9781316646243

DOI: 10.1017/9781108159883

© Deganit Paikowsky 2017

This publication is in copyright. Subject to statutory exception and to the provisions of relevant collective licensing agreements, no reproduction of any part may take place without the written permission of Cambridge University Press & Assessment.

First published 2017
First paperback edition 2023

A catalogue record for this publication is available from the British Library

ISBN   978-1-107-19449-6   Hardback
ISBN   978-1-316-64624-3   Paperback

Cambridge University Press & Assessment has no responsibility for the persistence or accuracy of URLs for external or third-party internet websites referred to in this publication and does not guarantee that any content on such websites is, or will remain, accurate or appropriate.

The Power of the Space Club

Deganit Paikowsky
Tel Aviv University

CAMBRIDGE
UNIVERSITY PRESS

Shaftesbury Road, Cambridge CB2 8EA, United Kingdom

One Liberty Plaza, 20th Floor, New York, NY 10006, USA

477 Williamstown Road, Port Melbourne, VIC 3207, Australia

314–321, 3rd Floor, Plot 3, Splendor Forum, Jasola District Centre, New Delhi – 110025, India

103 Penang Road, #05–06/07, Visioncrest Commercial, Singapore 238467

Cambridge University Press is part of Cambridge University Press & Assessment, a department of the University of Cambridge.

We share the University's mission to contribute to society through the pursuit of education, learning and research at the highest international levels of excellence.

www.cambridge.org
Information on this title: www.cambridge.org/9781316646243

DOI: 10.1017/9781108159883

© Deganit Paikowsky 2017

This publication is in copyright. Subject to statutory exception and to the provisions of relevant collective licensing agreements, no reproduction of any part may take place without the written permission of Cambridge University Press & Assessment.

First published 2017
First paperback edition 2023

A catalogue record for this publication is available from the British Library

ISBN 978-1-107-19449-6 Hardback
ISBN 978-1-316-64624-3 Paperback

Cambridge University Press & Assessment has no responsibility for the persistence or accuracy of URLs for external or third-party internet websites referred to in this publication and does not guarantee that any content on such websites is, or will remain, accurate or appropriate.

To my grandparents, Holocaust survivors who rebuilt their lives in Israel and were a source of inspiration for their will to overcome, live, and do, precisely because it is hard; and to my sons, the shining stars of my life.

I sent the club a wire stating, PLEASE ACCEPT MY RESIGNATION. I DON'T WANT TO BELONG TO ANY CLUB THAT WILL ACCEPT ME AS A MEMBER.

Groucho Marx, 1959

Contents

List of figures		*page* viii
List of tables		ix
Acknowledgments		x
1	Introduction	1
2	Nation-State Clubs in World Politics	28
3	The Evolution of the Space Club	48
4	A Multilateral Race for Space Club Membership	74
5	France and Britain	92
6	Canada and Australia	115
7	India and Israel	145
8	The Space Club in the Post–Cold War Era	178
9	Conclusions and Future Directions	210
	Bibliography	230
	Index	248

Figures

1.1.	The Space Club Pyramid in the Cold War	*page* 23
1.2.	The Space Club Pyramid in the Post–Cold War Period	24
1.3.	A Potential Future Structure of the Space Club Pyramid	24
2.1.	The Life Cycle of Clubs	41

Tables

1.1	Nuclear Programs and Space Programs	*page* 12
2.1	Types of Clubs and Their Characteristics	35
2.2	Comparison of International Regimes, Security Communities, and Nation-State Clubs	39
3.1	US Investment of Resources in Military and Civilian Activity in Space, 1959–1969	62
5.1	Comparison of France and Great Britain, Selected Parameters	93
6.1	Comparison of Canada and Australia, Selected Parameters	116
7.1	Comparison of India and Israel, Selected Parameters	146

Acknowledgments

My greatest debt in writing this book is to Isaac Ben Israel and Yossi Shain, who patiently guided me through the "waters" of conducting this research. Their invaluable help, dedication, and support got me through this and made it as enjoyable and painless as possible.

I am very grateful to the Space Policy Institute at George Washington University, to the History of Space Department at the National Air and Space Museum of the Smithsonian Institution, and to their staff members for their generous hospitality and cooperation. The time I spent in each of them, at different stages of my research, provided a stimulating environment and invaluable friendships. John Logsdon has been an endless source of knowledge and support, providing useful and thoughtful feedback. Scott Pace, Michael Neufeld, David DeVorkin, Valerie Neal, and Monique Laney were always good partners for discussion and consultation. Special thanks to Roger Launius for playing devil's advocate; no doubt, this allowed me to provide a better product. I am also grateful to the heads of the Leonard Davis Institute of International Relations at the Hebrew University, Dan Miodownik and Piki Ish-Shalom, for awarding me a fellowship and for their friendship. The time I spent there was utilized to expand, refine, and finalize the manuscript. I also want to express my gratitude to Israel's Ministry of Science and Technology for its support for my research in its early stages, through the Eshkol Doctoral Scholarship.

The NASA Headquarters History Office as well as the NASA Library and their dedicated staffs opened their doors and allowed me to search through invaluable, seemingly endless collections. Jane Odom, Richard Spencer, Colin Fries, and John Hargenrader enthusiastically shared their knowledge in locating documents and records.

In Israel, Chaim Eshed and his dedicated staff at the Israeli Ministry of Defense made innumerable efforts to assist in any possible way. Zvi Kaplan and his staff at the Israel Space Agency provided access to records and collections. Israel Aerospace Industries Ltd. allowed me to search for treasures in their archives.

Acknowledgments

My colleagues and friends deserve my gratitude and appreciation for their thoughtful comments, attention, and encouragement, especially Ethel Solingen, who was a source of inspiration as well as a role model; Azar Gat and Stephen Biddle for their good advice and encouragement, ensuring that I didn't give up; Glen Asner, who was always eager to assist in any possible way; Peter Hays for his thoughtful comments and attention; Dima Adamsky, Daniel Barok, Ofer Lapid, Keren Shachar, Deane Peter-Baker, Daniel Levine, Ehud Eiran, Cameron Brown, Elisabetta Brighi, Sergio Catignani, Shain Smith, Brett Biddington, Emanuel Adler, Barry Posen, Ariel (Eli) Levite, Galia Peres Bar-Nathan, Patrick Jackson, Larry Martinez, Yael Shomer, Or Honig, Gil Baram, and Ram Levi. All the interviewees and interlocutors, who patiently answered my questions, deserve my gratefulness. I am also deeply appreciative to Marsha Brown who did so much more than copyediting.

This is also an opportunity to sincerely thank those who helped along the way: The Yuval Neeman Workshop for Science, Technology and Security at Tel Aviv University for being a professional home for so many years; the Goldberg Family for their generosity in bringing me to Canada; Sheldon Lerman, whose knowledge and curiosity were of great help; Guy Ben Ari and Ayala Peled for providing me a home away from home; and the Piver family for their love and attention while I was in D.C.

I am deeply grateful to the editor John Haslam and to the staff of Cambridge University Press for their interest and faith in this project, as well as their guidance at all stages of the work. I appreciate the anonymous reviewers, whose thoughtful and considerate comments and suggestions were very helpful.

Finally, this mission would not have come to a happy end without the love and endless support of my family. My parents, Zeev and Yael Paikowsky, who taught me the value of knowledge, encouraged me to excel, and did everything in their power to allow me the needed time to write; my brother Nir, who was a source of encouragement; and Shuly and Eitan Haberman, with whom I had endless talks.

Finally, all of those mentioned here deserve my appreciation and gratitude, but above all, I owe the most to Uri, who was a constant source of advice, emotional support, and motivation. Without you, this would never have come to an end.

Deganit
Tel Aviv, 2017

1 Introduction

> The exploration of space will go ahead, whether we join in it or not, and it is one of the great adventures of all time, and no nation which expects to be the leader of other nations can expect to stay behind in the race for space.
>
> John F. Kennedy, September 12, 1962

In different eras in history, certain qualities or areas of expertise are identified as indicators of power and symbols of high standing. Usually, acquiring and developing these qualities require massive investments of resources and large-scale national efforts. Despite the difficulties, risks, and high costs, or because of them, nations that aspire to power and high standing often invest valuable resources and efforts in acquiring expertise in these areas. The nations that have succeeded in this task are recognized by many as an elite group – a club. In line with this reality, decision-makers and state officials often choose to emphasize the political aspect of their country's accomplishments and justify national efforts to acquire such qualities by arguing for membership in the club.

Historically, we can identify several nation-state clubs. At the end of the nineteenth century and into the early twentieth century, acquisition of battleships was an indicator of power and high standing. Each country that had battleships, or dreadnoughts (as they were later referred to), was considered a world power, and as a group, they were perceived as a superior club. After World War I, the dreadnought club declined. Total mechanization of air and ground warfare became an indicator of power and a symbol of high standing. The introduction of nuclear weapons at the end of World War II changed the rules of the game again. As of the 1950s, the group of countries that possessed nuclear weapons was recognized as the nuclear club. In the 1960s, the status of this superior group was somewhat formalized with the signing of the Non-Proliferation Treaty (NPT), by which means the international community formally accepted the N5, i.e. the five nuclear nations, as a legitimate, superior, and elite group – the nuclear club. At the same time, the countries reaching outer space were also recognized as a superior and exclusive group under the axiom developed in the Cold War space race: "Control of space means control of the world."[1]

This reality raises a number of questions: What are nation-state clubs? What role do they play in world politics? What is their life cycle? And what distinguishes a nation-state club from other models organizing the international system? Journalistic and historiography references to a "club" of nation-states when discussing expertise in areas of space technology, nuclear weapons, and other fields are frequent. Despite that, for the most part, the concept of such a "club" has been neglected or discounted by the vast majority of contemporary international relations (IR) scholars. IR scholars have not developed a comprehensive analytical or theoretical foundation to identify the behavioral and theoretical implications of states' activities in clubs. This book is designed to respond to this neglect by providing a systematic overview of the role of nation-state clubs in world politics. It explores the aforementioned questions using the case study of the space club.

This book focuses on the space club and on the national logic to join it, because space affects our terrestrial life far more than we often realize. A large diversity of applications and services are useful and sometimes even crucial for daily military, civil, and commercial functioning on Earth. The world space industry is an evolving international business. Space capability helps states to develop areas of commercial expertise, which diversifies their economies and enhances their global competitiveness.[2] Advanced space technologies, especially when used for spreading information, are believed to be the means for a quick transition from a traditional undeveloped society to an industrial and post-industrial nation.[3] Communication satellites today are like the railroads of the nineteenth century, enabling desolate parts of a country to be settled and connecting them with the center of the country.[4] Data that come from space or pass through space enable us to run a global and modern economy. We communicate with each other from every point on Earth, use financial systems throughout the world, and continuously access news from around the world via communications satellites.

---

[1] Johnson, Lyndon B., Summary Statement, Hearings of the Preparedness Subcommittee, Senate Armed Services Committee, Senate Inquiry on Missiles, January 8, 1958.
[2] Pace, S., "Emerging Challenges: National Security Requirements and Economic/Commercial Interests," in D. Johnson and E. Levite, (eds.), *Toward Fusion of Air and Space: Surveying Developments and Assessing Choices for Small and Middle Powers.* (Washington, DC: RAND & Fisher Institute, 2003), 48.
[3] Mistry, D.," The Geo-Strategic Implications of India's Space Program," *Asian Survey*, 41:6, (2001), 1034.
[4] Pacey, A., *Technology in World Civilization.* (Cambridge, MA: MIT Press, 1990), 141.

Weather forecasts come from satellite imagery; sea, air, and ground transportation are based on satellite navigation (global positioning). We study and learn about the Earth's geology and geography, maintain the environment, observe what is happening anywhere on Earth for various civilian purposes, and react to natural disasters with the aid of observation satellites.

Space technology and applications are also used extensively for national security and defense missions during war and peace. In fact, the very first uses of space were for intelligence purposes. Remote sensing satellites fulfill military and security intelligence requirements, without violating the sovereignty of any rival nation and without risk to human life. To a certain degree, during the Cold War, military intelligence satellites were viewed as a stabilizing force, preventing direct confrontation between the two powers.[5] In the last few decades, information gathered from and transferred through space is used extensively for tracking and pinpointing targets on earth; it is used for guidance and positioning, as well as for communications to forces engaged in combat and to weapons systems. In fact, space technology is considered one of the central factors of modern warfare that is based on information and knowledge superiority, better known as the Revolution in Military Affairs (RMA).[6]

In this context, exploring the origins and features of the space club is important in order to understand its role in world politics. The space club

---

[5] Gaddis, J. L., *The Long Peace: Inquiries into the History of the Cold War*, (New York, NY: Oxford University Press, 1987); Day, D. A., Logsdon, J. M., and Latell, B., *Eye In the Sky: The History of the CORONA Spy Satellites*, (Washington, DC: Smithsonian Institution Press, 1998).

[6] RMA is a concept of warfare that was developed in the 1980s and early 1990s in the United States. It is based on four main components: information warfare, dominant maneuver, precision strike (precise and guided attack capability), and space control. RMA aims at synchronizing all four components into one "System of Systems." Full synchronization can be obtained by using space technologies such as GPS satellites, surveillance and reconnaissance satellites, and communications satellites. Toffler, A., and Toffler, H., *War and Anti-War: Survival at the Dawn of the 21st Century*. (Boston, MA: Little, Brown, 1993); Ben Israel, I., "The Revolution in Military Affairs in the War in Iraq," in S. Feldman and M. Grundman, (eds.), *After the War in Iraq*. (Tel Aviv, Israel: Jaffe Center for Strategic Studies, Tel Aviv University Press, 2004), 55–74; Tilford, E. H., *The Revolution in Military Affairs: Prospects and Cautions*, (Carlisle, PA: Strategic Studies Institute, US Army War College, 1995); Cohen, E., "A Revolution in Warfare," *Foreign Affairs*, 75:2 (March/April 1996), 37–54; Gray, C., "Space Power and the Revolution in Military Affairs: A Glass Half Full?," *Aerospace Power Journal*, 13:3 (Fall 1999) 23–38; Nye, J., and Owens, W., "America's Information Edge," *Foreign Affairs*, 75:2 (March/April 1996), 20–36; Owens, W., "The Once and Future Revolution in Military Affairs," *Joint Force Quarterly*, 31:3, (Summer 2002), 55–61; Paikowsky, D., *The Impact of Space Technologies on Warfare and Force Build-Up in the USA Military Forces and the IDF*, M.A. thesis, Tel Aviv University, 2005.

is not a formal international organization. Nevertheless, despite the absence of a formal organization, it has an actual and significant role in world politics. The first evidence that the expression "space club" was used in the context of states' competition over space achievements can be traced back to the early 1960s. Surprisingly, one of the earliest occasions, if not the first one, referred to the United States' first man in space as an act of joining the "space club": "The United States now can claim membership in the space club, with the 11-minute flight of Alan B. Shepard paving the way for many more ventures beyond the limits of earth."[7] This reference to a club is a bit peculiar; a club is a social entity, therefore, at a minimum, it must consist of two members. This statement refers to the space club of that time as being composed of only one member, the Soviet Union.

From the early days of the race to space, state officials referred to a space club when discussing international activity in space technology and exploration. For example, in 1965, Arnold Frutkin, the Assistant Administrator for International Affairs at NASA, used the term "club" in his book *International Cooperation in Space*. In referring to an initiative to use India's sounding-rocket range for international cooperation, he wrote, "What began as a bilateral effort, with relatively narrow technical objectives, has grown through a process of inexorable technical and political appeal to the point where major nations, including the Soviet Union, find it important to join in ... Important was the fact that an unequivocal set of requirements for 'joining the club' was established."[8]

Observing current space activity shows that the space club is significant to world politics as well as to space politics. In December 2013, India successfully launched the Mangalyaan Mars Mission, which entered Mars' orbit in late September 2014. Several days later, the *New York Times* published a cartoon showing a traditionally dressed Indian man with a cow knocking at the door of the "Elite Space Club." Inside, white male members of the club are reading a newspaper with a headline about India's Mars mission and seem to be surprised and unhappy. Many readers felt that the cartoon was offensive and did not rightly reflect India's role in current space exploration. A few days later, the *New York Times* published an apology in a Facebook post, explaining that the

---

[7] "Space Problems Are Many," *Quebec Chronicle Telegraph*, May 8, 1961, 4.
[8] Frutkin served as NASA's Director of International Programs from its inception. In 1963, he became Assistant Administrator for International Affairs. He retired in 1979. During his career, he was involved in almost every negotiation process of important international space agreements. Arnold W. Frutkin, Biographical File, NASA Historical Reference Collection, NASA History Office, NASA Headquarters, Washington, DC; and Frutkin, A., *International Cooperation in Space*, (Englewood Cliffs, NJ: Prentice-Hall, 1965), 35, 62–63.

cartoonist's intention "was to highlight how space exploration is no longer the exclusive domain of rich, Western countries."[9] This cartoon highlights the significance of the "space club" in world politics, and its worldwide acknowledgment as a concrete entity. This reality raises several questions, which this book aims to answer. On the international level, in the absence of a formal organization called "space club," what is the space club, how did it develop, and how did it change over time? On the national level, why do states seek to join the club? And why do they construe their accomplishments in space as an act of joining it?

A nation-state club is a political structure that separates a small number of countries from the rest of the world because they have exclusive and unique capabilities that others do not have and cooperate with each other, even if on a limited scale. The basis for the separation between the haves and have-nots is in the fact that these unique capabilities are widely accepted as force multipliers or as currencies of power and high standing. By producing a distinction between powerful and less powerful nations, a club, formal or informal, serves as a structural expression of the distribution of power, stratification of status, and role in global governance.

The process by which nation-state clubs emerge begins when unique skills and capabilities are promoted by key players, usually the superpowers, to be the benchmarks for competition over power and high standing. Once the others acknowledge the high potential and strategic value of these skills, they perceive the group of haves as an elite group. Clubs make it easier to identify the stronger, higher-status players and distinguish them from weaker states. In return, states absorb the actions and characteristics expected of great powers and what it takes to be one. Individual states learn of the skills they are expected to develop and which specific superior group they should join in order to maintain their power and status or to achieve the power and position to which they aspire.

The dynamic that occurs within the club is usually characterized by an inherent tension between competition and cooperation among its members. Members of the club compete with each other over capabilities, achievements, and status in a highly visible and competitive but non-aggressive way. At the same time, they cooperate with each other for several reasons. Together, they develop the governance mechanisms of the club. They also cooperate to maximize the tangible goods and

---

[9] "New York Times Slammed for 'Racist' Cartoon about India's Mars Mission," *Mail Online India*, October 2, 2014, available at: www.dailymail.co.uk/indiahome/indianews/article-2778703/New-York-Times-slammed-racist-cartoon-India-s-Mars-mission.html, accessed on December 29, 2014; "India Mars Mission: New York Times Apologizes for Cartoon," *BBC*, October 6, 2014, available at: www.bbc.com/news/world-asia-india-29502062, accessed on December 29, 2014.

intangible benefits that accrue to them from the fact that they have the capabilities required, and that they are members of the club.

Analysts have explained why states want and develop expertise in highly demanding fields such as space technology, nuclear energy, and so forth. However, they have not carefully examined the role of nation-state clubs, such as the space club or the nuclear club, in shaping preferences, policies, and behavior. Rationalists explain state behavior through cost/benefit calculations of security considerations, the desire to achieve a high level of development in order to obtain economic benefit, or even the need for international prestige. According to their logic, it would be irrational to assume that states make tremendous efforts out of any arbitrary motivation to be a member of a club. Nevertheless, their reasoning fails to completely explain how and why certain qualities are perceived by many as indicators of power and symbols of high standing while others are not. They also fail to explain national investments in "impractical" projects or indigenous development of expensive capabilities for practical use that are available through foreign or commercial suppliers at much lower costs. Furthermore, these explanations are also inadequate when juxtaposed with the fact that these qualities and this expertise are often associated with an exclusive group of states – a club.

This book challenges this conventional wisdom. The phenomenon of grouping into clubs or cliques is a widespread human activity. Therefore, this book draws on the disciplines of sociology, psychology, and economics, in which the phenomenon of clubs in humans was comprehensively explored. Based on what is known about human clubs and the perception that nation-states are social entities operating in a social environment,[10] the general premise of this book is that the phenomenon of states clustering in clubs is applicable to the field of international relations.

Clubs enable us to reach a better understanding of the reasons leading states to develop indigenous capabilities in certain fields or the lack thereof, as well as the logic of the communicative strategies adopted regarding these capabilities. In addition, examining the interaction between members of the club, especially between the gatekeepers, as well as between them and the newcomers or those who wish to join the club, sheds light on major international tensions and struggles for power in the international system. States that join clubs accept and act according to conventions about the current means of power and symbols of high standing. Their decision to embark on

---

[10] Finnemore, M., *National Interests in International Society*, (Ithaca: Cornell University Press, 1996), 2; Wendt, A., *Social Theory of International Politics*, (Cambridge: Cambridge University Press, 1999), 20.

large-scale projects and join clubs is the result of strategic logic to fulfill what they perceive to be others' expectations of them or their own aspirations for empowerment and high status. Nevertheless, in order to be a member of the club, they need to be recognized and accepted into the club by the other members; acceptance is achieved through cooperation and joint ventures.

The primary argument is that joining nation-state clubs is a legitimate rational and significant consideration, which explains decision-making and national preferences. Nation-state clubs play a significant, and usually unrecognized, role in world politics. Exploring the phenomenon of states' activities in clubs enriches our overall understanding of the interaction between states and illuminates the factors affecting national decision-making and prioritization.

In general, by claiming membership in a club, national decision-makers and officials try to convince others to adopt their social and political interpretation of the achieved capability in terms of power, status, and esteem. Membership in the club provides a conceptual tool to evaluate a country's achievement. Nevertheless, the strategic rationale changes according to the power and status of the actor. For the strongest players or superpowers, the club is a highly valuable tool to project power and to claim the status of a superpower, by which they aspire to strengthen their impact on global governance and politics. They use the club as an arena in which they compete with each other over world leadership. In addition, they take advantage of the attractiveness of the club to less powerful players, allies, and others, to gain recognition for their claims for world leadership. The superpower club members offer other countries cooperation on joint ventures in order to placate these weaker countries and attract them as allies. The club members thus cooperate with these potential or new member nations to further their own national interests, maintain leadership positions, and increase control over the weaker countries.

Nevertheless, the superpowers are concerned that cooperation could lead to a rapid proliferation of these skills, which would reduce the exclusivity and attractiveness of these skills in terms of power and standing. This situation strategically threatens the superpowers because it erodes their superiority and reduces their tangible and intangible benefits. In order to prevent massive proliferation of these capabilities, the leading countries make it difficult for others to acquire the capabilities necessary for high international status by imposing significant restrictions and by barring proliferation and transfer of knowledge and technologies. The variety of tools used range from limited cooperation, export controls, suppliers groups, etc.

In summary, the superpowers' strategy of interweaving competition and cooperation on a limited scale and restrictions on the proliferation of these capabilities turned the countries that acquired these capabilities into an elite group – a club – in which the original members, the superpowers, served as its gatekeepers.

Powerful and high-status nations, as well as states in an empowerment process, choose to emulate the superpowers by embarking on national large-scale projects to develop indigenous expertise in the subject area. For them, club membership serves as a credible message of power, justifying their aspirations to have a seat at the table. Less powerful nations choose more moderate paths or make coherent decisions to refrain from developing their own capacity, and instead rely on others. The very weak or small nations use club membership to empower themselves and be placed in a higher category of capability and power than the one to which they actually belong.[11] In this process, the club has a twofold purpose: (a) it is a socializing mechanism and (b) an arena in which states rationally interact and negotiate over the distribution of power, status, and influence, using strategies of exclusion and inclusion.

Dual-Use Technology and the Space Club

Focused on the case of the space club, this book shows that global space activity developed via a similar process. In the late 1950s and 1960s, because of the potential immediate devastating consequences of a nuclear weapons attack using intercontinental ballistic missiles (ICBMs), the superpowers did almost anything possible to avoid direct military conflict that could escalate to a nuclear war. Among other actions taken, the superpowers channeled their hostilities into proxy wars and non-violent public competitions. The race to space was one of the prominent examples of this international rivalry. It should be noted that in addition to the public competition for achievements in space, the two superpowers each engaged in defense or military space programs aimed at preventing nuclear escalation. They developed and used space-based intelligence-gathering capabilities to obtain important information regarding the capabilities and developments of their opponents and to monitor arms control agreements.

Research and development of space technology is similar in many ways to research and development of nuclear energy and nuclear weapons technology. This led the superpowers to use space exploration and

---

[11] Jervis, R., *The Logic of Images in International Relations*, (New York, NY: Columbia University Press, 1989), 14, 55.

technology as a somewhat peaceful substitute for obtaining and demonstrating power and global leadership.[12] The two fields of research – nuclear and space – are at the cutting edge of human knowledge. They each have phenomenal potential for civil purposes as well as for military ones. They each spark the human imagination concerning the potential for development, progress, and understanding the universe. Each requires a huge national investment, drawing on the many scientific and technological fields, national entities, and human resources that the nation possesses. And space research and development, like nuclear development, involves a great deal of risk and a high chance of failure. Another important aspect linking nuclear development and space development is the technological relationship regarding the means of launching. Inter-Continental Ballistic Missiles and Space Launch Vehicles (SLVs) share fundamental core technologies, and thus are characterized as dual-use.[13]

The primary distinction between ICBMs delivering nuclear warheads and SLVs delivering payloads into space is the purpose of development. SLVs are designed to put a satellite in orbit. For this reason, they are generally classified as a civil technology for peaceful uses. Missiles, on the other hand, are designed to place warheads on targets and, therefore, are classified as technology for military purposes, or simply as weapons. The difference in objectives demands different technological functions. A ballistic missile is designed to accelerate the warhead to a very high speed. The warhead then follows a path through space, but it is not in orbit. Instead of orbiting Earth, it re-enters the atmosphere and, unless intercepted, hits a spot on the surface of the Earth.

Space-launch vehicles lift a payload to a desired altitude above the Earth and then give that payload enough forward speed to remain in orbit at that altitude. With enough speed (significantly faster than that of a missile), the payload moves forward and stays in orbit while resisting Earth's gravity. When its mission is done, the payload, similar to a missile warhead, becomes a ballistic object whose path is determined by the force of gravity. Unlike a missile that returns to the atmosphere with its cargo (its warhead) intact so as to strike its target, the thermodynamics of space-launch vehicles and satellites is different, and until recently were not

---

[12] McDougall, W., *The Heavens and the Earth: A Political History of the Space Age*, (New York, NY: Basic Books, 1985), 405.

[13] Dual-use technology supports applications that can be used for both civil, peaceful purposes, and defense purposes. For a comprehensive discussion of the dual-use of space technologies, see Johnson-Freese, J., *Space as a Strategic Asset*, (New York, NY: Columbia University Press, 2007); and Mineiro, M. C., *Space Technology Export Controls and International Cooperation in Outer Space*, (New York, NY: Springer Press, 2012).

designed for re-entry. Most space objects burn up when they re-enter the atmosphere. Other differences between missiles and SLVs have to do with the amount of time required before launching. The preparation time for a space launch is relatively long, lasting several weeks, during which the various components are tested and the ideal weather conditions are awaited. By contrast, a ballistic missile launch has to be very rapid and reliable; it must be capable of launching under a variety of conditions.

The technological proximity of ICBMs to SLVs makes it relatively easy to turn one into the other. Therefore, a country capable of launching a satellite into space is seen by others as having the potential ability to launch a ballistic missile to any point on Earth's surface, as well as to develop kinetic anti-satellite capabilities.[14] The major difference is that launching a ballistic missile is considered aggressive, while launching a satellite into space is considered peaceful and legitimate. For this reason, launching a satellite into space sends a clear, albeit peaceful message of deterrence and power because it can also serve as a cover for a missile test. Under these circumstances, space capability was perceived as complementary to nuclear capability, and the conquest of space was considered to be a substitute for war. Based on this rationale, the axiom that the nation that dominates space will dominate the world developed in the late 1950s and early 1960s.

The advantage of conventions and norms lies in the fact that they are collectively held. Therefore, the superpowers had to convince other nations to perceive accomplishments in space as indicators of national might, political power, and ideological supremacy. Both superpowers used displays of spectacular space projects constructed through language, along with strategies of competition and international cooperation to create conventions and norms to show that national space capability and its accomplishments further proved their right to claim world leadership.[15] On September 12, 1962, a year after he announced the Apollo program to land a man on the Moon, President John F. Kennedy delivered his famous address at Rice University in which he outlined the rationale for the United States to undertake space exploration. He stated, "The exploration of space will go ahead, whether we join in it or not, and it is one of the great adventures of all time, and no nation which expects to be the leader of other nations can

---

[14] The development of ASATs also requires the development of the capability to track and pinpoint targets moving at high speeds in orbit.

[15] John Logsdon and, later, Walter McDougall clearly show this in their comprehensive works: Logsdon, J., *The Decision to Go to the Moon: Project Apollo and The National Interest*, (Chicago, IL: University of Chicago Press, 1970); McDougall, W., *The Heavens and The Earth: A Political History of The Space Age*, (New York, NY: Basic Books, 1985).

expect to stay behind in the race for space."[16] In these simple words, Kennedy summed up the political logic that became the premise of the space club: Space technological development and exploration is what powerful countries do. Therefore, a country that sees itself as a power deserving of a seat at the table of world governance is expected to race for space.

The United States and the Soviet Union were very much aware of the impact their behavior had on other states. They acknowledged that they were setting an example of how a modern and progressive country should act in that era, creating a set of expectations and encouraging others to emulate their deeds. Indeed, other nations followed and initiated national space programs of their own. This process turned space development into a political practice that reflected on other good qualities of the space-capable state, providing it with tangible goods and intangible benefits. Taking advantage of this trend, each of the two superpowers initiated cooperative programs to attract allies. At the same time, they had concerns about the development of programs to independently launch satellites into space by other countries. Their concerns were rooted in the strategic implications of the intertwined relationship between space capability, especially launch capability, and the development of nuclear weapons and their delivery systems, as described above. Their concerns were justified: The countries developing launch capability were the same ones that were developing nuclear programs or intended to do so. Indeed, almost all of the countries that developed nuclear weapons capabilities also developed space programs with the capability to independently launch rockets into space.

The fact that space technology is dual-use and, as such, has significant military implications played a significant role in the process by which the space club evolved. The superpowers rejected fast proliferation of space technology and knowhow. Consequently, very early in the Cold War, they set many controls and restrictions on their cooperation with other countries in space development, primarily, but not limited to, the transfer of knowhow and technology of space launch. They also demanded commitments from the cooperating partners that they would control any transfers of technology derived from such cooperation to third countries. Later on, these controls were codified in the Missile Technology Control Regime (MTCR), which was originally established in 1987 to deal with the proliferation of nuclear weapons by limiting the export of missile

---

[16] John, F. Kennedy, Moon Race Speech, Rice Stadium, September 12, 1962. The text of the speech is available at: er.jsc.nasa.gov/seh/ricetalk.htm, accessed on June 1, 2015.

Table 1.1 *Nuclear Programs and Space Programs*

Country	Space Launch	Space Program	Nuclear Weapons	Ballistic Missiles
Russia	+	+	+	+
US	+	+	+	+
France	+	+	+	+
Japan	+	+	−	−
China	+	+	+	+
Britain	(1971)*	+	+	+
India	+	+	+	+
Israel	+	+	Ambiguity	Ambiguity
Iran	+	+	Remains uncertain	+
North Korea	+−**	−	+	+
South Korea	+	+	−	−
Pakistan	−	+	+	+

*Competency abandoned; ** Satellites were launched in 2012 and 2016 but failed to operate

technology.[17] This approach was based on the assumption that nations that have nuclear weapons programs wouldn't be able to destabilize the world without means of launching and delivering them.

Thus, limiting the distribution of launching technology and missile development was added as another defensive ring to pre-empt nuclear attacks. In the context of space, the MTCR thereby sets severe limitations on countries that are interested in developing the ability to independently launch a rocket into space, even for purely civilian purposes. In 2002, the MTCR was supplemented by the Hague Code of Conduct (HCOC). The code is a political initiative aimed at enhancing efforts to restrain ballistic missile proliferation worldwide and to further delegitimize such proliferation.[18]

Controls and restrictions were also imposed on the transfer of other dual-use sensitive space technologies that were considered strategically valuable, such as high-resolution imagery, satellites, systems and subsystems, components, etc. The rationale was that the use of such technologies by other countries could reduce the military advantage that the

---

[17] It was established by Canada, France, Germany, Italy, Japan, the United Kingdom, and the United States. Since that time, the number of MTCR partners has increased to a total of thirty-four states. For further reading on the MTCR, see www.mtcr.info/english/index.html, accessed on May 23, 2015.

[18] Martin, J., "Review of the Hague Code of Conduct Against Ballistic Missile Proliferation [HCOC]," *Center for Nonproliferation Studies*, available at: icns.miis.edu/inventory/pdfs/hcoc.pdf, accessed on May 23, 2015.

superpowers had over their allies and adversaries. As a result, space activity became a strategic and prestigious practice that powerful countries are expected to take upon themselves, and it turned the countries that successfully developed the expertise into an elite group known as the space club.

Despite the restrictions and controls imposed by the superpowers, or because of them, other countries have made conscious efforts to become more independent regarding access to and utilization of outer space.[19] The strategic significance of the technology and its dual civil-military nature made the space challenge even more appealing to them. As a result, space capability became an important mark of great powers. Formally, the superpowers did not form a "space club." Nonetheless, their strategies of a balanced game of competition and restricted cooperation distinguished between the haves and have-nots, producing the components of the "space club."

Since then, membership in the space club is a significant indicator of power in the international system. Demonstration of indigenous capabilities in space, especially the capability to launch satellites into orbit, usually intends to send a message of power, albeit a legitimate and peaceful one that does not pose a direct threat to others. As such, it can preclude the risk of a potential security dilemma. If a country upgrades its military force or allies itself with a strong country in order to increase its status, its efforts may boomerang; it may find itself threatened and insecure.[20]

The communicative strategy of club membership provides a political context that enables adversaries as well as allies to more easily accept the new reality of empowerment without having to publicly and directly address the very build-up of power that may pose a threat. For adversaries, membership in the space club is quite a "peaceful" message of deterrence, deflecting attention away from potential threatening military implications. For allies and other like-minded countries, membership in the club is intended to attract others to cooperate, in order to gain tangible material advantages and intangible benefits. By accepting the interpretation of peaceful membership in the space club, others, especially the rivals of the club-joining state, do not have to address its empowerment process head on and can plausibly deny it.

---

[19] Williamson, R., "International Cooperation and Competition in Space," in D. Papp and R. McIntyre, (eds.), *International Space Policy*, (New York, NY: Quorum Books, 1987), 105–118.

[20] Jervis, R., "Cooperation Under the Security Dilemma," *World Politics* 30:2, (January 1978), 167–174; Jervis, R., *Perception and Misperception in International Politics*, (Princeton, NJ: Princeton University Press, 1978), 58–113; and Davis, Z., "The Realist Nuclear Regime," *Security Studies*, (Spring/Summer 1993), 80.

In this context, the strategy of undertaking national space activities to gain membership in the space club is aimed at creating proximity to other club members in order to legitimize actions that otherwise would be considered threatening and aggressive. The framing of the development of delivery systems in the context of the peaceful space club makes it difficult for others to object to the new technological reality. Club members are co-opted into accepting the newly attained capabilities as a legitimate build-up of capabilities and high standing. Nevertheless, the claims for membership in the space club are sometimes used as a cover for the development of military capability, such as ballistic missiles.

From these basic arguments, one can derive the following hypotheses about the conditions under which states will be more or less likely to join nation-state clubs and, in the context of this study, the space club.

The first hypothesis is that states that define themselves as powers will emulate the superpowers by developing indigenous space capabilities. These states will justify their decision by arguing that this action is expected of them due to their status. In order to reinforce their status and message of power, they will claim membership in the space club. Following this rationale, declining powers that are no longer interested in restoring their status or states with modest or low aspirations for status and influence will relinquish their capabilities and places in the club, or they will not join the club at all. In practice, these states settle for the status of consumers of space technology and applications.

The second hypothesis is that states that are not powers but aspire to upgrade their power and international standing will develop national space capabilities and thereby try to join the club. Space capabilities are the condition for joining the space club, which they perceive as a prerequisite for claiming the status of a power.

The two hypotheses can be summarized as follows. Countries develop space programs for two reasons: they assume that this is expected of them to maintain their power and international standing, or they aspire to higher power and status for geo-political and/or domestic reasons, regardless of clear tangible cost/benefit considerations.

The Controversy over the Reasons for the Development of National Space Programs

Accepted explanations for the motivation of states in their quest for space capability are tangible materialistic or practical, functional reasons, which fall into three main categories: national security and military considerations; economic growth and prosperity, development, and benefit to society; and/or the desire for international prestige. These considerations may be intuitively appealing; nevertheless, they are challenged by empirical evidence. These considerations may explain nations' interest in using space applications. However, they are inadequate for solely explaining national decisions to undertake large-scale space programs and to develop indigenous capacities in space technology, let alone projects that do not provide immediate tangible benefits. Carrying out an indigenous space program requires enormous efforts, massive investments of resources, a high level of technology, and a large scientific infrastructure. Relying on the purchase of satellites and services for space applications is much cheaper, especially as space technology becomes a commodity and many space applications that provide tangible/functional benefits can be purchased at a sensible per unit cost, or are available through cooperation.

The decision to indigenously develop space technology is not trivial. Nevertheless, a large number of states are active in space and seek their own capabilities. They attribute strategic value to a variety of technological and scientific missions, as well as to national records and visible achievements. Furthermore, their decision-makers and state officials often emphasize the political achievement of their country's accomplishments in space by arguing for membership in the space club. The above explanations do not account for the patterns of space club membership and do not provide sufficient answers to a variety of questions. Among them are

- How can we explain the differences in space policies between similar countries?
- How can one explain space projects that do not provide security or direct service to the citizens?
- For example, what benefit did the Chinese leadership find in having a Chinese Taikonaut perform a space-walk while waving the Chinese flag in 2003;[21] or in landing Chang'e-3 on the Moon in December 2013? In what way do the Indian Moon and Mars probes meet Indian objectives of using space for India's development and the welfare of the Indian people?[22]
- By contrast, how can we explain a space policy that relies on procurement of services rather than on indigenous development of capabilities in countries with security problems or with high technological capacity and economic levels?

[21] Ramzy, A., "The Moment," *Time*, (October 13, 2008), 9.
[22] Traditionally, the Indians argued that they operate out of a functional need to provide their people with better service and objected to investing resources for intangible reasons. However, this idea has changed in the last few years.

In short, the general controversy this book presents is why would a rational actor choose to develop expensive programs when cheaper options, available on the commercial market or through international cooperation, might provide the same services? In what way does membership in the space club serve these actors?

States often engage in indigenous development of large-scale space programs with no direct cost-benefit security or economic considerations. This is not to say that tangible security and economic considerations are irrelevant to states' decisions to embark on large-scale projects. In most cases these considerations do exist. Nevertheless, the evidence provided in this book is that states are unlikely to pursue the development of indigenous capacity only for clear tangible cost/benefit considerations. As noted above, they are likely to do so when such behavior is consistent with a wider set of domestic and national perceptions of what is expected of them, given their power and position. States may also endeavor to attain power and status, which they seek for national and international reasons. In this context, indigenous development of space expertise and club membership is driven by a techno-nationalist approach.[23]

Techno-nationalism has many faces. Usually it refers to the development and use of advanced technologies to achieve a state's domestic or international objectives.[24] In practice, this means that the government identifies certain areas of expertise, usually involving advanced technology and high-tech (such as space), as valuable for achieving national and international objectives, and provides various governmental supports to the scientific community and industries involved in developing the technology in order to develop an indigenous capacity. Governmental support is awarded in a variety of ways: government procurements, import restrictions, subsidies, government-funded research and development, tax credits, etc.[25]

---

[23] According to Johnson-Freese, space technology development is driven by nationalism to serve as an indicator of geostrategic power and leadership. This is usually triggered by a threat or perception of a threat. Johnson-Freese, J., "The Geostrategic Techno-Nationalist Push into Space," *OASIS*, 20, (2014), 11.

[24] For further reading, see Edgerton, D. E. H., "The Contradictions of Techno-Nationalism and Techno-Globalism: A Historical Perspective," *New Global Studies*, 1:1, (2007), 1–32; Nakayama, S., "Techno-Nationalism versus Techno-Globalism," *East Asian Science, Technology and Society: an International Journal*, 6:1, (2012), 9–15; Hughes, C. W., "The Slow Death of Japanese Techno-Nationalism? Emerging Comparative Lessons for China's Defense Production," *Journal of Strategic Studies*, 34:3, (2011), 451–479; Sulfikar, A., "Nationalist Rhetoric and Technology Development: The Indonesian Aircraft Industry in the New Order Regime," *Technology in Society*, 29:3, (2007), 283–293.

[25] Yamada, A., "New-Techno-Nationalism: How and Why It Grows," paper presented at the International Studies Association Convention, Los Angeles, 2000.

Governments adopting such techno-nationalist policies emphasize the importance of in-house development instead of relying on foreign assistance. The motivations include attaining economic growth, which is a primary objective of most governments in their attitudes toward science and technology, military empowerment, domestic politics, and social development.

Technological progress is clearly the key to national prosperity. Therefore, large-scale domestic technological capability is an important goal, especially in achieving sustained and balanced growth. Economic growth that is totally reliant on foreign technology, management, and skilled personnel on an ongoing basis is inefficient. National capability in advanced technologies is perceived as a means to achieve fast development, as well as promoting local industry internationally.[26] However, governmental policies to preserve and upgrade strategic advantages provided by the technology and to protect local industry often include restrictions on technological development and export. Such steps often hinder the competitiveness of the local industry.

This book shows that clubs have a strong impact on the definition and meaning of power and international standing, the ways to achieve them and construct them. They contribute to the discussion of the changing character of power, emphasizing the superior role of symbolic power, status, and esteem in states' perceptions, preferences, and behaviors. Membership in clubs attests to the high capabilities, lofty positions, and power of states, which in turn affects the interaction between members and non-members. Although this research focuses on the case study of the space club, it offers a theoretical framework and methodology that can be applied to other political areas as well, particularly regarding capabilities or areas of expertise that are considered to be means of power and symbols of high standing, and which are developed for national reasons.

The key contribution of this book is in providing theoretical and empirical analyses of the role of nation-state clubs in world politics. It appeals to those who seek to understand where the theoretical and empirical study of "club membership" fits into and complements existing theories of international relations. The book offers a response to the weaknesses of other scholarly approaches while taking their strengths into account. Drawing from clubs in human society, the analytical lens of nation-state clubs enables a better understanding of processes and incentives shaping preferences, policies, and behaviors of states and their leaders. It suggests that understanding the phenomenon of nation-

---

[26] Kazuto, S., *Policy Logics and Institutions of European Space Collaboration*, (Burlington, VT: Ashgate Publishing, 2003), 25.

state clubs like the "space club" relies on the realist premise that a state operates out of a need and desire for power. But it asks further, "What kind of power and for what end?" The book supports the argument that states' perception of power and the means of its attainment are shaped by international norms and conventions, as well as by specific national characteristics, objectives, and domestic needs. The state's domestic sphere modifies these perceptions and transforms them into actual preferences, priorities, and programs that correspond to the principles of techno-nationalism. Stressing this point further, the framework of nation-state clubs enables the integration of international factors and domestic political discourse into one structure and thus provides better causal explanations and a much more complete picture than does artificial theoretical separations. In this way, the place that states allot to social, political, and other intangible factors in their calculations and aspirations is illuminated.

This study also corresponds to the discussion of the changing nature of power, emphasizing the superior role of symbolic power, status, and esteem in states' perceptions, preferences, and behaviors. Evidence provided in this book shows that in their interactions, states measure one another by what they have or have not accomplished in certain areas; space is one of these. Achieving technological capability is measured not only by the actual benefits it brings, but also by what it symbolizes. Nation-states that aspire to have an indigenous technological capability in space, for example, are motivated by its symbolic power and somewhat peaceful image as much as they are motivated by its instrumental capability. In fact, symbolic power may be an even greater motivation. Membership in the space club is a symbol of statehood, modernity and national capability; elements which are not for sale.

In summary, geo-strategic and material needs and conditions may be primary but inadequate on their own to convince decision-makers to embark on a large-scale project like a national space program. States' preferences and behaviors are also shaped by narratives of expectations and aspirations. A state acts in keeping with its perceptions of what others expect of it, what is necessary according to geo-strategic factors, and its national aspirations rooted in its domestic discourse of politics, national narratives, history, and culture.

In the growing discipline of space politics, an examination of the motivations and factors leading states to engage in this demanding field is important for better cooperation, in addition to improving understanding of competition and conflicts in this field. Literature that deals with space politics and policies focuses primarily on the Cold War space race, the policies and programs of the United States and Russia[27] or on China and Europe (represented as a single bloc).[28] Another aspect addressed in the literature is the potential for contemporary military applications.[29] Very little notice is taken of small and medium-sized

[27] McDougall, *The Heavens and the Earth*; Oberg, J., *Red Star in Orbit*, (New York, NY: Random House 1981); Brzezinski, M., *Red Moon Rising*, (New York, NY: Times Books, 2007); Shelton, W., "The United States and the Soviet Union: Fourteen Years in Space." *Russian Review*, 30:4, (1971), 322–334; Mowthorpe, M., "The Soviet/Russian Approach to Military Space," *The Journal of Slavic Military Studies*, 15:3, (September 2002), 24–48; Hardesty, V., and Eisman, G., *Epic Rivalry: The Inside Story of The Soviet and American Space Race*, (Washington, DC: National Geographic Society, 2007); Kash, D. E., *The Politics of Space Cooperation*, (West Lafayette, IN: Purdue University Studies, 1967); Siddiqi, A., *Challenge to Apollo: The Soviet Union and the Space Race, 1945–1974*, (Washington, DC: National Aeronautics and Space Administration, 2000). Johnson-Freese, J., *Heavenly Ambitions: America's Quest to Dominate Space*, (Philadelphia, PA: University of Pennsylvania Press, 2009); Van Dyke, V., *Pride and Power*, (London: Pall Mall Press, 1965); Logsdon, J., *The Decision to Go to the Moon: Project Apollo and the National Interest*, (Chicago, IL: University of Chicago Press, 1970); Roland, A., (ed.), *A Space-Faring People: Perspectives on Early Spaceflight*, (Washington, DC: The NASA History Series, 1985); Dick, S. J., and Launius, R. D., (eds.), *Societal Impact of Spaceflight*, (Washington, DC: NASA History Division, 2007); McCurdy, H., *Space and the American Imagination*, (Washington, DC, and London: Smithsonian Institution Press, 1997); Launius, R. D., Logsdon, J. M., and Smith, R. W., (eds.), *Reconsidering Sputnik*, (Amsterdam: Harwood Academic Publishers, 2000); Karash, Y., *The Superpower Odyssey: A Russian Perspective on Space Cooperation*, (Reston, VA: American Institute of Aeronautics and Astronautics, 1999); Smolders, P., *Soviets in Space*, (Guildford and London: Lutterworth Press, 1970).

[28] Sheehan, M., *The International Politics of Space*, (London: Routledge, 2007); Johnson-Freese, J., *The Chinese Space Program: A Mystery within a Maze* (Malabar, FL: Krieger Publishing, 1998); Harvey, B., *The Japanese and Indian Space Programs: Two Roads into Space*, (London: Springer Praxis Publishing, 2000); Lambright, H. W., (ed.), *Space Policy in the Twenty-First Century*. (Baltimore, MD: Johns Hopkins University Press, 2003); Suzuki, K., *Policy Logics and Institutions of European Space Collaboration*, (Burlington, VT: Ashgate Publishing, 2003); Kulacki, G., and Lewis, J. G., *A Place for One's Mat: China's Space Program 1956-2003*, (Cambridge, MA: American Academy of Arts and Science, 2009); Kulacki. G., "Chinese Intentions in Space: A Historical Perspective for Future Cooperation," *Space and Defense*, 4:1, (Winter 2010), 101–113; Moltz, J. C. *Asia's Space Race*, (New York, NY: Columbia University Press, 2012); Cheng, D., "China's Military Role In Space," Strategic Studies Quarterly, 6:1, (Spring 2012), 55–77; Cheng, D., "Meeting the Chinese Space Challenge," Web Memo, *Heritage Foundation*, Washington, DC, January, 18, 2012, available at www.heritage.org/research/reports/2012/01/us-needs-to-meet-chinas-space-challenge-of-the-next-5-years, accessed on June 3, 2015.

[29] Zhuk, E.I., "Astronautics: The Military-Political Aspect," *Military Thought*, (March–April 2003), available at: www.highbeam.com/doc/1G1-107201419.html, accessed on June 6, 2016; Serale, T. R., "The Air Force of the Future," *Air and Space Power Journal*, 18:2, (Summer 2004), 19–26; Watts, B. D., *The Military Use of Space: A Diagnostic Assessment*, (Washington, DC: Center for Strategic and Budgetary Assessments, 2001); Hays, P. L., *United States Military Space: Into the Twenty-First Century*, USAF Institute for National Security Studies Occasional Paper 42 (USAF Academy, CO and Maxwell AFB, AL: Air University Press September 2002); Lupton, D. *On Space Warfare: A Space Power Doctrine*, (Maxwell Air Force Base, AL: Air University Press 1998); Gray, C., "Space Power and the Revolution in Military

states. By examining the factors involved in joining the space club, this study offers a better understanding of the motivations to embark on national space programs. It also provides a detailed examination of the effect the race to space had on less powerful or medium-sized states, and their part in it.

Entry into the Space Club

The space club is a competitive informal club growing out of the Cold War, based primarily on technological capability. Therefore, by definition, the borderline between club members and non-members should be drawn so that it includes states that demonstrate indigenous space capability and excludes those that don't.

In general, space capability is open to all, and acquiring it is mostly dependent on the political will of a country's leaders. Club members attempting to prevent a country from acquiring the necessary capabilities may impose restrictions and difficulties on it, such as refusing to sell needed materials, implementing export controls to this country, and so forth. Trying to completely ban efforts to acquire a technological capability is nevertheless impossible. And yet, this does not mean that every country that demonstrates that it developed space capability automatically becomes a member of the club.

Joining the club is usually done in three stages. First, by a public demonstration of space capability or expertise, such as successfully launching a satellite into orbit; second, by a formal statement in which leaders and state officials characterize the event as "joining the space club." In the third and final stage, membership in the club is acknowledged by recognition from other club members and their willingness to accept it as a legitimate member. In practice, members welcome the new country into the club by entering into joint ventures and by sharing knowledge and technology with it. Alternatively, club members can deprive a country with space capabilities of membership by refusing to cooperate with it. Such a move is aimed at delegitimizing that country's achievements and capabilities and to prevent it from gaining the tangible goods and intangible benefits associated with the membership. For

Affairs: A Glass Half Full?," *Aerospace Power Journal*, 13:3, (Fall 1999), 23–38; Rumsfeld, D., "Transforming the Military," *Foreign Affairs*, 81:3, (May/June 2002), 20–32; Scott, W., "Strategic Space," *Aviation Week & Space Technology*, 161:16, (October 25, 2004), 83; Huntley, W. L. "Smaller State Perspectives on the Future of Space Governance," *Astropolitics*, 5:3, (2007), 237–271; Johnson-Freese, J., *Space as a Strategic Asset*, (New York, NY: Columbia University Press, 2007); Moltz, J. C. *The Politics of Space Security*, (Stanford, CA: Stanford University Press, 2008).

example, in the aftermath of the Cold War, the United States attempted to prevent China from gaining membership in the club but was unsuccessful. Similarly, in 2009, Iran launched a satellite into space, and North Korea did so in late 2012. Nonetheless, they were not welcomed into the space club by the other members. By contrast, in January 2013, South Korea successfully put a satellite into orbit and was widely accepted as a new member of the space club, with which other members are glad to cooperate.[30] These examples are further discussed in Chapter 8.

It should be noted that, often, the leading members of the club reach out to developing countries and engage in cooperation with them. These partnerships do not affect the club's structure because the cooperation usually takes place in areas that, in the eyes of the leading countries, do not pass the threshold for entry into the club. Still, cooperative projects between club members and non-member countries actually help to define the boundaries and structure of the club.

Structure of the Space Club

Countries involved in space research and technology differ in their investments and capabilities. Therefore, a pyramid-shaped model is the most suitable to describe the hierarchical structure of the space club, in which club membership costs and benefits are unequal. The basis of the pyramid is wide and contains a large number of actors relative to the number of actors on the highest level. At the bottom, costs and benefits are much lower than the costs and benefits of the actors on higher levels of the pyramid.

Due to the fact that the space club is not a formal institution, it has a fluid and dynamic structure. The levels of membership of the space club pyramid change according to progress in technology, as well as changes in geo-politics. Especially affected is the borderline separating members from non-members. This is in contrast to the much more static structure of the nuclear club in which having nuclear weapons and being part of the N5 (the five nuclear powers) are the criteria for membership in the club.

Evidence shows that in the early 1960s, when space technology was in its earliest stages, nearly every achievement in the field was considered a breakthrough and received considerable attention in global media. Even the launch of sounding rockets, let alone the development of simple satellites, was enough to claim membership in the space club. For

---

[30] Hewitt, G., "South Korea Joins Global Space Club with Satellite Launch," *Globe and Mail*, January 30, 2013, available at: www.theglobeandmail.com/news/world/south-korea-joins-global-space-club-with-satellite-launch/article7997644/, accessed on January 31, 2013.

example, on July 5, 1961, Israel successfully launched the Shavit-2 sounding rocket. Media reports described this achievement as an act of joining the "meteorological rocket launching club" or the "space club."[31] France was declared a new member of the club when it indigenously launched a French-made satellite on November 26, 1965.[32] A few weeks later, Brazil's test of a sounding rocket was described as an entry into the space club.[33] Japanese and Chinese efforts to launch their own satellites were similarly characterized.[34] Interestingly, there is no evidence that Britain's first launch, in November 1971, was acknowledged as an act of joining the space club. The reason for this may be that, by then, it was publicly known that the British government had decided that the project would be discontinued, making this Britain's first and last launch simultaneously.

As space technology developed and expanded across many countries, the entrance bar was raised; it became necessary to develop and demonstrate greater capabilities and more advanced technologies in order to be considered a member of the space club. By the end of the 1960s, launching sounding rockets was no longer considered a minimum for entrance into the space club. Countries had to demonstrate their ability to develop, build, and operate their own satellites.

As described in Figure 1.1, throughout the Cold War, states at the top level of the space club pyramid had indigenous capabilities to send humans into space. The states with indigenous capabilities to launch satellites into space were located on the next level down. The third level consisted of states with the indigenous capability to develop, maintain, and control their satellites. On the bottom level were states with a collective capability to develop, maintain, control, and launch satellites into space, such as the members of the European Space Agency. Excluded were states that depended on others for space applications.

In the post–Cold War era, progress in technology and changes in geo-politics led to the evolvement of the space market, and made the

---

[31] Israel, Media Coverage of Shavit 2 Launch, July 7, 1961, BBC Collection: Israel, Microfilm 51567-474, (Washington, DC: Library of Congress).
[32] Report, "France Soars into Space Club with Diamond A," *St. Petersburg Times* (Florida), November 27, 1965.
[33] "Brazil successfully launched a second N.A. rocket early today, completing the first phase of meteorological soundings that marked her entry into the space club," ("Brazil Launches 2nd Nike Apache," *Washington Post*, December 19, 1965, A25).
[34] "Japan stands on the threshold of joining the world's exclusive space club," (S. Jameson, "Japanese Sure of Success in Space Projects," *Chicago Tribune*, October 9, 1966); Willis, D., "Japan Joins Space Club," *Christian Science Monitor*, February 14, 1970, 1; "[Chinese] scientists have successfully orbited their first satellite, making China the fifth member of the international space club," ("Great Leap Forward," *New York Times*, April 26, 1970, E12).

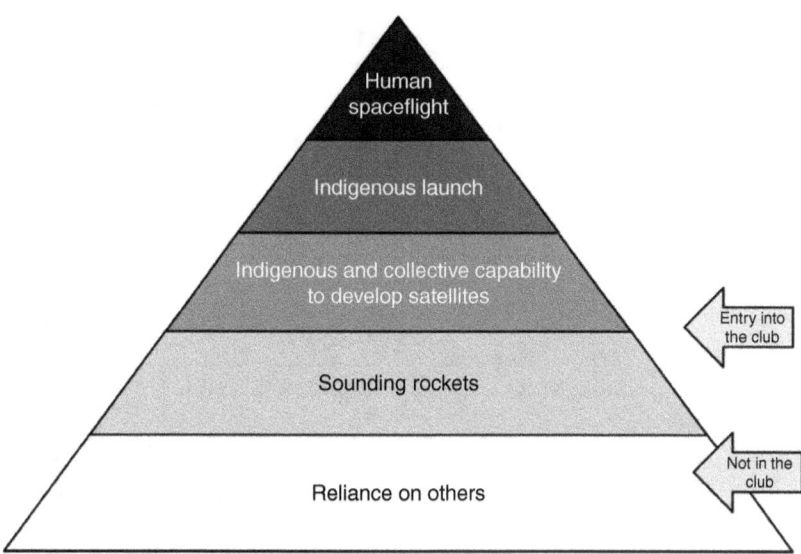

Figure 1.1 The Space Club Pyramid in the Cold War

task of developing simple satellites much easier. CubeSat (miniaturized cubic satellite) technology further broadened access, and the number of countries with space assets increased rapidly. In addition, these satellites could be launched through a commercial launch service at a much lower price. As a result, the borderline between club members and non-members blurred, and the status of the space club eroded. Gradually, the development of a single and simple satellite was no longer enough to earn club membership. In order to be considered a member of the club, countries needed to demonstrate that they had a broad, advanced capacity to develop, construct, integrate, operate, and control their satellites. The structure of the space club pyramid in the aftermath of the Cold War is described in Figure 1.2.

Contemporary dynamics of global space activity continue to shape the status of the space club and affect its future. Technological and economic developments taking place during the past several years, especially the growth in commercial activities to develop launch capabilities, and flying cargo and humans to low earth orbit (LEO) and beyond, threaten the value of the space club. This process shakes the structure of the pyramid, changes the borderline between members and non-members, and forces existing club members to expand and upgrade their capabilities. They must advance their space programs in new directions in order to preserve

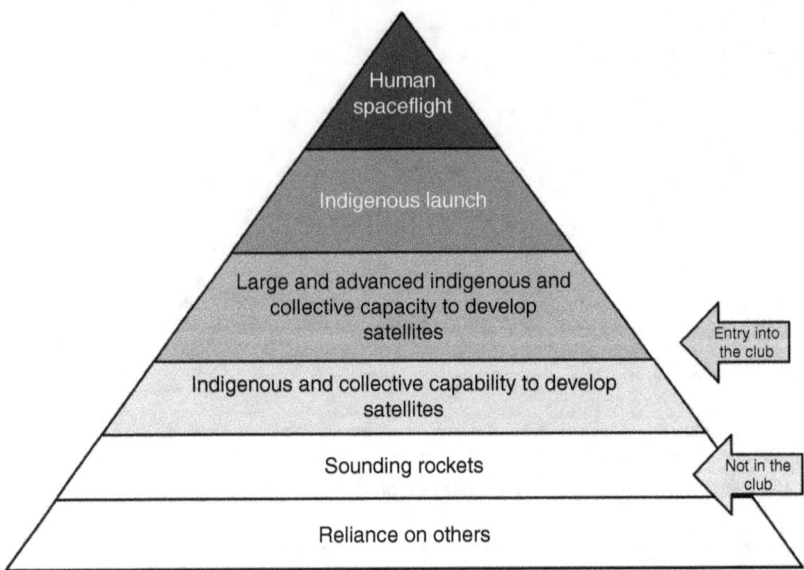

Figure 1.2 The Space Club Pyramid in the Post–Cold War Period

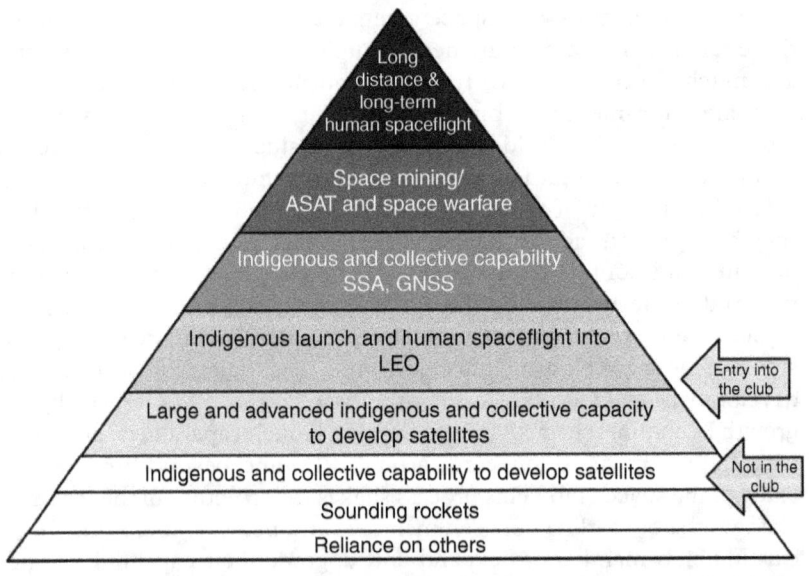

Figure 1.3 A Potential Future Structure of the Space Club Pyramid

the exclusivity and uniqueness of the space club and their own membership in it. These directions may include, among others, the development of complicated, long-term, and long-distance robotic and human space exploration missions; large-scale national infrastructures of satellites, for example, indigenous satellite navigation systems; or space situational awareness systems, which require tremendous investments of national resources. Other intriguing directions are space mining, anti-satellite capabilities (ASATs), and space warfare. These potential trends are discussed in depth in Chapter 8. Figure 1.3 describes a potential structure of the space club pyramid in the near future.

Aim and Outline of the Book

The purpose of this book is twofold. First, it presents an analytical account of the emergence of the space club in the early days of the Cold War race to space. Then it offers an explanatory framework for the variation in states' space policies and membership in the club. The methodological strategy used is a contrastive comparison of pairs of states with similar characteristics but with different preferences, policies, and behaviors vis-à-vis space club membership.

In order to achieve the first objective, the history of the development of the space club, which resulted from the Cold War space race between the United States and the Soviet Union, is reviewed. That history is presented together with an analytical examination of different national space programs. The various space programs serve as illustrations, highlighting and elaborating different points and issues related to the space club. As such, the book examines historical data that indicate the influence of international conventions and social and political motivations on national space policy, or the lack thereof.

In order to achieve the second purpose of this book and provide a valid assessment of the different reasons affecting states in shaping their policies and approaches to space activity, the book then follows a qualitative research design.[35] The methodological strategy is a focused contrastive comparison of pairs of states with similar

---

[35] George, A., and Bennett, A., *Case Study and Theory Development in the Social Sciences*, (Cambridge, MA: Harvard University Press, 2005); Klotz, A., and Lynch, C., *Strategies for Research in Constructivist International Relations: International Relations in a Constructed World*, (Armonk, NY: M. E. Sharpe, 2007); Mahoney, J. "Qualitative Methodology and Comparative Politics," *Comparative Political Studies*, 40:2, (2007) 122–144; Bennett, A., "Case Study Methods in the International Relations Subfield," *Comparative Political Studies*, 40:2, (2007), 170–195; Kacowitz, A., "Case Study Methods in International Security Studies," in D. F. Sprinz and Y. Wolinsky-Nahmias, (eds.), *Models, Numbers,*

characteristics but with different (or even diametrically opposed) preferences and space policies. The question is asked: "Why does State A have a different space policy than State B?" The purpose of the comparisons is not to produce rules or generalizations. Rather, they attempt to elucidate how mechanisms and processes work in practice in shaping preferences, policies, and decision-making. This empirical analysis of "contrastive why questions" provides a precise and reliable causal explanation. Eric Grynaviski best explains the contribution of such contrastive analysis in his methodological work:

> [The] Contrastive why-question focuses attention on a specific set of causes, screening off non-explanatory responses ... By screening off non-explanatory responses, contrastive why-questions focus research on politically and theoretically important causal explanations. Choosing contrastive questions means choosing the puzzle that interests the researcher, and using that puzzling variation on a dependent variable to motivate the search for causal explanations.[36]

By using a methodological strategy of contrastive comparison, better known as "compare and contrast," the variation in the countries examined in the case studies emerges clearly.[37] Each nation's definite needs for space applications are highlighted; an understanding of the underlying motivations in each case is thus attained.

When compared and contrasted, the cases chosen reflect different perceptions and behavioral patterns and even anomalies regarding space capabilities of three pairs of nation-states. In the first pair, Britain, a large power that relinquished its capability to launch objects into space and descended the levels of membership, is compared to France, a state with similar characteristics that adopted a very ambitious space program. In the second pair, Australia, a developed and capable state that chose not to join the club, is compared to Canada, a state with similar characteristics that adopted a very ambitious space program. Finally, the space programs and policies of Israel and India are contrasted and compared. Intuitively, the choice of comparing these cases may seem peculiar. In terms of size and geo-politics, a more reasonable comparison may seem to be of India and China. However, comparison

---

and Cases: Methods for Studying International Relations, (Ann Arbor, MI: University of Michigan Press, 2004), 107–128.

[36] Grynaviski, E., "Contrasts, Counterfactuals, and Causes," *European Journal of International Relations*, 19:4, (December 2013), 831–832.

[37] Mitchell, R., and Bernauer, T., "Beyond Story-Telling: Designing Case Study Research in International Environmental Policy," in D. F. Sprinz and Y. Wolinsky-Nahmias, (eds.), *Models, Numbers, and Cases: Methods for Studying International Relations*, (Ann Arbor: University of Michigan Press, 2004), 81–106.

of these two countries is not compatible with the methodology used in this book, of pairs of countries that share many similarities but differ in their activities and policies and vis-à-vis space. This is not the case with India and China, which in general share many similarities in their space policies. At the same time, they are very different in other significant parameters, which are important for the comparison. A more interesting examination is that of India and Israel. Although they differ in demography and geo-political aspects of size and GDP, they have many characteristics in common, and their space policies are different. Israel has a very pragmatic program, which is motivated mainly by security considerations. India, on the other hand, was motivated at first by pragmatic considerations but changed its policy and has become very ambitious about space.

The cases were selected for their ability to plausibly demonstrate the theoretical perspectives in question, and the richness of the data they presented on the subject in English (and Hebrew), including scholarly books, articles, and primary documentation.

The case studies examined provide valid and strong evidence supporting the argument that membership in the club does matter. Furthermore, they highlight and explain the circumstances under which it is likely to matter most. The case studies also examine how the motivation to join the club influenced events in a manner likely to be applicable in other cases. The analysis is focused on the crucial years in which the overall national approach to space and resulting policies were formulated.

The book contains nine chapters. Chapters 1 and 2 set out the foundations for the club model framework, elaborating on the unique concept of nation-state clubs. Chapters 3 and 4 apply this framework to the case study of the space club and explain why global governmental space activity is compatible with the framework of nation-state clubs. Chapter 3 delineates the process under which expertise in space was recognized as an indicator of power and high standing and how the space club developed. The role played by the superpowers in the development of the space club is highlighted, while the reaction of other countries is discussed in Chapter 4. The examples used throughout the chapter serve as illustrations of the logic other states have in joining the space club by undertaking large-scale national space programs, which in many ways resemble the principles of techno-nationalism. The variations in the space policies and decision-making of six countries – France, Britain, Canada, Australia, India, and Israel – are comprehensively explored in Chapters 5–7. Chapter 8 provides a discussion about the space club in the post–Cold War era, its current status and its potential future. A summary of the principal conclusions is presented in Chapter 9.

2 Nation-State Clubs in World Politics

Joining together in clubs or cliques is a widespread and important human dynamic that defines and shapes social standing and self-perception. Clubs entail important social functions in the organization of the structure of social power.[1] This chapter provides a systematic overview of the conceptual framework that shows how the concept of clubs is applicable to the field of international relations. The analysis concentrates on the characteristics of clubs and on the dynamic in which nation-states or their leaders often frame their efforts to develop large-scale indigenous capabilities and expertise as joining an exclusive club.

The chapter begins with a short outline of the role played by clubs in human society. It then deals with the conceptualization of nation-state clubs in world politics. The role of clubs in world politics is discussed in relation to other explanations for state behavior; a definition and typology of clubs is provided as well as an analysis of the differences between clubs and other types of groupings in world politics. The life cycle of nation-state clubs is presented, and the use of clubs by different types of countries is explored.

Clubs in Human Society

In human society, a club is a primary group, a set of actors in a network who are connected to one another by relationships. Usually, they have intimate face-to-face association and cooperation that result in interdependent relations.[2] Formal clubs or informal cliques fulfill a variety of functions in different stages of the human life cycle. In childhood, the popular and exclusive clique structure organizes children's social worlds and teaches them about society's differentiation between in-groups and

---

[1] Ridgeway, C., "Where Do Status Value Beliefs Come From? New Developments," in J. Szmatka, J. Skvoretz, and J. Berger, (eds.), *Status, Network, and Structure: Theory Development in Group Processes*, (Stanford: Stanford University Press, 1997), 137.

[2] Burt, R., "Models of Network Structure," *Annual Review of Sociology*, 6, (1980), 97.

out-groups, and about social elitism.[3] In adulthood, exclusive societies, whether secret[4] or publicly known, are a part of religious, political, and academic life.[5] They provide their members with exclusivity, elevated status, and a prestigious image.

Scholars of sociology, psychology, and economics observe that, in human society, joining a club or a clique is a means to define and visually display "who we are," shaping and reflecting one's power and reputation in a way that will elevate one's status, image, and self-esteem in non-violent, but competitive ways. Thus, individuals are willing to pay high admission fees, often higher than the instrumental goods generated by membership, in order to signal their capabilities and intentions to their surrounding environment and to themselves. From a sociological perspective, the social order of society is based on a hierarchy of status groups, just as classes are part of the economic order.[6] This hierarchy reflects the perceived distribution of power within a community, i.e. a high place grants more power.[7] Therefore, membership in clubs is a visible symbol of one's high position and status.[8] Thus, clubs are regarded as status organizations.[9] The desire to join an exclusive club is an expression of the human desire and need to "belong." Nevertheless, the perception of "us" is always in contrast to the other, the "them."

---

[3] Adler, P., and Adler, P., "Dynamics of Inclusion and Exclusion in Preadolescent Cliques," *Social Psychological Quarterly*, 58:3, (1995), 145, 160; Brown, B., "The Role of Peer Groups in Adolescents' Adjustment to Secondary School," in T.J. Berndt and G.W. Ladd, (eds.), *Peer Relationships in Child Development*, (New York: Wiley & Sons, 1989), 188–215.

[4] The most famous group is the Freemasons.

[5] Fraternities and sororities are an integral part of college life. Another example is the Ivy League, which implies academic excellence and social elitism.

[6] Roth, G., and Wittich, C., (eds.), *Economy and Society: An Outline of Interpretive Sociology by Max Weber*, (Berkley: University of California Press, 1978), ixxxvii.

[7] Gerth, H. H., and Mills, C. W., (eds.), *From Max Weber: Essays in Sociology*, (London: Routledge and Kegan Paul, 1948), 181.

[8] Roth, G., and Wittich, C., (eds.), *Economy and Society*, 347.

[9] This observation derives from a wide range of scholarship in economics. Although a few studies focused on clubs in the 1950s, e.g. those by Charles Tiebout and Jack Weisman, Economist James Buchanan is most associated with the "Club Theory" he developed in the 1960s. For further reading, see Buchanan, J. M., "An Economic Theory of Clubs," *Economica*, 32:125, (1965), 1–14; Tiebout, C., "A Pure Theory of Local Expenditures," *Journal of Political Economy*, 65:5, (1956), 416–424; Hansmann, H., "A Theory of Status Organization," *Journal of Law, Economics and Organization*, 2:1, (Spring 1986), 119–130; DeSerpa, A. C., "A Theory of Discriminatory Clubs," *Scottish Journal of Political Economy*, 24:1, (1977), 33–41; Bergals, E., "On the Theory of Clubs," *American Economic Review*, 66:2, (1976), 116–121; Sandler, T., and Tschirhart, J., "Club Theory: Thirty Years Later," *Public Choice*, 93, (1997), 335–355; McGuire, M., "Private Good Clubs and Public Good Clubs: Economic Models of Group Formation," *Swedish Journal of Economics* 74:1, (1972), 84–99; Sorenson, J., Tschirhart, J., and Whinston A., "Private Good Clubs and the Core," *Journal of Public Economics*, 10:1, (1978), 77–95.

By joining an exclusive club, individuals distance themselves from low status actors or groups to which they want to appear superior, and they try to include themselves in high status groups of equal or greater status to their own. Apart from drawing a clear distinction between haves and have-nots, the act of joining a club provides legitimacy and justification of one's ability and status, as well as of the order and structure of the exclusive group.[10]

Another way of understanding the phenomenon of grouping into clubs is through the prism of human motivations and group behavior.[11] Current psychological research on nationalism shows that people aspire to join clubs and be identified with other club members because belonging to clubs improves and increases their self-worth.[12] Membership in exclusive clubs, so explained, improves self-esteem and pride, which are basic human needs and motivations. Self-esteem is both a general sense of one's proper dignity and value, and it is a specific pleasure or satisfaction taken from (actual or expected) achievement or possession.[13] Maslow (1943) described two forms of esteem: the need for respect from others and the need for inner self-respect.[14] The recognition and acceptance embedded in club membership provide respect and appreciation by others, which are important for one's sense of self-esteem and pride. To summarize this section: Exclusive clubs operate as agencies of socialization and stratification in various dimensions of human society.[15]

---

[10] Knottnerus, J. D., "Social Structure Analysis and Status Generalization: The Contributions and Potential of Expectation State Theory," in J. Szmatka, J. Skvoretz, and J. Berger, (eds.), *Status, Network, and Structure: Theory Development in Group Processes*, (Stanford: Stanford University Press, 1997), 128–129.

[11] Jackson, J. M., "A Space for Conceptualizing Person-Group Relationships," *Human Relations*, 12:1, (1959), 3–15; Hornsey, M. J., "The Individual within the Group: Balancing the Need to Belong with the Need to Be Different," *Personality and Social Psychology Review*, 8:3, (2004), 248–264; Hogg, M., Hohman, Z., and Rivera, J., "Why Do People Join Groups? Three Motivational Accounts From Social Psychology," *Social and Personality Psychology Compass*, 2, (2008), 1269–1280; Sheldon, K. M., and Bettencourt, B. A., "Psychological Need-Satisfaction and Subjective Well-Bring within Social Groups," *British Journal of Social Psychology*, 41, (2002), 25–38.

[12] Greenfield, L., *Nationalism: Five Roads to Modernity*. (Cambridge, MA: Harvard University Press, 1992); Migdal, J. S., *Boundaries and Belongings: States and Societies in the Struggle to Shape Identities and Local Practices*, (Cambridge: Cambridge University Press, 2004); Hall, R. B., *National Collective Identity: Social Constructs and International System*. (New York: Columbia University Press, 1999), as cited in Lebow, R. N., *A Cultural Theory of International Relations*, (New York: Cambridge University Press, 2008), 17.

[13] Hymans, J., *The Psychology of Nuclear Proliferation*, (Cambridge: Cambridge University Press, 2006), 33.

[14] Maslow, A., "A Theory of Human Motivation," *Psychological Review*, 50:4, (1943), 370–396.

[15] Smucker, O., "The Campus Clique As An Agency of Socialization," *Journal of Educational Sociology*, 21:3, (November 1947), 163–168.

People join clubs to win tangible goods and intangible benefits, and to fulfill social aspirations as well as inner needs.

Conceptualizing Nation-State Clubs in World Politics

A widely accepted truism among IR scholars, realists, or liberalists is that states operate rationally and are therefore expected to adopt policies that maximize their interests while minimizing costs. They explain decisions (and behavior) to develop indigenous capabilities and investments of resources in fields like space technology and nuclear energy through cost/benefit calculations of security and self-reliance, the desire to achieve a high level of development for economic goods, or even the need to gain international prestige.[16] According to this logic, it would be irrational to assume that states make tremendous efforts and invest invaluable resources out of an arbitrary motivation to be a member of a club. Nevertheless, realists fail to explain why states often decide to invest large-scale resources in "impractical" projects that do not have conspicuous material benefits for their national security, like scientific missions to deep space, human space missions, etc. They also do not completely explain indigenous development of expensive capabilities for practical use that are available through foreign or commercial suppliers at much lower costs. Liberalists attribute value to the impact of domestic politics on state behavior, the implications of interdependency among states,[17] and the role of global norms and institutions in promoting international cooperation. For them, the explanatory mechanism for states' behavior is a struggle for consensus, progress, economic development, societal welfare, and mutual gain, rather than a struggle for power and survivability.[18] However, their arguments are also based on the premise that states are rational actors operating according to tangible cost-effective calculations. They too fail to explain national decisions to embark on large-scale national projects that do not provide concrete tangible cost-effective benefits.

---

[16] Prestige is a strategy in the quest for honor and standing in world politics. It should be regarded as a means to an end, not an end in itself. Lebow, R. N., *A Cultural Theory*, 15–16, 22, 71–72; Stein, A., *Why Nations Cooperate?* (Ithaca, NY: Cornell University Press, 1990), 4; Keohane, R., (ed.), *Neo-Realism and Its Critics*, (New York: Columbia University Press, 1986), 7; Morgenthau, H., *Politics among Nations*, Fourth Edition, (New York: Alfred Knopf, 1967); Deutsch, K., *The Analysis of International Relations*, Second Edition, (Englewood Cliffs, NJ: Prentice Hall, 1978).

[17] Keohane, R., and Nye, J., *Power and Interdependence: World Power in Transition*, (Boston: Little, Brown, 1977).

[18] Kegely C., and Wittkopf, E. R., *World Politics: Trends and Transformation*, (Belmont, CA: Thomson Wadsworth, 1999), 32.

National decisions to develop large-scale projects such as space programs or nuclear programs may also be explained by aspirations for status and self-esteem.[19] Nevertheless, how and why are certain qualities perceived as indicators of power and symbols of high standing while others are not? These explanations are also inadequate when juxtaposed with the fact that such qualities and expertise are often associated with an exclusive group of states – a club. Moreover, they do not provide sufficient answers to situations wherein certain states aspire to "join clubs" while others, similar to them, do not.

Means and symbols of power change over time. Their meaning and effect depend on the social structure of the system and its norms.[20] Norms and conventions about power shape the goals of states, their perceptions of their interests, and the means they use to achieve those goals.[21] The basis of this is communitarian knowledge, which enables sharing meaning and understanding through learning ideas, perspectives, and norms.[22] Therefore, an understanding of the logic, interests, and behavior of states in world politics can be obtained by examining the international structure of meaning and social values that shape policymakers' conception of the international system and the position of their states in that system. As Finnemore pointed out, "States are *socialized* (italics in original) to want certain things by the international society ... interests are often not the result of external threats or demands by

---

[19] Status as a motivation has been extensively explored in IR and so was the issue of roles. For further reading, see Deng, Y., *China's Struggle for Status*, (Cambridge: Cambridge University Press, 2008); Heimann, G., "What Does It Take to Be a Great Power? The Story of France Joining the Big Five," *Review of International Studies*, 41:1, (January 2015), 185–206; Lake, D. A., *Hierarchy in International Relations*, (Ithaca, NY: Cornell University Press, 2009); Larson, D., and Shevchenko, A., "Status Seekers: Chinese and Russian Responses to U.S. Primacy," *International Security*, 34:4, (2010), 63–95; Lebow, R. N., *Why Nations Fight* (New York: Cambridge University Press, 2010); Onea, A. T., "Between Dominance and Decline: Status Anxiety and Great Power Rivalry," *Review of International Studies*, 40:1, (January 2014), 125–152; Paul, T. V., Larson, D., and Wohlforth, W., (Eds), *Status in World Politics*. (Cambridge: Cambridge University Press, 2014); Volgy, T., Corbetta, R., Grant, K., and Baird, R., (Eds), *Major Powers and the Quest for Status in World Politics*, (New York: Palgrave Macmillan, 2011).

[20] Wendt, A., *Social Theory of International Politics*, (Cambridge: Cambridge University Press, 1999), 20.

[21] Florini, A., "The Evolution of International Norms," *International Studies Quarterly*, 40:3, (September 1996), 365–366.

[22] One of the mechanisms affecting this process is the epistemic community, which coordinates or structures international politics by implementing expectations and values in the policy-making process. For further reading, see Adler, E., and Hass, P. M., "Conclusion: Epistemic Communities, World Order, and the Creation of International Policy Coordination," *International Organization*, 46:1, (Winter 1992), 367–390; Adler, E., *Communitarian International Relations: The Epistemic Foundation of International Relations*, (London: Routledge, 2004).

domestic groups. Rather, they are shaped by internationally shared norms and values."[23] For example, Eyre and Suchman (1996) argued that the proliferation of high-technology weaponry throughout the world occurs due to the socially constructed meanings that have become associated with them.[24]

Similarly, states learn to perceive certain qualities as more powerful and valuable than others. The development of these qualities is respected because the process of development is long, difficult, uncertain, and dangerous. It involves a high level of risk and many failures along the way, an outcome that affects the state's capabilities, status, and image.[25] Nevertheless, success of development brings significant tangible capabilities, usually of a dual-use nature, meaning capabilities that carry implications for the society and economy as well as for national security. Therefore, the act of choosing to develop indigenous national expertise is interpreted, understood, and acknowledged in terms of a struggle for power, high standing, and self-esteem. Under this shared meaning of what grants power and high status, and what it takes to achieve it, states acknowledge the ones that develop those qualities as more powerful and together defines them as an elite club. Building on this reasoning and on what is known about human clubs, the primary argument of this work is that joining nation-state clubs is a legitimate, rational, and significant national consideration.

Nation-State Clubs: Definition and Typology

A nation-state club in world politics is a structure that separates a small and limited number of countries from the rest of the world because they possess unique capabilities that do not exist in most countries. Nevertheless, these capabilities are widely perceived as strategic assets having qualities that provide tangible goods for national security as well as for the economy and thus enhance power, high standing, and prestige. The club has a significant role in organizing the social structure of the international system because it allows countries to interact, compare, and compete with each other for power and status, and to evaluate each other

---

[23] Finnemore, M., *National Interests in International Society*, (Ithaca, NY: Cornell University Press, 1996), 2–3.
[24] Eyre, D., and Suchman, M., "Status, Norms and the Proliferation of Conventional Weapons: An Institutional Theory Approach," in P. Katzenstein, (ed.), *The Culture of National Security*, (New York: Columbia University Press, 1966), 86.
[25] Hirschman, A., *Development Projects Observed*, (Washington, DC: Brookings Institution, 1967); Flyvbjerg, B., Brizelius, N., and Rothengatter, W., *Megaprojects and Risk: An Anatomy of Ambition*, (Cambridge: Cambridge University Press, 2003).

according to these parameters. These interactions provide tangible goods as well as the intangible benefits of power and elevated status.

In addition to the tangible and intangible club good shared by club-member states, they also share responsibility for their actions and are expected to act in accordance with the norms and standards developed in the club. For example, the space club members jointly act to mitigate and prevent the increase of space debris in order to assure a sustainable space environment.[26]

This brings us to the question: What makes club members accept new members into the club and risk erosion of its exclusivity? Sometimes, despite the risk of losing some of the club's reputation and exclusiveness, accepting a new capable state into the club is a better choice than declining it membership, because it allows for better control of the new member's activities and forces some rules on it. It also strengthens the existence of the club and the position of its gatekeepers. For example, aside from the benefits entailed, the members of the "nuclear club" also carry responsibilities, explained Walter Slocombe, former Undersecretary of Defense during the Clinton Administration: "When India detonated its nuclear device in 1998, there was a sense in the United States, and in other states as well, that they finally came out of the closet and we need to come and talk to them about command and control, about targeting, about issues of security and so on."[27] India was eventually evaluated by the United States, the gatekeeper of the club, as having more power, but initially, India had been severely criticized by the United States. A decade later, under the Bush Administration, there was a change. India was recognized as "powerful," and thus should be rightly regarded as a power. In other words, it was "counted" by the key players.[28] That was an important source of pride and national esteem.

The typology of nation-state clubs includes two first-level categories: formal clubs, for example, the UN Security Council, the OECD, etc.; and informal clubs like the space club or the nuclear club. At the second level of the typology, clubs are categorized based on various characteristics of the management, admission, and interactions among its members, as explained in Table 2.1. Formal nation-state clubs may take the form of international organizations. Such clubs have a secretariat charged with implementing policies and other decisions of the governing body. Joining

---

[26] China's 2007 experiment in ASAT capabilities intensified the international process concerning debris mitigation.
[27] Interview with Walter Slocombe, former Undersecretary of Defense during the Clinton Administration, November 22, 2007, Tel Aviv, Israel.
[28] For a comprehensive analysis of India's case, see Rabinowotz, O., *Bargaining on Nuclear Tests: Washington and Its Cold War Deals*, (Oxford: Oxford University Press, 2014).

Table 2.1 *Types of Clubs and Their Characteristics*

	Formal Club	Informal Club
Organizing mechanism	Yes	No
Process of joining a club	Structured process of admission defined by the organizing mechanism	Public demonstration of associated qualities and declaration of joining the club by the state itself
Club membership	Pending approval by other members or acceptance committee	Self-joins, but pending the recognition by key members of the club
Interaction among members	Continuous and direct interactions	Loose and indirect interactions

a formal and organized club is similar to the process states undergo when joining other international organizations. The "wannabe" member-state has to apply for membership and follow a structured acceptance process. Its membership is pending upon approval by an acceptance mechanism, such as an acceptance committee. Informal nation-state clubs carry no legal authority. They are not structured by an international arrangement or established by formal international agreements, they have no secretariat, and the members are not closely linked. Their legitimacy is rooted in broad acknowledgment of the unique capabilities or qualities around which they center.

As explained above, the process a state has to follow in order to join an informal nation-state club is usually composed of three stages. The first stage requires a public demonstration of capability or expertise in the area associated with the specific club, for example, launching a satellite into space or detonating a nuclear device. The second stage involves a public statement by leaders and/or state officials that their state has joined the club. In the third stage, other members of the club acknowledge the efforts of the joining state and welcome the new member into the club. In principle, in an informal club such as the space club, there are no official entry restrictions, but each country relies on national capability and political will to pull it off. Other members of the club are able to exclude a country from the club and deny its membership by refusing to cooperate with it in various ways, such as refusal to sell needed materials or the imposition of export controls on commerce and cooperation with this country, among other measures.

Acceptance into the club is granted to new members through joint ventures, exchange of information, and other methods of cooperation. This process has no legal meaning; instead, it has a political meaning. Without recognition, nation-states that claim to have achieved the qualities and capabilities at stake are not granted the status or afforded club benefits, including material advantages reserved exclusively for members.

The nature of interactions among club members derives from the structure of the club. Members of formal clubs interact and collaborate in a variety of ways, for example, determining the club's code of conduct or establishing admission requirements. Members of informal clubs do not always interact directly. Loose relationships often exist, even among rival countries. Such interactions have to do with the duties that club members take upon themselves in addressing collective challenges, setting norms of behavior, and so forth. For example, even during the Cold War, there was always some collaboration regarding space activity between the United States and the Soviet Union. Today, despite tense relations, interactions take place between the United States and China, although to a much lesser extent than the interactions that took place between the United States and the Soviet Union. The interaction between them mainly involves diplomatic coordination activities regarding the sustainability of the space environment and small-scale cooperation. In October 2015, the first meeting between the United States and China, as part of the official dialogue on space, took place in Beijing. Both sides agreed on the need to strengthen the ties between the two countries vis-à-vis space.[29]

Clubs also differ in the structure of their membership. Clubs may provide homogenous membership in which members are equal in their costs, privileges, and responsibilities, or they may provide heterogeneous or hierarchical membership. In the latter form, members are unequal in their investments, capabilities, and ensuing benefits and duties. Such clubs have levels of membership. Membership at the lower level requires only moderate costs and provides moderate benefits, while membership at higher levels involves high risks and costs but provides more valuable benefits.

A nation-state club is related to other forms of international institutions, such as international regimes, international organizations, or security communities, in which nation-states often tend to group. The primary

---

[29] Staff Writers, "The First Meeting of the US-China Space Dialogue," *Space Daily*, October 1, 2015, available at: www.spacedaily.com/reports/The_First_Meeting_of_th e_U_S__China_Space_Dialogue_999.html, accessed on February 8, 2016.

characteristic differentiating a club from these types of groupings is its purpose and role.

International organizations (IOs)[30] and international regimes[31] are formed in order to coordinate behavior among several countries regarding a certain issue. A security community is an integrated group of states that do not fight each other physically and is designed to settle disputes and conflicts among its members using other, more peaceful means.[32] It develops when several states share values, meaning and identity, and establish a peaceful order between them. Unlike these types of groupings, a nation-state club is not designed to coordinate behavior. A club of states is a competitive institution, which exemplifies the means and symbols of power of that period and reflects the perceived distribution of power. The cub is designed to allow nations to evaluate one another's power, status and influence, and compete over it. For the most part, international organizations, regimes, security communities, and clubs are based on a broad consensus regarding shared ideas and perceptions. For example, these perceptions may regard the means and symbols of power, mutual interests regarding these means, etc. Another feature they have in common is that the broad-based consensus is achieved through means of attraction rather than coercion. This feature enables members to

---

[30] For literature on international organizations, see Rochester, J. M., "The Rise and Fall of International Organizations," *International Organizations*, 40:4, (Autumn 1986), 777–813; Keohane, R., *International Institutions and State Power*, (Boulder, CO: Westview Press, 1989); Finnemore, M., "International Organizations As Teachers of Norms: The United Nations Educational, Scientific, and Cultural Organization and Science Policy," *International Organization*, 47:4, (Autumn 1993), 592; Katzenstein, P., Keohane, R., and Krasner, S., "International Organization and the Study of World Politics," *International Organization*, 52:4, (Autumn 1998), 645–685; Barnett, M., and Finnemore, M., "The Politics, Power and Pathologies of International Organizations," *International Organizations*, 53:4, (Autumn 1999), 699–732.

[31] Steven Krasner defines international regimes as "implicit or explicit principles, norms, rules and decision-making procedures around which actors' expectations converge in a given area of international relations." Krasner, S., (ed.), (1983), *International Regimes*, (Ithaca, NY: Cornell University Press), 2. For more literature on regimes, see Hass, E. R., "Words Can Hurt You, or Who Said What to Whom about Regimes," *International Organization*, 36:2, (Spring 1982), 207–243; Hass, E. R., "Why Collaborate? Issue-Linkage and International Regimes," *World Politics*, 32:3, (April 1980), 357–405; Jervis, R., "Security Regimes," *International Organization*, 36:2, (1982), 357–378; Haggard, S., and Simmons, B., "Theories of International Regimes," *International Organization*, 41:3, (Summer 1987), 491–517.

[32] Security communities were first introduced as a theoretical framework in IR by Karl Deutsch. In the post–Cold War era, the concept was adopted by constructivist scholars and further developed, especially by Emanuel Adler and Michael Barnett. For further information, see Deutsch, K., Burrell, S., Kann, R., Jr., and Lee, M., *Political Community and the North Atlantic Area: International Organization in the Light of Historical Experience*, (Princeton, NJ: Princeton University Press, 1957); Adler, E., and Barnett, M., (eds.) *Security Communities*, (Cambridge: Cambridge University Press, 1981).

experience a sense of community. Membership in a club does not eliminate existing tensions between competing members, but the interaction is usually neither aggressive nor conducted through military force. Nevertheless, while IOs, regimes, and security communities derive their authority, power, legitimacy, and effectiveness from the widest possible adherence and participation of the target population, and they are, therefore, based on broad accessibility.[33] The club's uniqueness is that, as an elite group, it must preserve a wide and clear gap between the haves and have-nots. Only by keeping the gates closed does the exclusivity and appeal of the club in terms of power, standing, and esteem remain. Access to all grants no significance to the achievement of joining a club. Therefore, the club must provide a barrier that separates members from non-members and create among the members a sense of belonging to a special superior group.[34]

In this sense, the club exemplifies an inherent tension between competition and cooperation. Countries compete with each other to enter into the club. Members of the club compete with other members of the club in order to win power and status, but they also cooperate with each other. Cooperation among them is important in order to set the boundaries between members and non-members. Recognition in other nation's membership in the club is awarded through cooperation. In addition, limited cooperation with countries that are not members of the club often highlights the boundary for entrance into the club, since cooperation of this kind will not take place in areas that constitute a criterion to enter the club.

When it comes to structure, unlike international regimes and IOs, clubs and security communities may take the form of informal associations. Informal clubs and informal security communities are not structured by international arrangement or established by formal international agreements, have no secretariat, and members are not closely linked together. With time, though, they may develop into formal institutions or organizations. The Non-Proliferation Treaty (NPT) regime, in contrast to the "nuclear club," is a good example of this distinction. In both cases, broad consensus is formed around the tangible and intangible benefits provided by nuclear capability and the risks of its proliferation. The NPT grants relatively easy access to nuclear energy to the states that follow its rules, while nuclear weapons knowhow is not easily accessed because of barriers put up by the international community – especially by the states possessing these weapons,

---

[33] There are several unique regimes that are exclusive because their members control which states are allowed to join, for example, the Missile Technology Control Regime.
[34] Wendt, A., "Collective Identity Formation and the International State," *American Political Science Review*, 88:2, (1994), 384–396.

i.e. the nuclear powers. Thus, there is no club of states with nuclear energy capabilities, while there is a "nuclear club" of states that possess nuclear weapons.

The primary variables differentiating clubs from other types of groupings are summarized in Table 2.2.

Table 2.2 *Comparison of International Regimes, Security Communities, and Nation-State Clubs*

	International Regime	Security Community	Nation-State Club
Purpose/ functionality	Coordinate behavior among several countries regarding a specific issue	Solve conflicts peacefully	Structural expression of the distribution / competition of power & status; serves as an arena for interaction
Authority and power are derived from	Broad consensus on shared ideas and perceptions		
Normative base of Authority	Attraction allowing a sense of community		
Principle of accession	Inclusion	Inclusion	Exclusion
No. of members out of target population	Large number	Large number	Small number

The Life Cycle of Nation-State Clubs

The process by which nation-state clubs emerge has five stages and involves a variety of actors, each of which competes for power and standing. In the *first stage*, key players, usually the superpowers, develop unique capabilities in order to project power and achieve leadership and competency. Nevertheless, the status of pre-eminence and leadership rests on legitimacy from other nation-states, which accept this interpretation as true reality. Therefore, it has to be earned. The way to earn it is through what Nye refers to as soft power[35] and attraction, i.e. by convincing others

---

[35] Josef Nye developed the concept of "soft power" in the early 1990s in order to explain the ability to influence and persuade through attraction rather than by coercion or the use of military force. Nye first coined this term in his 1991 book, *Bound to Lead: The Changing Nature of American Power*, (New York: Basic Books, 1991). Nye further developed the concept in his 2004 book, *Soft Power*; in his 2011 book, *The Future of Power*; and in

to follow.[36] In this regard, Bially Mattern (2005) observed that " ... the most fundamental way to 'harvest' soft power is to spread social knowledge about one's values."[37] Based on these observations, I argue that in order to win primacy, superpowers must socially construct means and symbols of power, using a communicative strategy in an attempt not to leave any room to refuse their interpretation of power.

For this reason, in the *second stage*, the superpowers socialize states to accept their interpretation of power and adopt collectively held norms about power, standing, and prestige. In practice, the development of skills is followed by public demonstrations of capability and rhetoric concerning their superior qualities. Bially Mattern referred to such a process as coercion of attractiveness through verbal fighting.[38] Attraction is even more successful when others respond to the construction of power and wish to follow it, not only in accepting the ideas but also by emulating deeds. Thus, *the third stage* is realized when a positive reinforcement cycle of these conventions and norms ensues. In their struggle for power and standing, large- and medium-sized nations seek to obtain similar qualities and means of power because they understand and believe that, in order to sustain their status or improve it, they are expected to demonstrate indigenous expertise of the unique capability. Nevertheless, this is not enough to create a club. Clubs will not develop if such capabilities are widespread. The relative advantage that grants primacy is in its small numbers. Consequently, in the *fourth stage* of this process, although the key players offer cooperation to allies and others in order to attract nations to their side, they must strictly control the proliferation of the capabilities at stake in an attempt to win the competition and preserve their tangible and intangible advantage and competency. Therefore, the key players impose severe restrictions on the diffusion of knowledge and the transfer of technology and other critical elements.

In the *fifth stage*, the process of attraction on one hand and control on the other hand, which is aimed at setting boundaries to exclude others from joining, marks the individual states that acquired the means and symbols of power and separates them from the others. Together, they are perceived by others, as well as by themselves, as an exclusive group – a club. The actions of the superpowers limit the number of those that have

---

numerous articles. Since then, the term has been widely used, and discussed and debated extensively in IR.

[36] Nye, J. S., *Bound to Lead*.

[37] Bially Mattern, J., "Why Soft Power Isn't So Soft: Representational Force and the Sociolinguistic Construction of Attraction in World Politics," *Millennium – Journal of International Studies*, 33, (2005), 589.

[38] Bially Mattern, J., "Why Soft Power Isn't So Soft," 602.

the capability (even though they cannot totally control it) and shape the image of the group as an exclusive club. By controlling proliferation of knowledge and technology, they become the club's gatekeepers.

Finally, the *sixth stage* in the life cycle of a club is its demise. A club will cease to operate if it loses its attractiveness in the eyes of the large powers and wannabes as a symbol for defining a powerful country. This will happen when the number of actors with proven indigenous capabilities associated with the specific club dramatically increases. Such a process would lead to a drop in the added value and intangible benefits that come with having expertise in the area at the heart of the club. In such a case, the greatest challenge faced by the leading members of the club is to maintain a clear and excludable boundary between members and non-members of the club. Therefore, the future of a club depends on the willingness of its leading members to preserve its small size by redesigning a higher barrier between the haves and have-nots. If they fail, the club would cease to exist.

Another option that may lead to the demise of a club is the rise of a new club, which would replace it as the benchmark for acquiring a seat at the table of the large powers that affect global governance. In such a case, the superpowers and other large powers would lose interest in preserving a clear boundary between the haves and haves-not in the subject matter, and shift their efforts to another field that would better serve their interests in power and status.

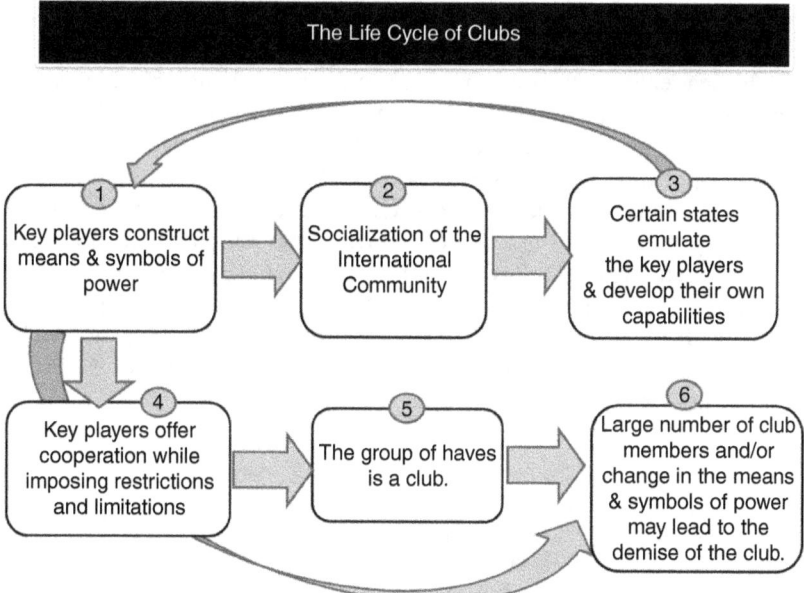

Figure 2.1 The Life Cycle of Clubs

The demise of the "club of dreadnoughts" is an example of this process. In past centuries, battleships were means and symbols of power. In World War I, the ability to put a fleet of dreadnoughts to sea was still a powerful quality, which had an effect on the war. But by World War II, this club no longer existed. The dreadnought was no longer a symbol or a prestige weapon, and other, newer weapons had become means and symbols of power. The club of dreadnoughts lost its place to the total mechanization of war, which was then replaced by the nuclear club and the space club (see Figure 2.1).[39]

Nation-State Clubs as Arenas for Interaction between States

In order to better understand the role of clubs in the interaction between states, we need to understand what club membership provides and how it is used by club members and wannabes in world politics. Club membership is used to construct a situation, such as a new technological reality, and communicate it to an international audience and the domestic population as a strategic achievement. In general, by claiming membership in a club, decision-makers and state officials try to convince others to adopt their social and political interpretation of the achieved capability in terms of power, status, and esteem, and provide them with a conceptual tool to evaluate the achievement. Nevertheless, the strategic rationale changes according to the power and status of the actor. Strong players or superpowers need the recognition of less powerful countries in their claims for world leadership. Without recognition, their claims for power and leadership are meaningless. For them, the club is a highly valuable structure to use to claim the power and status of superpowers. They use its appeal to smaller states in order to further their interests and maintain leadership and superiority. They do so by convincing less powerful states that high values would result for them, if only these smaller states would follow in the their footsteps. Thus, the stronger states win legitimacy and acknowledgment of their greater power and status as leaders. International recognition of the existence of the club is a significant message of support and acknowledgment of their capability, leadership, and superiority.

---

[39] Space is perceived as the arena replacing the seas in its importance to global dominance and world leadership. For further reading, see France, M., "Back To The Future: Space Power Theory and A.T. Mahan," *Space Policy*, 16, (2000), 237–241.

Nevertheless, the great powers have conflicting interests regarding the spread of capabilities. As explained above, they have a great interest in convincing others about the great potential of these capabilities. However, if these capabilities are accessible to everyone, the actual benefit the great powers derive from these capabilities for their national security and for their economy will be harmed, and their leadership would be challenged. For this reason, they do not favor an expansion of the number of countries possessing these capabilities. As a result, they take the role of gatekeepers of the club. In this role, they preserve the boundaries of the club by imposing strict controls on access to it and by offering only limited cooperation in areas that are not considered criteria to enter into the club.

In the hands of less powerful states, carrying the heavy burden of developing indigenous capability (even if it does not necessarily provide immediate or direct benefits) while framing the achievement in the context of club membership serves as a credible message of power. When intended for adversaries, it is a message of deterrence. When aimed at more powerful allies or other like-minded countries, it is a message of capability that projects power and the determination to achieve national goals. The aim of the joining state is to convince the members of the club to take it seriously and to grant greater power and higher status to it, which will come as its considerations are taken into account. On a more practical level, the aim is also that club membership will induce cooperation, which will provide material advantages.

The procurement of artillery cannons and battleships are fine examples. In the late sixteenth century, cannons were, according to Pacey (1991), "... too heavy to maneuver for aiming, and took so long to reload that they were of very little military use [But] ... They were also status symbols, they expressed dreams of power and they could represent the more formidable of manly virtues for that time."[40] Despite their burden or the handicaps they imposed on their users in the battlefield, states acquired artillery. The cannons served as a signal, a way of communicating the intent, aspirations, and capability of their holders to other states. In the late nineteenth and early twentieth centuries, battleships or dreadnoughts were perceived as means and symbols of power because they provided their holders advanced military capabilities and valuable economic benefits. The nations that acquired this expertise – Great Britain[41],

---

[40] Pacey, A., *Technology in World Civilization*, (Cambridge, MA: MIT Press, 1991), 78.

[41] Britain's navy played a significant role in the build-up and expansion of the British Empire. As a military power, the navy defended the Empire's borders and allowed its economy to flourish.

France, Russia, and later Germany – were perceived to be a superior group.[42]

In the hands of the weak or small, club membership is a tool to gain empowerment, get attention, and be placed in a higher category of capability and power than the one to which they actually belong; this is often done at the expense of the strong and powerful. In some cases, the attempt to enhance and glorify the mere declaration of membership in a club is no more than a substitute for a real achievement, and it may even cover failures or a lack of achievement. To further stress this point, some may argue that club membership is a form of swaggering behavior, because it provides high and powerful status "on the cheap."[43] Swaggering behavior seeks to enhance national pride or satisfy the personal ambitions of a state's ruler. The state and its leaders want to look and feel more powerful and important in order to be taken seriously by others in the councils of international decision-making. If a state's swaggering causes other states to take its interests more seriously, then the state will benefit.[44]

The discussion of credible empowerment and swaggering behavior leads us to address the importance of acquiring recognition and legitimacy of empowerment efforts by other club members as well as by non-members. Without recognition, claims for power and club membership are meaningless; club members are not granted the status or afforded material advantages reserved exclusively for members. International recognition, therefore, is a significant message of support and acknowledgment of the capability of the state. The status of the joining state, compared to states that aspire to join the club, is enhanced, and the morale of its professional community and population is strengthened. In general, the claim for membership in the club is aimed at creating proximity to other club members in order to make it difficult for them to object to the new reality and even to convince club members to accept the new situation as a legitimate build-up of capabilities and high standing.

These characteristics of a nation-state club and the interactions among its members correspond with the security dilemma that states are often challenged with regarding their efforts and aspirations for empowerment and provide at least a partial solution to the problem. A security dilemma refers to a situation in which a country that aims to increase the level of its

---

[42] Moll, K., "Politics, Power, and Panic: Britain's 1900 Dreadnoughts 'Gap'," *Military Affairs*, 29:3, (Autumn 1965), 133–144.

[43] Jervis, R., *The Logic of Images in International Relations*, (New York: Columbia University Press, 1989), 14, 55.

[44] Art, R., "To What Ends Military Power?" *International Security*, 4:4, (Spring 1980), 10–11.

security by upgrading its military force or by getting the support of a strong ally ultimately finds itself threatened and insecure. This is because the desire for increased power can bring with it too much power, which could force an increase in the power of both opponents and friends who are concerned by its empowerment efforts in a way that could put the country that began the process in danger. Thus, in the end, instead of solving a security problem, the process can exacerbate it.[45] The result of this dynamic could be a chain reaction or what Robert Jervis referred to as a "spiral model," in which empowerment efforts could escalate into direct conflict that would lead to a war, even when it is undesirable to all involved parties; during the Cold War, many analysts feared that the nuclear arms race could result in outright war.[46]

International relations scholarship deals extensively with the security dilemma to search for effective ways to solve it. Strategies for dealing with the dilemma are mainly focused on reducing the fear and uncertainty, especially in relation to the intentions of the opponent. For example, a defensive approach followed by defensive technologies instead of an offensive approach.[47] This idea tracks back to Clausewitz's seminal work *On War*, in which he argued that it is in the power of defensive measures to reduce the desire of both parties to launch an attack.[48] Following this logic, adoption of offensive measures may increase the likelihood of war because it could serve as a catalyst for arms races.[49] To stress this further, defensive strategies and technologies offer a solution to the security dilemma in several ways. First, defensive measures upgrade capability to deal with and prevent surprise attacks.[50] Second, defensive measures can raise the cost of an attack and, therefore, discourage an opponent from attacking.[51] Third, defensive measures can help increase the sense of security while not decreasing the sense of security of the other side. When the other side also takes

---

[45] Davis, Z., "The Realist Nuclear Regime," *Security Studies*, 2, (Spring/Summer 1993), 80.
[46] Jervis, R., "Cooperation under the Security Dilemma," *World Politics*, 30:2, (January 1978), 167–174; and Jervis, R., *Perception and Misperception in International Politics* (Princeton, NJ: Princeton University Press, 1978), 58–113; and Davis, Z., "The Realist Nuclear Regime," 80.
[47] Glaser, C. L., "The Security Dilemma Revisited," *World Politics*, 50:1, (1997), 171–201
[48] Clausewitz, C., *On War*, (Princeton, NJ: Princeton University Press, 1976), 83–84
[49] Levi, J., "The Offensive/Defensive Balance of Military Technology: A Theoretical and Historical Analysis," *International Studies Quarterly*, 28:2, (1984), 221. Levi also provides a detailed discussion of the literature about the delicate balance between defensive measures and offensive measures.
[50] Oye, K. A., (1986), *Cooperation under Anarchy*, (Princeton, NJ: Princeton University Press, 1986), 10.
[51] Oye, K. A., *Cooperation under Anarchy*, 10.

defensive measures, the status quo can be maintained, bringing about a reversal of the dilemma.[52]

Sometimes, it is difficult to distinguish between offensive measures and defensive measures. Technological means can be used for defensive purposes and even for civil uses; at the same time, they can be useful for achieving military offensive objectives. The use of such measures for defensive purposes does not guarantee that they will not be used in the future for offensive purposes. Jervis (1978) argued therefore that the use of defensive-only measures is more valuable for the recession of the security dilemma. Defensive-only measures reduce the chance of defensive measures being misinterpreted as offensive measure and vice versa, thus helping to prove the peaceful intentions of their holder.[53] Among the measures that can be used effectively are technologies for verification and arms-control agreements, as well as the adoption of policies imposing self-restrictions on power.[54]

Similar to the strategy of adopting defensive measures, showing off civil and peaceful capabilities – even of dual-use technologies such as space technologies – that have significant military implications and framing them as a peaceful action of joining a club helps to keep the focus away from its potential threatening implications. Instead of showing off military strength, an action that may be interpreted as a direct threat and exacerbate a security dilemma, membership in clubs, such as the space club, and the display of capabilities in this context, is a non-violent strategy for evaluation and projection of power, as well as achieving high-standing. In this context, the demonstration of ASATs capability is counterproductive.

Moreover, the claim for club membership provides a non-threatening, but competitive context that enables adversaries, as well as allies, to more easily accept the new reality without having to directly address the very build-up of military power because in the absence of a direct military threat, they do not have to publicly respond and can therefore deny it. In the present age, in which military force and offensive measures can no longer be used for deterrence and for projection of power,[55] membership in clubs is a plausible alternative that can serve as a peaceful way of applying deterrence without developing a security dilemma.

Other than that, joining clubs by accomplishing impressive visible achievements and declarations is often a strategy of socially constructing

[52] Jervis, R., "Cooperation under the Security Dilemma," 167–214.
[53] Jervis, R., "Cooperation under the Security Dilemma," 201.
[54] Glaser, C. L., "The Security Dilemma Revisited," 171–201.
[55] Lebow, R. N., *Why Nations Fight*, (New York: Cambridge University Press, 2010), 21–22.

domestic messages of internal encouragement for the scientific community and for the industrial sector, as well as a message of high national esteem and patriotism, aimed at improving and increasing the overall solidarity and support of the people in their state, its bureaucratic system, and its leadership. In this context, the recognition, legitimacy, and elevated status that club membership entails at the international level also serves domestic objectives, because it improves the image of the regime and popularity of its leaders in the eyes of its citizens.[56] In this respect, it is compatible with techno-nationalism.

To summarize, membership in clubs helps to identify the stronger players and to differentiate between them and others. Membership is one of the criteria by which states measure and evaluate power, standing, and national proximity to other club members. It allows greater association between members, makes it easier to gather information, and encourages cooperation and opinion sharing. This enables club members to widen the gap between them and the outsiders and to deliberately delay – and even prevent – non-member states from acquiring capabilities and achievement in that area, hindering their efforts to join the club.

---

[56] Steinberg, G., "Large Scale National Projects as Political Symbols," *Comparative Politics*, 19:3, (April, 1987), 333.

3   The Evolution of the Space Club

The dropping of atomic bombs over Hiroshima and Nagasaki in August 1945, the launch of Sputnik in October 1957, and the Apollo 11 Moon landing in July 1969 were spectacular and visible scientific events of the twentieth century. These events ignited the imagination of millions throughout the world regarding the potential to challenge forces of nature as well as the potential of its destruction. Decision-makers as well as the population in many countries (even small or developing ones) were and still are convinced that investments in science and technology are indispensable instruments of national security, development, prosperity, and progress. Science and technology became critical elements of military power and political power, as well as a symbol of superiority in the modern era.[1] In the 1950s, UNESCO contributed to this process with the development of an international norm that "the coordination and direction of science is a necessary task of the modern state."[2]

In this context, the main argument of this chapter is that a threefold and sometimes conflicting techno-nationalist strategy, which was implemented by each of the superpowers separately, led to the emergence of the space club. The first strategy was to compete with each other using the displays of spectacular space projects, which were then constructed through language to strengthen the message of power and international standing. The second strategy was to perform international cooperation

---

[1] Lakoof, S., "Scientists, Technologists and Political Power," in I. Spiegel-Rosing, and D. de Solla-Price, (eds.), *Science, Technology and Society*, (London: Sage Publications, 1977), 365–366; Brodie, B., and Brodie, F. M., *From Crossbow to H-Bomb*, (Bloomington, Indiana University Press, 1973); Van Creveled, M., *Technology and War: From 2000 B.C. to the Present*, (New York: The Free Press, 1989); Pacey, A., *Technology in World Civilization*, (Cambridge: MIT press, 1991); Howard, M., *War and the Nation State*, (Oxford: Clarendon Press, 1978); Toffler, A., *The Third Wave*, (New-York: W. Morrow, 1980); Toffler, A., and Toffler, H., *War and Anti-War: Survival at the Dawn of the 21st Century*, (Boston: Little, Brown, 1993).

[2] Finnemore, M., *National Interests in International Society*, (Ithaca: Cornell University Press, 1996), 36–37. Finnemore states that before 1955, only fourteen countries had state science bureaucracies. By 1975, eighty-nine countries had established offices for this function (pp. 38–39).

on a limited scale to attract others to their side. Third was a strategy of restriction and control over the transfer of sensitive space technologies and knowhow with a civil-military dual-use potential. The logic of this strategy was to prevent proliferation of these technologies and knowhow in order to preserve the superpowers' strategic advantages over their allies, in addition to various national security, economic, and industrial needs they had.

This chapter deals with several issues. First, it describes the process by which national space programs became a means and a symbol of power and national might in the Cold War race to space. Second, it portrays and analyzes the strategies adopted by the Soviet Union and the United States in the early stages of the space age. Both superpowers used public strategies aside from their military and secretive ones. The performed strategies were characterized by an inherent tension between public competition and international cooperation in space in order to convince their domestic populations and other states of their supremacy over the other, and to justify their claim for world leadership. Nevertheless, in order to maintain a leading position, they performed strategies that were aimed to restrict proliferation of these technologies. Their behavior served as the foundation from which the "space club" evolved. Third, this chapter provides more insight regarding the fact that the superpowers were interested in determining the identity of the members of the club.

National Space Capability as a Symbol and as a Means of Power

In the minds of millions, space achievements have become today's symbol of tomorrow's scientific and technical supremacy.

James Webb, NASA Administrator[3]

The space age emerged from the last phases of World War II. The use of V-2 rockets by Nazi Germany and the demonstration of the first atomic bombs by the United States, although separate events, offered new meanings of power and of war. The A-bomb's ability to create total destruction combined with the ability to rapidly hit remote targets using ballistic missiles, as demonstrated by the V-2 rockets (later upgraded to intercontinental ballistic missiles), exposed the world to a new and frightening situation. Power and war were no longer about massed

---

[3] Webb, J., Address to the Annual Convention of the Federal Bar Association, Mayflower Hotel, Washington, DC. (September 13, 1961), NASA News Release, No. 51–205, 10, NASA HQ Historical Reference Collection, History Office, Digital Records.

armies and the industrial capability to fight a long war. Instead, war was about highly advanced scientific and technological capabilities to develop non-conventional weapons. Nevertheless, the superpowers feared a direct nuclear attack. They also realized that claims for global leadership and superiority were not enough; leadership had to be earned. For this reason, the superpowers channeled their hostility and antagonism into war by proxy and into non-violent competitions. The race to space is one of the conspicuous examples of this challenge. The reason for that was that space, which could be used for military and civil purposes, and its delivery systems had significant strategic implications; it offered new ways of obtaining and demonstrating power and global leadership. Achievements in space were a clear message of national might and deterrence in a rather peaceful manner.

The objective of both the Soviet Union and the United States was to impress and convince their allies, adversaries, other actors, and their own citizens of their claims for ideological superiority and power. Demonstrations of accomplishments in space were used by each country as proof of its right to claim world leadership. The competition over space achievements, the propaganda that followed, and other means of public diplomacy – together with the fact that it provided significant strategic capabilities – led to the emergence of international conventions that national space capability was critical to power and competence of the superpowers as world leaders. Space programs became a political practice that reflected on other good qualities of the capable state. In the late 1950s and early 1960s, it was debated that the nation that dominated space would be in a position to dominate the world.

An American report on the Soviet space program from 1962 expresses the attitude towards the political values of space achievements. Although it describes actions taken by the Soviets, it reflects on the way space advancements were professed by the Americans as well:

Achievements in space are an asset in international politics, related directly to prestige and power. The Soviets have appreciated the political utility of space. They have exploited their successes in order to (1) enhance their world position and lessen that of the United States; (2) change favorably the world image of the Soviet Union as a great power; (3) divide the Western alliance system; and (4) further their propaganda campaign of "peaceful coexistence."[4]

---

[4] Report on Soviet Space Programs: Organization, Plans, Goals, and International Implications, prepared for the use of the Committee on Aeronautical and Space Sciences of the United States Senate, May 31, 1962 (Washington, DC: US Government Printing Office), 45–46.

This approach was also accepted by other countries that followed in the footsteps of the United States and the Soviet Union and initiated national space programs of their own. Taking advantage of this trend, each of the two superpowers initiated cooperation programs to attract allies to their side. Engaging with other countries in limited cooperation allowed the superpowers to control and closely monitor the advancement of other countries in this field – especially with regards to their military capabilities or its potential to be used for military purposes – and put their methods and rules into practice, as well as advance their industries.

But then again, mastering the military implications of space technology was critical to the national security of the United States and of the Soviet Union; from this perspective, proliferation of critical space technologies and knowhow was a threat. For this reason and also in order to protect their industries from competition, each of them put constraints on technology transfer and carefully limited the spread of knowhow. These somewhat contradicting techno-nationalist strategies of using public technological demonstrations, performing limited cooperation, and the imposition of controls highlighted the exclusivity and high profile of space capability that other countries found so appealing. This inherent tension between cooperation and competition and restrictions served as a mechanism of exclusion, which distinguished between the small group of countries that had access to the development of space capability and the ones that did not.

The Beginning of the Race to Space: Secretive versus Public Space Policies

For both of them, my father and Korolev, the launch of the satellite (Sputnik) signified the affirmation of our, and their own personal, leadership in competition with the most highly developed country in the world.

Sergey Khrushchev, the son of Nikita Khrushchev[5]

In the 1950s, the Soviet leaders were more interested in ballistic missiles that would carry nuclear warheads than in space rockets or satellites. Sergey Korolev, the chief designer of the Soviet rocket program, wanted to send a satellite into space but knew that it would be difficult to convince the Soviet leadership to invest in impractical missions unless a new world record could be set. In February 27, 1956, Korolev met with Nikita Khrushchev, First Secretary of the Soviet Communist Party, to introduce

---

[5] Khrushchev, S., "The First Earth Satellite," in R. D. Launius, J. M. Logsdon, and R. W. Smith, (eds.), *Reconsidering Sputnik: Forty Years Since the Soviet Satellite*, (Amsterdam: Harwood Academic Publishers, 2000), 269.

his idea. Khrushchev granted Korolev his support, and the project was set in motion.[6]

Khrushchev was motivated by three interrelated issues to support Korolev's idea to start a space program. He thought a satellite would (a) signal that he was leading the Soviet Union to a glorious future; (b) enable a reorganization of the armed forces, as it would overawe traditionalists; and (c) demonstrate national long-range missile capabilities.[7] By launching a satellite into space, Khrushchev wished to signal to his domestic population, and send a message to other states, that the Soviet Union was superior to the United States. This message was meant to convince others to accept the Soviet Union as the most powerful country in the world and to join its side in the Cold War. Domestically, it was aimed at the enhancement of Soviet pride and self-esteem as well as to increase Khrushchev's influence within the Communist Party and ensure his political standing. The third motivation was aimed to project hard-power capabilities of launching long-range ballistic missiles for deterrence and other military purposes.

The successful launch of Sputnik received extensive coverage, especially by the West.[8] At first, Soviet leadership did not fully realize the political effect of Sputnik. Once Sputnik's effect was acknowledged, it was used by the Soviet regime to justify its ideology and philosophy, to raise the self-esteem of the Soviet people, and to affirm its supremacy over the capitalist West. This achievement was also used to draw non-aligned states and even Western states closer to the Soviet Union. In this sense, it was not different from previous Soviet strategies that had used technological achievements for political and social purposes.[9]

The Soviet press widely covered the launch of Sputnik in the days following the launch. *Pravda* printed the praises of allies and adversaries under a big headline that ran across the page: "Russians Won the Competition."[10] For home audiences, the Soviet press emphasized the

---

[6] Oberg, J., *Red Star in Orbit*, (New York: Random House, 1981), 29–30.
[7] For further information on the development of Sputnik and the early days of the Soviet space program in the 1950s, see: Oberg, J., *Red Star in Orbit*; Siddiqi, A., "Korolev, Sputnik, and the International Geophysical Year," in R. D. Launius, J. M. Logsdon, and R. W. Smith, (eds.), *Reconsidering Sputnik*, 43–72.
[8] Khrushchev, S., "How Rockets Learned to Fly," in V. Hardesty, and G. Eisman, (eds.), *Epic Rivalry: The Inside Story of The Soviet and American Space Race*, (Washington, DC: National Geographic Society, 2007), xi–xiii.
[9] In the 1930s, Joseph Stalin and his associates used world records in aviation as a means of winning support for the Soviet regime at home and abroad. For a detailed and comprehensive discussion of this issue, see Bailes, K. E., "Technology and Legitimacy: Soviet Aviation and Stalinism in the 1930s," *Technology and Culture*, 17:1, (January 1976), 55–81.
[10] Harford, J., "Korolev's Triple Play: Sputniks 1, 2 and 3," in R. D. Launius, J. M. Logsdon, and R. W. Smith, (eds.), *Reconsidering Sputnik*, 74.

success of the Soviet scientific community, which had been achieved due to the government's heavy investment in scientific and technological research and development, and having made science and technology a very high priority. For foreign audiences, the emphasis was on Soviet supremacy and on opportunities for international scientific cooperation.[11] In contrast to this emphasis on scientific achievement, there was little mention made of its military significance.[12]

The Soviets wished to fully exploit their achievement in space for propaganda purposes. Therefore, Sputnik 2 was set to be launched a month later, on the fortieth anniversary of the Bolshevik Revolution. The Soviet leadership wanted to beat the Americans in all spheres of life and to prove that their socialist system was better. The high visibility of spaceflight served this strategy well.[13]

On the American side, the Eisenhower administration explicitly rejected prestige as a motive for national space development. Its inclination was to speak of only two reasons for going into space: military and "pure scientific" pursuits.[14] Nevertheless, in the mid-1950s, secretive and public debates were held over the idea that aerospace technology was one of the principal means by which the Cold War would be won. For example, in 1954, Wernher Von Braun[15] and others publicly discussed the "psychological warfare value of a satellite."[16] On May 20, 1955, the Executive Secretary to the National Security Council issued NSC-5520 on the subject of the US scientific satellite program. The report outlines the general considerations for a US satellite program. It focuses on the benefits that could be accrued as well as the necessary steps that should be taken, including the examination of the principles and practices of

[11] Moscow in French: October 8, 1957, BBC Collection, USSR, The Soviet Satellite, Microfilm 5167-246, 15–16, (Washington, DC, Library of Congress).
[12] Use of Comments from Foreign Sources Summary by the BBC, October 8, 1957, BBC Collection USSR, The Soviet Satellite, Microfilm 51567-246, 16 (Washington, DC: Library of Congress).
[13] Hardesty, V., and Eisman, G., *Epic Rivalry*, 78, 89–90; Harford, J., "Korolev's Triple Play, 86.
[14] Van Dyke, V., *Pride and Power*, (London: Pall Mall Press, 1965), 101, 120.
[15] Von Braun was the head of the group of German scientists that developed the V-2 rockets in Nazi Germany. From a young age, Von Braun was interested in space travel and rocketry. He found a fruitful soil to pursue his dream in the German Army, which, as of the mid-1930s, was interested in rocketry for military purposes. In 1945, Von Braun and members of his group surrendered to the American Army. After the war, they were brought to the United States to develop rockets and missiles. Later, it was this group that developed the first American satellite, Explorer 1. Von Braun became a key figure in the American space program. For a detailed and comprehensive work on Von Braun, see Neufeld, M., *Dreamer of Space, Engineer of War*, (New York: Knopf, 2007).
[16] Neufeld, M., "Orbiter, Overflight and the First Satellite: New Light on the Vanguard Decision," in R. D. Launius, J. M. Logsdon, and R. W. Smith, (eds.), *Reconsidering Sputnik*, 234.

international law regarding freedom of space. The report clearly indicates that a small scientific satellite will provide a test to the principle of freedom of space and serve as a political demonstration of capabilities, especially in light of its direct relationship to ICBMs.[17]

On the other hand, it is indicated in the report that the Joint Chiefs of Staff have stated:

> From a military standpoint, their belief that intelligence applications strongly warrant the construction of a large surveillance satellite. While a small scientific satellite cannot carry reconnaissance equipment and therefore will have no direct intelligence potential, it does represent a technological step towards the achievement of a large surveillance satellite, and will be helpful to this end so long as the small scientific satellite program does not impede development of the large surveillance satellite.[18]

Several weeks later, on June 8, 1955, NSC-5522 addressed the psychological aspect of placing an artificial satellite in orbit. The authors of the report stated that:

> The psychological warfare value of launching the first earth satellite makes its prompt development of great interest to the intelligence community and may make it a crucial event in sustaining the international prestige of the United States .... The successful launching of the first satellite will undoubtedly be an event comparable to the first successful release of nuclear energy in the world's scientific community, and will undoubtedly receive comparable publicity throughout the world ... The nation that first accomplishes this feat will gain incalculable prestige and recognition throughout the world.[19]

Despite the clear understanding of the values of a public demonstration of national development of space capabilities, President Eisenhower saw no reason to think in terms of public competition with the Soviet Union.[20] Eisenhower's approach to space-technology development was primarily motivated by national security reasons, especially the need for accurate intelligence about Soviet technological progress, military R&D, and deployment. Historian Walter McDougal argued in his seminal work *The Heavens and the Earth* that Eisenhower found the solution to the US intelligence and early-warning problems in space-based reconnaissance,

---

[17] National Security Council NSC 5520, May 20, 1955, available at: marshall.wpengine.com/wp-content/uploads/2013/09/NSC-5520-Statement-of-Policy-on-US-Scientific-Satellite-Program-20-May-1955.pdf, accessed on May 28, 2015.

[18] National Security Council NSC 5520, May 20, 1955.

[19] National Security Council NSC 5522, June 8, 1955, Comments on the Report to the President by the Technological Capabilities Panel, p. A-55–56, cited in Day, D., "Cover Stories and Hidden Agendas: Early American Space and National Security Policy," in R. D. Launius, J. M. Logsdon, and R. W. Smith, (eds.), *Reconsidering Sputnik*, 170–171.

[20] Day, D., "Cover Stories, 180.

which would allow the United States to equal Soviet capabilities and ensure credible deterrence without developing and investing excessively.[21] Eisenhower's space policy was therefore secretive and not publicly oriented, an exception to that was the activity as part of the International Geophysical Year (IGY).[22]

The Soviet Union's successful launches of Sputnik 1 on October 4, 1957 and, a month later, Sputnik 2 (November 1957) were precipitating events that challenged Eisenhower Administration's attitude towards space. The US government and public clearly understood the military consequences of Sputnik as the ability of the Soviet Union to bombard the United States with nuclear warheads; they also understood the symbolism in the loss of American technological superiority over the Soviet Union. The reactions of other countries, including US allies, to the successful soviet launches intensified this notion. British media expressed the view that the Soviet Union now had immense technical skill. They noted the threatening military and strategic implications. French media also admired the Soviet achievement, making the observation that the United States had lost.[23] According to BBC files, considerable publicity was given in Chinese broadcasting to the launching of the first man-made satellite by the Soviet Union.[24] For example, various Chinese officials lauded the event, pointing out that the launch marked the beginning of a new era: "It provides outstanding proof of the incomparable superiority of the socialist system and shows that the Soviet Union is the most advanced country in the world in the field of science and technique."[25] The report continued by quoting an article in *Jemin Jin Pao* by the president of the Chinese Academy of Science, who urged Chinese scientists to make full use of their potential and catch up with their Soviet colleagues.[26]

Similar comments were expressed in the Eastern European bloc, praising the achievement as evidence of the superiority of the Soviet socialist system.[27] In Iran, officials of the government

---

[21] McDougall, W., *The Heavens and the Earth: A Political History of the Space Age*, (New York: Basic Books, 1985), 133.
[22] The IGY from July 1957 to December 1958 was intended to focus global scientific efforts on the study of large physical forces that affected Earth.
[23] Hardesty, V., and Eisman, G., *Epic Rivalry*, 76.
[24] China, Media Coverage of Sputnik, October 10, 1957, BBC Collection: China, Launching of Soviet Satellite, Microfilm 51567-381, (Washington, DC: Library of Congress), p. 2.
[25] China, Media Coverage of Sputnik, October 10, 1957, p. 2–3.
[26] China, Media Coverage of Sputnik, October 10, 1957, p. 3.
[27] Poland, Media Coverage of Sputnik, October 9, 1957, BBC Collection: Poland, Launching of Soviet Satellite, Microfilm 5167-870, (Washington, DC: Library of Congress).

considered the satellite such a blow to US prestige that they displayed uneasy embarrassment in discussing it with Americans. Representatives of the Western European Union Assembly meeting in Strasburg severely criticized the United States for falling behind in the arms race ... The satellite is, of course, most readily accepted as proof of scientific and technical leadership by those with the least scientific and political sophistication.[28]

The United States was extremely sensitive to these reactions, which suggested that any other state that could demonstrate an ability to place a satellite into orbit would, consciously or unconsciously, be transmitting both political and military signals to allies and adversaries. This concern of the United States intensified after its first attempt to launch the Vanguard satellite failed in front of TV cameras on December 6, 1957. Newspapers around the world covered the American failure in light of the Soviet success, naming the American satellite "Flopnik" or "Kaputnik."[29] Finally, the United States successfully launched Explorer 1 on January 31, 1958. These events led to a change in US space policy, which now also had to include the pursuit of ambitious public space activities.[30] Two months later, on March 26, 1958, Eisenhower's Advisory Committee, chaired by Dr. James Killian, produced one of the early efforts to identify reasons and motivations for the American space program, a report entitled "Introduction to Outer Space."[31] The report listed four factors that gave "importance, urgency, and inevitability to the advancement of space technology," among which national prestige was third.[32]

In order to meet international public goals such as preserving the leadership of the United States over Western countries, the United States developed a civil and public channel of national space activity, separated from its secretive national security activity, which was focused

---

[28] Office of Research and Intelligence, US Information Agency, Report: World Opinion and the Soviet Satellite – A Preliminary Evaluation (October 17, 1957), in Portree, D., (ed.), *NASA's Origins and the Dawn of the Space Age, Monographs in Aerospace History #10* (Washington, DC: NASA History Division, September 1998).

[29] Harford, J., "Korolev's Triple Play," 87.

[30] Logsdon, J., "Opportunities for Policy Historians: The Evolution of the US Civilian Space Program," in A., Roland, (ed.), *A Space-Faring People: Perspectives on Early Spaceflight*, (Washington, DC: The NASA History Series, 1985), 83; Van Dyke, V., *Pride and Power*, 120–121; McCurdy, H., *Space and the American Imagination*, (Washington, DC, and London: Smithsonian Institution Press, 1997), 54, 101; Launius, R. D., "What Are Turning Points in History and What Were They in The Space Age?," in S. J. Dick, and R. D. Launius, (eds.), *Societal Impact of Spaceflight*, (Washington, DC: NASA History Division, 2007), 19–40.

[31] A scanned copy of the report is available online at: www.fas.org/spp/guide/usa/intro1958.html, accessed on February 22, 2009).

[32] Van Dyke, *Pride and Power*, 5. The goals were as follows: space exploration and discovery, defense objective, national prestige, and scientific observation of Earth.

on the development of space capabilities, especially for intelligence and early warning. For this mission, the Eisenhower Administration created NASA in 1958 as a separate civilian space agency to carry out an open program of scientific activities and to engage in international cooperation. Many countries followed in the footsteps of the United States and adopted an organizational model that separates their civil space activities from their military space activities. The reasons for that included a need to preserve a secretive military activity, a need to establish international cooperation in space on a scientific and technological basis, and a need to preserve the space development, especially space research and exploration, as a legitimate and peaceful activity. In countries in which there is no such separation, the distinction between civil activity and military activity is much more difficult to determine and civil space activity is often considered as a cover for military activity.

One of the motivations for the establishment of NASA as a civil space agency was that it would contrast with the closed and secretive Soviet space effort[33] and attract other countries to the United States. The Space Act that created NASA in 1958 clearly stated that international cooperation was one of its main missions. A primary objective was to strengthen the Western alliance by consolidating the political and cultural solidarity of the West.[34] This was also one of the reasons that the Eisenhower administration pushed for the establishment of the Committee on the Peaceful Uses of Outer Space (COPUOS) by the United Nations.

Another highly important reason for the establishment of COPUOS was to diplomatically and legally support the principle of freedom of space; a crucial principle for the secretive US national space program in which reconnaissance satellites were developed and were used to provide significant intelligence on the Soviet Union. The role of COPUOS was to safeguard the rights of people of all nations to beneficial results from space exploration, by providing assistance for research, exchange, and dissemination of information, encouraging national research programs and studying legal problems arising from space exploration. COPUOS had a universal message of equal opportunity to all countries and humans to

---

[33] Logsdon, J., "Ten Presidents and NASA," in *NASA – 50 years of Exploration and Discovery*, (Tampa, FL: Faircount LLC, 2008), 226.

[34] In an article on NASA as an instrument of US foreign policy, John Krige also addressed this issue. A French scientist who was interviewed by Krige noted that despite the admiration of the Soviet success in space, the open policy of information of the United States attracted France to cooperate with the United States, because the Russians maintained a closed and restricted policy of information flow. Krige, J., "NASA as an Instrument of US Foreign Policy," in S. J. Dick and R.D., Launius (eds.), *Societal Impact of Spaceflight*, (Washington, DC: NASA History Division, 2007), 210–211.

explore and benefit from space exploration. In practice, space was controlled by those who had access to it – the superpowers.[35]

Strategies of Visible Competition

After Sputnik and Explorer 1 were launched into space, the public competition in the years 1958–1961 continued with many other "space firsts," which included the launch of animals into space. In 1961, the competition further intensified and included setting records of human flights into space. Here too, the Soviet Union came first by launching Yuri Gagarin on April 12, 1961. Three weeks later on May 5, 1961, the United States sent the first American astronaut, Alan Shepard, on a sub-orbital flight into space. Both men became national and international heroes.

The Soviet Union placed enormous emphasis on the importance of science as a vehicle for national progress and as a symbol of the superiority of socialism. The public space program, therefore, effectively served Soviet interests.[36] It demonstrated the existence of a modern scientific, technical, and industrial base in the Soviet Union[37]. Soviet propaganda was aimed directly at foreign populations, hoping that citizens would force their governments to act in a manner that would favor Soviet interests.

The American civil and public space policy, which was designed in the early 1960s, was a reaction to the series of Soviet technological firsts, which attracted international attention that put great pressure on the United States to equalize. The United States feared that publicly it was losing its leading status and aimed to preserve and maintain US leadership and supremacy.[38] The American fear of losing power and prestige in the eyes of the "watching world," as Kennedy later phrased it, is well expressed in the following report that was prepared by the American Embassy in Tehran in 1959 and sent to the State Department bearing the title "Significance of Outer Space Operations in Relation to the Iranian Political Situation":

---

[35] Initially, the Soviet Union, Czechoslovakia, and Poland refused to participate in COPUOS, which was created as an ad hoc committee based on majority voting. They became members a year later, when it was decided that all of COPUOS's decisions would be made by consensus (Galloway, E., "Sputnik and the Creation of NASA: A Personal Perspective," *NASA 50 Years*, 49).

[36] For an excellent detailed overview and analysis of the Soviet Union's space program, see Siddiqi, A., *Challenge to Apollo: The Soviet Union and the Space Race, 1945–1974*, (Washington, DC: National Aeronautics and Space Administration, 2000).

[37] Sheehan, M., *The International Politics of Space*, (London: Routledge, 2007), 21–22.

[38] Logsdon, J., "Space in the Post–Cold War Environment," in S. J. Dick and R.D., Launius, (eds.), *Societal Impact of Spaceflight*, (Washington, DC: NASA History Division, 2007), 89–102 and Van Dyke, V., *Pride and Power*, 5.

Soviet satellite operation had a very harmful effect on Iranian opinion in that they tended to greatly reduce an opinion previously widely held (even among Communists) to the effect that Russians are quite backward, scientifically and technically, as compared with the West. US operations of the same nature reduced the amount of damage done by this disillusionment ... The "race for space" is a convenient, though inaccurate, measuring gauge for the relative scientific and technological status of the United States and the USSR. A spectacular Soviet leap into space tomorrow would have a serious and possibly even decisive effect in the present psychological battle for Iran, which has been touched off by the current Soviet propaganda offensive.[39]

The author of the report concluded that manned landings on the Moon, a bright and visible satellite to be seen from earth, or a manned orbital flight would be most impressive and would have a maximum political effect on Iran, whether accomplished by the United States or by the Soviets. These words emphasize the public and visible aspects of going into space and their significance to American foreign policy.

The words of Lloyd Berkner, former chairman of the Space Science Board of the National Academy of Sciences, also exemplify the importance attributed to civil and public space activity and its potential implications on the status and international image of the United States at that time:

Man prizes the idea of escape from the earth as the highest symbol of progress ... Therefore, the nation that can capture and hold that symbol will carry the banner of world leadership. Consequently, leadership in space exploration has a real political meaning. Failure in that leadership means inevitably falling into the status of a second class nation with the heavy costs to our way of free enterprise which subjugation to others would involve.[40]

Before taking office, President Kennedy appointed an ad-hoc committee on space issues chaired by Dr. Jerome Wiesner. The report of the committee included the following statement:[41] "In addition to the need to develop ballistic missiles to provide our military security, there are five principal motivations for desiring a vital, effective space program ... National prestige, National security, Scientific observation, Economy and civil application, and International cooperation in the world." Indeed, and especially due to the numerous Soviets' firsts, the Kennedy Administration became

---

[39] Stelle, C., (May 11, 1959), "Significance of Outer Space Operations in Relation to the Iranian Political Situation," Foreign Service Dispatch no. 827 from the American Embassy in Tehran to the Department of State in Washington, DC, (Washington, DC: NASA Headquarters, NASA Historical Reference Collection, International file: Iran).

[40] Berkner, L., "Space Research – A Permanent Peacetime Activity," in S. Ramo, (ed.), *Peacetime Uses of Outer Space*, (New York: McGraw-Hill, 1961), 7, cited by Van Dyke, V., *Pride and Power*, 151–152.

[41] Berkner, L., "Space Research – A Permanent," 5–6.

explicitly concerned with prestige in relation to space, and was willing to emphasize space accomplishments as a source of prestige.[42]

After Gagarin's flight into space on April 12, 1961, and the failure of the invasion in the Bay of Pigs, which occurred a week later, Kennedy had developed a deep commitment to the political goal of beating the Soviets. For this reason, NASA Administrator Webb and Secretary of Defense Robert McNamara recommended that Kennedy embark on a lunar mission as a national objective. Vice President Lyndon B. Johnson[43] pushed hard for the decision to go to the Moon, writing in a memo to the president about the international implications that "this country should be realistic and recognize that other nations, regardless of their appreciation of our idealistic values, will tend to align themselves with the country which they believe will be the world leader – the winner in the long run. Dramatic accomplishments in space are being identified as a major indicator of world leadership."[44] Kennedy adopted this approach, and on May 25, 1961, he declared that the United States would send a man to the Moon by the end of the decade.[45] His unsuccessful meeting with Khrushchev on June 4, 1961, increased his determination to achieve this goal.

In this context, in the late 1950s and through the 1960s, the United States had a secretive space program and a public civil space program. The American civil space policy had two different aspects. The first was focused on a direct competition with the Soviets over the development of spectacular capabilities and setting national records, which would get great international visibility, such as landing a man on the Moon. The second aspect focused on the encouragement of international initiatives for cooperating with other countries, which would highlight the United States' leading position.

The competitive facet was set as the highest priority, while cooperation in space activity was only secondary. The political objective of the civil space program was to establish a position of international leadership in this field.[46] After the Cuban missile crisis, Kennedy's approach to this issue only intensified. At a White House meeting[47] on November 21,

---

[42] Van Dyke, V., *Pride and Power*, 123.
[43] Vice President Lyndon B. Johnson replaced Kennedy after his assassination and served as president in the years 1963–1969.
[44] Logsdon, J., "Ten Presidents," 229.   [45] Logsdon, J., "Space," 92.
[46] Logsdon, J., "Opportunities for Policy Historians: The Evolution of the US Civilian Space Program," in A. Roland, (ed.), *A Space-Faring People: Perspectives on Early Spaceflight*, (Washington, DC: The NASA History Series, 1985), 84, 86, 99.
[47] The full transcript of the meeting and its recording is available online at: history.nasa.gov/JFK-Webbconv/pages/transcript.pdf, accessed on February 25, 2009. The recording was released in August 2001.

1962, Kennedy told Webb that winning the Moon race "is the top priority of the agency and except for defense, the top priority of the US government. Otherwise, we shouldn't be spending this kind of money, because I'm not that interested in space."[48] Henceforth, NASA was transformed from an agency with goals of space engineering, technology and science, into an agency with almost one single mission – landing a man on the Moon. Achieving this mission "would be a spectacular achievement that would get America going again, reestablish its world prestige, and help it feel better about itself and its leaders."[49]

In July 1969, Apollo 11 astronauts walked on the Moon. This spectacular achievement marked the end of the first stage of the Space Age that was mainly characterized by the competition between the superpowers. After the Apollo 11 Moon landing, the rhetoric of political competition in space was dampened and then largely replaced by an approach that stressed international collaboration between the United States and Europe and even between the United States and the Soviet Union.[50]

The Apollo Moon landing was more than a technological or scientific effort; it was also the culmination of a twelve-year campaign to sell America as the greatest power of the world; an advertisement that was much about impression and impressing.[51] It was also an overall human achievement of conquering outer space and challenging the laws of nature. As such, it was met with much acclaim by almost everyone, including the Soviet Union and the Warsaw Pact countries.[52] It allowed for greater cooperation with the Soviet Union. The Americans had proven their leadership and were more willing to cooperate, while for the Soviets, cooperation with the United States served as an opportunity to catch up and portray themselves as equal partners with the United States.[53]

An examination of the breakdown of resources allocated to American activity in space between NASA and the Defense Department from the end of the 1950s until 1969 teaches us a great deal about the US policy and its primary motivations at that time. At the end of the 1950s, the majority of investments were allocated to the Department of Defense

---

[48] Logsdon, J. "Ten Presidents," 229.
[49] DeVorkin, D., *Race to the Stratosphere – Manned Scientific Ballooning in America*, (New York: Springer-Verlag, 1989), 321.
[50] Logsdon, J., "Outer Space and International Space Policy: The Rapidly Changing Issues," in D. Papp and R. McIntyre, (eds.), *International Space Policy*, (New York: Quorum Books, 1987), 33.
[51] Smith, M., "Selling the Moon," in W. Fox and J. Lears, (eds.), *The Culture of Consumption*, (New York: Pantheon Books, 1983), 175–210.
[52] USSR, Media Coverage of Apollo-11 Moon Landing, Collected by the BBC, July 21–22, 1969, BBC Collection: Russia, Luna-15 – Apollo-11, Microfilm 51567-654, (Washington, DC: Library of Congress).
[53] Karash, Y., *The Superpower Odyssey*, 78.

Table 3.1 *US Investment of Resources in Military and Civilian Activity in Space, 1959–1969 (In Constant FY2014 $)*

Year	NASA	NASA%	DOD	DOD%	Other	Other%	Total Space
1959	1639	33.23869	3078	62.42142	214	4.33989	4931
1960	2858	43.33586	3471	52.63078	266	4.033359	6595
1961	5650	51.21929	4966	45.01858	415	3.762125	11031
1962	10815	54.55508	7812	39.40678	1197	6.038136	19824
1963	21601	66.73979	9234	28.52994	1531	4.730273	32366
1964	29518	73.46258	9410	23.41903	1253	3.118389	40181
1965	29872	74.2309	9151	22.73992	1219	3.029174	40242
1966	28941	72.69051	9651	24.24022	1222	3.069272	39814
1967	27016	72.01386	9308	24.81141	1191	3.17473	37515
1968	24043	67.8759	10432	29.45062	947	2.67348	35422
1969	20058	63.64386	10564	33.51948	894	2.836654	31516

(DOD), while only about a third was allocated to NASA. In the 1960s, this trend changed, and the emphasis was on the civilian program – the Apollo program whose objective was to put a man on the Moon. Throughout the 1960s, national investments in NASA's activities greatly exceeded the national investments in the DOD's space activities. In 1959, the DOD's space budget constituted 62.4 percent of the US total space budget, while in 1965, its share was only 22.7 percent of the total national investment in space. In this period, the scientific race for Space was the central expression of the direct struggle between the superpowers.[54]

International Cooperation versus Technology Proliferation Controls

> *The space effort ... represents Americans as the world has long thought of Americans and as the world wishes to think of Americans.*
>
> Arnold Frutkin[55]

In addition to the strategies of public competition for records and achievements, each of the superpowers adopted a strategy of scientific

---

[54] Data were obtained from Aeronautics and Space Report of The President – Fiscal Year 2014 Activities, NASA, p. 178. Available at: history.nasa.gov/presrep2014.pdf, accessed on June 25, 2015.

[55] Frutkin, A., Address by Assistant Administrator for International Affairs, NASA, to the American Academy of Political and Social Science, Philadelphia, PA, (April 16, 1966), (Washington, DC: Frutkin Biographic Files NASA Historical Reference Collection, NASA History Office, NASA Headquarters), 6.

international cooperation with allies and others. Nevertheless, the superpowers feared that the transfer of strategic technologies and knowhow could be used not only for peaceful uses but also for the development of strategic and military capabilities. In order to avoid this outcome, cooperation was conducted under strictly defined rules and restrictions.

The tools for controlling the flow of technology and knowhow include restrictions on commercial activity as well as on international cooperation. The first step is to provide security classification to areas of technological development and its knowhow. The second step involves the development of national and international regulation, such as control by export licensing and by setting country category. Licensing applies to technology, data, and knowhow. On the international level, in an attempt to impose restrictions on the international flow of technology and knowhow, countries may cooperate in the use of mechanisms such as suppliers groups, treaties, and bilateral agreements.

Bilateral agreements of technological cooperation are subject to the security classification of the potential areas for cooperation and do not include areas of strategic importance. Often there is also a prohibition on foreign funding, which is intended to make it more difficult for others to develop their own capabilities. An important issue is the demand of a commitment from the cooperating partners not to transfer technology derived from the cooperation at stake to third parties. Finally, there may also be a demand of a commitment not to pursue indigenous development of certain capabilities.

The Soviets offered international cooperation in order to convince states of Soviet supremacy and leadership and attract them to their side. For example, in June 1966, seven months after France demonstrated its capability to place a satellite in orbit in November 1965, French President Charles de Gaulle became the first Westerner to witness a Soviet launching and visit the Baikonur installation.[56] The Soviets also cooperated with scientists from other socialist countries starting in 1957. At first, this cooperation was mainly restricted to operating observation posts in the various countries, where the trajectories of Soviet satellites were recorded. In 1967, a concrete program for space exploration, Interkosmos,[57] was

---

[56] "De Gaulle Sees Soviet Satellite Launched," *Washington Post*, (June 26, 1966), 5.
[57] Interkosmos was initiated as a formal organization to bring together scientists of the Soviet bloc countries to consider mutually useful opportunities for cooperation. Bulgaria, Hungary, Poland, Romania, East Germany, Czechoslovakia, and the Soviet Union participated. The satellites developed under this initiative were primarily used for the study of solar radiation, Earth's atmosphere, and cosmic radiation. Later, Interkosmos was extended to include geophysical rockets. Another plan of cooperation, although less productive, was Intersputnik, which was aimed at offering the Soviet bloc countries an array of communication satellites similar to Intelsat.

developed. The Soviet Union did not encourage its Communist allies to develop their own programs, but through such initiatives, Soviet bloc countries developed instruments for Soviet satellites and participated in various aspects of the Soviet space program. Their participation was limited in scope. It did not include domestic development of satellites or transfer of rocket and missile technological knowhow.[58]

In the late 1970s, Interkosmos was extended, and the Soviet Union invited Socialist states to send their own cosmonauts aboard Soviet spacecrafts. The impetus for this Soviet initiative was the American agreement with the European Space Agency that stipulated that Europeans would build the Spacelab module to be flown on the shuttle in the 1980s. West European astronauts would be trained so that they could operate the lab and be a part of the project. In order to counter the American initiative, Soviets hurried to invite socialist and Third World countries to fly cosmonauts aboard their spacecrafts as of 1978 (prior to the United States doing so). These flights were mainly political and symbolic, and were used to strengthen relations with friends and allies. Only one person from each country got a chance to fly. Upon returning to earth, he and his backup cosmonaut were dismissed from the cosmonaut program.[59] The identity of the countries selected, and the order in which their cosmonauts flew in space, was highly politicized. The first such flight was Soyuz 28 in March 1978, taking Vladimir Remek.[60] Initially, the guests were from the Soviet bloc countries, but the Soviet Union widened the program to include a French cosmonaut in 1982 and an Indian cosmonaut who went to space in 1984.[61]

---

[58] For further information on Interkosmos activity, see Oberg, J., *Red Star*; Smolders, P., *Soviets in Space*, (Guildford and London, England: Lutterworth Press, 1970); Senate Science Policy Research Division and Foreign Affairs Division of the Congressional Research Service and the European Law Division of the Law Library, Library of Congress Report on Soviet Space Programs, 1966–1970 (December 9, 1971), Staff Report prepared for the Use of the Committee on Aeronautical and Space Sciences United States Senate (Washington, DC: US Government Printing Office); Caidin, M., *Red Star in Space*, (New York: The Crowell-Collier Publishing Company, 1963).

[59] Oberg, J. *Red Star*, 185–189.

[60] Remek, a Czechoslovak, was deliberately chosen first because 1978 was the tenth anniversary of the controversial Soviet invasion of Czechoslovakia, the "Prague Spring," which had brought Alexander Dubcek's liberal Communist regime to an end in 1968. The Soyuz flight, therefore, sought to emphasize the closeness of Soviet-Czechoslovak cooperation and the USSR's recognition of Czechoslovakia as a sovereign equal of the USSR within the Warsaw alliance (Sheehan, M., *The International Politics of Space*, 59–60).

[61] For more information on the first flight of an Indian cosmonaut see: Harvey, B., *The Japanese and Indian Space Programs: Two Roads into Space*, (London: Springer Praxis, 2000), 163.

The Soviets, however, were not willing to share their knowhow. They refused to provide information on Soviet satellites to other states or to share data. The Soviets feared that sharing information and facilities with other states that did not have space programs or facilities of their own would fritter away the Soviet advantage.[62] For example, China expected the Soviet Union to assist it in building its missile program, which was later used to develop space vehicles.[63] In August 1957, the Soviet Union agreed to supply missile models, technical documents, designs, and specialists. Despite that, the Chinese soon felt that the Soviets were not very open and cooperative, as requests for information were often denied.[64] Political tensions between the two countries led the Soviet Union to restrict its assistance to China. Soviet refusal to cooperate with China influenced Chinese aspirations to develop their own capabilities.[65]

The United States engaged in international cooperation in space as part of its strategy to preserve and improve its image and regain some of its lost stature in the eyes of allies and others after the successful launch of Sputnik and the other Soviet achievements that followed. By cooperating with other countries, the United States hoped to make the free world identify with the American space program and accept its leadership.[66] In 1959, a report by the Select Committee on Aeronautics and Space Exploration of the Congress described the advantages of international cooperation: "The best way to solidify this confidence [in the scientific leadership of the US] is by a program of general and genuine free world cooperation. Future misfiring there will be. And free world reactions to them will be far different, morally, and psychologically speaking, if other nations have a direct stake in at least some of the project."[67]

---

[62] Karash, Y., *The Superpower Odyssey: A Russian Perspective on Space Cooperation*, (Reston, VA: AIAA, 1999), 21–23.

[63] A comprehensive and detailed study on the early days of the Chinese space effort and its rationale was conducted by Yanping Chen in 1999. This is one of the first studies on this topic that was done by a Chinese and relies on Chinese sources; see Chen, Y., *China's Space Activities, Policy and Organizations, 1956–1986*, unpublished Ph.D. dissertation, George Washington University, 1999.

[64] While there, some of the students spied on behalf of their country; they copied documents and other restricted information. Harvey, B., *China's Space Program – From Conception to Manned Spaceflight*, (Chichester, UK: Springer Praxis, 2004), 24.

[65] Chen, Y., *China's Space Activities*, 69–73.

[66] Kash, D. E., The Politics of Space Cooperation, (West Lafayette, IN: Purdue University Studies, 1967), 16–17.

[67] US Congress House of Representatives, Select Committee on Aeronautics and Space Exploration, International Cooperation in the Exploration of Space, Report, No. 2709, 85th Congress, 2nd Session, 1959, p. 11, cited in Kash, D. E., *The Politics of Space Cooperation*, 17.

One of the first moves in the direction of international cooperation came in March 1959, when the American delegation to UN COSPAR[68] announced that the United States would be willing to launch scientific experiments proposed by foreign scientists on American-built satellites. The British were the first to accept the American offer. On April 26, 1962, NASA launched Ariel 1, which contained components and instruments that had been designed by British scientists. A few months later, Alouette 1, a Canadian satellite, was launched aboard an American launcher. The American incentive to assist Britain and Canada resulted from the American desire for a Western country, an ally rather than a Communist country, to be third in space.[69]

Cooperation was based on mutual scientific benefits and mutual funding. NASA was not sponsoring the activities of other countries.[70] Under the foreign policy guidance of the president, NASA had the ability to conduct international cooperation in less formal arrangements.[71] For this reason, interested countries were asked to designate a central, civilian government or government-sponsored authority to deal with NASA. NASA's philosophy for international cooperation required literal cooperation without the passing of dollars, solid rather than token program content, a project-by-project procedure, negotiations with central and authorized civil agencies on a direct technical basis rather than a diplomatic one, encouragement of foreign scientific interests, and finally, purely experimental projects. Furthermore, countries were not pressed to divert energies and resources to space activity. The decision to embark on a space program had to be their own.[72]

By 1965, NASA had entered into collaborative arrangements with about seventy countries. Collaboration included the United States launching satellites developed by other nations, competitive selection of individual experiments submitted by foreign scientists or other nations for inclusion in US satellites, joint sounding-rocket projects,[73] ground-based activities in various fields, accommodation or joint operation of US tracking and data acquisition facilities abroad, and training of

---

[68] UN Committee on Space Research was established in 1958.
[69] Krige, J., "NASA as an Instrument," 208–210.
[70] Logsdon, J., "Opportunities for Policy," 100.
[71] Among the earliest agreements were those covering tracking and telemetry stations, data from satellites and probes, exchanges of scientific and technical information, training programs and exchanges with foreign scientists (Galloway, E., "Sputnik and the Creation of NASA," 49).
[72] Frutkin, A., *International Cooperation*, 34–35, 60.
[73] Argentina, Australia, Canada, France, Germany, India, Italy, Japan, New Zealand, Norway, Pakistan, Sweden, and the United Kingdom were engaged in projects utilizing sounding rockets. See Frutkin, A., *International Cooperation*, 54–59.

personnel.[74] Although these collaborative missions did not include any transfers of funds, countries of all sizes and levels of development were interested in cooperating with NASA.

Despite their scientific nature, these collaborations were very much embedded in the Cold War struggle and served important foreign policy objectives such as increasing American political power and projecting the image of the United States as the leader of the free world.[75] A memo by Arnold Frutkin to Mr. Julian Scheer, Assistant Administrator for Public Affairs at NASA, on September 8, 1965, is a good example. In this memo, Frutkin suggested that the White House should take an active part in celebrating the first launch of a French satellite aboard an American launcher: "The satellite [FR-1] is almost certainly to be the first French satellite . . . It now remains to determine whether the White House has an interest in holding open the possibility of the President's receiving the principal French (and American) personnel the day following the launch."[76] By hosting a French delegation at the White House after the launch to celebrate the French achievement, the role of the United States in assisting France and other countries would be highlighted. France, however, preferred not to be seen as dependent on the United States and wanted to demonstrate greater capability and self-reliance by launching its first satellite on a French launcher. Only days before the expected launch of FR-1 aboard an American launcher, France successfully launched a French-made satellite aboard a French-made launcher known as Diamond A.[77]

Another interesting example of a cooperative effort is the case of the sounding-rocket range at Thumba in India. The original objective of building the range was to create a bilateral cooperative project between NASA and the Indian Committee for Space Research (INCOSPAR). A suggestion was later made to India that the range be offered for international use and that UN sponsorship be sought.[78] As the idea developed, France joined India and the United States on a triple-partner project, and

---

[74] Frutkin, A., *International Cooperation*, 41.
[75] Krige, J., "NASA as an Instrument," 209.
[76] Frutkin, A., Memorandum of Understanding to Mr. Scheer, Subject: FR-1 Launch Ceremonies, (September 8, 1965), (Washington, DC: NASA HQ History Division Archives, Frutkin Files).
[77] In the literature, Diamond A is also referred to as Diamant A.
[78] The United States introduced a resolution to the Technical Subcommittee of the United Nations Committee on the Peaceful Uses of Outer Space. The resolution called for UN sponsorship of sounding rockets ranged in scientifically critical locations; the ranges would be available to member nations interested in using them for open projects. The resolution was accepted. In the course of this procedure, India formally offered its proposed range at Thumba for sponsorship under the resolution. See Frutkin, A., *International Cooperation*, 62.

the Soviet Union discussed joint sounding rockets with INCOSPAR.[79] Thus, explained Frutkin, "what began as a bilateral effort, with relatively narrow technical objectives, has grown through a process of inexorable technical and political appeal to the point where major nations, including the Soviet Union, find it important to join in."[80] Frutkin's words exemplify the notion that had developed in which countries were expected to be involved in space activity.

In a paper published in July 1966, Frutkin elaborated on American engagement in space cooperation with other countries. He remarked that it provided significant opportunities for foreign scientists to contribute and develop their talents, and at the same time, allowed other nations "a chance to share not only in the published results of space research, but in the doing and the achieving."[81] Frutkin's words show that the Americans were fully aware of the political values ascribed by other countries to having their own share of this attractive activity. They wanted to exploit their aspirations in order to make political gains in favor of the United States' image, international position, and interests. The United States, however, was not keen on sharing and spreading strategic space capabilities, such as launch capability, high-resolution imagery, etc., and was looking to keep the space club rather small.[82] For this reason it focused mainly on Europe. There, too, cooperation was restricted mainly to purely scientific projects.[83]

NASA's efforts to stimulate bilateral and multilateral cooperation on space activity had another incentive; they were part of the overall

---

[79] In the late 1960s and early 1970s, the United States, USSR, France, and other countries launched sounding rockets at Thumba.

[80] Frutkin, A., *International Cooperation*, 35, 62–63.

[81] Frutkin, A., (July 1966), "The United States Space Program and Its International Significance," *The Annals of the American Academy of Political and Social Science*, Volume 366, (Washington, DC: NASA HQ History Division Archives, Frutkin Files).

[82] At that time, only France had demonstrated the indigenous capability of launching satellites into space. It was to take several more years for Japan, China, and Britain catch up.

[83] In the mid-1960s, cooperation was extended and included developing countries such as India and Brazil. In the late 1960s, the United States also negotiated with Japan over space cooperation. Despite US policy aimed at banning the proliferation of launch vehicles, it did assist Japan in this field. The rationale was to assure access to and knowledge of the Japanese program and capabilities. In that case, Americans were willing to share technology in order to prevent Japan from developing its own space rocket; otherwise the United States would be ignorant of Japan's progress. See Logsdon, J., "The Development of International Space Cooperation," in J. Logsdon, D. Day, and R. D. Launius, (eds.), *Exploring the Unknown – Selected Documents in the History of The US Civilian Space Program Volume II: External Relationships*, (Washington, DC: The NASA History Series, NASA History Office, 1996), 4; and Logsdon, J., *Learning From the Leader – The Early Years of US-Japanese Cooperation in Space*, (Washington, DC: Space Policy Institute, George Washington University, 2002), Unpublished paper, 8–9.

American effort to limit proliferation of nuclear capability. In order to maintain a small and exclusive "nuclear club," the United States advocated that space be perceived as an eligible substitute. In this respect, NASA was asked to stimulate foreign involvement in space technology as a means of diverting energies from the development of nuclear weapons systems. On March 23, 1966, the National Aeronautics and Space Council [NASC],[84] chaired by Vice President Hubert Humphrey, met to discuss cooperation in space exploration.[85] Considerable attention was given in this discussion to the potential value of the substitution of space technology for weapons proliferation and production on the part of other countries. In the discussion, Secretary of Defense Robert McNamara said, "many countries felt they should make technological progress through military hardware programs. A divergence to a space program would be wholesome for all concerned."[86] McNamara also said that the United States should continue preventing other countries from gaining access to ballistic weapons. Nevertheless, he also emphasized that the restrictive policies should be reviewed with the aim of encouraging the export of technology, particularly space technology. In summarizing the discussion, Vice President Humphrey wrote that such activities could serve as a substitute for developing weapons systems in certain countries.[87]

In a letter to McNamara dated April 28, 1966, NASA Administrator James Webb referred to a meeting that was held several weeks earlier on this issue and expressed his support of this political objective: "We in NASA are anxious to contribute in any way we can to policies which assist the Departments of State and Defense to meet difficult pressures from

---

[84] The National Aeronautics and Space Council is anchored in the 1958 law that established NASA. At first, it was chaired by President Dwight Eisenhower. The Council members included the Secretary of Defense, the head of NASA, the head of the Atomic Energy Commission, and others appointed by the president. Eisenhower did not initiate frequent meetings of the council. Toward the end of his term, he thought that it should be disbanded. Upon entering office, President Kennedy asked that the law be changed, and that the vice president head the Council. Edward Cristy Welsh was appointed as the first secretary of the council under Kennedy, and continued to serve in that position for six years. During that period, he was also the senior advisor to the White House on space matters.

[85] Among those who took part in the discussion were the vice president; Secretary of Defense Robert McNamara; Secretary of State Dean Rusk; the head of NASA, James Webb; and others.

[86] Memorandum for the Record (Washington, March 25, 1966). Department of State, S/PC Files: Lot 72 124, Scientific and Technological Development, 1966. Drafted by James E. Goodby.

[87] Space Council Meeting March 23, 1966, Memorandum for the President From the Vice President, March 28, 1966, 1. Johnson Library Archives, White House Central Files Exec FG 11-4 6/1/65-1/4/166 Box 62.

abroad."[88] Nonetheless, shifting energy toward space activity did not mean rapid and unlimited proliferation of space technologies. In this respect, Webb indicated in his letter that restrictions imposed on technology exports made it difficult to progress on this issue and recommended a considerable change in US attitudes toward the spread of space vehicle technology.

However, the United States was concerned with proliferation of strategic delivery technology. Therefore, it set strict limits on the export of technologies that could help other states develop nuclear weapons delivery capabilities, including on the technology of launch into space. In the mid-1960s, almost all American and Soviet space launchers were based on ballistic missiles, and the United States did not want other countries to be able to develop nuclear delivery systems from space launchers. For this reason, the United States restricted and controlled the transfer and flow of launching technology and knowhow.[89]

Given the sharp competition between the two superpowers and the civil-military dual-use nature of space capabilities, as well as the interest in maintaining the monopoly of American industries, restrictions and controls on the transfer of sensitive space technology were not only imposed on means of launching into space, but also on other space technologies. Consequently, the United States offered limited international cooperation. Arnold Frutkin provides a close look at NASA's external relations in the early 1960s in his 1965 book in which he explains the rationale that made NASA mainly engage in civil scientific space activities by stating that because the tools, techniques, and objectives of space exploration were in good part common to military and civilian interests alike, NASA's international activities were limited in scope. US foreign policy encouraged international cooperation, but due to national security considerations, cooperation had to be mainly scientific. Transfer of launch technology was especially restricted because such technology had clear military benefits.[90]

In the late 1960s and early 1970s, the United States tried to discourage Europe from developing indigenous launchers to put satellites into orbit. On September 1, 1971, the United States crafted a policy that made its launchers available for European satellites.[91] According to Logsdon

---

[88] Webb, J., A letter by NASA Administrator to Secretary of Defense Robert McNamara, (April 26, 1966), (Washington, DC: NASA HQ History Division Archives, file: Miscellaneous Correspondence from CODE I- International Relations 1958–1967).
[89] Logsdon, J., *Learning From the Leader*, 5.
[90] Frutkin, A., *International Cooperation*, 35–36.
[91] For a comprehensive work on US cooperation and involvement in Europe after WWII, see Krige J., *American Hegemony and the Postwar Reconstruction of Science in Europe*, (Cambridge, MA and London: The MIT Press, 2006).

(1996), one reason for this approach was to maintain the American monopoly on access to space.[92] At about the same time, the United States put pressure on Europe to not commercialize its series of communications satellites (Symphonie 1 and 2), which were to be launched using an American launcher, in order to avoid competition with the United States-led Intelsat. Johnson-Freese (2007) argued that eventually, American pressure reached the opposite outcome, because it helped convince European governments of the necessity of a European launcher.[93]

The United States perceived its assistance to foreign space programs as rather generous. On the European side, however, there was reluctance about the dominant role of the United States in almost every project. Often, NASA and American scientists would define the objectives and content of a scientific mission and only then approach foreign scientists to participate.[94]

In addition, the United States paid close attention to the motivations and interests of the participating states to be engaged, making sure that these projects coincided with other US interests and perceptions, and did not contradict or damage other US efforts. For instance, in the early 1960s, Egypt approached NASA and suggested a cooperative project that would include the launch of sounding rockets. NASA officials refused this offer; it appeared to them to be nothing more than a political attempt to intimidate Israel, rather than a scientific experiment.[95]

While the United States and the Soviet Union restricted transfer of strategic space technologies, each of them wanted one of its allies to be the next to join the club. The United States assisted European countries and Japan while the Soviet Union assisted China. This issue was seriously discussed in a special CIA report in 1965. The report, entitled "The Race for Third in Space" reviewed the space programs of Japan, China, and France, stating that "the satellites involved will almost certainly be small and will probably carry little instrumentation other than a radio transmitter to broadcast the achievement to the world. A successful satellite launch by any of these countries using a native-designed rocket would

---

[92] Logsdon, J., "The Development of International Space Cooperation," 7–8.
[93] Johnson-Freese, J., *Space as a Strategic Asset*, (New York: Columbia University Press, 2007), 46.
[94] Logsdon, J., "The Development of International Space Cooperation." 4.
[95] Oral History Transcript, Arnold Frutkin, Interviewed by Rebecca Wright, Washington, DC, January 11, 2002, (Washington, DC: NASA HQ, History Office, Historical Reference Collection), 16–20.

undoubtedly be exploited to show that that country was approaching the scientific abilities of the US and the USSR."[96]

The report pointed out the political motives of pursuing the capability of launching a satellite. The authors explicitly stated that the United States acknowledged the political and social benefits that follow such an impressive achievement and regarded it as very significant, especially in terms of public image. The report clearly indicated that winning the title "third in space" is important to these countries: " ... the Japanese are still very much in the running for third in space ... If one of these [Japanese satellites] achieves orbit and neither the French nor the Chinese Communists have succeeded by that time, the Japanese intend to give wide publicity to their claim of being third in space."[97] Eventually, the authors of the report made the assumption that France would be third in space.

Indeed, the CIA assumption became reality. Only a few months after the report was submitted, France became third in space on November 26, 1965. Japan was next to follow, launching its first satellite on February 11, 1970. China came fifth, launching its first satellite on April 24, 1970. The attitude reflected in this report and especially the remarks on the desire to identify and associate with the existing spacefaring nations illustrates the values, benefits, and functions associated with being a "club member."

Conclusions

The early years of the space age show that the Soviet Union and the United States learnt that they cannot treat space activity only as a technical matter and as a military matter. They learnt to value the public elements of space activity and approached space exploration and applications as an important component of national and international politics. Through their public rivalry and competition, the superpowers created an understanding that expertise in space was a first-rate symbol of ideological, military, and economic superiority. This turned space into an overall measure of political power. An advanced space program had a "halo effect"[98] on the overall image, power, and reputation of the

---

[96] CIA Special Report, (July 23, 1965), The Race for Third in Space, President Johnson's Library, NSF Subject Files, Box 37, Outer Space, Vol. 2, 1 (the report was declassified by the National Archives and Record Administration [NARA] in January 1993).

[97] CIA Special Report, (July 23, 1965), 3.

[98] This process is similar to the process that takes place in human society and is referred to in social psychology as the "halo effect." In this situation, society adopts a comprehensive view regarding an individual based upon a positive or a negative quality that the individual possesses.

Conclusions

superpowers, and it positively projected other characteristics, abilities, and qualities they presumably had.

The strategy of international cooperation was used to bring allies and others into some form of closer relationship to each of the superpowers in order to expand and affirm its spheres of influence that could prove its world leadership. Cooperative and collaborative projects also allowed greater influence on these states, as well as monitoring and control of their activities and development in a way that sustained the superpower's overall influence over them, forcing them to meet standards and regulations promoted by their patrons. Nevertheless, the potential to use the technologies at stake not only for peaceful uses, but also for military purposes, backed by economic motivations, forced strict controls and restriction on international cooperation. As a result, the number of countries that gained access to the technology and its knowhow was low.

The superpowers acknowledged the fact that their behavior affected the perception and behavior of other states regarding the question of how a modern and progressive country should act. The challenge of overcoming the political and technological obstacles made space even more appealing to many of them. Indeed, despite the restrictions and controls imposed by the superpowers, or because of them, other countries made conscious efforts to become more independent regarding access to and utilization of outer space, which are important qualities for great powers.[99]

The politics of space, characterized by an inherent tension between competition, limited cooperation, and controls on the transfer and flow of technology, produced the ingredients of what has been termed the "space club." The spacefaring nations became a closed community that shared a "secret" that inspired millions around the world to develop expectations and aspirations.

Although there was no formal organization or association, club rules and regulations, admission board, nor central management, the countries that had demonstrated this capability enjoyed proximity that resulted in cooperation and the exchange of ideas (even between the Soviet Union and the United States). The superpowers served as its leaders and as its gatekeepers.

---

[99] Williamson, R., "International Cooperation and Competition in Space," in D. Papp and R. McIntyre, (eds.), *International Space Policy*, (New York: Quorum Books, 1987), 105–118.

4   A Multilateral Race for Space Club Membership

The Cold War race to space is usually referred to as a bilateral competition. But in practice, a multilateral competition over space achievements took place, and it still takes place. The competitive atmosphere, propaganda, and public diplomacy of the two superpowers over space exploration created norms and conventions about the importance of space for national might and stressed the exclusivity of national space capability. Other states adopted the message and were, and still are, interested in catching up by demonstrating similar capabilities in order to win tangible economic and development goods and enjoy the added strategic, political, and social values attributed to space expertise.

This chapter provides insights on the perceptions held by decision-makers and state officials of emerging spacefaring nations, as well as medium-sized and small states, concerning the politics of space and the values they attribute to achievements in this field. These weaker states accepted the interpretation offered by the superpowers that space programs are means and symbols of power and used it for their own national and international purposes. Medium-sized and small states aspire to emulate the superpowers in deeds and in declarations by stressing the importance of developing a leading indigenous position. Their behavior resembles a techno-nationalist approach and so does their rhetoric when justifying and vindicating investments and national efforts to develop a national space capacity. They socially construct their achievements as an act of joining the space club, while stressing their self-reliance to distinguish themselves from lower-status states or creating proximity to higher-status or equal-footing states in order to achieve the lofty status and gains that are reserved for members only.

They link the technical achievements to national narratives in order to upgrade national esteem and to support the domestic scientific and industrial community; they compete for national achievements and take pride in setting their own national records. These records have significant political meaning, as they are important to national history and collective memory; they are also used in political conflicts over power and status. Setting such records assists in assimilating states into the group of high-status and powerful states and draws clear distinctions between themselves and low-status, weaker states. For example, China takes pride in being third in the world to send humans into space[1] and in softly landing on the Moon. Canada takes pride in being third in the world to develop its own satellite. France takes pride in being third to develop and launch its own satellite.[2] Japan takes pride in being fourth to demonstrate capability to launch its own satellite.[3] Australia takes pride in being fourth to have a satellite launched from its territory. Israel takes pride in being seventh to launch a sounding rocket and eighth to develop and launch its own satellite. Brazil takes pride in being the first in South America to develop a satellite.[4] Iran declared its ambition to be the first Islamic country to launch a satellite[5] and greatly emphasized this fact when it accomplished this mission in February 2009. South Korea declared its ambition to be among the top spacefaring states of the world and ninth to launch a satellite into space using its own technology; eventually Iran preceded South Korea in setting this record.[6] In 2014, the European Space Agency took pride in being the first to land on a comet.

In most of the states that made the effort of putting a satellite into space, the political and strategic aspects were no less important than the scientific and practical ones. Usually, the motivations behind these impressive achievements were explained as an aspiration to serve humanity, enhance scientific knowledge, and expand space exploration. But many of the satellites launched as "national firsts" were unsophisticated and only equipped to perform a series of "national beeps" that could be picked

---

[1] NTIS, World News Connection, Xinhua, "News Analysis: China To Fortify Presence in World's Space Club," *Xinhua Saturday*, October 15, 2005.
[2] AP, "French Proud of Satellite Despite Its Loss of Voice," *Sunday Times*, November 28, 1965, A4.
[3] Far East, World Broadcasts, Media Coverage of Japanese Satellite Launch, February 11, 1970, BBC Collection, Microfilm 51567-693, (Washington, DC: Library of Congress).
[4] Brooke, J., "Brazil's 'Window on Space' Broken," *New York Times*, August 2, 1993, A4; Cole, R., "Brazil Begins the Countdown on its Entrance into Space race," *Philadelphia Inquirer*, July 12, 1982.
[5] "Iran will be the first Islamic country to go into the space beyond the Earth's atmosphere with its indigenous satellite and launch pad system," ("Shamkhani: Iran will launch its own satellite within 18 months," *Global Security Forum*, January 5, 2004, available at: www.globalsecurity.org/space/library/news/2004/space-040105-irna01.htm, accessed on August, 1, 2007).
[6] NTIS, World News Connection, ROK Daily, "Korea To Build First Space Launch Vehicle," *Chosun Ilbo WWW-Text Friday*, September 14, 2007. Iran was the ninth country to launch a satellite into space in 2009. South Korea successfully launched a satellite into space in January 2013.

up by tracking stations around the world;[7] they were not scientifically meaningful,[8] a fact that puts these motives in doubt. Rather, this reality implies that other factors, such as the need or aspiration to demonstrate national might through space expertise, overtook scientific incentives. After all, demonstration of strategic capability to launch satellites into space has clear international and national implications; when followed by claims of joining an exclusive group of states – the space club – the national and strategic nature of this achievement is further emphasized. This way, state officials and leaders construct the reality of the material achievements and provide them a political context and meaning in order to leverage the power and status to which they aspire, and to upgrade their state's national esteem in a competitive but non-violent way. In this manner they aim to avoid the exacerbation of a potential security dilemma and to win national gains.

Motivations for the Development of Space Capability

Ezell (1985) recognized political, military, scientific, and practical motivations as basic categories.[9] Suzuki (2003), in his work on the policy logics of European space collaboration, identified six types of policy logics for space development: science, technology, commerce, military, autonomy, and finance. [10] He argued that in order to affect decision-makers' objectives, space experts usually form "policy logic coalitions" around common policy logics, such as the ones mentioned above. Each country has its own distinctive institutional setting, which grants power to certain logic coalitions and has a different degree of influence on principal decision-makers.[11] The perspective of policy logic coalition places emphasis on observed practical and material motivations, which are advocated as rational and justifiable. This view does not address other policy logics and motivations that affect preferences and policy-making, such as domestic and international social and political aspects, which are important to the overall identity and social standing of a country in the world community.

---

[7] The Chinese, for example, outdid themselves by playing their national hymn, "The East Is Red," on their first launch.

[8] Explorer 1, the first American satellite, which was launched on January 31, 1958, was the only one that made an actual scientific contribution. An experiment on this satellite by the physicist James Van Allen documented the existence of radiation zones encircling Earth. These are known as the Van Allen Radiation Belts.

[9] Ezell, E. C., "Space Activities in the Soviet Union, Japan, and The People's Republic of China," in A. Roland, (ed.), *A Space-Faring People: Perspectives on Early Spaceflight*, (Washington, DC: The NASA History Series, 1985), 118.

[10] Kazuto, S., *Policy Logics and Institutions of European Space Collaboration*, (Burlington: Ashgate, 2003).

[11] Kazuto, S., *Policy Logics and Institutions*, 24–29.

Parkinson (1998) outlined motivating groups that advocate for space programs out of the rationale for scientific knowledge, adventure, challenge, human evolution, survival, technology advancement, commerce, and security.[12] Gerard Brachet, the chairman of UN COPUOS[13] in 2006–2007, surmised that the prime motivations for national development of space program are scientific/research or exploration, applications to societal needs, and security and defense.[14] In his seminal work on Asia's space activity, Moltz (2012) referred to science-technical motivations, security-based motivations, and prestige as possible factors shaping preferences and priorities.[15] Other work identified social welfare, economical and industrial development, national and international prestige, environmental concerns, and modernity among the reasons and reasoning for national development of space technology.[16] These ideas are expressed in many space agencies' declared visions or mandates. The guiding principles are usually to promote the peaceful use and development of space, to advance scientific knowledge, to utilize space technology to improve life on Earth, and to promote international cooperation.[17] All of these observations cannot be disregarded, but when constructed as an act of joining the space club, it is clear that states operate in this realm out of less tangible motivations.

In this respect, it is important to realize that each state has its own complex set of motivations leading it toward a national space program. However, because of the significant implications that space expertise provides for the security, economy, and the overall international standing of a state, in many cases, objectives regarding space and space policies are

---

[12] Parkinson, R.C., "Review of Rationales for Space Activity," *Journal of the British Interplanetary Society*, 51, (1998), 275–280.
[13] UN Committee on the Peaceful Uses of Outer Space.
[14] Brachet, G., *The Future of Space Activities and The Role of UN COPUOS*, Presentation at CSIS, October 16, 2006, Washington, DC.
[15] Moltz, J. C., *Asia's Space Race*, (New York: Columbia University Press, 2012).
[16] Ocampo, A., Friedman, L., and Logsdon, J., "Why Space Science and Exploration Benefit Everyone," *Space Policy*, 14, (1998), 137–143; Mistry, D., "The Geo-Strategic Implications of India's Space Program," *Asian Survey*, 41:6, (2001), 1034; Knorr, K., "On the International Implications of Outer Space," *World Politics*, 12:4, (July 1960), 564–584; Logsdon, J. M., "A Sustainable Rationale for Human Spaceflight," *Issues in Science and Technology*, (Winter 2004), 31–34; Van Dyke, V., *Pride and Power: The Rationale for the Space Program* (Urbana: University of Illinois Press, 1965).
[17] For more examples and information see the following documents and websites: ESA Purposes on ESA's website, www.esa.int/SPECIALS/About_ESA/SEMSN26LARE_0 .html, accessed on March 21, 2009; Canadian Space Agency Mandate on CSA's website, www.asc-csa.gc.ca/eng/about/mission.asp, accessed on March 21, 2009; UK's space center website, www.bnsc.gov.uk/5550.aspx, accessed on March 22, 2009; Brochures of space agencies of Italy, South Korea, India, Hungary, and France.

usually linked to nationalism and are affected by the principles of techno-nationalism.

Since the end of the Cold War, the space industry has become an international business. Thus, space capability helps states to develop areas of commercial expertise, which diversify their economies and enhance their global competitiveness.[18] In addition, advanced space technologies are believed to be the means for a quick transition from a traditional undeveloped society to an industrial and post-industrial nation. One of the reasons is that space is of crucial importance for quickly transmitting information from one place to another.

In the Cold War, techno-nationalism of space expertise was practiced by the superpowers in order to achieve leadership. For medium-sized countries that emulated the superpowers, the objective was not leadership: it was to use technological advancement and expertise for industrialization, which would develop a strong leading economy and by that provide them a higher status, global power, and greater influence. Today, developing countries use techno-nationalist techniques to achieve faster development. Their objective is usually to leapfrog stages of development for a stronger economy and for military empowerment, which they too aspire to translate into a higher status and greater influence on the international system and on their own future.[19] Membership in the space club and its rhetoric serve these aspirations.

Club Membership and the Quest for Empowerment, Development, and Lofty Status

Since the early days of the space age, states (other than the superpowers) use space programs to demonstrate their powerful capability in order to convince the world, as well as their own citizens, of their power and high status. In the 1960s, France and Britain initiated space programs and developed launchers and satellites in order to preserve their historical status as world powers and leaders of Europe.[20] Possessing nuclear

---

[18] Pace, S., "Emerging Challenges: National Security Requirements and Economic/Commercial Interests," in D. Johnson, and E. Levite, (eds.), *Toward Fusion of Air and Space*, (Washington, DC: RAND & Fisher Institute, 2003), 48.

[19] For further reading on techno-nationalism of space technology see: Johnson-Freese, J., "The Geostrategic, Techno-Nationalist Push into Space," 20, *OASIS*, 9–22; and Johnson-Freese, J., "How does IR relates to space exploration in the 21st century?," *E-International Relations*, July 19, 2013, available at: www.e-ir.info/2013/07/19/how-does-ir-relate-to-space-exploration-in-the-21st-century, accessed on June 26, 2015.

[20] The cases of France and Britain's space efforts are discussed in depth in Chapter 5.

weapons, and later the capacity to launch a satellite into space, was perceived by France as means to demonstrate to the world and to its citizens, that France was still an important and influential actor in the international system.[21] British leaders sought ways to restore Britain's special relationship with the United States, which they believed would ensure Britain's security and protection.[22] Acquiring expertise in these fields was Britain's way to signal to the United States that it should not be ignored.[23]

Throughout the 1960s, Japan invested great efforts in advancing its knowledge and capability in space technology. Many in the Japanese government, industry, and research community believed Japan should develop indigenous space capacity.[24] Suzuki (2005) argued that "[Japan] was motivated by a desire to 'join the club of advanced industrial states,' instead of by a desire for competition with other states."[25] In the 1960s and 1970s, one of the primary motivations of Japan on the space path, was the drive toward parity with the great powers. For many among Japanese leaders, a national space program was a symbol of prestige, pride, and Japanese power.[26] In January 1965, United States' President Lyndon B. Johnson and Japanese Prime Minister Eisaku Satō[27] met in Washington. Discussing space technology, Satō told Johnson that Japan aspired to be third in space by developing indigenous capabilities to launch objects into space. On this meeting the Japanese even raised the possibility of Japan developing nuclear capacity.[28]

---

[21] Kolodziej, E. A., "Revolt and Revisionism in the Gaullist Global Vision: An Analysis of French Strategic Policy," *The Journal of Politics*, 3:2, (May 1971), 448–454; Thomson, D., "General de-Gaulle and the Anglo-Saxons," *International Affairs*, 41:1, (January, 1965), 11–12, 16–21.
[22] Wallace, W., "Foreign Policy and National Identity in the United Kingdom," *International Affairs*, 67:1, (1991), 65.
[23] For a comprehensive discussion of Britain's nuclear policy after WWII, and especially on Churchill's agenda, see Best, G., *Churchill and War*, (London and New York: Palgrave/Hambledon and London, 2005).
[24] Harvey, B., Smid, H., and Pirad, T., *Emerging Space Powers: The New Space Programs of Asia, the Middle East and South America*, (Chichester, UK: Springer-Praxis, 2000), 24.
[25] Suzuki, K., "Administrative Reforms and the Policy Logics of Japanese Space Policy," *Space Policy*, 21, (2005), 15.
[26] Sato, Y., "A Contested Gift of Power: American Assistance to Japan's Space Launch Vehicle Technology, 1965–1975," *Historical Scientiarum*, 11:2, (2001), 178.
[27] Prime minister from 1964–1972, Eisaku Satō was considered the highest-level Japanese leader to support Japanese development of nuclear weapons.
[28] Satō expressed his aspiration in his meeting with President Lyndon Johnson in Washington on January 13, 1965. Memorandum of conversation between President Johnson and Prime Minister Sato, Washington, January 13, 1965, 11:30 AM, Foreign Relations of the United States, 1964–1968, Volume XXIX, Part 2, Japan, available at the National Archives and Records Administration, RG 59, Central Files 1964–66, POL JAPAN–US; also available at: history.state.gov/historicaldocuments/frus1964-68v29p2, accessed on May 20, 2016.

In the late 1960s, Japan was concerned with potentially losing its world standing. In a telegram sent to the Department of State on March 1, 1967, US Ambassador Alexis Johnson well explains that status considerations are significant in Japan's decision-making regarding the nuclear issue: "The drive toward parity with the great powers has been one of the most consistent themes of Japan's modern history. In spite of its present attitudes on military and nuclear affairs, an implied relegation of Japan to second-class status because of her non-possession of nuclear arms would ultimately constitute a powerful incentive to go after an independent nuclear capability."[29] A similar incentive affected Japan's space policy.

In late 1967, despite Japan's reluctance to rely on foreign assistance for the development of its space capabilities, serious talks began when the United States, which was concerned about the possibility of Japan developing nuclear weapons along with their delivery system, became willing to discuss sensitive space cooperation with Japan. In January 1968, the United States formally proposed to Japan cooperation that included American rocketry technology. At the end of 1968, the Japanese government decided to accept the American offer. Diplomatic notes were exchanged on July 31, 1969, under the administration of President Richard Nixon.[30] Japan's first launch of a satellite into space, using a Japanese rocket,[31] took place on February 11, 1970. The successful launch made Japan the fourth country to independently launch a satellite into space, only two months ahead of China.[32] In the years to come, the cooperation with the United States helped Japan boost its space program, especially its launch capability.[33]

---

[29] Telegram From the Embassy in Japan to the Department of State, Tokyo, March 1, 1967. The Department of State copy is in the National Archives and Records Administration, RG 59, Central Files 1967–69, POL 7 US/GOLDBERG. Foreign Relations of the United States, 1964–1968, Volume XXIX, Part 2, Japan, Available at the National Archives and Records Administration, RG 59, Central Files 1964–66, POL JAPAN–US; also available at: history.state.gov/historicaldocuments/frus1964-68v29p2, accessed on May 20, 2016. Document 84 The Telegram was attached to a memorandum from the President's Special Assistant (Rostow) to President Johnson. The memorandum indicates that the president saw it.

[30] Harvey, B., Smid, H., and Pirad, T., *Emerging Space Powers*, 24; and Logsdon, J., Day, D., and Launius, R.D., (eds.), Exploring the Unknown – Selected Documents In The History of The US Civilian Space Program Volume II: External Relationships, (Washington, DC: The NASA History Series, NASA History Office, 1996), 46.

[31] The first satellite was launched aboard a Lambada 4S rocket. The L-4S rocket is a four-stage solid propellant rocket. For further information, see www.isas.jaxa.jp/e/japan_s_history/detail/challenge.shtml, accessed September 1, 2013.

[32] Willis, D., "Japan Joins Space Club," *Christian Science Monitor*, February 14, 1970, 1.

[33] The Japanese N-I, N-II, and H-I rockets were developed on the basis of the US Thor-Delta rocket technology.

The approach of using space technology development for the achievement of a powerful higher status was adopted by other less powerful states as well. Egypt for example, which perceived itself as a regional power in the Middle East and as one of the leaders of the non-aligned states, declared in the mid-1960s that it was planning to launch a satellite into orbit as a concrete example of the state's growing political-military strength and its general technological surge under the aegis of President Gamal Abdel Nasser.[34] Brazil's space program was developed in the 1970s under the military government.[35] This era was known as "Brazil Grande" or Great Brazil. The space program was only one of a series of projects initiated by the government to demonstrate Brazil's power and increase its status in the region and the world. Brazil built the world's longest bridge, the world's longest dam, the Trans-Amazon Highway, and nuclear energy installations. By the end of the 1980s, the military predicted confidently that Brazil would "join the club" of the world's space powers, launching a Brazilian-made satellite on a Brazilian-made rocket.[36] Major General Hugo de Oliveira Piva, Vice Director of the Institute for Space Activities, said, "If we want to be an important country, we would have to use space extensively – for remote sensing, communication, meteorology and for data collection."[37] His words exemplify the significance attributed to the development of indigenous capabilities for national reasons, far beyond their tangible value.

In India, the space program was and still is perceived as an important component of statehood.[38] Already in the early 1960s, Indian officials expressed their view that space should be used for the development of India and for making it an important state.[39] The following was published in the Indian media after the successful launch of the PSLV-C1 in 1997 that put the 1,200 kg Indian Remote Sensing Satellite IRS 1-D into orbit: "This is a stupendous achievement by any means and a rebuff to the untiring efforts of the big powers to constitute a technological cartel ... India, with the PSLV-C1 launch, has now emerged as a major global

---

[34] Brownlow, C., "Egypt Plans Satellite Launch Within A Year," *Aviation Week & Space Technology*, September 9, 1963, 32–33; "Germany Seen Big Help to Egypt in Space," *Washington Daily News*, June 2, 1964; "Egypt Planning Satellite Launch," *Washington Post*, June 4, 1964.

[35] The first research center was established in the 1960s.

[36] Brooke, J., "Brazil's 'Window on Space' Broken," *New York Times*, August 2, 1993, A4.

[37] Michaels, J., "Brazil's Fledging Space Program Jolted by Chances to Join a US Shuttle Mission," *Wall Street Journal*, February 15, 1983, 36.

[38] For a comprehensive discussion of this subject, see Kinsella, D., and Chima, J., "Symbols of Statehood: Military Industrialization and Public Discourse in India," *Review of International Studies*, 27, (2001), 353–373.

[39] For an analysis of the Indian space policy and motivations, see Chapter 8 of this book.

power in the satellite launching business."⁴⁰ This statement exemplifies a techno-nationalist approach to space development.

After the demise of the Soviet Union, the Soviet bloc states initiated national space agencies. Ukraine was fortunate to be left with part of the Soviet launch infrastructure, which is now a part of its space program. The words of Andriy Zhalko-Tytarenko, Deputy General Director of Ukraine's National Space Agency in 1993 that "we are one of the strongest space powers ... If we lose the possibility to work in the aerospace sphere, we will automatically turn into an ordinary third-world country with all the consequences of such a status,"⁴¹ well express Ukraine's approach regarding its space capacity, perceiving it as its calling card for the developed world.

In Israel, too, the achievements of the space program are perceived as important elements of statehood and as indicators of elevated status and power in the international sphere. For example, after the first Israeli satellite was launched on September 19, 1988, Professor Yuval Neeman, chairman of Israel's Space Agency, said that Israel must not be left behind in this significant field.⁴² In 2001, Israeli Minister of Science and Technology Matan Vilnai expressed his view on the motivation of Israel to be among the spacefaring nations by saying "Any nation that isn't part of the world's space community is essentially a handicapped nation."⁴³ In 2005, shortly after Ofeq 5, a remote sensing satellite was successfully launched off the Israeli shore, Prime Minister Ariel Sharon and other senior government officials explained that the launch was not aimed only at intelligence gathering, but also to project Israel's power.⁴⁴

In South Korea, national space activity is perceived in a similar way. In the 2000s, the Korean government identified space technology as a national strategic issue. In 2008, Kim Chang Woo, Director General for Space Technology at the Ministry of Science and Technology of Korea explains Korea's international ambitions in using space: "In the last ten years, the gap between us and the space powers has been greatly reduced ... It is said that those who rule space will rule the world ...

---

⁴⁰ NTIS, World News Connection, India: Article Praises Country's 'Space Prowess', Article by Soumyajit Pattanik: "A Great Leap Forward," *Delhi, The Pioneer in English*, October 1, 1997, 8.
⁴¹ Space Agency Official Interviewed on Program, (August 3, 1993), FBIS, Kiev, MOLOD UKRAYINY in Ukraine.
⁴² Sadeh, D., "Professor Yuval Neeman, Chairman of ISA: 'Israel Must Not be Left Behind in the Conquest of Space'," *Yediot Aharonot* [Newspaper], September 20, 1988, (Hebrew).
⁴³ Opall-Rome, B., "Israel Approves Six-Fold Increase in Space Funding," *Space News*, October 1, 2001, 9.
⁴⁴ Ben, A., "Shihab-3 Versus Ofeq-5," *Haaretz*, June 6, 2002, (in Hebrew).

Therefore, it is obvious that Korea should aim to be a competitive force in space development."[45]

The objectives of national empowerment and achieving high status are also desired through emphasizing self-reliance, which serves as an indicator of power and as a somewhat peaceful message of deterrence. When a state does not possess an independent capability, it is subject to the good will of the country from which it receives information or products. Nevertheless, the issue of a state's self-sufficiency is a complex one. States, even the most powerful ones, are far from being totally self-reliant; they depend on other states for economic and commercial interests, political support in international arenas, and in the field of defense and security. The development of space technology is risky and highly expensive. Even superpowers have trouble sustaining such projects independently because it puts a considerable burden on the national economy. Nevertheless, beyond the benefits of the actual ability, limited as it may be, it sends a message of national might and intent to its citizens, allies, and adversaries alike.

States often choose to engage in space development, even on a limited scope that obviously does not allow them full independence, just to prove their ability and by that to strengthen their sovereignty and overall statehood, upgrade their overall international standing, and gain material goods. For example, in South Africa, independence and self-reliance play a role in the renewal of the space program. Under its former rule, South Africa had an ambitious space program that was aimed at developing indigenous capability to launch and develop satellites. In 1994, when the apartheid government ceased operations and the new government took over, the space program was stopped. In the last decade, the government decided to renew its program, this time on a more moderate scale; nonetheless, it attributed value to having some extent of local capability and is willing to carry the burden in order to project a message of capability.

Such an action can be treated as merely a quest for international prestige. Nevertheless, the image a nation seeks to be identified with in the eyes of other states is not an end in itself; it is a means to achieve tangible goods, as well as a high position in the world, which further upgrades the tangible goods and intangible benefits. Scientific and technological capability in space is a tool for shaping a prestigious image in the

---

[45] Chang Woo, K., "Space Development, Korean Dream and Hope," *Korea Net – Gateway to Korea*, February 17, 2008, available at: www.kois.go.kr/News/News/newsprint.asp?serial_no=20080205006, accessed on February 18, 2008.

international system, as well as the regional system.[46] It implies that a state has a reputation as an advanced country or as a power; nevertheless, this reputation is meaningless, unless it represents substantive underlying factors. "It is precisely because space achievements are consciously or unconsciously recognized as infinitely more important than stunts that they have meaning in the world today," said Arnold Frutkin in 1965.[47] Indeed, space technology is an advanced technology that requires expertise in a variety of scientific and technological fields. Such capability reflects the overall national technological and scientific capability of a state, which is highly significant for its development, as well as for its potential military power.[48]

Space capability has prominent visibility. The launch of a satellite into space cannot be hidden, and in the age of worldwide and live television broadcasts, it is even more visible and public. The combination of these two aspects has the potential of upgrading the image of a state as developed and modern. The capability itself projects on the fact that the state has advanced scientific and technological skills, or at least is on its way to achieve that. The visibility of "space events" attracts attention because it demonstrates national skills and sends a message of intent and ability. This has the potential to increase confidence in the skills of that state, its level of development and modernity, which can in turn upgrade its image.[49] Improved image may lead and contribute to an actual process of development, because it serves as a symbol of development. For

[46] Dinshaw Mistry argues that India's space program was guided by strong political motivations for development of the nation in the international system: "It was intended to symbolize India's high-technology achievements and enhance New Delhi's international status ... The Indian space program also caters to a domestic constituency – successful satellite deployments and launches are national morale boosters" (Mistry. D., "Geo-Strategic Implications," 1034). The president of India, Dr. Abdul Kalam, published a book in 2004 in which he refers to India's space program as a means of empowerment: Kalam, A., and Pillai, S., *Envisioning an Empowered Nation – Technology for Societal Transformation*, (New Delhi: Tata MacGraw-Hill Publishing, 2004).

[47] Address by Arnold Frutkin, Assistant Administrator for International Affairs, NASA, to the American Academy of Political and Social Science, Philadelphia, PA, April 16, 1966, NASA HQ History Office Historical Reference Collection Archives, Frutkin Biographic files, Washington, DC, 12–13.

[48] More evidence on this argument may be found in: McDougall, W., The Heavens and the Earth: A Political History of the Space Age, (New York, NY: Basic Books, 1985); Logsdon, J. M., "A Sustainable Rationale, 31–34; Logsdon, J. M., "Human Space Flight and National Power," *High Frontier*, (March 2007), 11–13; Van Dyke, V., *Pride and Power*; Spaey, J., Defay, J., Ladriere, J., Stenmans, A., and Wautrequin, J., (1971), *Science for Development*, (Paris: UNESCO), 15.

[49] In 1960, Klaus Knorr attempted to evaluate the extent to which advancement and development of space technology would affect the intentions and/or capabilities of actors in the international system, and perhaps the operation of the system itself. Knorr claimed that scientific and technological achievements are highly valued. Therefore, scientific and technological prestige would be a major objective motivating states to participate (and

example, it may encourage other states to cooperate or invest in that state, not necessarily in space technology per se, but because a space program is identified as a real potential of development.

A CIA report from 1964 on the motivations of Western European states to pursue space capability on a national level pointed out that "national and cooperative programs are motivated both by the promise of industrial, scientific, and commercial benefits, and by considerations of national prestige."[50] The motivations of developing states to be involved in space in recent years are not much different. Their behavior resembles the Handicap Principle, in which a reliable signal must be costly to the signaler in order to convince others of his capabilities and sincere intentions and commitment to achieve his goals.[51] Independent development of expertise in space technology, which is highly expensive and risky, serves as a credible signal of the ability, intent, and decisiveness of a state to achieve its goals. This credibility makes others take the state's considerations into account in international forums as well as extend it cooperation, which is extremely important for the development of its industry, scientific community, and overall economy. For example, Brazil's space program is part of Brazil's undertaking to achieve a degree of technological independence and project a message of decisiveness. Himilcon de Crvahlo, former Head of the Department of Space Policy at the Brazilian Space Agency, explained the importance of independence and self-reliance in Brazil's eyes for achieving a better position in the international system: "Being able to have real access to space means we must have our own capabilities to put things in space and not being subject to either economic or political decisions of third parties ... If you have some space capabilities you have some degree of development, so you must be heard in multilateral forums or negotiations."[52] Nevertheless, so far, Brazil has not achieved its goal.

When asked to elaborate on the motivation and rationale of developing states to embark on a national space program from his experience, Professor Sir Martin Sweeting[53] replied that

excel) in space activities. See Knorr, K., "On the International Implications of Outer Space," *World Politics*, 12:4, (July 1960), 564–584.

[50] CIA Special Report on Western European Space Program, May 1, 1964, 1, available at CIA FOIA database, www.foia.cia.gov/browse_docs_full.asp, accessed on November 17, 2008.

[51] For a comprehensive and detailed discussion of the Handicap Principle in evolutionary biology, see Zahavi, A., and Zahavi A., *The Handicap Principle: A Missing Piece of Darwin's Puzzle*, (New York: Oxford University Press, 1997).

[52] Interview with Himilcon de Crvahlo, former Head of the Department of Space Policy at the Brazilian Space Agency, September 25, 2007, Hyderabad, India.

[53] Professor Sweeting from the University of Surrey is the founder of Surrey Satellite Technology Ltd. SSTL is a company that specializes in the development of small satellites. Over the last two decades, SSTL has concluded more than two dozen cooperative projects

as part of the prestige aspect you have also the option of sitting at the table of COPUOS[54] as a head of a space agency together with other heads of space agencies like NASA. If you have a program, you are more credible and it changes your position. If you do not have a program or a satellite, you are only an observer. They [the states] see that as important. It is not only prestige, but it gives them also a channel of communications with people and allows them to establish later interactions and exchanges, perhaps in other fields; and the developed states see them as slightly more developed than the other undeveloped states and they are more likely to give them other things.[55]

Professor Sweeting's words highlight the tangible benefits countries expect to gain by joining the club. He summed up by adding that a space program in these developing countries is also an internal message of self-esteem:

If we look at the experience that we have had with Algeria, Nigeria, Thailand, Malaysia, Singapore, Korea, Portugal, and more, there is an element of national pride, a statement of not necessarily national capability but national intent .... People in those countries aspire for something better. They want to show that they are not as underdeveloped as perhaps some of their neighbors.[56]

His observation leads us to the discussion of domestic national considerations for the development of space programs.

Domestic Considerations for Club Membership

From the beginning, space programs were nationalist projects and were used to enhance the sense of pride within the nation[57] because they reinforce the notion that space exploration is a powerful vehicle for expressing a nation's broader aspirations. Space events represent "pride in history, a consensus that the present is a moment to be celebrated, and confidence in a bright tomorrow."[58] The following examples, from different countries at different eras, show that national space activity and especially visible achievements are often used to forward to the people a message of internal encouragement, esteem, and patriotism; and an important message of support and encouragement to the scientific community and industrial sector.

---

with developing states, in which the SSTL team taught and trained local teams from these states in space engineering, assisting them in developing small national satellites.

[54] UN Committee on the Peaceful Uses of Outer Space.
[55] Interview with Professor Sir Martin Sweeting, January 31, 2008, Tel Aviv, Israel.
[56] Ibid.
[57] Van Dyke, V., *Pride and Power*; Sheahan, J.T., and Hoban, F.T., (2004), "Spaceports", in: Button, K., Lammersen-Baum, J. and Stough R., (eds.), *Defining Aerospace Policy – Essays in Honor of Francis T. Hoban*, (England: Ashgate), pp. 98–117.
[58] Siddiqi, A., "Spaceflight in the National Imagination," in S. Dick, (ed.), *Remembering the Space Age*, (Washington, DC: NASA History Office, 2008), 17–21.

When Israel launched its first sounding rocket on July 5, 1961, media reports and statements emphasized the fact that Israel joined a superior group of six states that had accomplished this before and are members of the "meteorological rocket launching club."[59] Other statements on this event stressed the fact that despite Israel's size and young age, it had succeeded where others have failed.[60]

After China launched its own satellite in April 1970, the headlines of the Chinese newspapers quoted Mao's statement after the Soviet Union launched Sputnik: "'We Too Should Produce a Man-made Satellite' [has] Come True." They also stressed China's ability to do it on its own. One of the published articles of the *People's Daily* was entitled "Work with Our Own Hands, Rely on Our Own Efforts."[61] Other reports stressed that by demonstrating this capability, China showed it could catch up with and surpass the advanced world.[62] Shortly after India demonstrated its capability to launch satellites into space in the summer of 1980, Prime Minister Indira Gandhi said that "This is a notable achievement of India and Indian science. I am sure the house will join me in congratulating our scientists and technicians of the department of space on their achievement. The nation is proud of them and wishes them further success."[63] Israeli Prime Minister Yitzhak Shamir said similar things after Israel launched Ofeq 1 in 1988: "All the citizens of Israel should be proud of their country, which is capable of displaying such an achievement."[64] In 2008, the Iranian President, Mahmoud Ahmadinejad, expressed the same feelings while touring Iran's launch site: "A deep sense of self-belief, positive authority, and hope for a clear and bright future and a sense of joy and power is something that fills one's being when one witnesses the work of Iranian young scientists and experts."[65]

The message of national esteem and pride is especially embedded in human spaceflight missions. Having one of your own people in space is

---

[59] Israel, Media Coverage of Shavit-2 Launch, July 7, 1961, BBC Collection Israel, Microfilm 51567-474, (Washington, DC: Library of Congress).
[60] Ibid.
[61] Far East, China, Media Coverage of China's First Satellite, April 28, 1970, BBC Collection Microfilm 51567-694, (Washington, DC: Library of Congress).
[62] Far East, China, Media Coverage of China's First Satellite, April 27, 1970.
[63] FBIS, (July 18, 1980), "Gandhi Makes Statement on 18 July, Satellite Launch," *Delhi ISI Diplomatic Information Service*, in English, 08:31 GMT, July 19, 1980.
[64] Telephone Interview with Prime Minister Shamir by Shalom Qital and Oded Ben Ami (live), on Jerusalem Domestic Service in Hebrew, September 19, 1988, FBIS-NES- 88-182 (September 20, 1988).
[65] NTIS, World News Connection, "Iran President Visits Satellite Carrier Launch Site," Vision of the Islamic republic of Iran Network 1, August 17, 2008, translated from Persian.

perceived as a national achievement in and of itself, regardless of the actual scientific value of the mission. The superpowers launched foreign astronauts and cosmonauts into space beginning in March 1978. Czechoslovakia was the first such state to have one of its citizens fly in space on another country's spacecraft. The motivation for such a mission is aimed at boosting national morale and sense of national achievement. Astronauts and cosmonauts, especially those who are the first from a state to be launched into space, become national heroes.

Malaysian Prime Minister Abdullah Ahmed Badawi expressed his admiration and stressed that the flight of a Malaysian into space in October 2007 was a moment of pride for his nation.[66] Given their economic stature, Koreans found the fact that hundreds of astronauts flew to space but none of them were Korean to be humiliating.[67] In April 2008, just before the launch of the first South Korean into space, South Korean President Lee Myung-bak said in a TV address that "this day will go down in history as the day when South Korea reached the outer space."[68] When the first Saudi astronaut, Prince Sultan, arrived in his country after returning to Earth, ethnic emotions exceeded national ones, as Prince Sultan was perceived as the first Arab astronaut. In this context, Clovis Maksoud, the Arab League Ambassador to the UN, said that "the flight is a symbol of the resilience of our people ... and the determination of the Arab people to cope with the latest scientific challenges."[69]

In addition to the objective of increasing self-esteem, national achievements in space technology and exploration are often used to increase the popularity of the government or individual leaders. Because governments or leaders of non-democratic states usually rule for long periods of time, they are more likely to enjoy the fruits of their investments in large-scale national projects like space programs and receive the credit for it. Therefore, this consideration most clearly exists in such regimes. However, it does not mean that this is a prime motive for embarking on such a program, or that it does not happen in democracies. Unlike the motive of international prestige, there is no clear evidence that this consideration has a direct effect on capacity development. Instead, once the

---

[66] "Malaysians Over the Moon as their Astronaut Blasts into Space," *Space Travel*, October 10, 2007.
[67] Sang Hun, C., "Kimchi Goes to Space, along with First Korean Astronaut," *Herald Tribune*, February 22, 2008.
[68] NTIS, World News Connection, "South Korean President Congratulates Nation On Space Flight," *ITAS-TASS*, Tuesday, April 8, 2008, T13:02:09.
[69] Storey, K., and Fitchett, J., "Down to Earth," *Saudi Aramco World*, (January–February 1986), 30–40.

state successfully demonstrates its capability, its leaders are more likely to take the credit for the achievement.

For example, the Soviet space program was crucial for Khrushchev's domestic political context. He alone would receive the credit for the success of the space program. For this reason, it was equally important that failures were hidden both from the Soviet population and the rest of the world.[70] The early days of the Chinese space program were similar. After China successfully launched its first satellite on April 24, 1970, Chinese media coverage of the launch focused on thanking and praising the great leader Mao Tse-tung for this impressive achievement. A press communiqué, for example, announced that China's first man-made satellite was a great victory for Mao Tse-tung's thinking and another fruitful result of the Culture Revolution.[71] The following description of the Chinese celebrations sheds more light on the use of this event to empower the leader and strengthen Communist rule in China:

> Thousands upon thousands of people, carrying huge portraits of our great leader Chairman Mao, and singing and dancing, streamed into the streets and public squares from all directions, for meetings and parades. They proudly declare the successful launching of China's first man-made earth satellite has greatly strengthened the military of the Chinese people and the revolutionary people of the world and deflated the arrogance of imperialism, modern revisionism and all reaction. This achievement is a great victory of invincible Mao Tse-tung thought, a great victory for Chairman Mao's proletarian revolutionary line and another fruitful result of the great proletarian Cultural Revolution![72]

Sometimes, such events are timed to coincide with political events like national elections, and are used in domestic political struggles, to prove and demonstrate that the leadership is boosting the nation forward. For example, President de Gaulle timed the first French launch only days before national elections, which he won. In Israel, the Shavit 2 sounding rocket was launched a month before the elections for the Knesset (Parliament), which took place on August 15, 1961. The opposition and the media accused the government of conducting the launch for propaganda purposes, calling it an election stunt.[73] The ruling party lost six seats in the Knesset, which cast doubt on the political effectiveness

---

[70] Sheehan, M., The International Politics of Space, (London, UK: Routledge, 2007), 32.
[71] Far East, China, Media Coverage of China's First Satellite, April 25, 1970, BBC Collection Microfilm 51567-694, (Washington, DC: Library of Congress), Press Communiqué, NCNA in English.
[72] Far East, China, Media Coverage of China's First Satellite, April 27, 1970, BBC Collection Microfilm 51567-694, (Washington, DC: Library of Congress), NCNA in English 0610 GMT 27.4.70.
[73] Not much information was provided after the launch and only a handful of pictures were released. One of them shows Prime Minister and Minister of Defense David Ben-Gurion

of the launch, if it was a political stunt. Coincidentally, Ofeq 1, Israel's first satellite, was scheduled to be launched a short time before the national elections were to take place on November 1, 1988. Concerned by the memory of the Shavit 2 incident, Yitzhak Rabin, Minister of Defense, decided not to be present at the launch site, in order to avoid political criticism for performing another political stunt.[74]

The first Iranian launch into space, in February 2009, may also be analyzed in this light. The then Iranian president has made Iran's scientific development and particularly the space and nuclear programs one of the main themes of his presidency.[75] In his campaign for a second tenure of presidency, he stressed the achievements of Iran in these fields under his leadership. He was also present at the launch site on the day of the successful launch, exploiting the national achievement for his campaign.[76]

Conclusion

The examples provided in this chapter show that since the Cold War years, decision-makers and state officials see significance in the political and social meaning of a national space program and its achievements for domestic and international considerations. They perceive projects of this kind as means and symbols of power and glory in the overall context of their state's struggle for power and survivability. Indeed, in many states that made the effort to put a satellite into space, the strategic and national aspects were no less important than the material and scientific ones, perhaps even more.

Aspirations to great-power status and greater national esteem through self-reliance, association with other powerful states, and national pride by demonstrations of highly visible spectaculars were expressed in the claims for membership in the space club in the years of the Cold War – and continue to be after it ended. In the years that followed, medium-sized and small states often claimed high rank and powerful status in this field by stressing their affiliation to a superior, exclusive group of states that had already demonstrated national capability in the field of space activity and exploration. By making these claims, they strive to be included in

standing next to the rocket, in: Shalom, D., Beyond Horizon, (Private printing, 2004), 12–15, Hebrew.

[74] Barzilai, A., "A Force-Multiplier is Being Built Here," *Haaretz*, September 26, 2001, (in Hebrew), available at: www.hayadan.org.il/wp/double-power-260901/, accessed on March 30, 2009.

[75] Peter, N., Space Policies Issues and Trends, 2007–2008, Report 15, (Vienna: European Space Policy Institute, 2008).

[76] The elections in Iran took place in June 2009.

Conclusion

a high-status group that either equals their status or even exceeds it. Concomitantly, they exclude themselves from low-status states, to which they wish to be superior.

The superpowers raced for space, but they also raced for the attention of small and medium-sized states. The superpowers needed the support of the latter, and recognition of their claims for power and legitimacy, to operate as world leaders. The aforementioned examples show that these messages were clearly understood and adopted. Even today, a national advanced space program is perceived as a key to a powerful status; great powers and states that aspire to be great regional or global powers are expected to pursue a space program. For this reason, the rhetoric used by decision-makers and officials of small and medium-sized states is very similar to the rhetoric used by the superpowers. It elaborates on the processes, interests, and logic that motivate decision-makers to embark on such projects and on the values they ascribe to achievements in this field.

The space club has been an important part of the global interaction over space politics in the past several decades and provides the context in which these political processes take place. A national space program remains a symbol and a means of statehood and of projecting power. The emphasis that small and medium-sized states, as well as superpowers, put on the national and international meaning of these capabilities and achievements, through the prism of a club, shows that it is more than a cynical attempt to maximize political gains. The space club became an integral part of the international political discourse over status, power, esteem and identity. For those who perceive themselves as members, it means that they are a cut above ordinary states, allowing them to identify their status as comparable to larger and more powerful states. For the superpowers, it was an important arena in which they exercised their leadership, interacted, and competed with one another in a civilized manner. Overall, it was used (and is still being used) as a credible signal of decisiveness, intent, and high capability. By claiming membership in the elite space-club, states participate in the political game and fulfill what they observe to be expected of them in the international social environment – a message that is clearly understood in-house and abroad.

5 France and Britain

France and Great Britain are both important actors in the international system and share many similarities. They have similar gross domestic products per capita, their populations are similar in size, and their people enjoy a high standard of living and national economic productivity. In terms of history and culture, they are two traditional world powers that controlled parts of the New World and still maintain strong ties to the countries that emerged out of their former empires. France and Britain are both open and democratic societies that were part of the Western alliance during the years of the Cold War and, hence, were under the American strategic umbrella. Each of them has nuclear weapons. They are both UN Security Council member states. Nonetheless, when it comes to space activity, France and Britain have chosen different paths. Succeeding British governments opposed a national space agency because they did not attribute much significance to space or having national indigenous expertise in Britain's overall strategy. Britain's approach to space activity is in striking contrast to France's, which perceived space as a prominent part of its grand strategy and consistently granted priority status to its space programs.[1]

To date, France has the most advanced national space program in Europe and is the largest contributor to the European Space Agency (ESA). France takes pride in being the third country to indigenously launch and orbit its own satellite, and it has a high-profile space industry. In the 1960s, Britain was one of the leading nations in space activity, especially in rocketry, and developed a capability to launch satellites into space. The British launch into space in October 1971 took place after the British Government decided to discontinue its launch program in the late 1960s. Since then, Britain's main effort was to make space technology more cost effective. Over the years, British space activity has centered on areas with high commercial potential, such as earth observation,

---

[1] MacLean, A., and Sheehan, M., "A Hare Turned Tortoise: 40 Years of UK Space Policy," *Quest*, 6:4, (Winter 1998), 15.

Table 5.1 *Comparison of France and Great Britain, Selected Parameters*

	France (Metropolitan)		Great Britain	
Total area	545,630 sq. km		244,820 sq. km	
Population (July 2015)	66,553,766		64,088,222	
GDP per capita in US$ (2015 est.)	$41,400		$41,200	
(a) GDP composition by sector (2015 est.)	Agriculture:	1.7%	Agriculture	0.6%
	Industry:	19.3%	Industry:	19.7%
	Services:	79%	Services:	79.7%
Internet users (2014 est.)	56.8 million		57.3 million	
Military expenditure	1.8% of GDP (2014 est.)		2.49% of GDP (2012 est.)	

communications, navigation, and space science for environmental and economic advances.[2] In recent years, Britain had gained much more interest in space activity. In 2010, the British government established a national space agency as part of its new space policy, which is aimed at the development and enhancement of Britain's space sector. However, the incentive for this change is mostly commercial and not strategic.[3]

The different policies and programs each country has pursued on its path to space raise important questions regarding the underlying motivation in each case. This chapter examines the different British and French perspectives on national space activity, and it outlines and analyzes the factors that led these two countries to choose almost contradictory space policies. It consists of three sections. The first section provides a short historical background on Britain's and France's nuclear weapons development and their space efforts. The second section examines the perspectives, aspirations, and objectives that led each country to pursue a different path. Finally, the third section points out several conclusions drawn from the comparison of the two cases. The investigation of British and French space programs stops in the early 1970s, after Britain performed its first launch and declined to develop its capability further.

---

[2] Burleson, D., *Space Programs Outside the United States*, (Jefferson, NC: McFarland & Company Publishers, 2005), 306.

[3] Data presented in Table 5.1 were obtained from the online site of the CIA World Fact-Book: "France," available at www.cia.gov/library/publications/the-world-factbook/geos/fr.html; and "United Kingdom," available at www.cia.gov/library/publications/the-world-factbook/geos/uk.html, accessed on March 20, 2016.

Are We Still Great Powers after World War II?

We must do it. It's the price we pay to sit at the top table.
Winston Churchill, on the H-bomb[4]

Before World War II, Britain had been a major world power with considerable military might and global political influence. When the war ended, Britain was on the winning side. Nevertheless, due to enormous expenditures on the war effort, Britain came close to collapsing economically. It found itself overstrained and dependent on the United States for its armament, military industry, and strategic defense. But the fact that Britain's industrial infrastructure was not heavily damaged, along with the psychological boost from the fact that Britain had won the war, led the British people and its leaders to continue thinking of Britain as a great power.[5]

France had a different story. In June 1940, France endured a German invasion for the second time in thirty years. Over the years of the war, France lost nearly a million and a half people. Its industrial infrastructure was destroyed, and its economic situation was dreadful. France had lost its standing among world powers and its self-respect. French leaders turned their efforts to restoring the grandeur and the radiance of France.[6]

Under these circumstances, both countries wanted to restore their status as great powers that were independent of the United States. They initiated development of rockets (the British developed the Blue Streak[7] and Black Knight[8]; the French developed the Veronique)[9], nuclear weapons, and space programs because they believed this was expected of great powers.

In 1946, the United States discontinued its partnership with Britain on atomic research and development due to the US Atomic Energy Act, known as the McMahon Act, which decreed that transmission of any restricted atomic information to another country was a criminal offense. Britain, which aspired to restore its partnership with the United States,

---

[4] Hannesey, P., *The Secret State*, (London: Penguin, 2003), 44.
[5] See the discussion on Britain's situation after the war in Boyd, L., *Britain's Search for A Role*, (Westmead, Farnborough, Hants: Saxon House and Lexington Books, 1975), 15–26.
[6] Hecht, G., *The Radiance of France – Nuclear Power and National Identity after World War II*, (Cambridge, MA: MIT Press, 1998), 2.
[7] Blue Streak, a liquid-fueled missile, was initiated in 1954 as a medium range ballistic missile (MRBM). For more information on the politics of Blue Streak, see Clark, I., *Nuclear Diplomacy and the Special Relationship*, (Oxford, UK: Clarendon Press, 1994), 157–189; MacLean, A., and Sheehan, M., "A Hare Turned Tortoise," 15.
[8] Black Knight was a test bed for developing re-entry vehicles for the nuclear warheads carried on Blue Streak.
[9] A liquid-fueled sounding rocket.

had to impress the Americans with its willingness to defend itself, rather than hide under the American nuclear umbrella. Britain was third to develop a nuclear capability and test a nuclear device, Hurricane, on October 3, 1952. Despite its acclaim as a great scientific and technical achievement and as proof of Britain's status as a major power, it did not provide Britain greater military security or increased respect from the United States: "Barely a month later the Americans tested their first thermonuclear device ... Britain had to do much more to prove her worth as a partner."[10]

Hence, Britain moved on to develop the H-bomb. The rationale was well expressed by the Chiefs of Staff in their general strategic assessment to the Defense Policy Committee on June 1, 1954: "We must maintain and strengthen our position as a world power so that Her Majesty's Government can exercise a powerful influence in the counsels of the world."[11] At an official dinner party in Ottawa on June 29, 1954,[12] Winston Churchill expressed similar thoughts, pointing out that, among other reasons, the British government had decided to make the hydrogen bomb because it would allow Britain greater legitimacy when intervening in world affairs, far more than if it did not have the bomb.[13]

Britain's aspirations to become a member of the nuclear club were based on two assumptions. First, at that point, despite the decline of its empire, it still perceived itself as a great power with a right to "dine at the top table" with the Soviet Union and the United States. Second, a nuclear capability seemed the perfect response to the problems facing Britain in the aftermath of World War II: an uncertain relationship with the United States, the threat of the Soviet Union, an unstable empire, a devastated economy, and a new strategic environment dominated by the H-bomb. "Status," concluded Gerard DeGroot, "gave Britain the right to a Bomb, and the Bomb underlined that status. It was a symbol, not a weapon."[14]

In July 1952, France initiated a five-year plan for its nuclear program. The last sentence in the preface to the plan made France's intentions clear: "It depends on us, today, that France still be a great modern

---

[10] Arnold, L., *Britain and the H-Bomb*, (Hampshire, Palgrave: The Ministry of Defense, 2001), 35–37.
[11] Arnold, L., *Britain and the H-Bomb*, 53.
[12] In discussions of the costs of the H-bomb, it was noted that production could be started soon if tritium could be obtained from Canada. Hence, it was decided that Prime Minister Churchill would discuss this on his forthcoming visit to North America, and that no official statement of government policy should be made.
[13] Eventually, no deal was reached with Canada (Arnold, L., *Britain and the H-Bomb*, 54).
[14] DeGroot, G., (2004). *The Bomb: A Life*, (Cambridge: Harvard University Press), 217–221.

country in ten years."[15] The return to power of General Charles de Gaulle in the Fifth Republic in 1958 elevated the status of the French nuclear program. For de Gaulle, it marked the essence of the great power that France thought it ought and deserved to be. National nuclear capability was believed to bridge the strategic and diplomatic gap between France and the other nuclear powers.[16] The following words by de Gaulle, several years after France had acquired nuclear capability and "joined the nuclear club," illuminate the French attitude toward its strategic capability:

> ... it is clear there is no independence imaginable for a country that does not have its own nuclear weapon, because if it does not have such a weapon it will be forced to rely for its security, and consequently for its policy, on another country which does ... For France, which has no intention of handing over responsibility for her own fate to a foreign nation, no matter how friendly, it is absolutely necessary that she should have the wherewithal to act in any war, in other words, that she should have nuclear arms.[17]

Britain: "To Be or Not to Be" in Space

At the beginning, many in Britain accepted the premise that great powers must be involved in space activity. For them, having a space program was a means to upgrade Britain's special relationship with the United States. For this reason, the successful launch of Sputnik on October 4, 1957, did not evoke a sense of crisis in Britain like it did in the United States. For Britain, the American crisis was a window of opportunity that worked to its advantage on a broad political and technological front; to show the Americans that the United States was not invulnerable and that they needed their allies.[18] In a telegram sent from Washington following the launch, British Ambassador Sir Harold Caccia predicted that "with luck and judgment, we should be able to turn this in some way to our special advantage."[19] On October 10, 1957, British Prime Minister Harold Macmillan sent a personal message to President Dwight Eisenhower. His goal was to exploit this event to re-establish the cooperation enjoyed

---

[15] DeGroot, G., *The Bomb*, 233.
[16] Kolodziej, E., *French International Policy Under De Gaulle and Pompidou – The Politics of Grandeur*, (Ithaca, NY: Cornell University Press, 1974), 79.
[17] Speech by de Gaulle at the Ecole Militaire, February 15, 1963, available at: www.charles-de-gaulle.org, accessed on January 14, 2008.
[18] Krige, J., "Building a Third Space Power," in R. D., Launius, J. M., Logsdon, and R. W., Smith, (eds.), *Reconsidering Sputnik*, (Amsterdam, the Netherlands: Harwood Academic Publishers, 2000), 291.
[19] Whyte, N., and Gummett, P., "Far Beyond the Bounds of Science: The Making of the United Kingdom's First Space Policy," *Minerva*, 35, (1997), 142.

between the two countries in the days of World War II. In his message, Macmillan argued that this was the time to pool efforts to meet the Soviet threat. In his diary Macmillan wrote, "The Russians' success in launching the satellite has been something equivalent to Pearl Harbor. The American cocksureness is shaken."[20] Nevertheless, Macmillan rejected calls to utilize the country's rocket capability in the development of a national space program. On November 14, 1957, he said, "I do not consider the advantages to be gained by this country from launching an earth satellite at present, justify the duplication of scientific effort and the large expenditure that would be involved."[21]

In September 1958, American officials suggested launching British instruments on American-built satellites, more or less free of charge. A month later, the US government released a report praising British achievements thus far and emphasizing the virtues of international collaboration in space. The impetus for the United States to pressure Britain to embark on a satellite program came from the State Department, which wanted the next nation to enter space to be from the "Free World," not the Communist Bloc. According to Krige (2000), Britain was then the only allied power in Europe potentially capable of playing this role.[22]

In the context of local and American pressure, the British Royal Society and the Ministry of Supply decided to re-evaluate the question of a British satellite program.[23] Sherwood (1991) claimed that the great debate in Britain over space activity was not about whether or not Britain should become a space power, but when it would become a space power.[24] In May 1959, Macmillan decided to initiate a delegation to the United States to discuss specific cooperative projects.[25] The decision to accept the American offer shaped the overall British attitude on space activity in Britain, which, as Millard (2005) expressed so well, was a "blending of skepticism and pragmatism."[26]

---

[20] Ashton, N., "Harold Macmillan and the 'Golden Days' of Anglo-American Relations Revisited, 1957–1963," *Diplomatic History*, 29:4, (September 2005), 699.

[21] Millard, D., "Dusting off the Roots of Consistency: British Space Policy 1957–1959," (October 7, 1997), 1, Presented at IAA-97, NASA HQ, History Office, Historical Reference Collection, International Files: UK, Washington, DC.

[22] Krige, J., "Building a Third," 294.

[23] Krige, J., "Building a Third," 296.

[24] Sherwood, R., "Britain in Space," *Spaceflight*, 33, (May 1991), 174.

[25] Logsdon, J., "The Development of International Space Cooperation," in J. Logsdon, D. Day, and R. D. Launius, (eds.), *Exploring the Unknown – Selected Documents in the History of The US Civilian Space Program Volume II: External Relationships*, (Washington, DC: The NASA History Series, NASA History Office, 1996), 3.

[26] Millard, D., *An Overview of United Kingdom Space Activity 1957–1987*, (ESA Publications, April 2005), 4.

In April 1960, the Macmillan Government canceled the Blue Streak Medium Range Ballistic Missile Program and instead decided to buy Polaris, a submarine-launched ballistic missile, from the United States. At that time, Britain was a European leader in rocket engineering. British policy-makers were therefore not fully ready to give up on that capability. Britain persuaded France, Italy, and West Germany to join in the European Launcher Development Organization (ELDO), an attempt to build a European satellite launcher using Blue Streak as a first stage. ELDO was also driven by Macmillan's pro-European policy, which assumed that the Common Market would allow Britain to join it.[27]

During the 1960s, Britain worked its way into space on two parallel paths. First, it worked closely with the United States, while at the same time promoting the European joint venture under ELDO and ESRO (European Space Research Organization). Despite these diverse and multiple activities, Britain was not fully committed to a comprehensive national space program, and the government support was not assured. In April 1962, NASA successfully launched Ariel 1. The satellite contained British-made devices.

A year later, on March 29, 1963, the British government announced that Britain had decided to go ahead with a space program, but on a commercial basis that it hoped would be less costly. Both sides of Parliament supported the decision to go into space. For example, F. W. Farey-Jones, a conservative backbencher, said the choice for Britain now was "to take our place in the vanguard of progress or to finish up as a small 'off-shore island'[28] on the edge of nowhere."[29] The climate changed under the government of James Harold Wilson, who took office in 1964. Wilson's government did not approve of large-scale, expensive, defense-oriented programs. It did not continue to provide large sums of public financing for space projects and decided not to pursue national or European launcher activity any further. Eventually, this led Britain to withdraw from ELDO.

Despite calls to put greater emphasis on national space activity rather than on international programs, Britain devoted about 80 percent of its space budget to international activity.[30] For example, the Science and Technology Sub-Committee of the House of Commons Estimates Committee argued in its July 1967 report that "the United Kingdom

---

[27] Spufford, F., "Operation Backfire," *London Review of Books*, (October 28, 1999), 22.
[28] "Off-shore island" is a phrase that was used to capture the feeling of unimportance and exclusion from a world rushing ahead that had descended on many Britons.
[29] Lewis, F., "British Will Go Ahead With Space Program," *Washington Post*, (March 30, 1963), n.p.
[30] MacLean, A., and Sheehan, M., "A Hare Turned Tortoise," 18.

has quite as much skill and technical resources as France, yet we have been worsted time and time again by the French in the field of space, simply because the French have a centrally directed, planned national space program and we have not ... There should in future be a British space program."[31] Furthermore, while space science was always considered a worthy activity by successive British governments, other fields of space activity, such as launch vehicle development and manned exploration, were not.[32]

In sum, the British space activity in the 1950s and 1960s excluded human spaceflights and also excluded orbital defense systems. It did include science, civil applications, military communications, and meteorology. At the policy level, the aim was to provide national expertise sufficient to keep Britain effectively in the exploitation of space, at modest cost, and to be in a position to collaborate efficiently with other states.[33] On October 28, 1971, a British Black Arrow rocket put the British satellite Prospero in orbit. This was the first and last launch by Britain. On January 17, 1973, the US Department of State reached an agreement with Britain to provide launch services for the latter's satellites aboard American launchers. The agreement granted Britain access to American launchers operated by NASA at launch sites in the United States.[34]

During the 1970s, Britain's position changed little. Although it became more inclined to participate in collaborative ventures in Europe and joined the European Space Agency when it was formed in 1975, no real attempt was made to expand its national space program. The prevailing view was that participation in ESA effectively removed the need for an autonomous British space program.[35] It took the British government more than thirty years to reach a different conclusion. In 2008, in light of the growing space market, the British government initiated a process to re-evaluate its space policy. Consequently, it adopted a new space policy aimed at stimulating the domestic industry. As part of this process, in April 2010, a national space agency was established, and it replaced the BNSC, which had coordinated British space activity since 1985.

The new space policy is much more ambitious, but it is still very pragmatic and is guided by commercial objectives; as explained by David Willetts, Britain's minister for Universities and Science, "Space

---

[31] MacLean, A., and Sheehan, M., "A Hare Turned Tortoise," 19.
[32] Millard, D., *An Overview*, 14.
[33] Simmons, N., "The British National Space Program," *Spaceflight*, (January 1971), 6, 9.
[34] News Release by NASA on January 18, 1973, Subject: US Launch Services for UK Satellites, the information was issued for release on January 17, 1973, NASA HQ, History Division Archives, International Files, Country File: UK.
[35] MacLean, A., and Sheehan, M., "A Hare Turned Tortoise," 20.

is one of our most promising sectors and the government is determined to foster innovation and help companies invest in R & D to drive long-term growth."[36] The British government is working to achieve this goal and improve the space sector. In 2013, the funds allocated to ESA were increased significantly. ESA's department of R&D in satellite telecommunications was set to move from the UK from the Netherlands.[37] In 2014, it was announced that the government would adopt "more user friendly" approach to its space industry.[38] Among the steps the government took was an announcement that it would exempt the space industry from the 6 percent tax on insurance for launches and orbiting satellites.[39] The British government also announced that it intended to build its first spaceport, based on expectations of increased space tourism and growth of the space industry by 2030.[40]

France in the Space Age

In the early 1950s, the issue of an "artificial satellite" was widely discussed in France.[41] The greatest interest was expressed by the military. Once the International Geophysical Year was announced, the French Defense Minister formed a research group to set the agenda for satellite-related research. Toward the end of August 1955, the group set out the results of its research, estimating that France would be able to develop a satellite within a few years. Therefore, the group proposed an outline for

---

[36] Staff Writers, " UK Space Companies Benefit from Investment in Research and Development," *Space Mart*, December 5, 2012, available at: www.spacemart.com/reports/UK_space_companies_benefit_from_investment_in_research_and_development_999.html, accessed on June 6, 2016.

[37] Amos, J., "Two New Centers to Drive UK Space Activity," *BBC*, May 14, 2013, available at: www.bbc.com/news/science-environment-22524233, accessed on June 6, 2016.

[38] For details, see National Space Technology Strategy, April 2014, available at: sec.kingston.ac.uk/uklaunch/docs/National%20Space%20Technology%20Strategy%20April%202014.pdf, accessed on March 20, 2015.

[39] de Selding, P. B., "Britain Looks to End Tax on Satellite and Launch Insurance," *Space News*, March 24, 2014, available at: www.spacenews.com/article/financial-report/39963britain-looks-to-end-tax-on-satellite-and-launch-insurance, accessed on March 26, 2014.

[40] Coppinger, R., "UK to Launch Commercial Spaceport by 2018," *Space.com*, August 6, 2014, available at: www.space.com/26749-uk-spaceport-commercial-space-plane.html, accessed on August 08, 2014. For more information on the subject, see Supporting Commercial Spaceplane Operations in the UK – Consultation on Criteria to Determine the Location of a UK Spaceport, Department for Transport, 2014, available at: www.gov.uk/government/uploads/system/uploads/attachment_data/file/360448/spaceport-consultation.pdf, accessed on March 10, 2015.

[41] Space travel was part of French culture and literature for many years, especially in the context of the science fiction work of Jules Verne.

a national program. But, because of the heavy costs and significant resources required to be actively involved in space research, the group also recommended that an international federation be established. It strongly emphasized that "...the countries represented would increase their international standing in actually bringing space projects to fruition."[42]

Following the successful launches by the United States and the Soviet Union, French officials began to take notice of space technologies and their potential applications. In 1959, a government committee was formed to evaluate the potential benefits of space development. As a result of this process, the French government included space in its first programs of national scientific projects. The government also created a special committee for space research. The committee was to formulate and coordinate space policy and activities on a national scale. The committee's work, reinforced by developments in French rocketry,[43] encouraged the government to establish the National Centre for Space Studies (CNES)[44] in 1961 to conduct the nation's activities in space.[45]

In the early 1960s, the French government decided to invest in several scientific fields that were identified as highly important; among them was space. According to Gilpin (1968), the motivation behind the selection of these fields was not to solve immediate problems for France, but to develop national expertise in areas that were under rapid development in the United States and the Soviet Union in order to exploit expected technological potential and high prestige in a way that would serve the state.[46] Pierre Chiquet, founder of the space centers of Bretigny and Toulous and the rocket-launching platform of Kourou, expressed this idea when he said that

when [De Gaulle] returned to power in 1958, he wished to return France to the role its past had assigned it... At the time the CNES was launched... we had no money, and we did not know at the outset what we should do or where we were

---

[42] Moulin, H., "The Question of the Artificial Satellite in The Mid-1950s," Paper presented at the International Astronautical Congress, Amsterdam, the Netherlands, October 4–8, 1999, 3.
[43] By mid-1960, designs had been completed for a small, three-stage launch vehicle utilizing indigenous liquid and solid propellant technologies as the first and upper stages, respectively.
[44] CNES was created in light of NASA, on a scientific basis.
[45] Gilpin, R., *France in the Age of the Scientific State*, (Princeton, NJ: Princeton University Press, 1968), 277–278; Wells, D., *France and Japan in Space: Niche Market Players with Evolving Assets and Roles*, Unpublished M.A. dissertation, MIT, 1991, 20.
[46] Gilpin, R., *France in the Age*, 209, 217.

going to go. But we had unshakable faith in our country, and were supported by a lucid and determined president.[47]

De Gaulle was determined to restore the "glory" of France by stressing its independence in a variety of ways, including in technology.[48] He was generous toward science, particularly regarding highly visible, spectacular projects. In the years 1958–1969, allocations of funds for R&D soared from 2.5 percent to 6.2 percent of the national budget.[49]

In order to highlight France's independence, de Gaulle's administration emphasized French nuclear *force de frappe* as the only means to be respected. Then, it decided to develop launch technology so that France could become a partner in the conquest of space, along with the Soviet Union and the United States.[50] Within just a few years, the French space program showed remarkable growth. On November 26, 1965, France's first satellite was successfully launched from Algeria on Diamant A[51], a French booster.

The launch took place only days before another French satellite, FR-1, was to be launched aboard an American booster.[52] As explained earlier, it was important for France and for de Gaulle to successfully launch France's first satellite on its own; a move that would reinforce its political standing in the world as third in space, and would enhance its people's self-esteem and support of the regime. A few days before the launch, the French weekly *Figaro* pointed out that "at a time when great power status is achieved in the skies, France becomes third in the space race."[53] A few moments after the launching, General de Gaulle issued a jubilant statement: "The placing in orbit of the first French satellite launched by a French rocket is an important success, which will give our entire nation joy and pride'."[54] The headline of *Le Monde* called France the "third space power," emphasizing the fact that France was ahead of Britain and

---

[47] Chiquet, P., "Great Projects Are What the World Needs" (testimony of Pierre Chiquet at the Schiller Institute Conference that took place on September 15–16, 2007, Kiedrich Germany, and published in the EIR conference report dated October 12, 2007, 59).

[48] For discussion on de Gaulle's agenda to make France more independent of the United States, see Morse, E., *Foreign Policy and Interdependence in Gaullist France*, (Princeton, NJ: Princeton University Press, 1973).

[49] Sullivan, W., "Ideas & Trends," *New York Times*, August 15, 1982, 8E.

[50] Chiquet, P., "Great Projects," 59.

[51] For more information on the development and specifications of the Diamant A (Diamond) rocket, see Sanders, B., "The French Diamant Rockets," *Quest*, 7:1, (Spring 1999), 18–22.

[52] The launch took place on December 6, 1965.

[53] Braesrup, P., "France to Orbit First Satellite," *New York Times*, November 21, 1965, 10.

[54] Report, "France Soars into Space Club with Diamond A," *St. Petersburg Times* (Florida), November 27, 1965.

Japan. Also a last-minute rush to launch before the December 5, 1965, presidential election was revealed,[55] providing a domestic and political perspective to this event.

In the following years, France continued to launch satellites into space and even built a new launching facility in French Guiana, Kourou, when it had to withdraw from Algeria.[56] Up until today, France maintains a coherent and consistent national space program. France continues to position independence in access to space and in space technology as significant elements of its national strategy and space policy. France is also committed to space exploration and is the leading force in the European Space Agency, its largest contributor, and the pillar of its launching program. Approximately 40 percent of CNES's budget and the French funding for ESA are allocated to launch activities.[57] After all, the European launcher Ariane is based on the French Diamant.[58]

European Collaboration: To (Efficiently) Lead the Way to Space

In the early 1960s, the European technological and financial capabilities were limited compared to those of the superpowers. Western European governments were facing two options: collaborating with the United States as inferior partners or forming a European collaborative venture that would counter the dominant American position.[59] Britain, in fact, was the most advanced country in Europe and already had most of the technological resources required to develop a three-stage launcher capable of placing satellites in orbit.[60] Nevertheless, because the government

---

[55] AP, "French Proud of Satellite Despite Its Loss of Voice," *Sunday Times*, November 28, 1965, A4.
[56] The French launch pad in Kourou is ESA's launch pad, from which all of its satellites are launched aboard an Ariane launcher.
[57] Bochinger, S., (ed)., Profiles of Government Space Activities 2012, Euroconsult, (Paris, Euroconsult, March 2012), pp. 193–199.
[58] For further information on the technological background and history of the French space program, see Gire, B., and Schibler, J., "The French National Space Programme, 1950–1975," *JBIS*, 40, (1987), 51–66; Laidet, L., "The French Space Program," in W. Thompson and S. Guerrier, (eds.), *Space: National Programs and International Cooperation*, (Boulder, CO: Westview Press, 1989), 63–78; Moulin, H., "D-1 French Satellite Program (1962–1967)," Paper presented at the 47th International Astronautical Congress, Beijing China (IAA-96-IAA.2.3.06), October, 7–11, 1996; Moulin, H. "The Question of the Artificial Satellite."
[59] Suzuki, K., *Policy, Logics and Institutions of European Space Collaboration*, (Burlington, VT: Ashgate, 2003), 3.
[60] Blue Streak was available as the first stage, and the Black Knight sounding rocket was available as a second stage. Britain only needed to develop a small third-stage booster.

did not agree that there was a need for a British launcher, it turned to collaborative projects.[61]

In January 1961, British Prime Minister Macmillan met with President de Gaulle. In their meeting, de Gaulle said he was attracted by the idea of Europe becoming "the third space power."[62] A few days later the European conference on launcher development was held. The conference concluded that a European launcher would be developed, but only France and Britain made commitments of financial and technological contributions.[63] Following discussions, ELDO[64] was established in February 1964, and three weeks later, ESRO was formed as well.[65] Soon thereafter, France and Britain slowly diverged. Britain's rationale for the establishment of ELDO was mainly a national financial concern and desire to share costs. The French, however, were especially motivated by the need to reinforce Europe's autonomous capability, which would challenge American dominance in the "Free World." For France, this was a natural extension of their national space program.[66] France was frustrated by the delays in development and naturally preferred that the ELDO launcher be based on French Diamant rocket technology, rather than on British Blue-Streak technology.

Gradually, Britain lost interest in ELDO; Britain focused more on the financial and commercial aspects of space activities. Frequent delays and failures of ELDO programs convinced the British that it was inefficient.[67] In April 1968, the British government decided to withdraw from ELDO.[68] It announced that developing a purely European launcher was "nonviable," and that Europe should depend upon American

---

[61] Britain also considered the option of collaborative projects with Commonwealth countries. Canada, Australia, New Zealand, and India expressed an interest in scientific space research collaboration with Britain in 1959, but they did not express much interest in developing and sharing the costs of space boosters. See MacLean, A., and Sheehan, M., "A Hare Turned Tortoise" 16; Suzuki, K., *Policy, Logics and* Institutions, 42–43.

[62] Krige, J., "Building a Third, 303–304.

[63] Suzuki, K., *Policy, Logics and Institutions* 48–49.

[64] European Launch Development Organization.

[65] For a comprehensive and in-depth examination of the historical process that led to the formation of ESRO and ELDO, see Krige, J., and Russo, A., *A History of the European Space Agency 1958–1987*, (Noordwijk: European Space Agency, 2000).

[66] Back in 1965, France spent US$56 million on space activities (two-thirds of which was on its national program), and Britain spent only US$43 million (only US$5 million of which were allocated to national space activities). See MacLean, A., and Sheehan, M., "A Hare Turned Tortoise," 16–17.

[67] Suzuki, K., *Policy, Logics and Institutions*, 57–61.

[68] It is not unlikely to assume that the British government was motivated by a twofold rationale. First, the United States invested great efforts in convincing the Europeans to decline the initiative to develop a European launcher. Second, they wanted to force an American commitment to launch British satellites.

launchers.⁶⁹ Minister of Technology Anthony Wedgwood Benn announced that Britain would cease contributing to ELDO at the end of 1971, arguing that all government-financed research programs must be cost effective and economically justifiable.⁷⁰

In 1969, when NASA suggested that Europe should use American launchers, the French government objected to the idea and stressed the importance of having autonomous European access to space. According to French Minister for Defense Michel Debré, France was willing to bear the costs alone to ensure Europe's access to space and prevent the superpowers from monopolizing space. In the French perspective, assured European access to space by a European launcher was inevitable. The British government adopted the opposite perspective and thought Europe could count on the United States to provide it with launch services.⁷¹ Krige (2008) argued that the French rationale combined a Gaullist determination to become independent of the United States with recognition that space could close the technological gap that had opened up between Europe and the United States.⁷² According to Johnson-Freese (2007), the French motivation to develop a European launcher was further intensified after the United States attempted to restrict Europe from commercializing the Symphonie communication satellites, which were planned to be launched aboard an American launcher. The American demand was intended to protect Intelsat, an intergovernmental consortium of commercial communication satellites led by the United States, from competition with the European Symphonie.⁷³

This incident with the United States helped France to convince other European countries of the necessity of developing a European launcher. In December 1972, a ministerial meeting of the European Space Conference took place. The French proposal for an independent European launcher was accepted. CNES provided the management and 63.4 percent of the funding for what eventually became known as the Ariane launch vehicle.⁷⁴ In 1975, ESRO and ELDO were replaced by one

---

⁶⁹ Marriott, J., "Britain's Space Program – A Respectable Past and a Future Yet Uncharted," *Air Force Magazine*, (August 1970), 63.
⁷⁰ The first and last launch of Britain into space took place in October 1971. MacLean, A., and Sheehan, M., "A Hare Turned Tortoise," 18.
⁷¹ Suzuki, K. *Policy, Logics and Institutions*, 72–73.
⁷² Krige, J., "Building Space Capability through European Regional Collaboration," in S. Dick, (ed.), *Remembering the Space Age*, (Washington, DC: NASA History Office, 2008), 46.
⁷³ Johnson-Freese, J., *Space as a Strategic Asset*, (New York: Columbia University Press, 2007), 46.
⁷⁴ Wells, D., *France and Japan*, 23.

organization, the European Space Agency (ESA). The first launch by ESA took place in 1979.

Motivations to Go into Space

For hundreds of years, France was considered a great power, one of Europe's and the world's leaders. But in the first half of the twentieth century, within one generation, France was occupied twice for several years and then liberated by allies. After World War II, France slowly realized it had lost its empire, and it suffered difficulties defending its far-flung colonies and interests.[75] France refused to accept the fact that it was now, at best, only a secondary power that could no longer defend itself by its own means. French leadership especially resented France's dependence on the strategic umbrella of the United States for its very existence, fearing that it would lead to the loss of European identity.[76]

In the first part of the Cold War and especially under the presidency of General de Gaulle, France aspired to restore its national unity and its world status. The restoration of France required rebuilding the economy, the military force, and its society. French leaders had to restore French dignity, esteem, and faith in its power – in the eyes of the world and more importantly, in the eyes of its own population. Hence, it adopted a policy of grandeur.[77] To further stress this point, de Gaulle said in an interview on January 8, 1958, before his return to power, "The French no longer have any spur to action. The thing which spurs a people on is ambition. And France cannot do without a great national ambition."[78] France did not aspire to equal the superpowers, but to reduce the gap and decrease its dependence on the United States. "Maintaining France's international 'rank,' power and prestige has been a fundamental foreign policy goal of all French governments since WWII."[79] The way to achieve these aspirations was by striving for a leadership position in Europe and by taking a position as independent as possible of the United States in political issues and actual deeds.[80]

---

[75] France faced revolt in Algeria in the 1950s, which eventually forced it to leave Algeria and grant it independence. It lost the war in Indo-China, which later on led to the American intervention in Vietnam.
[76] Gilpin, R., *France in the Age*, 9.
[77] Cerny, P., *The Politics of Grandeur*, (Cambridge, Cambridge University Press, 1980), 80.
[78] Ibid.
[79] Grant, R., "French Defense Policy and European Security," *Political Science Quarterly*, 100:3, (Fall 1985), 411. For more information on French foreign policy, see Tint, H., *French Foreign Policy since the Second World War*, (London: Wiedenfeld and Nicolson, 1972).
[80] In this context, France withdrew from NATO in 1966.

The imbalance between France and the United States, especially the growing technological gap, was perceived as threatening French values, traditions, independence, and sovereignty, which might lead France to become an undeveloped nation. The fear of the technological gap fits into the French narrative, going back in French history to the nineteenth century, when the Third Republic reformed education in order to catch up with German science and technology. This concept was intensified after France's failures in World War I and even more so after the devastating defeat to the Germans again in 1940.[81] De Gaulle's return to power in 1958 rested on fruitful soil. As Gilpin (1968) put it, "He was as much an instrument of these deeper economic, political, and psychological forces as he has been their master; his role has been primarily that of accelerating their effects and giving them direction."[82]

Accepting the premise that scientific and technological expertise is a key to political independence, along with the desire to play a significant part in world affairs, led France to rapidly expand its scientific and technological level while preserving its autonomy. The American reluctance to transfer technology and knowhow further encouraged a broad French effort to develop local capabilities in defense technology and other scientific fields. The development of national programs in nuclear technology and later space were important elements of this agenda. The aim was not to disengage from the United States, but to produce a new French position of power that would force the United States to take French and European interests and views into account.[83] Dr. Raymond Hamelin, Scientific Attaché to the Embassy of France in the United States in the mid-1960s, explained this incentive by saying, "Not to have a space program would be inconsistent with the general French policy, since it would lead to considerable dependence on other countries in some major industrial fields."[84] Indeed, still today, the space program is a symbol of statehood for France and a means to an independent Europe led by France. For example, it was stated in the 2011–2015

---

[81] Gilpin, R., *France in the Age*, 442.
[82] Gilpin, R., *France in the Age*, 9; Philip Cerny also expressed this idea in his book *The Politics of Grandeur*, 74.
[83] Wahl, N., *The Fifth Republic – France's New Political System*, (New York: Random House, 1959), third printing; Kolodziej, E., "Revolt and Revisionism in the Gaullist Global Vision: An Analysis of French Strategic Policy," *The Journal of Politics*, 3, 2, (May 1971) 468.
[84] Presentation by Dr. Raymond Hamelin, Scientific Attaché to the Embassy of France at the Second Space Congress at Cocoa Beach Florida, April 5–7, 1965, Embassy of France, US, (NASA HQ, Historical reference collection, History Office Archives Washington, DC, country files, France, Washington, DC), 4.

multiyear contract between CNES and the French government that it contributes to the emergence of the EU as a major player in space.[85]

It is important to note that French governments were motivated to take on this agenda also from the desire to regain the confidence of the French people. In the 1960s, General Aubinierge, Director of CNES, has said that "space technology touches so many disciplines that to neglect it would signify for our people, formerly masters of the world, a decadence and underdevelopment, an unacceptable economic servitude, no matter whence it comes."[86] Accomplishments in science and technology, especially in spectacular fields such as nuclear energy and space, were thus perceived as primary catalysts for social change.

In Britain, the approach to space was affected by a process in which Britain adjusted to a decline in its status from that of a world power to the status of a medium-power. Over the years of the British Empire, Britain thought of itself quite literally as the center of the world: "The headquarters from which decisions were made for the whole world about international trade and communications; the 'workshop of the world' in which all of the most advanced industrial products were manufactured; and the place from where most new ideas and inventions emanated."[87] At the dawn of the twentieth century, Britain stood as the pre-eminent global power. Then, following two awful world wars, it became a secondary power, ceding its eminence to the United States and Soviet Union.

In the first two decades after World War II, Britain underwent a slow process of acknowledgment of its decline and adjustment to its new status. At first, Britain was under the illusion of still having great power status and did not fully accept its decline.[88] However, its leaders understood the necessity of a strategic partnership with the United States. Hence, Britain's decision-making on large-scale national projects was, to a great extent, aimed at convincing the United States to take British interests into serious consideration. For this reason, as well as for other national security reasons, Britain became the first country after the United States and the Soviet Union to test both atomic and hydrogen bombs. Britain had the first commercial nuclear power reactor dedicated to civilian energy production in the free world; it built the first commercial

---

[85] Profiles of Government Space Programs 2012, Euroconsult, 193–194.
[86] CIA Special Report on Western European Space Program, May 1, 1964, 3, CIA FOIA database available at: www.foia.cia.gov/browse_docs_full.asp, accessed on November 17, 2008.
[87] Mandler, P., *The English National Character*, (New Haven, CT, and London: Yale University Press, 2006), 65.
[88] Kennedy, P., *The Rise and Fall of The Great Powers*, (New York: Vintage Books, 1987), 368; and Krige, J., "Building Space Capability," 47.

jet passenger aircraft, and was the most advanced European country in rocketry and space science.

The debate in British society over Britain's position in the world and its view of itself involved many groups and issues, including the issue of a national space program. In the 1950s, several scientists and officials at the Foreign Office insisted that Britain would be "classed as an undeveloped country" if it did not launch its own satellite: They believed that Britain could gain "political, psychological and prestige advantages by taking a lead in relation to its allies on the continent of Europe, in proposing joint development of a West European Earth satellite."[89] Krige (2000) explained, "This appeal to national prestige and world status touched a sore nerve in a country trying to adjust to its diminishing influence in a world increasingly dominated by the superpowers ... In short, it seemed that any government which wanted to have some weight in the international affairs, had to have a space program."[90] Krige continued by arguing that for this reason, at that time, space was perceived by many British scientists and officials as a place where Britain would confirm to itself and to others "that it was still a major power to be reckoned with ... This dream of British grandeur soon proved to be illusory."[91] In the same spirit, in 1960 the *Sunday Times* newspaper published the following editorial statement about the meaning of space activities in Britain: "It is not, indeed, a question of whether we can afford a modest space research program, but whether we can afford, as a major and a scientific engineering nation, to be without one ... This is no time for resignation into second-class status."[92] Nevertheless, no senior British politician saw space as important in its own right. The only real driving force behind British policy was a vague fear that it might be unwise to be left behind by other nations; this was not sufficient motivation to inspire determined action or point to any specific program objectives.[93]

In the 1960s, Britain had to painfully adjust to the realities of being a medium-sized world power. Former United States Secretary of State Dean Acheson best explained Britain's situation at that time, when he remarked in a speech on December 5, 1962, that "Britain had lost an Empire and not yet found a role."[94] This was especially true, because it was matched by an increase in self-reliance, industrial maturity, and a sense of independent identity in the Commonwealth countries, fostered

---

[89] Whyte, N., and Gummett, P., "Far Beyond the Bounds," 152–153.
[90] Krige, J., "Building a Third," 294.
[91] Krige, J., "Building a Third," 299.
[92] *Sunday Times*, May 15, 1960, cited in MacLean, A., and Sheehan, M., "A Hare Turned Tortoise," 17.
[93] MacLean, A., and Sheehan, M., "A Hare Turned Tortoise," 19.
[94] Cited in Stone, L., "Britain and the World," in D. Mackie and C. Cook, (eds.), *The Decade of Disillusion: British Politics in the Sixties*, (Bristol, UK: Macmillan St. Martin's Press, 1972), 122.

by wartime developments.[95] Eventually, Prime Minister Macmillan decided that it was time to acknowledge that Britain was no longer a great power and, as a result, should draw closer to Europe.[96] One of Britain's first moves in this direction came in June 1961, when it requested approval to join the European Common Market.[97] Britain exercised similar moves in the field of space activity as well, shifting its focus from a national program to European ventures and bilateral projects with the United States.

During the 1960s, Britain went from being ten years ahead of the rest of Europe in developing satellite launchers to a country that lagged behind others. In October 1971, when Britain placed its first satellite, Prospero, in orbit, it was only the sixth nation to launch a satellite using its own launcher. The reason for this drastic shift was not a lack of scientific and technological expertise. It was a lack of the political will to devote the economic capacity needed to match the ambitions and capabilities of its scientists.[98]

Part of the explanation for this lack of political will rests on Britain's overall pragmatic and economic perspective. The British perspective in general was, and still is, very pragmatic and dedicated to cost-effective calculations. Decision-making on space activity was no different. In this respect, Suzuki (2003) observed that finance was the major policy logic in Britain in the early 1960s, especially with regard to a national program. However, in the process of choosing between collaboration with Europe rather than with the United States, the relative autonomy and strategic concern for leadership became the deciding factor for the European option.[99]

Unlike France, Britain did not perceive its cooperation with and reliance on the United States as a threat to its sovereignty. Britain and the United States had enjoyed a special relationship based on their shared history, language, and cultural heritage over the course of many years. For

---

[95] Blaxland, J., *Strategic Cousins – Australian and Canadian Expeditionary Forces and the British and American Empires*, (Montreal and Kingston: McGill-Queen's University Press, 2006), 3.

[96] For more on Britain's foreign relations and policies at that time, see Vital, D., *The Making of British Foreign Policy*, Second Edition, (London: George Allen and Unwin Ltd., 1971); Wallace, W., *The Foreign Policy Process in Britain*, (London: The Royal Institute of International Affairs, 1975); Capet, A., (ed.), *Britain, France and the Entente Cordiale Since 1904*, (Hampshire: Palgrave Macmillan, 2006); Boyd, L., *Britain's Search for a Role*, (Westmead, Farnborough, Hants: Saxon House and Lexington Books, 1975).

[97] Krige, J., "Building Space Capability," 47.

[98] Wright, D., "What Went Wrong with Dan Dare? The Failure of England's Space Program," *History Today*, 47:7, (July 1999), available at: www.historytoday.com/dave-wright/what-went-wrong-dan-dare, accessed on June 1, 2016.

[99] Suzuki, K., *Policy, Logics and Institutions*, 43.

example, the United States regularly shared its most highly classified intelligence source, CORONA reconnaissance satellite photos, with Britain.[100] Roy Gibson, the first director general of the BNSC (1985–1987), argued that it was perfectly safe for Britain to rely on the United States for the provision of launch opportunities, either on a cooperative or a commercial basis, as it viewed space from a very practical and pragmatic perspective. British perspective was that space was a tool, like many other tools.[101]

Membership in the Club: Final Note

The difference between French and British approaches to space activity is not in technical expertise and knowhow; the French were not technologically superior to the British. The difference, therefore, lies in the commitment shown by their national leadership to fulfill social functions such as standing, national esteem, and identity.[102] The cases of France's and Britain's space policies are compatible with the first hypothesis of this book, which proposes that states that define themselves as powers will emulate the superpowers by developing indigenous space capabilities. They do so because they believe that, as world powers, they are expected by other states as well as by their own population to demonstrate national capability in space.

In the first decade following World War II, British decision-makers did not adjust to the politics of decline.[103] Confident in Britain's status as a world power, they perceived Britain as a natural "member of the club" of the superpowers. Hence, to their understanding, it was expected of Britain to have a space program. Several years later, once they recognized that Britain could no longer measure up to the superpowers, their approach changed.[104] As a result, the focus of Britain's national strategy shifted from strategic missions to practical and pragmatic tasks; it lost interest in being a significant member of the space club. Britain saw significance only in providing national expertise that would be sufficient to keep Britain effectively in the exploitation of space at modest costs and to be in a position to collaborate efficiently with other states.[105]

---

[100] Day, D., "Taking the 'Special Relationship' to New Heights," *JBIS*, 52, (1999), 417.
[101] Gibson, R., "Britain and Space," The Eighteenth J.D. Bernal Lecture, Delivered at Birkbeck College, London, May 7, 1987, 2–3.
[102] MacLean, A., and Sheehan, M., "A Hare Turned Tortoise," 22.
[103] Kennedy, P., *The Rise and Fall,"* 367.
[104] Morgan, K. O., *The People's Peace – British History, 1945–1990,* (Oxford: Oxford University Press, 1992), 197.
[105] Simmons, N., "The British National Space Program," 9.

The results of World War II made it clear for France that it was a declining power. Unlike Britain, France attributed great value to restoring its previous position among the great powers. For this reason for France, membership in the space club in and of itself was of great value for international and domestic reasons. France wished to be recognized as a great power by the international community, but first of all by the superpowers.[106] On the domestic level, the French public had always perceived their program as a symbol of France's independence and its ability to be at the forefront of technology.[107] The French government felt it was necessary to invest large-scale resources in spectacular programs that could evoke the pride and enthusiasm of the population.[108] Therefore, the main motivation in France to develop space activity and join the club was of a strategic nature.

Over the years, French governments attributed great value to autonomous capability separate from that of the United States. Bell (1997) noted that on September 17, 1958, soon after he became president again, de Gaulle proposed to President Eisenhower the establishment of three-power directorate – made up of the United States, France, and Britain – to make decisions on world affairs. Eisenhower declined the offer. Thereafter, de Gaulle pursued a policy of asserting French independence from the United States, which came into fruition in the French withdrawal from NATO's integrated military command in 1966.[109] Separating France from the United States' hegemony over Western Europe was also achieved by the development of a direct relationship with the Soviet Union that matured into actual collaboration. For example, de Gaulle was the first Western leader to visit Soviet space launch facilities and witness a launch.[110] Years later, the first Westerner to fly into space aboard a Soviet spacecraft was the Frenchman Jean-Loup Jacques Marie Chrétien.[111]

As early as 1968, Tegger claimed that the French motivation to embark on a space program must be viewed as a political maneuver, an instrument of foreign and domestic policy. Her description of French ambitions

---

[106] Serfaty, S., *France, De Gaulle, and Europe*, (Baltimore: Johns Hopkins Press, 1968), 38–39.
[107] MacLean, A., and Sheehan, M., "A Hare Turned Tortoise," 20.
[108] Tegger, J. A., "The French Space Program: Political and Social Implications," AIAA Paper no. 68–898 Presented at the Impact of Aerospace Science and Technology on Law and Government Conference, Washington, DC, August 28–30, 1968, (NASA Head Quarters, History Office, Reference Collection, Country Files: France), 3.
[109] Bell, P. M. H., *France and Britain 1940–1994 – The Long Separation*, (New-York: Longman, 1997), 166.
[110] *Washington Post*, "De Gaulle Sees Soviet Satellite Launched," June 26, 1966, 5.
[111] He was launched into space on June 24, 1982.

and aspirations to power coincide with the characterizations of the "club" that allows weaker actors the powerful halo of stronger actors:

> France, under de Gaulle, has asserted a power, frequently felt to be far beyond its real capacities. Hence, rather than resting on a firm political and economic base, French assertions of power have often depended more on an illusionary base supported by an element of credibility, which de Gaulle has been able to establish ... To place France in the position of being the first nation besides the Great Powers to participate in outer space activities would have special significance in the eyes of the other nations of the world ... In so doing, the French leadership combines a deep understanding of *Realpolitik* with a large measure of idealization of the French cultural heritage, resulting in manifestations of nationalism that have had both beneficial and detrimental effects on France, Europe, and the world.[112]

In its attempt to restore its status as a large power, membership in the space club allowed France to project a much more powerful image than it actually had. This was primarily a component of France's efforts to maintain control over its own destiny and assert some influence on global politics.

The development of a nuclear striking force and an ambitious space program were not aimed only at increasing French prestige abroad, but at enhancing pride at home as well.[113] De Gaulle also used the visible spectaculars of nuclear testing and satellite launching in his own favor.[114] For example, he marshaled the image of the first launch of a French satellite in his 1965 presidency campaign. The successful launch on November 26, 1965, occurred only a few days before the elections.

Britain, by contrast, was motivated by much more pragmatic and financial motivations and showed greater confidence in collaboration with the United States. Adjusting to its new status as a declining power, British leadership realized that Britain was no longer expected to demonstrate advanced indigenous capabilities in space. For this reason, they concluded that heavy investments in the development of national space capabilities are no longer justified. For Britain, the aim was to provide national expertise that would be sufficient to keep Britain effectively in the space club at modest costs and to be in a position to collaborate efficiently with other states.[115] Throughout the years, Britain's space activity was measured by commercial and industrial return, while space activity in France was justified by geo-strategic and national factors. Despite the years that have passed and the change in the strategic environment, this

---

[112] Tegger, J. A., "The French Space Program," 1.
[113] Wells, D., *France and Japan*, 21.; and Cerny, P., *The Politics of Grandeur*, 125, 270.
[114] Cerny, P., *The Politics of Grandeur*, 86.
[115] Simmons, N., "The British National Space Program," 9.

basic difference did not change. The guiding principle prioritizing France's space activities is at large, political and industrial leadership. Contrary, in general, Britain's guiding principle prioritizing space activity is economic return. This principle guides Britain's new and ambitious space policy.

In summary, the different historical experiences, domestic needs, national narratives, and political cultures of France and Great Britain affected the way each country perceived its global status and the values of space technology and national space activity to their national interests. Their preferences and policies were shaped accordingly. As a declining power, Britain did not attribute much significance to demonstrating national capability. Hence, Britain's interest in space focused primarily on the tangible instrumental needs of space activity. Furthermore, this view enabled Britain to relinquish the expertise it had already achieved. In fact, even today, Britain's approach to space is rather selective. Even in the modest context of ESA, Britain does not invest in all of the optional programs.[116]

Aiming to restore its status as a world power, France attributed great value to the intangible, political, and social aspects of having a national space program. Club membership served as a source of projecting French power, boosting its standing and identity, and enhancing its development and industrial scale. Club membership was an internal and external message that France was a world power, which should be taken into account as an essential parameter in international affairs.

---

[116] House of Commons Science and Technology Committee, 2007: A Space Policy – Seventh Report of Seventh Session, 2006–7, Volume 1, (July 4, 2007), 41.

6 Canada and Australia

Canada and Australia are both large countries with relatively small and scattered populations.[1] They have a similar gross domestic product per capita, and their people enjoy a high standard of living and national economic productivity. By fostering a well-educated workforce, these two countries have developed high technology industries, which have contributed to an industrialized economy with a large service sector. In addition, both countries are heavily dependent on global trade.

In terms of history and culture, these are two relatively young countries that matured out of the British Empire and are still members of the British Commonwealth. They share a widespread use of the English language, although in each country there has been some anti-British sentiment.[2] Canada and Australia are both open and democratic societies that, following the demise of the British Empire, had shifted to come under the American strategic umbrella.[3] Both countries have sought to play global middle-power roles in various international affairs. Their armed forces are similar in size, and they both cooperate with the United States and Britain on intelligence matters, although each faces different threats and challenges.[4]

---

[1] In territory, Canada, with about 33 million people, is the second largest country in the world after Russia, while Australia is the sixth largest country in the world with only 21 million people.

[2] In Australia, this was primarily associated with the Irish Catholic Diaspora and post–World War II migration program that resulted in a diverse population less connected or attached to Britain. In Canada, it was expressed in the opposition of French-speaking Canadians to involvement in British and other foreign wars (Blaxland, J., *Strategic Cousins – Australian and Canadian Expeditionary Forces and the British and American Empires*, (Montreal and Kingston, Ontario: McGill-Queen's University Press, 2006), 254–256).

[3] Many Canadians view their country's membership in the British Commonwealth (especially the English-Canadians) and other international organizations, such as La Francophonie, as a means of asserting a national identity that is distinct from that of the United States. Australia also attaches symbolic importance to its affiliation to the Commonwealth despite the demise of the British Empire.

[4] Blaxland, *Strategic Cousins*, 258, 260–261.

Table 6.1 *Comparison of Canada and Australia, Selected Parameters*

	Canada	Australia
Total area	9,984,670 sq. km	7,686,850 sq. km
Population (July 2015 est.)	35,099,836	22,751,014
GDP per capita in US$ (2015 est.)	$45,900	$65,400
GDP composition by sector (2015 est.)	*agriculture:* 1.5% *industry:* 28.2% *services:* 70.3%	*agriculture:* 3.7% *industry:* 28.9% *services:* 67.4%
Internet users (2014 est.)	32.4 million	20.2 million
Military expenditure	1% of GDP (2015 est.)	1.71% of GDP (2012 est.)

When it comes to space activity, Canada and Australia have chosen different paths. Canada has been very ambitious about space, taking pride in: (a) being the third[5] nation to orbit its own satellite, Alouette,[6] on September 29, 1962; (b) building a high-profile space industry; (c) creating and operating an astronaut program; (d) partnering in the International Space Station with its contribution of the well-known Canadarm; and (e) providing its citizens with necessary space applications of Canadian-made technology.

Australia, on the other hand, has shown no interest in having a national capacity in this field. Throughout the years, it has made no major national effort to develop an indigenous space capability. As a result, Australia relies heavily on commercial suppliers to meet its needs, and it takes pride in being a "sophisticated user" of space applications.[7]

Each country has a definite need for the use of space application services. Nonetheless, the different policies and programs each has

---

[5] Several months earlier, Britain had launched Ariel 1 aboard an American launcher, making it the third country to have a satellite orbiting earth. Canada, however, claims to be the third nation to launch an indigenously developed satellite, since Ariel 1 was not made solely by Britain.

[6] The satellite was named after a lark in a popular French-Canadian children's song about plucking the feathers off a lark.

[7] Data presented in Table 6.1 were obtained from the online site of the CIA World Factbook: "Canada," available at: www.cia.gov/library/publications/the-world-factbook/geos/ ca.html; and "Australia," available at: www.cia.gov/library/publications/the-world-factbook/geos/as.html, accessed on March 20, 2016.

pursued on its path to space raise important questions regarding the underlying motivation in each case. This chapter examines the different Australian and Canadian perspectives on the use of space for national needs and attempts to outline and analyze the factors that led these two countries to choose almost contradictory space policies.

The main argument is that different national narratives and political cultures affect the way each country perceives the functions fulfilled by space activity. For Australia, space is more about fulfilling tangible instrumental needs with little, if any, importance assigned to demonstrating national capability. In Canada's case, space activity also fulfills social functions: "club membership" serves as a source of political power and international standing, and as an identity booster.

This chapter consists of four sections. The first outlines the history of Canada's space activity. The second discusses the motivations behind some of the major Canadian decisions in the field of space activity and exploration. A short history of Australia's space activity is presented in the third. Finally, the fourth section examines the differences between Canada and Australia that have produced these two different approaches.

Canada in Space

In the 1940s and 1950s, Canada's preliminary activities in space focused on ionospheric research in order to further develop its capability in the field of communications.[8] Such concern was understandable, considering Canada's size and scattered population. Canada is also a country with two official languages, many different cultures, and distinct regional identities. Efficient communication services were and still are vital for connecting Canadians to one another as well as to the rest of the world. Even before the official dawn of the Space Age, Canadian expertise in ionospheric research had already led to successful cooperation with the United States. The US Air Force invested large sums in this endeavor, much more than Canada was able to provide to its own scientists. This successful cooperation had a significant effect on space research in Canada, forming the scientific foundation on which Canada could later develop its space program.[9]

---

[8] Canadians were also interested in exploring this scientific field because back then, the only way to communicate with the Canadian north was by transmitting high frequency radio waves through the ionosphere. For a very informative and detailed book on this issue, see Shepherd, G., and Kruchio, A., *Canada's Fifty Years in Space*, (Burlington, Ontario: Apogee Books, 2008).

[9] Interview with Professor Gordon Shepherd, York University, October 30, 2008, Toronto, Canada.

The launch of Sputnik in 1957 by the Soviet Union both impressed and concerned Canada's Conservative government, headed by Prime Minister John Diefenbaker. It stimulated Canadian interest in the possibilities of expanding its own role in space exploration, with the dual aim of achieving its international goals and addressing important domestic needs.[10] Furthermore, the vulnerability of the United States to a possible Soviet attack over Canadian airspace and concerns regarding Soviet advances in satellite technology spurred further American cooperative programs with Canada,[11] one of which led to the successful development and launch of the first Canadian satellite, Alouette 1, on an American launcher.

Although Alouette 1's primary scientific mission was to study the ionosphere, it also fulfilled a fundamental need to better communicate with the Canadian north, thereby providing other benefits related to Canadian sovereignty and security, as well as fulfilling social and cultural needs.[12] The satellite was built by Canada's Defense Research Board[13] under the leadership of physicist Dr. John Chapman, who is considered the father of the Canadian space program.[14] The success of this mission led to closer cooperation between Canada and the United States.[15]

The 1960s witnessed a great increase in Canadian space activity. The government used the scientific interest in this field and the program as catalysts for developing a domestic space industry.[16] In 1966, the government commissioned a study of Canada's space program chaired by Dr. Chapman. The findings of this study were published in 1967 under the title of "Upper Atmosphere and Space Programs for Canada," but it is better known as the Chapman Report. The inherent

---

[10] Godefroy, A., "Canada's Early Space Policy Development 1958–1974," *Space Policy*, 19, (2003), 138.

[11] DeWitt, D., and Kirton, J., *Canada as a Principal Power*, (Toronto: John Wiley & Sons, 1983), 321.

[12] Interview with William (Mac) Evans, former head of the CSA, November 3, 2008, Ottawa, Canada.

[13] For more information on the involvement of the defense sector in the Canadian space program, see Godefroy, A. B., Defense and Discovery Science, National Security, and the Origins of the Canadian Rocket and Space Program 1954–1974, Ph.D. Dissertation, Royal Military College of Canada, March 2004.

[14] For further reading on the history of Alouette, see Franklin, C.A., "Alouette/ISIS: How it All Began," IEEE International Milestone in Engineering Ceremony, Shirley Bay, Ottawa, (May 13, 1993), available at: www.ieee.ca/millennium/alouette/alouette_franklin.html, accessed on January 8, 2009.

[15] Following the successful launch, the two countries signed a memorandum of understanding in which they agreed to construct, launch, and operate four additional satellites – the ISIS series – under the management of a joint working group.

[16] Many veterans of World War II who were highly qualified in communications joined the research and development projects. Interview with Professor Gordon Shepherd.

questions raised were "Make or buy?" and "Why should Canada involve itself in these expensive facilities?" Among the reasons the report provided were Canada's unique geographical position and the services needed to develop and manage this vast land. However, the report also concluded that a space program should be a part of "Canada's struggle to develop competitive technologies as part of its struggle to retain an independent identity while providing its people with an acceptable standard of living and preventing international control over the essential fabric of Canada's national structure."[17] Evans (2004) explained that the Chapman Report, and another independent Science Council report[18] issued the same year, made the case for a national Canadian space program that would concentrate on satellite communications and remote sensing, industrial development, and cooperation with other countries. It also recommended the establishment of a central coordinating and contracting agency for space research and development to oversee and manage the Canadian space effort[19], as well as a modest capability to put small satellites into orbit.[20] The latter recommendation was never adopted.[21]

These reports stimulated the Canadian cabinet to direct the Science Secretariat to set up a task force on a satellite communication system in August 1967. The ensuing efforts led to the publication of a white paper that was submitted to the government in March 1968 entitled "A Domestic Satellite Communication System for Canada." This paper paved the way for the enactment of legislation to establish Telesat Canada, which came into existence in June 1969. Two months earlier, the new Liberal government under Prime Minister Pierre Elliott Trudeau created the Department of Communications (DOC) to oversee all satellite communications development.[22] Eventually on November 9, 1972,

---

[17] Chapman, J. H, Forsyth, P.A., and Patterson, G. N., *Upper Atmosphere and Space Programs in Canada*, Special Study Number 1, Science Secretariat Privy Council Office, Ottawa, (Queen's Printer and Controller of Stationery: Ottawa, February 1967), 3–4.

[18] The report was entitled "A Space Program for Canada."

[19] It would take about twenty years for the Canadian government to finally accept this recommendation and establish a national space agency.

[20] The issues that were raised repeatedly were the need for a central Canadian organization for space, the need for Canadian communications satellites, and the need for a Canadian satellite launching capability (this was stated in the appendix of the report on page 115) (Chapman, J. H., Forsyth, P. A., and Patterson, G. N., *Upper Atmosphere*, 104–105, 109–113).

[21] Evans, W. M., "The Canadian Space Program – Past, Present, and Future (A History of The Development of Space Policy in Canada)," *Canadian Aeronautics and Space Journal*, 50, (2004), 24–25.

[22] This shifted Canada's space program out of the military and into civilian applications (Godefroy, A., "Canada's Early Space Policy Development," 39).

the first Canadian communication satellite, Anik A1, was developed by the American company Hughes and launched by NASA.[23]

Two years later, in July 1974, Canada's first formal comprehensive space policy was announced by the government. The policy called for a stronger Canadian role in basic space science; an indigenous capacity to design, develop, and construct operational systems in Canada; and a contracting and purchasing policy that would further promote Canadian industry. The policy affirmed Canada's continued reliance on foreign launch facilities[24] and the utility of its longstanding relationship with NASA. Apparently, Canada's decision to refrain from the development of an indigenous capability to launch satellites into space stems from its strategic relationship with the United States, which enables Canada to take advantage of the American space program, and shift valuable resources to other subjects of space development. Nevertheless, in order to avoid overreliance on the United States, Canada's policy also noted the establishment of substantial launching facilities in other countries and Canada's willingness to consider involvement in these countries' space programs in order to ensure access to those facilities. The policy received widespread government acceptance and was ratified several months later.[25]

In the late 1970s, it was this logic that led Canada to become involved in the American shuttle program by developing the robotic arm, known as Canadarm,[26] and join the European Space Agency (ESA) as an observer in 1979, although the mechanism for cooperation in this case was slightly different. The main impetus to join ESA, besides expanding partnerships to secure Canadian access to space, was to have the ability to influence policy and programs by having a seat at the table. This move also dovetailed with Prime Minister Trudeau's policy of the "Third Option.[27]

---

[23] Anik A2 followed shortly afterwards in April 1973, and Anik A3 was launched in May 1975.
[24] Canada has a launching range at Churchill, Manitoba, that was used by Canadian as well as American scientists to launch sounding rockets as of the mid-1950s. Canada's first scientific payload was launched on a sounding rocket on November 8, 1958 (Burleson, D., *Space Programs Outside the United States*, [Jefferson, North Carolina: McFarland & Company, 2005], 43).
[25] DeWitt, D., and Kirton, J., *Canada as a Principal Power*, 349; Godefroy, "Canada's Early Space Policy Development," 140.
[26] Interview with William (Mac) Evans.
[27] In 1972, the Trudeau Government developed a conceptual approach that rejected preserving the status quo or increasing integration of Canada and the United States. Hence, it called for Canada to turn its attention to ways of counterbalancing the growing continental integration by choosing a "third option" that is, co-operating with other international partners. Canada was seeking to strengthen its ties to other areas of the world beyond North America. During Trudeau's administration, the relationship with

The development of the Canadarm marked a significant change in Canada's space policy toward visible and popular projects. Pictures taken in space of the Canadarm, which had the word "Canada" and the red-and-white maple-leaf flag emblazoned on its side, generated a burst of national pride and support for the space program.[28] Soon it became clear that the Canadarm was only the visible tip of the Canadian space program as Canadian space activity and space policy in the 1980s shifted toward more visible, but less tangible projects. One of the best examples of this process was the Canadian astronaut program.

In 1982, NASA invited Canada to fly its own astronauts aboard the shuttle. The Canadian government immediately recognized the significance of this offer and a Canadian Astronaut Program Office was established.[29] William (Mac) Evans, a former president of the Canadian Space Agency (CSA) claimed that Canada entered the human spaceflight arena primarily to support the Canadian space industry. There was no Canadian user need for either the Canadarm or the astronauts, but the space industry needed a major program to follow.[30] After a country-wide competition involving more than 4,400 candidates, Canada's first six astronauts were announced in December 1983. Ten months later, in October 1984, Marc Garneau, a naval officer from Quebec, became the first Canadian to fly in space.[31] The strong and positive public reaction to the Canadarm and the astronaut program were noticed by politicians and led to human spaceflight becoming a permanent part of the Canadian Space Program. This would eventually lead to Canada's consent to accept an American invitation[32] to participate in the International Space Station[33] as of 1985, and to the creation of the Canadian Space Agency in 1989.

---

the United States was tense and troubled. (Sokolsky, J., "A Seat At The Table: Canada and Its Alliances," *Armed Forces and Society*, 16:1, [Fall 1989], 25).

[28] Interview with William (Mac) Evans.

[29] Evans, W., "The Canadian Space Program," 26.

[30] According to NASA's definition, the Canadian astronauts were actually payload specialists rather than astronauts. Later, they were trained to be mission specialists, which awarded them the title of "Astronaut" according to NASA's definition.

[31] Immen, W., "Perfect Launch for Eight Day Mission: Canadian in Space," *The Globe & Mail* (Canada), October 5, 1984.

[32] In 1982, the Reagan Administration adopted an overall policy statement with respect to international space relationships that provided the context for making the station an international project. In Logsdon, J. M. "The Development of International Space Cooperation," in J. M., Logsdon, R. D. Launius, and D. Day, (eds.), *Exploring the Unknown – Selected Documents In The History of The US Civilian Space Program Volume II: External Relationships*, (Washington, DC: The NASA History Series, NASA History Office, 1996), 9.

[33] The Canadian government announced its commitment to participate in the International Space Station program (ISS) at the "Shamrock" summit between President Reagan and

To summarize this section, during the 1960s, space activity in Canada had focused on scientific research. Toward the end of that decade and throughout the 1970s, the focus shifted to technology and applications by developing a domestic industry. In the 1980s, the focus of Canadian space activity was on highly visible projects, while providing Canadians with space applications to meet their needs also continued to be an important task. One of the major Canadian efforts in this direction was the RADARSAT project to develop Radar satellites.[34] During the 1990s, the mission of Canadian space officials was to stabilize the program by establishing the Canadian Space Agency as the governmental body responsible for Canadian space activity, and by developing long-term plans secured by a coherent budget.

In the past several years, Canada's space sector has suffered from uncertainty over a long-term space plan. The absence of a coherent policy and funding led to an attempt to sell the space division of "Canada's leading space company,"[35] MacDonald, Dettwiler and Associates Ltd. (MDA), which had developed the Canadarm, to the US defense contractor Alliant Techsystems Inc. Nevertheless, in light of Canada's growing concerns over its sovereignty in the arctic region, the Canadian government and public strongly objected to this move, which induced the government to block the deal and recognize Canada's space capacity as a strategic national asset that must be protected.[36] This event exemplifies the change in the approach of the Canadian government to space, which is to use Canada's capacity in space for broad strategic objectives of national sovereignty and security.[37]

In 2012, the Canadian government ordered David Emerson, a former Cabinet minister to study the state of the country's aerospace and space sectors. Emerson's review, released in November 2012, called on the government to recognize the importance of space to national security and economic prosperity. In 2014, the government announced its space plans for the coming years. Among the principal aspects of its plans is Canada's use of space to reinforce its sovereignty, strengthen national security, and create more jobs. Also emphasized is placing the private

---

Prime Minister Mulroney in Quebec City in March 1985. In Doetsch, K., "Canada's Role on Space Station," *Acta Astronautica*, 57, (2005), 665.

[34] RADARST is a constellation of Canadian remote sensing satellites composed of RADARSAT1 and RADARSAT2.

[35] Laghi, B., and Clarck, C., "Ottawa Rejects Space Firm's Sale to US," *The Globe and Mail*, April 10, 2008, available at: http://www.theglobeandmail.com/news/national/ottawa-rejects-space-firms-sale-to-us/article17983725/, accessed on December 23, 2016.

[36] Interview with William (Mac) Evans.

[37] Bochinger, S., (ed)., Profiles of Government Space Activities 2012, Euroconsult, (Paris, Euroconsult, March 2012), p. 43.

space sector as a first priority, promoting cooperation, and increasing the involvement of Canadians in space activities.[38]

Canada's Motivations

A Strategic Alliance with an Elephant

Canada and the United States have a special and strategic relationship. Their economies are intertwined, and their militaries work closely together, especially in operating NORAD.[39] Nevertheless, Canada's approach toward the United States is complex. On one hand, it is shaped by a desire to take advantage of the geographical and cultural proximity to its giant neighbor. On the other hand, it is overwhelmed by this giant and is concerned about becoming overly dependent on and overshadowed by it. Canada finds it important to emphasize its own independent and distinct identity in order to avoid being seen as simply an extension of the United States. As a result, Canada plays a calculated political game in which it cooperates with the United States in joint ventures while stressing its own unique, separate identity and contribution to the alliance. This behavior pattern also finds expression in Canada's space program.

The proximity to the United States was and still is an enabler and a motivator for the Canadian space program.[40] "The United States was looking for allies and it was willing to let [us] into the club with the low cost use of their facilities," explained Ambassador Jon Allen.[41] The Canadian program is so well integrated into the American space program that for some it may seem to be an integral part of it.[42] For this reason, Canada attempts to make its unique contribution to the American space program and international initiatives more noticeable. Canada does so by focusing on elements of high visibility and wide exposure that are meant to project Canadian capacity and indigenous achievements in an

---

[38] Pugliese, D., "Canadian Policy Outlines Broad National Goals for Space Program," *Space News*, February 7, 2014, available at: spacenews.com/39412canadian-policy-outlines-broad-national-goals-for-space-program/#sthash.pfePrqhk.dpuf, accessed on February 10, 2014.

[39] NORAD, the North American Aerospace Defense Command, is headed by a US Air Force General who simultaneously commands US Continental Air Defense Forces. His deputy is always a Canadian officer.

[40] Kirton, J., "Canada-United States Space Co-operation; Current Choices," in J. Kirton, (ed.), *Canada, the United States, and Space*, (Toronto: Canadian Institute of International Affairs, 1985), 79.

[41] Interview with Ambassador Jon Allen, Canadian Ambassador to Israel, August 19, 2008, Tel Aviv, Israel.

[42] Interview with Professor David Mutimer, York University, October 30, 2008, Toronto, Canada.

effort to enhance Canadian identity.[43] In this respect, much emphasis is given to the astronaut corps, as well as to the Canadarm that displays "Canada" and the Canadian flag on its side.

In the 1960s, Canada was especially concerned with its "brain drain" to the United States. The cancellation of the Avro Arrow venture[44] in 1959, in which thousands of technicians and engineers were laid off, was seen as a contributing factor to this trend because several of them moved south and joined NASA and other American enterprises. NASA made a major effort to hire many of them by offering various incentives, including assistance in a quick and smooth process of relocation.[45] The Diefenbaker government was severely criticized for its decision on this project.

When the Chapman Report was underway in 1966, Canada was undergoing social change influenced by a great patriotic wave, as well as by separatist unrest in Quebec. The report reflected the national atmosphere, expressing concern about Canada's proximity to the United States while recommending that this be utilized in Canada's favor. The report encouraged the government not to disregard space activity because of its high costs and risks for a small country, but rather to take advantage of its giant neighbor's space program to establish a national Canadian space program that would inspire Canadian scientists and prevent their exodus to the United States:

> Since the costs involved in space research are so great ... it is arguable that Canada, like many another smaller nation, should stay out of this activity and devote her comparatively slender resources to the study of other more immediately rewarding problems. The fact is that our contiguity to the US and our close involvement with the intellectual activity of the North American continent do not allow us to stand wholly aloof from such a major preoccupation of our immense southern neighbor ... It is quite unrealistic to think that Canadian scientists will not become active participants in this truly continental activity, seeing that it presents them with many of the greatest opportunities and most challenging problems of their professional disciplines. If Canada does not provide access to these challenges, the more eager and forceful of her scientists and technologists will be drawn to those places where that access is afforded, and her own mental climate will suffer.[46]

---

[43] Interview with Mr. Graham Gibbs Canadian Space Attaché at the Canadian Embassy in Washington, DC, March 18, 2008, Washington, DC; interview with Professor David Mutimer.
[44] A Canadian attempt to develop highly advanced interceptor aircraft by Avro Aircraft Ltd.
[45] For a detailed and informative book on this subject, see Gainor, C., *Arrows to the Moon – Avro's Engineers and the Space Race*, (Burlington, Ottawa: Apogee Books, 2001).
[46] Chapman, J. H, Forsyth, P. A., and Patterson, G. N., *Upper Atmosphere*, 93–94.

Canada's proximity to the United States also raises concerns of a cultural nature. Canadian politicians have always been alarmed by the tidal wave of American media that threatens to overwhelm Canadian consumers, especially those in English Canada.[47] A Canadian communications satellite, it was believed, would "enable the government to take major steps in protecting and strengthening Canada's cultural heritage."[48] In the 1970s, this perception intensified as part of Prime Minister Trudeau's overall strategy of the "Third Option." Canada's observer status in the European Space Agency (ESA) in 1979 reflected Trudeau's policy. This theme was echoed in a memorandum prepared by John Chapman, the DOC Assistant Deputy Minister for Communications, prior to a meeting with ESA officials in May 1976.

Chapman noted that Canada's interest in a relationship with ESA "stems from our intention to develop the Third Option in our Foreign Policy." Chapman further stressed that Canada was not self-sufficient in space technology and lacked a launch capability, so it needed a partner and, although the United States is Canada's natural partner, "we are overwhelmed by the size and depth of the US program, while the European program is comparable (relative to GNP) to the effort Canada is putting forward in space."[49] Another example of Canada's use of space to associate itself with the strength and capability of the United States, while distinguishing its contribution as an independent player, is the Canadian flag painted on the Canadarm. "It was a national pride thing to show the world that this was done by Canada and not by the United States, to get some recognition," explained Evans in an interview.[50]

The close and special strategic relationship shared by Canada and the United States allowed Canada to join the "space club" at a very early stage and at a relatively low cost. Canada's membership in the "space club," especially through highly visible projects, allows Canada to project a strong and autonomous image with regard to space activity. For example, Canada is putting major effort into preserving space as a peaceful environment that is free from weapons. According to Handberg (2004), by adopting this policy, Canada has created some distance from the United States and has also signaled to other countries that its space

---

[47] The Canadian government implemented "Canadian Content Regulations" in the early 1970s (Can-Con) that set specific quotas for Canadian content in Canadian media.

[48] Drury, Hon. C. M., "White Paper on A Domestic Satellite Communication System for Canada" (Ottawa: Queen's Printer, 1968), 38, cited in C., Gainor, "The Chapman Report and the Development of Canada's Space Program," *Quest*, 10:4, (2003), 3–18.

[49] Dotto, L., *Canada and the European Space Agency Three Decades of Cooperation*, (Noordwijk, The Netherlands: European Space Agency, May 2002), 1–2.

[50] Interview with William (Mac) Evans.

activities are not simply an extension of the activities of the United States.[51]

The Domestic Sphere: Canadian Identity and the Cultural–Political Divide

There seems no doubt that in the second century of Confederation, the fabric of Canadian society will be held together by strands in space just as strongly as the railway and telegraph held together the scattered provinces in the last century.

Chapman Report, p. 95

Canadian society is divided into several ethnic groups. The two main groups are British Canadians and French Canadians. Approximately a quarter of Canadians speak French as their main (and sometimes only) language. The needs and aspirations of French Canadians, who are concentrated in the province of Quebec but are also present elsewhere in the country, have placed special demands on Canada's communication infrastructure and policies. Furthermore, the scattered and remote population, especially in the north, requires national efforts to bring people together. In the nineteenth century, it was the Canadian Pacific Railway that brought people together and catalyzed the formation of Canada.[52] There are many similarities to be found between the application of space technology and the building of the Canadian Pacific Railway. At the time, the railway represented the most advanced technology available to bring the country together. "A lot has changed since then, but the need to build linkages in this vast country – for political, cultural, communications and economic purposes – remains an enduring priority of government."[53]

For the last fifty years, space communications, along with other aspects of the Canadian space program, are used for more than just providing connectivity services such as radio, internet, and telephone. Canada's high and visible membership in the "space club" fulfills important social needs of the Canadian community and plays a major role in promoting

---

[51] Handberg, R., "Outer Space As a Shared Frontier – Canada and the US, Cooperation Between Unequal Partners," *American Behavioral Scientist*, 47:10, (June 2004), 1251.

[52] On July 1, 1867, the Provinces of Canada, New Brunswick, and Nova Scotia became a federation. The construction of the Canadian Pacific Railway convinced the provinces in the west and in the north to join the federation and accept its authority. Manitoba joined the Dominion in 1870, British Columbia in 1871, and Prince Edward Island in 1873. Upset that the promises of the original agreement were not being met, British Columbia threatened to withdraw from the Confederation. In the end, it did not do so, because the railway was completed by 1885.

[53] Collin, A., (1985), "The Canadian Space Program," in J. Kirton, (ed.), *Canada, the United States, and Space*, (Toronto: Canadian Institute of International Affairs, 1985), 59.

national unity, boosting Canadian national identity, and creating a robust self-image.

National Unrest in Quebec and Canada's First Communication Satellite

In the 1960s, major social changes in the province of Quebec led to a rise in Quebecois nationalism, including calls for recognition of cultural dualism and even secession from Canada. Since then, the demands and problems of Quebec have been at the center of Canadian politics.[54] Canada's federal government "responded to this challenge with policies that promoted bilingualism, including the provision of broadcast services in both French and English to every part of the country."[55] This issue inevitably affected Canada's space program.

The provincial government of Quebec, where a majority of French Canadians live, made the argument that its responsibility for strengthening French language and culture enabled it to act internationally for the development of satellite communication programs. This served as a background to the Chapman Report's recommendation to develop a communication satellite infrastructure in Canada so as to preserve the fabric of the society, and to regard these satellites as essential systems that permit Canada to shape its own destiny, parallel to national transportation systems (rail and air), electric power services, and national telecommunications services that are owned by Canada.[56] "Bilingualism, national unity and sovereignty, which were the primary political imperatives of that time, made it impossible to ignore the benefits of satellite communications for Canadians, or to allow needed services to be provided by foreign satellites," explained Dr. Jocelyn Mallett, Director General of Policy and Planning at the Canadian Space Agency, in a 1990 article.[57]

The first response by the government of Prime Minister Lester Pearson to the claims made by Quebec's provincial government resulted in an

---

[54] Quebec had been calling for sovereignty and separation from Canada for many years. France was one of the first nations to recognize the distinctiveness of the Quebecois nation in the 1960s, and it has maintained diplomatic relations with the province independently of the federal government of Canada, allowing Quebec to open an office in Paris. French support of Quebec severely damaged relations between France and Canada. In the mid-1990s, a Quebec referendum on national sovereignty was narrowly defeated: 50.6 percent voted against sovereignty. In 2006, Canadian Prime Minister Harper recognized Quebec as a nation within Canada.
[55] Gainor, C., "The Chapman Report," 4.
[56] Chapman, Forsyth, and Patterson, *Upper Atmosphere*, 86.
[57] Mallett, J., "Canada's Space Programs," *Space Policy Journal*, 6:1, (February 1990), 54.

agreement with France on space matters.[58] In 1968, the Trudeau government took power and gave greater priority to this issue: "One of the reasons for the cabinet's concern was rooted in the French government's attempt to improve its relationship with the Quebec provincial government and to strengthen the hand of Quebec separatists.[59] The Quebec government agreed, in early 1969, to take part in the Franco-German Symphonie communications satellite program. This agreement added further to the Canadian government's desire to launch a Canadian communication satellite."[60] In 1969, the government created Telesat, a corporation that would build and operate Canada's satellites.[61] Eventually, despite loud domestic protest, the government awarded the contract to Hughes, an American satellite manufacturer,[62] and the Anik was successfully launched in late 1972. Soon after, the publicly owned Canadian Broadcasting Corporation established English and French television services in nearly every part of Canada. The federal government retained control of satellite broadcasting and beat back the Quebec government's challenge to its jurisdiction.[63]

High Visibility: An Astronaut Program for Greater National Esteem

In the 1980s, in order to further enhance the visibility of the Canadian space program to the public, it was decided that the astronauts would be selected by a nationwide contest. Evans, who was involved in the selection process, explained that it was all a part of the federal government's desire to show that being a Canadian is important: "It is part of demonstrating to ourselves that we are equal to the big guys in this area and, second, demonstrating to the world that we are playing in this geopolitical field."[64] Furthermore, because equality is considered an important Canadian value, it was also necessary to ensure (not only in fact, but also in appearance) equal opportunity for people of different geographic regions, ethnic backgrounds and gender.[65]

---

[58] DeWitt, D., and Kirton, J., *Canada as a Principal Power*, 335–336.
[59] It was part of the overall French effort to reverse the declining prestige and use of French in the world. Leaders of La Francophonie recognized that the strength of French as an international language depended on its status at the national and local level. See St.-Hilaire, A., "North America and the Francophonie: Local and Transnational Movements for the Survival of French-Speaking North America," *Language Science*, 19:4, (1997), 369–380.
[60] Gainor, C., "The Chapman Report," 5.
[61] Gainor, C., *Canada in Space – The People and Stories Behind Canada's Role in the Exploration of Space*, (Edmonton, Canada: Folklore Publishing, 2006), 37.
[62] Gainor, C., "The Chapman Report," 8.   [63] Gainor, C., "The Chapman Report," 6.
[64] Interview with William (Mac) Evans.
[65] Dotto, L., *Canada in Space*, (Toronto: Irwin Publishing Inc., 1987), 57.

It was widely acknowledged that Canada's first astronauts would become national figures whose role would also be to represent Canada to the world and Canadians to themselves.[66] This would be especially true for the first astronaut to actually fly. In this respect, Marc Garneau fulfilled the image of a national hero. Why Garneau was chosen to be the first of the group of six astronauts to fly has not been revealed. The policy from the outset had been that the astronaut corps as a whole would have facility in both official languages, but individual bilingualism was not mandatory.[67] Dr. Karl Doetsch, of the Canadian space program, said, "It is an ability that can be used so we did not ignore it. It is one of the things that we put into the mix."[68] Evans confirmed this, arguing that there was no political input to the selection process and that the selection of Garneau had nothing to do with his being bilingual. (It is worth mentioning that Garneau was not the only bilingual person in the group; Steve MacLean enjoyed this quality as well, but having been born in Ottawa, he was not recognized as a French Canadian.) "We looked at all the qualities, and one of the problems with [the flight] was the short notice.[69] We had to decide who would be able to do it in a short time and we had to decide who will be best prepared in such a short time [and Garneau] was the best ... The fact that he was bilingual did no harm. After all, he had to communicate to all Canadians, it was a useful aspect."[70] Dotto (1987) argued that Garneau's bilingual capability and his origin as a French Canadian born in Quebec was clearly an asset, both for practical and symbolic reasons.[71]

As of 2016, Canada has conducted only three public searches for astronauts, the third ended in 2009. Dr. Steve MacLean, CSA president in the years 2008–2013, said in an interview in November 2008 that the agency is primarily interested in professionalism and will work hard so that secondary factors do not matter. However, if the newly selected astronauts reflect the diversity of the Canadian society, it will paint a better picture, especially if the desire is for the astronauts to make space a source of inspiration for the whole country.[72]

[66] Dotto, L., *Canada in Space*, 58.
[67] In the second recruitment (1992) and the third, which began in May 2008, the bilingual requirement was not aimed [solely] to satisfy domestic considerations, but also to address a practical requirement of working in the multi-cultural environment of the International Space Station. Dotto, L., *Canada in Space*, 94–95.
[68] Dotto, L., *Canada in Space*, 94–95.
[69] Early in 1984, NASA informed Canada it would like the first Canadian astronaut to be launched in the fall of 1984, which allowed only several months for training.
[70] Interview with William (Mac) Evans.   [71] Dotto, L., *Canada in Space*, 94–95.
[72] Interview with Dr. Steve MacLean, President of the Canadian Space Agency and former Canadian astronaut, November 4, 2008, Montreal, Canada.

Canadians take much pride in their space program and see the Canadian astronauts and the Canadarm as national icons and important symbols that define their being. According to a survey conducted in 2001, eight of ten Canadians are proud of Canada's achievements in space and believe it is important for Canada to have an active space program and to be involved in the development of advanced technologies and science related space.[73] Furthermore, on June 30, 2008, Ipsos Reid published the results of a broad survey in which Canadians were asked to choose 101 things that best define Canada. The Canadarm came in fifth with 4,689 votes. In first place was the maple leaf with 14,523 votes, followed by hockey (5,612), the Canadian flag (5,417), and the beaver (5,040). Interestingly, space exploration only came in at 100 with 202 votes.[74] This suggests that Canadians may be more aware of, and take greater pride in, the visible elements of their space program.

High International Standing and a Role of Leadership in World Affairs

Canada pursues a global and visible foreign policy. For years, this has been an important tradition, as it allows Canada to fulfill its aspiration to play a significant and meaningful role in world affairs.[75] In part, Canada's strong international interest stems from its strategic location, neighboring both Russia and the United States. This unique position stimulated Canadian officials to direct Canada to seek a moderating role in American-Soviet relations during the Cold War years.[76]

Canada's ethnic diversity also contributes to the nation's vast interest in world affairs and cosmopolitan nature, as many regions of the world are represented in the Canadian society. Ambassador Paul Meyer described Canada as a "regional power without a region … It is not easy for us to limit ourselves to one region, and that puts us in a global perspective … It is also a part of Canadians' self-image that they would like to see their country make some contribution to global affairs."[77] This Canadian narrative is manifested in Canada's aspirations to have a "seat at the

---

[73] Canadian Space Agency, Report on Plans and Priorities, 2002–2003, Estimates, 19, available at:http://publications.gc.ca/site/archivee-archived.html?url=http://publications.gc.ca/collections/Collection/BT31-2-2003-III-93E.pdf, accessed on December 23, 2016.

[74] IPSOS REID, Defining Canada: A Nation Chooses The 101 Things That Best Define Their Country. June 30, 2008, available at: https://www.historicacanada.ca/sites/default/files/PDF/polls/canada101_part3_en.pdf, accessed December 23, 2016.

[75] Sokolsky, J., "A Seat At The Table, 11–12.

[76] Sokolsky, J., "A Seat At The Table, 24.

[77] Interview with Ambassador Paul Meyer, November 3, 2008, Ottawa, Canada.

table." It is of significance to Canada to participate in councils and organizations involved with global strategy and security; to join and actively participate in various international economic clubs and alliances; and to promote peacekeeping and global arms control.[78] The space program supports Canada's efforts to play an active, visible, and key role in international affairs. This perception is clearly evident in the Canadian Space Agency's 2003 space strategy:

> Space is a strategic priority that enables Canadians to meet their economic, social and political objectives ... Space is consequently recognized as a national priority by countries seeking to retain scientific, commercial, social and political leadership ... It is no longer an option for us to question whether a space program has a place in our future, but whether we have a future without a space program ... Canada must prepare to make vital, meaningful contributions to such multilateral efforts – not only to respond to our national needs, but also to take leadership in international collaborations, and promote Canadian values, as well as our scientific and technological capabilities.[79]

During the Cold War, the multilateral emphasis in Canada's space activity "was due in large measure to a pronounced dispersion of power within the international space club. The United States maintained its previous dominance through a rapidly expanding program, and quickly assumed leadership in the most sophisticated field. But the emergence of a serious Soviet challenge produced an urgent and sustained need for mediatory activity at the United Nations and for an international space order based on a broader range of states."[80] Canada sought to lead in that direction. The Canadarm, which was launched on the second mission of the shuttle on November 12, 1981, made the government realize its major international significance as a symbol of Canada's technological capability. The Canadarm soon became a part of Canada's efforts to build its image as a country that has a world-class space industry.[81]

The same logic motivated Canada to join the International Space Station (ISS). The ISS was a top priority of US foreign policy during the Reagan administration and was presented as a G7 initiative. As a G7 member, Canada was approached by the United States on this matter.[82]

---

[78] Sokolsky, J., "A Seat At The Table, 11–12.
[79] The Canadian Space Strategy was approved by the Canadian Space Agency on November 12, 2003 (from the brochure of the Canadian Space Agency [received 2008], 9, 11, 23).
[80] DeWitt, D., and Kirton, J., *Canada as a Principal Power*, 326–327.
[81] Interview with William (Mac) Evans.
[82] Canada was not an original member of the G6. Despite its strong ambition to join this elite group of countries, its appeal for membership had been rejected by France. It took major efforts to be included in this exclusive club, which then turned into the G7. Canada continued to feel the need to prove to itself and to the other members that it truly

Evans explained that Canada's decision to join the ISS endeavor had nothing much to do with space. Rather, it had a lot to do with Canada's relations with the United States:

> This is club politics of a very high level ... Canada could not be left outside ... There is no doubt in my mind that the Canadarm and the Astronauts, because of their visibility, planted in our psyche the belief that we were in the same class as all the other G7 countries. It was part of our identity. So when the space station came along and became a major initiative of the G7, we had no option and the decision was made.[83]

Having reviewed the background and development of Canada's space program, we now turn to Australia, which is frequently compared with Canada, to see what role, if any, space activity has played in there.

Australia: A Sophisticated User of Space Applications

Australia has been involved in space for many years. Like Canada, Australia's preliminary activities in space focused on ionospheric research and radio astronomy for communication reasons. Australia has various observatories, telescopes, and facilities similar to those of other countries, as well as a launch complex in its territory located in Woomera in southern central Australia.[84] Nonetheless, none of this was ever part of a coherent national space plan. Most of Australia's space activity since the 1950s was the result of initiatives and joint projects with Britain or the United States.[85] The Woomera Rocket Range was built by the British. After World War II, Britain rebuilt its armed forces and needed a place to test new weapon systems. The Australian government under Prime Minister Ben Chifley recognized the benefits of hosting this facility on Australian soil and accepted the British offer. Australia was especially interested in acquiring its own versions of the new generations of weapons, and in the immigration of talented and qualified people who would boost the economy, establish new

---

belonged (Hajnal, P., *The* G8 System and the G20 – Evolution, Role and Documentation, [England: Ashgate, 2007], 38).
[83] Interview with William (Mac) Evans.
[84] A woomera is a spear thrower in a language of Eastern Australia.
[85] Woomera was used to launch several British rockets and satellites. On October 28, 1971, the UK's Prospero satellite was launched on a Black Arrow rocket from Woomera; it was Britain's first and only indigenous launch. NASA built its first space tracking station at Woomera, which was later used to communicate with the Apollo 11 mission that landed on the moon.

industries, and expand scientific research. These expectations were only partially fulfilled.[86]

Several events in Asia in the years following World War II intensified Australia's threat perception. China became a communist state (1949), and North Korea attacked South Korea (1950). The then Prime Minister, Robert Gordon Menzies, feared that the circle of threat and violence was approaching Australia. He thought that Australia was incapable of defending itself. He therefore offered to host Britain's nuclear test facilities, binding Britain and the West to the defense of Australia. Menzies aspired to a more independent Australian security posture, but he did not move further to develop Australian nuclear capability.[87] He settled for aid from "friends and allies," as he referred to the United States and Britain.[88]

In the mid-1950s, Australia made plans to participate in the International Geophysical Year. Australia developed upper atmospheric research programs that included the development of a series of Australian-designed and -built sounding rockets, some of which used British motors and were launched from Woomera.[89] This program was under the auspices of the Weapons Research Establishment (WRE), the Australian Defense Scientific and Technical Research Organization that controlled the Woomera Range and oversaw Australia's space related activities.[90]

---

[86] The transfer of research and personnel from Britain to Australia was rather limited, but some of those who did move were later integrated into R&D organizations like the Defense, Science and Technology Organization. American Institute of Aeronautics and Astronautics, Historic Aerospace Site, Woomera, (2007), 2, 5, available at: www.aiaa.org/Participate/Uploads/07-0345%20Woomera.pdf, accessed on December 31, 2008; Morton, P., *Testing Blue Streak at Woomera: An Episode in Anglo-Australian Collaboration and Conflict*, Working Paper No. 32 (London: Sir Robert Menzies Center for Australian Studies, Institute of Commonwealth Studies, University of London, 1998), 4, available at: www.kcl.ac.uk/content/1/c6/01/51/32/WP32Morton.pdf, accessed on December 4, 2008).

[87] Hymans, J., *The Psychology of Nuclear Proliferation – Identity, Emotions, and Foreign Policy*, (Cambridge: Cambridge University Press, 2006), 116–117.

[88] For a comprehensive document on the strategic policy of Australia during the past several decades, see: Fruhling, S., *A History of Australian Strategic Policy Since 1945*, (Canberra: Defense Publishing Service, Department of Defense, 2009); and Drobik, I., "The Role of Defense Science in Achieving Australian Self-Reliance, Australian Defense College," *Monograph Series*, 3, (2003), 10, available at: www.defence.gov.au/adc/hqadc_mono.htm, accessed on May 20, 2009; Watt, A., *The Evolution of Australian Foreign Policy 1938–1965*, (London: Cambridge University Press, 1968), 339.

[89] For further reading on the Australian sounding rocket programs and the operation of Woomera Range, see Morton, P., *Fire across the Desert: Woomera and the Anglo-Australian Joint Project 1946–1980*, (Canberra: Australian Government Publishing Service, 1989).

[90] Dougherty, K., "Upper Atmospheric Research at Woomera: The Australian-Built Sounding Rockets," *Acta Astronautica*, 59, (May 2006), 55.

In April 1960, Britain canceled its Blue-Streak program[91] without consulting the Australian government that hosted the program at Woomera. Peter Morton described the Australian reaction as "a sense of betrayal and inferiority; the sense that scarce resources could be summoned up, consumed and then tossed aside according to decisions made in another country. And it was the Mother Country behaving thus!"[92] This was not the first incident in which Australia felt betrayed by Britain. In 1957, Britain agreed to integrate its nuclear forces into NATO in exchange for the prized atomic partnership with the United States. As part of this move, Britain agreed to shift its nuclear test zone to Nevada without consulting Australia on this issue.[93] Furthermore, the British government's decision to rationalize its military presence east of Suez stimulated anxieties about Australia's future position in Asia. These British moves, together with Britain's intention to seek entry into the European Common Market, shifted Australia's foreign policy from Britain and Europe toward the United States, especially as the latter became extensively involved in Southeast Asia.[94]

In the 1960s, Australia was considered an important player in world space activity, because Woomera was ELDO's[95] testing ground.[96] In this context, Australia was invited to join European nations in the exploration of space, and to make Woomera available for research projects by those nations. Nevertheless, Australian Prime Minister Menzies and his Cabinet expressed their view that the "price" Australia had to pay for membership in the "European Space Club"[97] was too high. According to a report by the *New York Times*,

Australia had expected to obtain "life membership" in the "club" without any financial obligation, in return for allowing its members to use the Woomera range and its facilities. Under the draft convention that was presented to the Federal Government, Australia was to have membership without financial obligation, but only for the research and development phase of the space program. It was expected to contribute its share if it wished to continue as a member and share

---

[91] Blue Streak was a medium-range ballistic missile.
[92] Morton, P. *Testing Blue Streak*, 17.
[93] Hymans, *The Psychology of Nuclear Proliferation*, 118.
[94] Kennedy, D. E. "The Debate on Distinctive Australian Foreign Policy," in M., Teichman, (ed.). *New Directions in Australian Foreign Policy – Ally, Satellite or Neutral?* (Victoria: Penguin Books, 1969), 66.
[95] European Launch Development Organization.
[96] Tonkin, R., and Mace, O., "Australia – A History of the Development of the Australian Student Built Satellite," Presented at the IAA 1998 Convention, September 1998.
[97] In the 1960s, the media referred to ESRO and ELDO (European initiatives to develop a launch vehicle and a space program) as a space club.

in the results of the telecommunications systems that the European countries planned to establish.[98]

This approach coincided well with the overall Australian approach that it would not be able to provide for its own security and hence should focus on protecting Australia by alliances with greater powers rather than by indigenous development. Furthermore, developing indigenous capability was not thought of as economical for a small country like Australia.

In late 1966, Australia's space activities progressed from sounding rockets to satellites. In that period, Australia was involved in a research project with the United States and Britain to investigate the physics of high velocity warhead re-entry into Earth's atmosphere. The project, named Sparta, used American Redstone boosters to launch the tested warheads. Over time, it was obvious that not all of the boosters that were brought to Woomera would be used. WRE officials suggested that the spare booster be used as a satellite launcher to launch an Australian-made satellite.[99] On November 29, 1967, the Australian scientific satellite WRESAT[100] was launched, making Australia the fourth nation in the world to launch a satellite into Earth's orbit from its own territory. Because Australia did not do so indigenously, it is not considered a "full" member of the space club. Eventually, due to a lack of national commitment by the Australian government and the cancellation of various British space projects, especially the cancellation of the British launch project, Woomera declined.[101]

At the end of 1969 and the beginning of 1970, NASA Administrator Thomas Paine toured Europe, Canada, Japan, and Australia for preliminary discussions on cooperative opportunities in the post-Apollo period. Early on, Australia specified that space was not among its highest priorities and that it was not able to spend the considerable amount of money required to cooperate with the United States on a meaningful basis.[102] In the mid-1970s, after more than fifteen years, the Australian sounding rocket program ceased operation. The Australian government decided to focus its spending on defense research rather than on upper

---

[98] "Australia Facing Decision on Space," *New York Times*, February 18, 1962, 43.
[99] Dougherty, K., "Upper Atmospheric, 55.
[100] The Weapons Research Establishment Satellite was slightly more than 2 meters long and weighed 72.5 kilograms. The satellite carried instruments to measure the Earth's atmosphere, solar radiation, and the temperature of the sun's outer atmosphere, and to study ozone concentrations at very high altitudes.
[101] Burleson, *Space Programs*, 16.
[102] Logsdon, J., "The Development of International Space Cooperation," in J. M. Logsdon, D. Day, and R. D. Launius, (eds.), *Exploring the Unknown*, 6.

atmospheric research. Existing cooperation with Britain declined as well, due to changes in the British attitude.[103]

In 1979, the Australian government created AUSSAT, one of the first national communications satellite systems in the world. Nonetheless, the demand for communication satellite services did not encourage the Australian government to embark on a national space program. Traditionally, Australian governments have been reluctant to commit to public investment in space activities.[104] A change of atmosphere occurred in the 1980s. The Australian Labor Party government, elected in 1983, aspired to reform industrial policy. In March 1984, the Department of Science and Technology convened a National Space Symposium,[105] which was set to examine possible new directions in space science and technology on a national level.[106]

Barry Owen Jones, then Minister for Science and Technology, said at that conference that it was "time for Australia to enter the 'space club' ... otherwise, the leading countries will be uncatchable, and by default Australia will be a mere spectator."[107] In July 1984, Minister Jones sought the advice of the Australian Academy of Technological Sciences regarding the appropriate form of an Australian space policy. The resulting report, known as the Madigan Report,[108] was published in 1985. Its main findings were[109]

- the need to formulate a national space policy;
- the need for the Australian government to play a leading role in facilitating the development of space science and technology capabilities;
- the identification of ground sector activities and remote sensing technology as areas of immediate potential; and
- the important role of international collaboration.

One of the report's main conclusions was that it was not possible for the private sector, from its own resources, to develop a space industry that would carry the rest of Australia on its back into the space age. The commitment to a space program must be a government decision,

---

[103] Dougherty, "Upper Atmospheric Research," 55.
[104] Middleton, B., "Australia's Space Development at the End of the 20th Century," *News Bulletin*, 20:8, (May 1995), 81–90.
[105] This was the first national symposium of its kind in Australia.
[106] Siemon, N., *Public Policy Planning And Global Technology Dependence: Strategic Factors for a National Space-related Innovation System*, unpublished Ph.D. Dissertation, University of Western Sydney, 2003, 139–140.
[107] Department of Science and Technology, 1984, 2, cited by Siemon, N., *Public Policy Planning*, 140.
[108] The academy's working group was headed by Sir Russell Madigan.
[109] Middleton, B. S., and Cory, E. F., "Australian Space Policy," *Space Policy Journal*, (February 1989), 41–42.

not a commercial one.[110] The report recommended, therefore, the establishment of a statutory body to draw together all of Australia's space efforts, with funding of AU$100 million over five years to finance participation in a number of space projects in which Australia would have a significant design and construction responsibility, and associated basic research.[111]

The Australian government adopted many of the Madigan Report recommendations, but it did not agree to establish an independent statutory body. Instead, it formed an Australian Space Board that reported directly to the Minister for Industry, Technology and Commerce.[112] A year later (1987), it also established the Australian Space Office within the Department of Industry, Technology and Commerce. Located in Canberra, this was the federal government body responsible for space industry development. As such, it was responsible for placing the majority of space contracts, encouraging greater local industry involvement in space-related R&D, and promoting the development of commercially viable industries based on space technologies.[113]

The mandate of the Australian Space Office was to actively encourage the development of a local space industry and commercial space activities that would compete internationally by encouraging greater involvement of local industry in space research and development activities.[114] In 1994, the Australian Space Council produced a "Five Year Plan," which was adopted by the minister. But funding for the program was withdrawn in 1995 and a year later, less than a decade after it was originally established, the Australian Space Office was closed.[115] The Cooperative Research Center for Satellite Systems CRCSS[116] was then considered to be the country's official national space body.[117] Its only project was FedSat, a 58 kg experimental satellite manufactured to demonstrate Australian space capability.[118] CRCSS ceased operations in December 2005 when

---

[110] Australian Academy of Technological Sciences, *A Space Policy for Australia*, (June 1985), 2.
[111] Middleton, B. S., and Cory, E. F., "Australian Space Policy," 42.
[112] The Senate Standing Committee on Economics, *Lost in Space? Setting a New Direction for Australia's Space Science and Industry Sector*, (November 2008), 48.
[113] Clark, P., "Australian Space Looking For A Direction," *Space*, (April–May 1992), 7.
[114] Heyman, J., "The Ups and Downs of Australia in Space," *Space Times*, (May–June 2001), 13.
[115] The Senate Standing Committee on Economics, *Lost in Space*, 51–52.
[116] It was established in 1998 to carry out research and training in space technologies. Its primary objective is to develop capability in design and operation of small satellites.
[117] Burleson, *Space Programs*, 10.
[118] It was launched in December 2002 by Japan's H2-A rocket. For a comprehensive work on FedSat, see Moody, J. B., *The Importance of Complex Product Systems to the Space Industry in Australia: A Small Satellite Case Study*, unpublished Ph.D. Dissertation, The Australian National University, Canberra, 2004.

its funding was not renewed, and the Department of Defense assumed responsibility for the satellite until its signal failed in 2007. This was the first satellite mission in thirty years that Australia actually conducted.[119]

In 2005, Senator Grant Chapman convened a Space Policy Advisory Group. This group prepared a report that emphasized Australia's dependence on space from the utility perspective and highlighted the associated vulnerabilities and risks. Chapman called for a national space policy assigned to a specific agency, which, among other things, would review the nation's space interests in order to reduce vulnerability to disruption or denial of space data and services. In April 2007, the Ministry for Industry issued a brief government response to the Chapman Report, stating that it did not intend to change its policy.[120]

Attempts to change the Australian policy continued in 2008. Several papers on this issue were published,[121] and the Senate Economics Committee released a detailed report on their space inquiry entitled "Lost in Space? – Setting a New Direction for Australia's Space Science and Industry Sector." The report called for the establishment of an Australian Space Agency to coordinate Australia's space activities and reduce its reliance on other countries in the area of space technology. The committee also recommended that the Space Industry Advisory Council be established to guide the development of the national agency. Such a council, chaired by the Minister for Innovation, Industry, Science and Research or his representative, would be composed of industry, government agencies, defense representatives, and academicians.[122]

In 2009, a space policy unit was established. Motivated by military as well as civil objectives, funding increased significantly. In 2011, the government's allocation to space was estimated to top AU$313 million.[123] The same year, Australia formed its new principles for a national space policy, which included placing a focus on space applications of national significance; assuring access to space capability; strengthening and increasing international cooperation; contributing to

---

[119] The Senate Standing Committee on Economics, *Lost in Space*, 52.
[120] Biddington, B., "Skin in The Game: Realizing Australia's National Interests in Space to 2025," The Kokoda Foundation, paper no. 7, (May 2008), 13–14; The Senate Standing Committee on Economics, *Lost in Space*, 53.
[121] Among these papers are Biddington, B., "Skin in The Game"; Holt, L., "Integrating Space Efforts into Australia's Joint Operations," *Australian Defense Force Journal*, 175, (2008), 51–65.
[122] Merrett, N. "New Directions for the Heavens From National Security Statements," *Australian Defense-Business Review*, (January–February 2009), 43–47.
[123] In the past decade, the funds the Australian government allocates to space, especially for defense, have been increased significantly, most of it to upgrade satellite communication capability. See Bochinger, S., (ed)., Profiles Of Government Space Activities 2012, Euroconsult, (Paris, Euroconsult, March 2012), pp. 407–411.

a stable space environment; supporting innovation, science, and skills development; and protecting and enhancing national security and economic well-being. Two years later, in 2013, the government published a policy in which it set the objective to strengthen Australia's use of space.[124] In 2013, the space policy unit became the Space Coordination Office within the Department of Industry, which serves as the mechanism coordinating Australia's civil space activities. Although these developments exemplify a greater interest in space by the Australian government, they do not reflect a major change in its overall approach to space. Australia is not interested in space exploration. Its focus remains on sophisticated utilization of space through international and commercial partnerships rather than through the indigenous development of capabilities.[125] Australia, therefore, remains a sophisticated user of space and not a producer.

Canada and Australia: Two Different Paths

Observing the Canadian space effort through the prism of a "space club" enables a better understanding of the political and social aspects that are part of Canada's policy-making. In accordance with the second hypothesis raised in this book – that states that are not powers but aspire to upgrade their power and international standing will develop national space capabilities – being associated with the elite group of spacefaring nations (the "space club") serves Canadian needs and goals of international status and national esteem. The space program is valuable to Canada in terms of its international position, community building, and support of the political regime.

Canada never "joined" the space club; rather, it acknowledged its membership in retrospect, using it to vindicate the efforts invested in its space activities. In the early 1970s, Canadians realized that the benefits of their space activity were more than the concrete daily uses of space applications. Mac Evans, who had been closely involved in Canadian space activities since the early 1970s, expressed his opinion that the celebration of the tenth anniversary of Alouette 1 was a turning point; the fact that Canada had produced a satellite that operated for a decade, at a time when most satellites ceased operation after a few months, had a tremendous impact on the public's perception of Canada's expertise in

---

[124] Australia's Satellite Utilisation Policy 2013, available at: www.space.gov.au/SPACEPOLICYUNIT/Pages/default.aspx, accessed on June 21, 2015.

[125] Freeland, S., "Australia National Space Law and Space Policy," presentation at the United Nations Workshop on Space Law, Beijing, November 2014, 17–20, available at: www.unoosa.org/pdf/spacelaw/activities/2014/pres09E.pdf, accessed on June 21, 2015.

this field.[126] It was from this point on that Canadian media, government publications, and official statements began to emphasize Canada's high position, stressing the fact that Canada was third to have a satellite in space. Thus, Canada's achievements in space were recognized in the context of "club politics."

In the 1980s, the idea of the "space club" was even more evident. Dr. Colin Franklin, Director General of Space Programs in the Department of Communications, said in a presentation on the industrial opportunities in space that "we in Canada are members of a small group of nations, which have mastered the technology of the space age. We would do well to capitalize commercially on our experience as other nations prepare to enter space."[127] Marc Garneau's flight was also recognized as an act of joining "the club."[128] Being a member of the space club and making it as visible as possible became essential to Canadian decision-makers. The words of Ambassador Raymond Chretien elaborate more on this issue: "[Canada] is a country that wants to belong to as many clubs as possible. We are only 32 million people and the generations have influenced the world through membership in clubs ... So to belong to the space club fits nicely with the overall policy of exerting our influence through membership in various clubs."[129] Dr. Steve MacLean, explaining that Canada is a middle-level player with respect to others, added, " ... but if we show that we are an innovation-driven spacefaring nation, then that puts us at the table with respect to space, but it also allows us to be at the table for other things and for other relations, and that is because space is cross cutting."[130] In sum, club membership addresses a Canadian need to be recognized by others as a high profile country, and its association with other high members in the club serves to intensify the people's national esteem and pride in their country and its achievements. Therefore, it is expected of Canada to invest in a national space program if it aspires to upgrade its position.

Australia, on the other hand, did not attribute much value to these factors. At large, Australia's aspirations to a high status in global

---

[126] Interview with William (Mac) Evans.
[127] Franklin, C., "Industrial Opportunities in Space," in B. MacDonald, (ed.), *Canada's Strategy for Space*, (Toronto: The Canadian Institute of Strategic Studies, 1983), 54.
[128] Wallace, I., "Canadians are Slow to Get into Orbit," *The Globe & Mail*, October 4, 1984, 17.
[129] Interview with Ambassador Raymond Chretien, Canada's Ambassador to the US 1994–2000; Canada's Ambassador to France 2000–2003, November 5, 2008, Montreal, Canada.
[130] Interview with Dr. Steve MacLean, President of the Canadian Space Agency and former Canadian Astronaut, November 4, 2008, Montreal, Canada.

politics were low. Due to its more homogenous society and remote geography, Australia perceived itself as isolated, and adopted a space strategy of reliance on the United States. Australian leadership sees no national imperative to launch or operate satellites. They perceive Australia as a user and a customer of space systems and applications, not as a space manufacturer of an indigenous capacity. Hence, Australia expresses no aspirations to join the "club."

The statement on the first page of the Australian Government Space Engagement report of 2006 manifests well Australia's approach to space activity: "Space is important for Australians – we are sophisticated users of space … The government and private sector secure access to the benefits of space by participating in a range of international cooperative arrangements and by purchasing products and services in the domestic and global market place."[131] In November 2008, the Australian Senate Committee on Economics published a report on Australia's direction for space activity. The report presented a comparison with other countries' space activities, stating that "Australia is becoming unusual among its peers in not having a space program" and is the only OECD country without a space program of any sort. Moreover, even developing countries have more advanced space activities than Australia.[132]

The absence of an Australian aspiration to "join the club" compared to Canada's eagerness to be associated with this group suggests that despite the fact that they share tangible needs for space technology, Canada's and Australia's approaches to space are affected by significant differences that derive from different perspectives on their role and status in global politics. As a result, their interests and priorities toward space are different.

One of the eminent differences between Canada and Australia is their strategic location; while Australia is almost isolated in the southern hemisphere, Canada is located between Russia and the United States. This substantial difference has several facets: First, neighboring the United States puts Canada in a better position than Australia. After all, in the Cold War, it was in America's interest to prevent Canada from becoming a strategic liability. "The United States does not help Canada defend Canada; it helps Canada defend the United States."[133] This proximity allowed Canada to take advantage of the American space activity. The United States more easily opened up to Canada and shared its

---

[131] Australian Government Space Engagement, *Policy Framework and Overview*, Australian Government Department of Industry, Tourism and Resources, (November 2006), 1.
[132] The Senate Standing Committee on Economics, *Lost in Space*, 55.
[133] Dr. Joel Sokolsky, interviewed and cited by Blaxland, J., *Strategic Cousins*, 272

knowhow.[134] This also allowed Canada greater confidence in developing its own capacity and encouraged it to catch up. Although Australia is a close ally to the United States, it was never in such a favorable bargaining, nor did it enjoy American funds for scientific research the way Canada did in the 1950s.[135]

In the atmosphere of the early days of the Cold War, Australia's distance intensified Australian threat perceptions. Although its isolation was to some extent an equivocal factor, traditionally, Australia's foreign policy was always based on close relations with a powerful ally. During and after World War II, Australia's geo-strategic position in Asia called for a major ally to stand by it. Once Britain lost its greatness and was no longer in a position to provide Australia with a sense of security, Australia turned to the United States[136] but had to work harder to win American friendship.[137]

Second, in some cases being remote is an advantage while being so close to the United States is a burden. Australia's geographically remoteness from its European/Western partners leaves it with a sense of relative isolation that result in fewer concerns about its sovereignty.[138] According to White (2007), Australia felt no need to build forces to help fight the Soviet Union, and the United States did not press it to do so. "It seemed clear that any Australian military contribution to a global superpower war would be too small and come too late to count. We hosted important American-Australian joint facilities instead."[139]

In respect to space, Australia has leveraged its geography to considerable advantage, as it hosts satellite ground-stations that are essential to the national security of the United States. Gyngell and Wesley (2007) argued that the security of distance provided Australia with the psychological capacity to take risks with fewer consequences than others would find

---

[134] For example, the unique cooperation through NORAD allowed spinoffs that Canadian industry could use to build national capacity that also served the civilian market (not only in the field of space). Interview with Ambassador Paul Meyer.
[135] Interview with Professor Gordon Shepherd.
[136] Gelber, H. G., *The Australian-American Alliance – Costs and Benefits*, (Baltimore: Penguin Books, 1968), 34–35.
[137] For this reason, Australia allowed the United States (and also Britain) to operate parts of their space and nuclear programs in its territory and sent troops to participate in the American effort in Vietnam, while Canada did not. Hymans, J., *The Psychology of Nuclear Proliferation*, 123–124.
[138] Blaxland, J., *Strategic Cousins*, 272.
[139] White, H., "Four Decades of the Defense of Australia: Reflections on Australian Defense Policy Over the Past 40 Years," in R. Huisken, and M. Thatcher, (eds.), *History as Policy – Framing the Debate on the Future of Australia's Defense Policy*, (The Australian National University Press, 2007), 169.

comfortable.[140] This observation may explain why Australia allows itself to not have a national space program or national space capacity, something that many middle powers or regional powers pursue. The difference is especially noticeable when compared to Canada's geo-strategic situation, which made it perceive national space capability as so vital.

As discussed above, Canada's proximity to the United States is a traditional Canadian concern. The fundamental fact that Canada lives directly next to its major trading partner and ally, and is almost overshadowed by the United States on the international stage, has certainly added to Canadian angst and its desire to project its imprint on world politics and seek a high position among the nations of the world.[141] A visible space program that strives for a great deal of exposure and recognition as an independent and meaningful contributor to international endeavors serves this desire.

Another striking difference between Australia and Canada is the divided and dualistic culture produced by the French majority in Quebec. This has an effect on Canadian foreign and domestic policies that cannot be ignored. Canadian concern about national identity-building is in contrast to the somewhat homogenous nature of Australian society;[142] Australia often takes its own national coherence for granted.[143] In part, this has influenced Canadian interest in forging an independent identity distinct from both the British Commonwealth and the United States. The Canadian space program and especially its visible elements are used to enhance Canadian national esteem. This need does not exist in Australian society, as "nationalism in Australia is a social issue, not a governmental or state-oriented phenomenon."[144]

Finally, Australians are considered more pragmatic in their perspectives and policies than strategic. Australia does not seem to be interested in reducing its level of technological dependence and prefers to buy and adapt the technology needed.[145] In contrast, Canadian perspectives may be considered to be more strategic, attributing added values to the development of national skills and perceiving space activity as strategically substantial. In this respect, Australia is more similar in its approach to Britain, which also took a very pragmatic approach towards space. It may

---

[140] Gyngell, A., and Wesley, M., *Making Australian Foreign Policy*, Second Edition, (Cambridge: Cambridge University Press, 2007), 9–10.
[141] Blaxland, J., *Strategic Cousins*, 267.
[142] Several years ago, Australia changed its immigration regulations, opening its doors to immigrants from Asia. This changed somewhat the homogenous nature of the society.
[143] Blaxland, J., *Strategic Cousins*, 265.
[144] Albinski, H. S., *Politics and Foreign Policy in Australia*, (Durham, NC: Duke University Press, 1970), 3.
[145] Siemon, N., *Public Policy Planning*, 210.

be argued that Canada was pulled up by the American ambitious space program and was very much inspired by it and tried to "catch up."[146]

To conclude, Australia and Canada are different in their perceived roles in global politics. Therefore, different national narratives and political cultures associated with their perceived roles affect the way each country observes the values of a national space program and advanced indigenous capabilities. While Canada is seeking a global role and impact on world politics, Australia shows less interest and is more focused on its region – Asia. Australia perceives itself as an important force in the Pacific, as a bridge to Asia, and as a source of development. As a result, Canada finds it important to participate in international space ventures such as the ISS, even if such participation does not provide immediate concrete benefits to its citizens, while Australia sticks to tangible concrete services.

---

[146] David Greasley and Les Oxley suggest that Canada's and Australia's links with the United Kingdom and the United States shaped the comparative economic development of the two countries; see Greasley, D., and Oxley, L., "A Tale of Two Dominions: Comparing the Macroeconomic Records of Australia and Canada Since 1870," *Economic History Review*, 2, (1998), 294–318.

7   India and Israel

At first glance, India and Israel do not seem to have much in common that would justify their comparison. While India has a very large territory of 3,287,263 square kilometers, making it the seventh largest country in the world, Israel covers only 20,770 square kilometers (154th in the world). Their populations are not similar in size either. In 2015, India had a population of more than one billion people (1,251,695,584), while Israel's population was about 8 million people. The two countries also have very different gross domestic products per capita: India's GDP per capita is only US$6,300, while Israel's GDP per capita is US$33,400. Nevertheless, India and Israel do have many things in common that justify the comparison.[1]

First, India and Israel are two open, liberal, and democratic countries located in an undemocratic region. This realization has drawn the two nations closer. In the words of Pant (2004), India is the "first close friend Israel has to its east and Israel [is] the first close friend India has to its west."[2] Second, both Israel and India are ancient cultures in new countries that gained independence from the British Empire in almost contemporaneous struggles: India in 1947 and Israel in 1948.

Third, for many years they were considered to be developing countries. In this respect, India and Israel share a similar perspective on the role and importance of national investments in science and technology for self-reliance, which they see as key elements in national development. Israel's first premier, David Ben-Gurion, and India's first premier, Jawaharlal Nehru, shared the philosophy that through serious national investment in science and technology, fast development, national security, and social improvement are achievable. Over the

---

[1] Data presented here and in Table 7.1 were obtained from the online site of the CIA World Fact-book: "India," available at: www.cia.gov/library/publications/the-world-factbook/geos/in.html; and "Israel," available at: www.cia.gov/library/publications/the-world-factbook/geos/is.html, accessed on March 20, 2016.
[2] Pant, H. V., "India-Israel Partnership: Convergence and Constraints," *Middle East Review of International Affairs (MERIA)*, 4, (December 2004), 63.

Table 7.1 *Comparison of India and Israel, Selected Parameters*

	India		Israel	
Total area	3,287,263 sq. km		20,770 sq. km	
Population (July 2015 est.)	1,251,695,584		8,049,314	
GDP per capita in US$ (2015 est.)	$6,300		$34,300	
GDP composition by sector (2015 est.)	*Agriculture:*	16.1%	*Agriculture:*	2.5%
	Industry:	29.5%	*Industry:*	27.5%
	Services:	54.4%	*Services:*	70%
Military expenditure (2014 est.)	2.4% of GDP		5.58% of GDP	

years, the two nations have invested a great deal in the development of science and technology in the hopes that it would speed up national development and bring prosperity. The technology-based industries developed in India and in Israel over the last two decades indicate how successful this approach was.

Fourth, in geo-political terms, India and Israel each play the role of a regional power in Southeast Asia and in the Middle East (respectively). During the Cold War, these two areas were seriously affected by the struggle between the two superpowers. Since their establishment, India and Israel have both been faced with severe national security challenges imposed on them by their neighbors and have suffered terrorist attacks by various local Muslim groups. During the years of the Cold War, both of them suffered several wars that brought about intervention of the superpowers, including arms embargos. In this context, the principle of self-reliance, especially in the development of arms, guides decision-making in both countries vis-à-vis defense issues and even serves as a strong impetus for collaboration between them.

India and Israel are not parties to some of the basic arms control treaties, in particular, treaties concerning weapons of mass destruction (WMD) such as the NPT, which is a universal international treaty joined by a very large number of countries.[3] In the nuclear

---

[3] The only countries that are not parties to this treaty are India, Pakistan, Israel, South Sudan, and North Korea, which withdrew from the NPT in 2003.

context, India tested nuclear weapons, leaving no room for doubt regarding its capabilities. Israel, on the other hand, maintains a policy of ambiguity.[4] India and Israel are commonly referred to as responsible countries concerning WMD. In addition, up until June 2016, both countries had not been members of the MTCR, but they had adhered to the regime by incorporating its lists into their national legislation.[5] In June 2016, India joined the MTCR, and Israel remains adherent to the regime.[6]

With regards to space, the rationale for a small state like Israel and a poor nation like India to bear the high costs and risks involved in undertaking such a large-scale project is not obvious. In spite of all difficulties, or as some may say because of them, in the 1980s, India was the seventh country to successfully put a satellite in orbit. In 1988, Israel became the eighth country to succeed in this mission. In India and in Israel, the journey into space was initiated by the need to increase capabilities for tangible and pragmatic uses, but their paths subsequently diverged. India's approach toward space activity became much more strategic and ambitious. Succeeding Indian governments perceived space activity as a prominent part of India's statehood and status in the international arena and as a key to its national development. For this reason, India's space program includes space exploration missions, heavy-lift space-launch vehicles, as well as the development of an Indian satellite navigation system, efforts which are not within the scope of Israel's space program. Understanding the logic and motivations in India and in Israel to undertake the mission of a national space program requires in-depth examination. This chapter seeks to inquire about and illuminate the logic and motivation in India and in Israel to develop national space programs and socially construct national achievements in space as an act of joining the space club.

---

[4] Cohen, A., *Israel and the Bomb*, (New York: Columbia University Press, 1998); and Cohen, A., *The Worst Kept Secret: Israel's Bargain with the Bomb*, (New York: Columbia University Press, 2010).

[5] India's national export control list (SCOMET) is on par with the MTCR lists. For more information, see India's 2013 report to the Security Council Committee established pursuant to resolution 1540. The report is available at: daccess-dds-ny.un.org/doc/UNDOC/GEN/N14/205/54/PDF/N1420554.pdf?OpenElement, accessed June 7, 2015; Israel's 2014 report to the 1540 committee indicates a similar approach and policies. The report is available at: daccess-dds-ny.un.org/doc/UNDOC/GEN/N13/201/01/PDF/N1320101.pdf?OpenElement, accessed on June 7, 2015.

[6] Bhattacherjee, K., "India Joins Missile Technology Control Regime," *The Hindu*, June 27, 2016, available at: http://www.thehindu.com/news/national/%E2%80%8BIndia-joins-Missile-Technology-Control-Regime.-Top-5-things-to-know/article14405165.ece, accessed on December 23, 2016.

India Goes into Space

In India, the scientific research of space can be traced back centuries. Rocketry, too, was mastered in India long before it was developed in Europe.[7] India's modern involvement in space research and technology goes back to the early days of the space age. In the 1950s, Professor Vikram Sarabhai, known as the father of India's space program, established the Physical Research Laboratory (PRL); when the International Geophysical Year (IGY) was announced, he got involved in space research.[8] After the first Sputnik was launched, Sarabhai suggested to the Indian government that it consider developing a satellite.[9] In 1958, about a year after the launch of Sputnik, Prime Minister Nehru approved a scientific policy resolution in the Indian parliament stating that "the key to national prosperity, apart from the spirit of people, lies in the modern age, in the effective combination of three factors– technology, raw material and capital– of which the first is perhaps the most important ... But technology can only grow out of the study of science and its applications."[10] The resolution clearly states that the Indian government's prime motivation for investing significant national resources in science and technology stems from the objective to catch up to the developed countries:

> The gap between the advanced and backward countries has widened more and more. Only by adopting the most vigorous measures and by putting forward our utmost effort into the development of science, can we bridge the gap ... Our national goals involve leapfrogging from a state of economic backwardness and social disabilities, attempting to achieve in a few decades a change which has historically taken centuries in other lands.[11]

---

[7] For further reading, see Moltz, J. C., *Asia's Space Race – National Motivations, Regional Rivalries, and International Risks*, (New York: Columbia University Press, 2012), 112–113; and Nair, K.K., *Space – the Frontiers of Modern Defence*, (New Delhi: Knowledge World: 2006), 2–3.

[8] Arnold Frutkin describes the positive effect of the IGY on acquiring public and governmental support in developing countries like India, in his 1965 book *International Cooperation in Space*, (Englewood Cliffs, NJ: Prentice-Hall, 1965), 23.

[9] Harvey, B., Smid, H. H. F., and Pirad, T., *Emerging Space Powers – The New Space Programs of Asia, the Middle East, and South America*, (Chichester, UK: Springer and Praxis Publishing: 2010), 143.

[10] Scientific Policy Resolution, New Delhi, India, (March 4, 1958). Available on the website of the Department of Science and Technology of India at: dst.gov.in/stsysindia/spr1958.htm, accessed on February 16, 2008.

[11] Scientific Policy Resolution.

In practice, the Indian government committed to offer "good conditions of service to scientists, according them honoured positions, by associating scientists with the formulation of policies."[12]

In 1961, the responsibility for space research was awarded to the Department of Atomic Energy (DAE) headed by Dr. Homi Bhabha.[13] The same year, Sarabhai presented a proposal to the Indian government to develop a small and focused space program oriented toward development. The government approved his proposal.[14] A year later, in 1962, the Indian National Committee on Space Research (INCOSPAR) was established under the auspices of the DAE. Chaired by Dr. Vikram Sarabhai,[15] INCOSPAR's task was to advise the government on space research, promote international collaboration, and participate in international activities.[16] Sarabhai focused India's efforts in space on applications of advanced technologies for mitigating real problems of the developing population. Sarabhai rejected India's involvement in a space race with other spacefaring nations.[17] Nevertheless, he proclaimed that in the field of applications, India should be second to none.

At the time, India suffered major problems of poverty, underdevelopment, and security. In 1962, a war took place between China and India, and India was defeated. The defeat took India by surprise and resulted in a quest for empowerment, triggering the need to use science and technology for defense purposes.[18] Against this background of the need and desire to develop India, the Indian space program began to operate. At first, many of its projects were within the framework of international cooperation. India collaborated with the United States, France, and the Soviet Union on various projects, including the development and launch of sounding rockets in the launch field of Thumba. In this capacity, Indian scientists and engineers were trained at NASA.[19]

---

[12] Rao, P. V. M., "No Ambiguity of Purpose – The Indian Space Programme," in P. V. M. Rao, (ed.), *50 Years of Space – A Global Perspective*, (Hyderabad: Universities Press, 2007), 212.

[13] Nuclear science in India began in the 1940s, before India's independence. It was led by Dr. Homi Bhabha, who is considered to be the father of India's nuclear program and is one of the country's leading scientists. For further reading on the early days of India's nuclear effort, see Marwah, O., "India's Nuclear and Space Programs: Intent and Policy," *International Security*, 2:2, (Fall 1977), 96–121.

[14] Harvey, B., Smid, H. H. F., and Pirad, T., *Emerging Space Powers*, 143.

[15] Rao, P.V.M., "No Ambiguity of Purpose," 212.

[16] Harvey, B., Smid, H. H. F., and Pirad, T., *Emerging Space Powers*, 144.

[17] Moltz, J. C., *Asia's Space Race*, 114.

[18] Krige, J., Callahan, A. L., and Maharaj, A., *NASA in the World*, (New York: Palgrave Macmillan, 2013), 213.

[19] For a comprehensive analysis of the cooperation between NASA and India, see Krige, J., Callahan, A. L., and Maharaj, A., *NASA in the World*, 211–248. Dr. A. P. J. Abdul Kalam, who is one of India's leading missiles and space scientists and from 2002 to 2007

On November 21, 1963, India launched its first sounding rocket from Thumba.[20] The rocket, Nike Apache, was made by NASA and assembled in India. After the successful launch, Sarabhai shared his dream of an Indian satellite launch vehicle with his colleagues.[21] For this reason, in 1966, Sarabhai set up the Space Science and Technology Center (SSTC); its mandate was to conduct R&D on rocket systems and components in order to eventually develop indigenous satellite launch capability.[22] A year later, in 1967, the first Indian-made sounding rocket, Rohini 75, was launched from Thumba. In order to upgrade space activity in India, Professor Sarabhai suggested to NASA that the Thumba launch field be offered for international use. Arnold Frutkin, who was the NASA executive responsible for cooperation with other countries during the 1960s and 1970s, argued in his 1965 book that "what began as a bilateral effort, with relatively narrow technical objectives, has grown through a process of inexorable technical and political appeal to the point where major nations, including the Soviet Union, find it important to join in."[23] Despite the successful launch of sounding rockets from Thumba, in the beginning, Sarabhai focused the Indian space program on the development of satellite communication services and on Earth observation; it was clear that satellites could be developed faster, especially with the help of one of India's international partners.[24] In the late 1960s and through the 1970s, India began to develop its own space launch capabilities.

After China performed its first nuclear test on October 16, 1964, India became deeply concerned about its security and about the positive effect the Chinese experiment had had on China's status and prestige.[25] Developing nuclear weapons was thus seriously considered. In order to

was president of India, describes his training at NASA in his autobiography *Wings of Fire*, (Hyderabad: Universities Press, 30th impression), 37–39.

[20] The rocket reached 200 kilometers. India's achievement was eclipsed by the assassination of US President John F. Kennedy the following day. Harvey, B., Smid, H. H. F., and Pirad, T., *Emerging Space Powers*, 146.

[21] As a young rocket scientist, Former President of India A. P. J. Abdul Kalam was in charge of rocket integration and safety. He describes this in his autobiography, *Wings of Fire*, (39–40).

[22] Rao, P. V. M., "No Ambiguity of Purpose," 217.

[23] Frutkin, A., *International Cooperation in Space*, (Englewood Cliffs, NJ: Prentice-Hall, 1965), 62.

[24] Harvey, B., Smid, H. H. F., and Pirad, T., *Emerging Space Powers*, 158.

[25] For example, in a conversation with American diplomats, former defense minister of India V. K. Krishna Menon accused the United States of enhancing the prestige China had won. He felt this helped prompt demands in India for a bomb. Retrieved from a report by First Secretary at the US Embassy, Harald Jacobson, to the Department of State on Krishna Menon's views, December 2, 1964, NARA, RG-59, DOS, Box 1655-Def-Armament.

prevent India from producing nuclear weapons, under the premise that the United States would not extend a strategic umbrella over India, the US Department of State focused on building up India's science and technology to afford it international prestige.

This was a strong impetus for the United States to enhance space cooperation with India. A telegram from the Department of State to the embassy in India, dated December 12, 1964, stated that "our first need is to probe and if necessary to direct GOI thoughts in this area. If GOI has recognized and weighed full dimensions of their prestige problem, they are probably looking for ways to deal with it and may be receptive to our help."[26] It was then specifically indicated in the telegram that the United States would be willing to "jointly explore the possibility of developing one or more ventures in fields [of] peaceful uses of nuclear energies and space technology that would serve [to] highlight India's capabilities."[27]

In February 1965, Dr. Homi Bhabha, Secretary of India's Department of Atomic Energy, in which the space program operated, met with United States Under Secretary of State George Ball and explained India's approach regarding nuclear proliferation. Bhabha argued that India needed to produce some dramatic "peaceful" scientific achievement to offset the prestige gained by China. He expressed his view that a way must be found for a nation to gain as much by not developing nuclear weapons as it might by developing them.[28] In talking to NASA officials, Bhabha and Sarabhai discussed the possibilities of cooperation between India and the United States in building a launch vehicle as a potential response to the loss of prestige to China; the discussion centered on procurement of the all-solid four-stage Scout rocket technology.[29]

On May 14, 1965, China conducted a second nuclear test. In late June 1965, it was reported that Bhabha was pressing Indian Prime Minister Lal Bahadur Shastri very hard for permission to test a nuclear device later that year.[30] In the summer of 1965, Pakistan invaded India, and a war broke out between the two countries over Kashmir. Although the superpowers imposed a ceasefire, it was clear

---

[26] Telegram from the Department of State to the Embassy in India regarding upcoming meeting with India's Prime Minister Shastri, dated December 12, 1964, NARA, RG-59, DOS, Box 1655-Def-12- Armament.
[27] Telegram from the Department of State to the Embassy in India.
[28] Memorandum of conversation, Washington, February 22, 1965. NARA, RG-59, Central Files, 1964–1966, DEF-12-1 India.
[29] Krige, J., Callahan, A. L, and Maharaj, A., *NASA in the World*, 226.
[30] Memorandum for the record on Indian nuclear capability from a luncheon conversation at the pentagon by nuclear theorist Herman Kahn, June 29, 1965, NARA, RG-59, DOS, box 1655-Def 12, India.

that India had been the victor, thus establishing itself as a regional power that could not be ignored by the international community.

A few months later, in January 1966, Bhabha died in a plane crash and was replaced by Sarabhai as Chairman of the Atomic Energy Commission. In March 1966, India's new prime minister, Indira Gandhi, was invited to Washington to conduct high-level dialogue on the future of Indo-US relations. A few days before her visit, in a meeting of top American officials from the National Aeronautics and Space Council (NASC) discussed ways to further space cooperation, giving considerable attention to the potential value of the substitution of space technology for weapons proliferation and production. They specifically discussed the possibility of offering cooperation on space to India.[31]

On May 9, 1966, China conducted its third nuclear test. Despite the United States' desire to prevent India from acquiring nuclear weapons, it was not willing to cooperate with India on strategic issues such as space launch technology. Therefore, cooperation in space was limited to scientific and technological projects. On May 19, 1966, NASA Administrator James Webb wrote to U. Alexis Johnson, Deputy Under Secretary for Political Affairs at the State Department, suggesting that NASA would cooperate with India on a communications satellite. The project would enable India to test the benefits of direct broadcasting as well as to reinforce the Indian electronics industry. As part of the project, the United States would construct and launch a geostationary communications satellite that would broadcast to India. For its part, India would set up receiving stations.[32] NASA and India began discussions on possibilities for cooperation, which eventually matured and became known as project Satellite Instructional Television Experiment (SITE).[33]

In 1967, talks began on the possible development of a 30-kg Indian satellite. The long-term goal was to indigenously develop a satellite that would carry a communication payload for television services or a remote-sensing payload. However, these kinds of payloads were too heavy. Therefore, it was decided to begin with a small scientific payload. In 1968, Sarabhai put together a unit under the Physical Research Laboratory to develop remote sensing capabilities in India.[34]

---

[31] Space Council Meeting March 23, 1966, Memorandum for the President From the Vice President, March 28, 1966, p. 1. Johnson Library Archives, White House Central Files Exec FG 11-4 6/1/65-1/4/166 Box 62.

[32] Logsdon, J., Day, D., and Launius, R.D. (eds.) (1996), *Exploring the Unknown – Selected*, 24.

[33] For more information on SITE see: Krige, J., Callahan, A. L., and Maharaj, A., 235–248.

[34] Harvey, B., Smid, H. H. F., and Pirad, T. *Emerging Space Powers*, 152, 158.

In August 1969, the Indian space program was separated from the DAE, and the Indian Space Research Organization (ISRO) was established. Professor Sarabhai prepared a ten-year profile for space research in India. The plan centered on the early ideas developed under INCOSPAR; it included utilizing satellites for television and developmental education, meteorological observations and remote sensing for managing natural resources, as well as the development of satellite launch vehicles.[35] Dr. Abdul Kalam, former president of India and one of its chief rocket scientists, who worked closely with Sarabhai, explained that the emphasis in the plan was on self-reliance and indigenous technologies and that active international cooperation, which was dominant in the early years, was gradually eased out.[36]

In April 1970, China launched its first satellite into space. China's achievement intensified India's need and aspiration to equalize its status with that of China. Perkovich (1999) argued that this raised the "specter of a significant Chinese ballistic missile capability to launch nuclear warheads at distant targets." He then cites the Indian Institute of Public Opinion: "We felt humbled for having lost a race we never chose to enter."[37] In May 1970, Sarabhai presented to the government his ten-year profile for the development of atomic energy and space research in India. In July 1970, it was published and became known as the Sarabhai Profile. The profile emphasized three objectives for space research: satellites for communications; development and utilization of meteorological satellites; and application of remote sensing technology. The plan was to launch India's first satellite in 1974 aboard an Indian-made launcher.[38]

In August 1971, India signed a twenty-year treaty of peace and friendship with the Soviet Union. In December 1971, India and Pakistan fought over Bangladesh. After the war, India strengthened its relationship with the Soviet Union to accelerate the modernization of India, decision made easy due to the Soviet's anti-Chinese policies. In 1972, in another outcome of the war, ISRO was placed under the Department of Space, which was under the office of the prime minister.[39] In 1974, India conducted a peaceful nuclear experiment.[40] On April 19, 1975, the Aryabhata, India's first satellite carrying a scientific payload, was launched by the

---

[35] For the history of space remote sensing in India, see Savant, S. S., and Seelan, S. K., "India's Remote-Sensing Program – A Historical Perspective," *Quest*, 24:4, 2005, 26–33.
[36] Abdul-Kalam, A. P. J., *Wings of Fire*, 52.
[37] Perkovich, G., *India's Nuclear Bomb*, (Berkeley: University of California Press, 1999), 151.
[38] Ibid., 152–155.
[39] Harvey, B., Smid, H. H. F., and Pirad, T., *Emerging Space Powers*, 158–159.
[40] India referred to this experiment as a peaceful test. Nevertheless, most countries perceived it as a nuclear weapons test.

Soviet Union. In 1979, India's second satellite, the Bhaskhara 1, was also launched by the Soviet Union. In July 1980, India successfully launched its first indigenous satellite aboard its indigenously built launcher.[41]

In the 1980s, the Indian program focused on larger, more powerful and mission-specific systems. India initiated the development of the Polar Space Launch Vehicle (PSLV), designed for the launch of remote sensing satellites. In 1988, India completed the development of its first remote sensing satellite, the IRS 1, which was launched by the Soviet Union. India also initiated the development of the heavy-lift Geosynchronous Space Launch Vehicle (GSLV), which was designed to launch geosynchronous communication and meteorological satellites.[42] In the 1990s, India upgraded its satellite technology and launch technology. In 1993, the PSLV was successfully tested. A year later, India successfully placed a satellite into orbit. In 1999, the PSLV carried its first commercial payload into space. In the 2000s, India improved its relations with the United States and entered into scientific cooperation with it. It also cooperated with other countries, including Israel: in 2008, India launched Israel's satellite TecSAR.[43]

For decades, the Indian space program was focused on projects that were designated to provide tangible goods, such as remote sensing on Earth, communications, weather forecasts, and so forth, all aimed at serving the developing Indian society and economy. On this basis, India expanded its program to include commercial space activity, including commercial launch service. Furthermore, in recent years India's pragmatic and development-oriented approach has changed to include objectives such as space exploration and strategic-military capabilities. India's military space actions include the launch of reconnaissance satellites, the development and deployment of precision navigation satellites, and the planning of ASAT capability.[44] On the organizational level, India initiated a military space command. Moltz (2012) explained the shift in the Indian approach toward military activity in space in (a) China's rise, (b) the US rapprochement with India, (c) the 1999 Kargil clash in which India did not have space

---

[41] For a detailed description of the history of the Indian space program in the context of developing the capability to launch objects into space, see Abdul-Kalam, A. P. J., and Tiwari, A., *Wings of Fire*, (Hyderabad, Universities Press, 1999).

[42] Mistry, D., "The Geo-Strategic Implications of India's Space Program," *Asian Survey*, (November–December 2001), 41:6, 1026.

[43] Moltz, J. C., *Asia's Space Race*, 121–125.

[44] For a review and discussion of India's shift toward military space activities, see the special issue of *India Review*, 10:4, 2011.

surveillance capabilities, and (d) India's general effort to increase its indigenous military technology.[45]

As for space exploration, Moltz asserted that China's increasing efforts and visible achievements in space exploration and human spaceflight put pressure on India to follow this path as well, in order to remain a leading space faring nation in Asia.[46] The Indian civil space program expanded, and it now includes missions to the Moon and Mars as well as other scientific endeavors. In 2008, India launched the Chandrayaan 1 mission, its first lunar mission. In December 2013, India launched the Mangalyaan Mars Mission, which entered Mars's orbit in September 2014, awarding India much international acclaim and prestige. The success of the mission proved that even with a modest budget, significant achievements can be accomplished.[47] As a result, India is advancing plans for an exploratory mission to Venus.[48]

Planning for the future, India wants to strengthen its domestic space industry.[49] India continues to reinforce its array of launchers, primarily the GSLV, which can be used to send astronauts into space.[50] In December 2014, India succeeded in launching a capsule, and it returned to earth, an important step in attaining human flights.[51] Regarding space security, India is getting closer to the United States.[52]

---

[45] Moltz, J. C., *Asia's Space Race*, 110, 122, 127–131.
[46] Moltz, J. C., *Asia's Space Race*, 110–111.
[47] Choudhury, S. and Sugden, J., "How India Mounted the World's Cheapest Mission to Mars," *India Real Time*, September 23, 2014, available at: blogs.wsj.com/indiarealtime/2014/09/23/how-india-mounted-the-worlds-cheapest-mission-to-mars/, accessed on September 30, 2014.
[48] Staff Writers, "After Mars, Indian Space Agency Aims at Venus," *Space Daily*, May 25, 2015, available at: www.spacedaily.com/reports/After_Mars_Indian_Space_Agency_Aims_at_Venus_999.html, accessed on February 8, 2016.
[49] de Selding, P. B., "For Airbus, Modi Visit Opens Door To Building Larger Satellites in India," *Space News*, April 13, 2015, available at: spacenews.com/for-airbus-modi-visit-opens-door-to-building-larger-satellites-in-india/, accessed on February 8, 2016.
[50] "India Test Fires New Engine for GSLV," *Spacenews*, 26:17, May 4, 2015, 9; Nowakowski, T., "ISRO Successfully Tests its GSLV Mk III Cryogenic Engine," *Spaceflight Insider*, March 16, 2015, available at: www.spaceflightinsider.com/organizations/isro/isro-successfully-tests-its-gslv-mk-iii-cryogenic-engine/, accessed on February 8, 2016.
[51] Staff Writers, "India Launches Biggest ever Rocket into Space," *Space Daily*, December 18, 2014, available at: www.spacedaily.com/reports/India_launches_biggest_ever_rocket_into_space_999.html Accessed on December 24.
[52] Rose, F. A. "US-India Space Security Cooperation: A Partnership for the 21st Century," *Space War*, March 13, 2015, available at: www.spacewar.com/reports/US_India_Space_Security_Cooperation_A_Partnership_for_the_21st_Century_999.html, accessed on February 8, 2016.

India's Motivations: National Development in Search of an International Role

Through the successful launching of SLV-3 in July 1980, India attained indigenous launch capability ... [and] became an exclusive member of the space club.[53]

A. P. J. Abdul Kalam

The key figures involved in the decision to develop India's space program were Dr. Vikram Sarabhai, Dr. Homi Bhabha, and India's first prime minister, Jawaharlal Nehru. The three viewed national investment in science and technology as a means to achieve national development and prosperity. Under their leadership, India began its journey into space. For Nehru, science and technology were key in enabling India to leap frog the years and become a developed country quickly. Bhabha, a world-renowned scientist, had tremendous influence on Nehru, convincing him that it was necessary for India to develop nuclear and space programs.[54] Sarabhai, who directed the program in its early days, focused India's space program on applications, but for what end? Was it merely to provide tangible goods to the Indian people?

Sarabhai's vision was to develop mass communication, particularly television, throughout India, and to use Earth observation satellites to monitor and manage the country's natural resources, so as to ensure that the country derived maximum benefit. Nevertheless, national development through space had another complementary objective. The space program offered India, still a developing country, the opportunity to bypass the intermediate-technology stage and move directly into the high-technology era. Thus, India would swiftly be recognized as having a lofty status in the community of nations.[55]

This was not purely for prestige reasons; Harvey (2000) asserted that "Sarabhai set himself resolutely against the use of space programs for prestige purposes, as some form of national virility symbol. Instead, they had to be harnessed for the immediate, practical needs of the people, an ever-greater imperative in the case of a developing country."[56] Nevertheless, it is evident from Sarabhai's words of that in addition to bringing tangible goods and prosperity to Indian people, India's space program was also guided by strategic motivations to place India in a high position in the international community:

---

[53] Kalam, A., and Pillai, S., *Envisioning an Empowered Nation – Technology for Societal Transformation*, (New Delhi: Tata McGraw-Hill Publishing Company, 2004), 124.
[54] Rao, P. V. M., "No Ambiguity of Purpose," 211.
[55] Sheehan, M., *The International Politics of Space*, (London: Routledge, 2007), 146
[56] Harvey, B., *The Japanese and Indian Space Programs: Two Roads into Space*, (Chichester, UK: Springer-Praxis, 2000), 129.

There are some who question the relevance of space activities in a developing nation. To us, there is no ambiguity of purpose. We do not have the fantasy of competing with the economically advanced nations in the exploration of the Moon or the planets or manned space-flight. But we are convinced that if we are to play a meaningful role nationally, and in the community of nations, we must be second to none in the application of advanced technologies to the real problems of man and society.[57]

In another statement, Sarabhai said that:

In appreciating the value of space activities to a developing nation, one should recognize some inherent problems. They arise from the glamour that is associated with space activities. There is a real danger that developing nations may adopt a space program largely for this glamour, devoting resources not through a recognition of the values of which we are talking about here, but from a desire to create a sham image nationally and internationally. International cooperation in space activities may stimulate this state of affairs.[58]

Sarabhai did not reject space development for political reasons. He refused to use the space program only for prestige, but it was clear that for him, tangible and advanced space capabilities should be used by India for political objectives.

Abdul Kalam took a similar approach when he explained why Nehru and Sarabhai decided to develop an indigenous space program in India. He argued that:

very many individuals with myopic vision questioned the relevance of space activities in a newly independent nation which was finding it difficult to feed its population. But neither Prime Minister Nehru nor Professor Sarabhai had any ambiguity of purpose. Their vision was very clear: if Indians were to play a meaningful role in the community of nations, they must be second to none in the application of advanced technologies to their real life problems. They had no intention of using it merely as a means to display our might.[59]

As a leader of the non-aligned group in the Cold War, India had to avoid a position of dependency. For this reason, Moltz (2012) argued that India worked its way to a middle ground between the two superpowers.[60] Achieving this goal demanded at least partial self-reliance in the scientific and technological fields of nuclear energy, space, and rocketry, the most

---

[57] Rao, U. R., "India's Space Program – Past, Present and Future," *Harvard Asian Pacific Review*, 9:2, (Spring 2008), 24.
[58] Sarabhai, V., "Space Activity for Developing Countries," in *Science Policy and National Development*, (New Delhi: Macmillan, 1974), 23 (series of Sarabhai's papers published after his death in 1971). This chapter appeared in the Impact of Space Exploration on Society, Vol. 8, Science and Technology, Series of the American Astronautical Society, California 1966.
[59] Abdul-Kalam A. P. J., and Tiwari, A., *Wings of Fire*, 43.
[60] Moltz, J. C., *Asia's Space Race*, 114.

significant means and symbol of power in the Cold War (and today). Indian leadership asserted that mastering these fields would assure India the freedom of action it needed as a non-aligned nation; as Indira Gandhi put it, "We want India to be self-reliant and to strengthen its independence so that it cannot be pressurized by anybody."[61] The wars experienced by India in 1962, 1965, and 1971, which were followed by great international pressure on India, enhanced this conviction among Indian leaders.[62] Abdul Kalam clearly explained this approach in his autobiography: "The bitter lessons of the two wars in 1962 and 1965 had left the Indian leadership with little choice in the matter of achieving self-reliance in military hardware and weapon systems."[63]

The tangible goods India accumulates from its space program have substantial benefits for its foreign policy and its defense strategy. For example, India's capability in space technology reinforces political and economic ties with other spacefaring nations that India considers to be its peers. India's technological autonomy in developing advanced satellites and launching them into space greatly enhances India's projection of power and serves as a force multiplier affecting the strategic balance in Asia.[64]

In addition, indigenous production capacity of arms and other highly advanced technologies, including space, has taken on symbolic importance for India. Although Kinsella and Chima (2001) focused on the Indian logic for military industrialization and nuclear development, their argument that indigenous development in India is a currency of power is relevant in the case of India's logic to develop a space program: "If India wants to become a 'first class nation', or even if India aspires to 'mini-power status', it cannot rely on imported weaponry because 'real' power requires something more."[65] Indian foreign policy under Indira Gandhi, they proclaimed, has received much attention on this score. To stress this point further, they cite the words of Sisir Gupta, an Indian diplomat and academician, who wrote about the nuclear issue in 1965. Gupta referred to India as the "sixth power in a world where only five are recognized to be great" and suggested that India could "either enter the club by defying the world and making a bomb or see to it that the

---

[61] Shashi, T., *Reasons of State: Political Development and India's Foreign Policy under Indira Gandhi, 1966–1977* (New-Delhi: Vikras, 1982), 88.
[62] Kinsella, D., and Chima, J., "Symbols of Statehood: Military Industrialization and Public Discourse in India," *Review of International Studies*, 27, (2001), 356–357.
[63] Abdul-Kalam, A. P. J., and Tiwari, A., *Wings of Fire*, 54.
[64] Mistry, D., "The Geo-Strategic Implications," 1042; Paikowsky, D., and Ben-Israel, I., "India's Space Program – An Israeli Perspective on Regional Security," *India Review*, 10:4, (October–December, 2011), 394–405.
[65] Kinsella, D., and Chima, J., "Symbols of Statehood," 368.

bomb as a status symbol loses its significance because of effective progress towards disarmament; he was skeptical regarding the latter option because 'military capability remains the most important source of a country's status, prestige and power'.[66] His observation of India's strategic situation illuminates the perception of the Indian leadership regarding India's international status; this observation is also relevant for India's space program.

Thirty years later, in 1998, India's Foreign Minister Jaswant Singh expressed the same rationale when he said in a radio interview that:

> we cannot have a situation in which some countries say, "We have a permanent right to these symbols of deterrence and power; all the rest of you ... do not have that right. We will decide what your security is and how you are to deal with that security." A country the size of India – not simply a sixth of the human race but also an ancient civilization – cannot in this fashion abdicate its responsibility.[67]

An analysis of India's space effort through the prism of the politics of clubs supports the second hypothesis, i.e. that nations that aspire to upgrade their power and international standing will develop national space capabilities and thereby try to join the club. The evidence provided above shows that Indian leadership accepted the perception that advanced national space capability is a prerequisite for claiming the status of a power. Therefore, India's motivation to embark on a national space program results from its perception of what the international community expects of it, and of what India and the Indian people expect of themselves. The Indian nation's motivation to excel in science and technology in general stems not only from a tangible objective to achieve fast development, but also from a more intangible objective: to upgrade India's role as a leader in scientific research. Although India is a young state, it is an old nation. India's people and its political, economic, and scientific leadership take pride in being the descendants of a people with a history of cultural and scientific achievement that goes back hundreds of years.[68]

For example, Kinsella and Chima (2001) also pointed out the role of domestic considerations and proclaimed that "domestic weapons production seems to have been partly motivated by the desire to enhance

---

[66] Gupta, S., "India and the International System," in M. S. Rajan and Shivaji Ganguly (eds.) (New Delhi: Vikas, 1981), 243, cited in Kinsella, D., Chima, J., "Symbols of Statehood," 357.

[67] His statement is cited in Tellis, A. J., *India's Emerging Nuclear Posture: Between Recessed Deterrence and Ready Arsenal* (Arlington, VA: RAND, 2001), 151.

[68] For example, the Indian astronomer Aryabhata, who lived in the fifth century, discovered that the Earth revolves around the sun about 1,000 years before the same conclusion was reached by Europeans.

India in the eyes of Indians themselves."[69] They asserted that this was a recurrent theme in Indira Gandhi's defense policy. For example, in a 1968 interview, Gandhi lamented that "our intellectuals, our industrialists and businessman do not yet feel proud of being Indians."[70] With regards to space, Sarabhai called upon Indian scientists abroad to return to India and participate in the process of nation-building.[71] They reached the conclusion, that in addition to self-image as a symbolic theme, "it is evident that in the public discourse in India, there is an apparent preoccupation with what it takes to become a member of the ... 'exclusive club' of nation-states."[72]

Israel's Space Program

Since the early days of the race to space, Israel's political and scientific leadership acknowledged the importance of space. As early as 1960, the Israeli Academy of Science and Humanities established the National Committee for Space Research. The Committee was responsible for research and educational projects in Israel, as well as for relations with similar institutions and organizations abroad. However, it did not form a national space program.[73] Back then, the only major national effort in the field of space was the launch of the Shavit 2 sounding rocket on July 5, 1961.

The launch was in response to Egypt's recruitment of German missile scientists to boost its missile program, which raised fear in Israel.[74] Israeli leadership decided to balance the situation and sustain Israel's deterrence by making sure that Israel would be the first to demonstrate such capability.[75] In a statement to *Haaretz* (an Israeli daily newspaper) Prime Minister David Ben-Gurion, who was present at the launch site, said that Israel's launching of Shavit 2 had no military significance. He continued by saying that the launch indicates the scientific abilities of Israel's young scientists and shows what they could achieve in the future.[76]

---

[69] Kinsella, D., and Chima, J., "Symbols of Statehood," 358.
[70] Quoted in Ibid.
[71] Harvey, B., Smid, H. H. F., Pirad, T., *Emerging Space Powers*, 142.
[72] Kinsella, D., and Chima, J., "Symbols of Statehood," 370.
[73] For a review of the history of Israel's space effort, see: Paikowsky, D., "From the Shavit-2 to Ofeq-1- A History of the Israeli Space Effort," *Quest*, 18:4, (Fall 2011), 4–12.
[74] Meir (Munya) Mardor, first General Director of Rafael, which developed the rocket, explains in his book that the launch was part of the "desire to stay ahead of the Egyptians and deny them the political, psychological, and morale benefits, especially in the eyes of other Arab states." Mardor, M., (1981), *Rafael – On the Path of R&D for the Security of Israel*, (Tel Aviv: Maarachot Ministry of Defense Press), 319.
[75] Interview with Israel's President Shimon Peres, January 18, 2008, Jerusalem.
[76] Also present were Deputy Defense Minister Shimon Peres, Minister of Foreign Affairs Golda Meir, Chief of Staff Lieutenant General Zvi Zur, Deputy Chief of Staff Major

The reports in the Israeli media echoed this message by emphasizing the fact that Israel was the seventh state to indigenously launch such a rocket. For example it was reported in the Israeli broadcasting service in Arabic that:

> at dawn today, the first Israeli space rocket was launched into space ... Israel, the dynamic country which is 13 years old and has accomplished more than what other countries have achieved in centuries, would not remain backward in the open field of science. Israel ... will spare no effort to stand on the same level with the countries whose scientific achievements speak for them."[77]

The use of club rhetoric was used to convey a communicative message to socially construct this achievement as a legitimate projection of capability and enhance national self-esteem.

Another twenty years would pass before a national space program would be established. During these years, several attempts were made by scientists and officials to push for a national research program that would include a satellite, but none of these plans matured. Things started to change in favor of a national space program after the 1973 "Yom Kippur War," which had a tremendous impact on Israel in many ways. The coordinated attacks of Egypt and Syria on Yom Kippur (The Jewish Day of Atonement) in 1973 took Israel by surprise, intensified the perception of threat, and deepened the need for a powerful Israel with strong deterrence to ensure Israel's survival. Consequently, Israel's Defense Forces (IDF) were bolstered. Large investments were made in the fields of development and procurement. This atmosphere served as fertile soil for large-scale technological projects such as the *Merkava* (Chariot) Main Battle Tank (MBT), the Lavi aircraft, reconnaissance satellites, and more.[78] Brigadier General (retired) Uzi Eilam described the era following the war as "a hysterical run for unprecedented and disproportional empowerment through the development and procurement in all directions, to ensure that a surprise attack like the one on Yom Kippur would not repeat itself."[79] Nevertheless, the large investments in military needs and capabilities entailed great economic burdens.

Prior to and during the war, Israel requested satellite intelligence information on Syrian and Egyptian troop movements from the

---

General Yitzhak Rabin and Ministry of Foreign Affairs Director General Asher Ben Natan. Israel, Media Coverage of Shavit-2 Launch, July 8, 1961, BBC Collection: Israel, Microfilm 51567-474, (Washington, DC: Library of Congress).

[77] Israel, Media Coverage of Shavit-2 Launch, July 7, 1961, BBC Collection: Israel, Microfilm 51567-474, (Washington, DC: Library of Congress).

[78] This project was initiated before the war but was boosted by its results.

[79] Interview with Brig. General (ret.) Uzi Eilam, November 18, 1988, Tel Aviv.

Americans, but these requests were denied.[80] At that time, the Soviet Union was apparently supplying the Arab states with satellite images of the deployment of Israeli forces.[81] "From time to time, the IDF received satellite imagery from the United States, but the resolution was degraded, the coverage was limited, and the images were not provided in real time."[82] The lack of information when it was needed heightened awareness among a few Israeli officials and scientists of the crucial need to be able to independently gather intelligence. The development or acquisition of a satellite was a suitable solution.[83]

In the mid-1970s, the military raised thoughts and ideas about using space for military and security needs. Director of Military Intelligence (DMI) General Shlomo Gazit approached Professor Yuval Neeman, who at the time was the scientific advisor to the minister of defense, about Israel's early warning problems and suggested developing or acquiring a satellite.[84] Neeman tried to promote this idea, but Prime Minister Yitzhak Rabin opposed his lobbying attempts.[85]

The trauma of the war also brought a tremendous change to the political scene, which reached its peak in the 1977 election. For the first time since the establishment of Israel, the Likud party, headed by Menachem Begin, won the election. Begin's government adopted policies very different from those of the previous Labor-led governments, which

---

[80] The Americans claimed that for technical reasons, it was impossible to produce the relevant data, and that the information was unavailable at that time. According to Israeli assessments, the Americans intentionally blocked transfer of the information. Former Chief of Staff Lieutenant General Mordechai (Mota) Gur was reported to have made this claim after the successful launch of Ofeq-1 on *Mabat*, Channel One's daily TV news broadcast, on the day of the launch, September 19, 1988, 9:00 p.m. (Hebrew).

[81] The Soviet Union launched several Cosmos satellites during the war that were apparently used to collect intelligence information on the course of the war. These satellites, however, were not used as primary intelligence sources, because the results could not make much contribution to tactical decision-making. Quandt, W., "Soviet Policy in the October Middle East War II," *International Affairs*, 53:4, (October, 1977), 587–603. Shalom, D., *Beyond the Horizon*, (Private printing, 2004), 57, (Hebrew).

[82] Nair, K. K., *Space: The Frontiers of Modern Defense*, (New Delhi: The Center for Air and Power Studies, Knowledge World Publishers Pvt., Ltd. 2006), 158.

[83] Zorn, E. L., "Israel's Quest for Satellite Intelligence," *Studies in Intelligence*, (10 Winter–Spring 2001), 33–38. This was also stressed by many Israeli officials in interviews: Moshe Arens, October 25, 2007, Tel Aviv; Chaim Eshed, November 11, 2007, Tel Aviv; Uzi Eilam, November 7, 2007, Tel Aviv; Zeev Bonen, October 7, 2007, Haifa; Yehoshua Saguy, October 17, 2007, Beit-Chanan.

[84] Professor Neeman, an elementary particle physicist, was one of the pioneering scientists in the field of space research and astronomy in Israel.

[85] This episode is described in Rabin's 1979 autobiography. Mrs. Dvora Neeman, Professor Yuval Neeman's widow, said in an interview with the author on June 24, 2007, that later on, Rabin acknowledged that his objection had been a mistake.

Israel's Space Program

viewed Jewish power as an idealized value in its own right.[86] Despite the fact that the Likud was more right wing, in 1979, it was under a Likud government that Israel signed the peace treaty with Egypt.

The political change and the signing of the Egyptian-Israeli Peace Treaty were significant factors in the decision to embark on an independent Israeli space program.[87] The withdrawal from Sinai distanced the IDF from Egyptian territory, causing it to lose much of its intelligence-gathering capabilities, including the ability to carry out manned reconnaissance overflights.[88] The peace treaty did not dispel Israeli fears of hostile Egyptian intentions, and it was essential to ensure adherence to the treaty.

In 1978, the DMI established a task force headed by Lieutenant Colonel Chaim Eshed,[89] to examine possible solutions for dealing with the enormous early-warning problems faced by Israel after the signing of the peace treaty. The team reached the conclusion that the best solution to ensure early-warning intelligence over Egypt was by using reconnaissance satellites. DMI Major General Gazit and his successor, Major General Yehoshua Saguy, accepted this conclusion and helped to promote it.[90] Saguy claimed that the trauma of the war resulted in an Israeli desire to be ultra-protected. For this reason, as head of DMI in the years 1979–1983, he supported the indigenous satellite option: "After what had happened in the Yom Kippur War, I came to the conclusion that we must follow the satellites option. I approached the Americans on this, but they refused, claiming the US does not share these essential sources."[91]

In 1979, Saguy approached the Minister of Defense Ezer Weitzman and Chief of Staff Rafael Eitan on this issue, but they dismissed the concept.[92] Nevertheless, together with Eshed, Saguy ordered feasibility studies on the production of launch vehicles, satellites, and payloads to be drawn up by Israel's Defense Industries. The studies, completed by December 1980, came out positive and were presented to senior

---

[86] Handel, M., "The Evolution of Israeli Strategy: The Psychology of Insecurity and the Quest for Absolute Security," in W. Murray, M. Knox, and A. Bernstein, (eds.), *The Making of Strategy: Rulers, States, and War*, (Cambridge: Cambridge University Press, 1994), 574.

[87] Interview with Yehoshua Saguy, Head of the Directorate of Military Intelligence, IDF 1979–1983, Israel, October 17, 2007, Beit Chanan, Israel.

[88] Such flights were considered a violation of Egyptian sovereignty and were a very sensitive issue in the embryonic relations between the two countries after the treaty was signed.

[89] Professor Eshed was then head of the DMI R&D unit. Later on, he was appointed to serve as head of the space program in the Ministry of Defense, a position he held until 2010.

[90] Barzilai, A., "The Goal: Five Israeli Satellites Will be Launched Into Space in the Next Five Years," *Haaretz*, August 3, 2003, 1, 9, (in Hebrew).

[91] Interview with Gen. (ret.) Yehoshua Saguy, Head of the Directorate of Military Intelligence, IDF 1979–1983, Israel, October 17, 2007, Beit Chanan.

[92] Barzilai, A., (September 26, 2001), "A Force-Multiplier is Being Built Here", *Haaretz*, available in Hebrew at: http://www.hayadan.org.il/wp/double-power-260901/, accessed on March 30, 2009. Interview with Gen. (ret.) Yehoshua Saguy.

officials at the Ministry of Defense.[93] At the end of June 1981, shortly after Israel successfully destroyed Iraq's nuclear installation, the concept for the initiative was presented to Premier and Defense Minister Menachem Begin.[94] Begin approved the project and demanded that the development begin immediately, even though funding was not yet secured.[95] On September 19, 1988, Ofeq 1 was indigenously launched from the shores of Israel.[96] Ofeq 2 was successfully launched in 1990. In 1995, Israel's space program became operational with the launch of Ofeq 3 satellite into space. The launch of Ofeq 4 in 1998 failed. In 2002, Ofeq 5 was successfully launched. Ofeq 7 was successfully launched in 2007, a year after the launch of Ofeq 6 failed. In 2008, Israel's Synthetic Aperture Radar (SAR) satellite TecSAR was launched from India, and in 2010, Ofeq 9 was successfully launched. The second SAR satellite, Ofeq 10, was launched in 2014 from Israel. Ofeq 11 was launched in 2016.

In parallel, commercial space activity developed in Israel, benefiting the national infrastructure and broadening the country's expertise and knowhow. Commercial electro-optic satellite EROS A was launched in 2000, followed by EROS B, which was launched six years later; the two satellites were launched aboard Russian launchers. In 1996, the Amos 1 communications satellite was successfully launched aboard the Arian launcher from Kourou. Amos 2 was launched from Kazakhstan in 2003; five years later in 2008, Amos 3 was successfully launched, followed by Amos 4, which was launched in 2013. Nevertheless, national security remained Israel's primary motivation to be involved in space.

In the mid-1990s, the idea of sending an Israeli astronaut on a NASA mission was raised. Many among the Israeli scientific community objected to this idea. They claimed that there was no justification for the effort because it would not provide Israel with any unique scientific contribution or other

---

[93] Discussion Summary in a letter to the Ministry of Defense Director General's Bureau Chief from Deputy Defense Minister's Bureau Chief, dated March 5, 1981, Ministry of Defense Archives.

[94] Operation Opera took place on June 7, 1981. Weitzman had resigned in May 1980, and Begin took over his position as Defense Minister until the elections held in the summer of 1981, when he appointed Ariel Sharon as Minister of Defense.

[95] Also present at the meeting were Deputy Defense Minister, IDF Chief of Staff, Deputy Chief of Staff, Ministry of Defense Director General and others. In Discussion Summary written by Minister of Defense's Military Secretary to Ministry of Defense Director General on June 28, 1981, (Ministry of Defense Archives). Eventually, IAI found a "foreign client" willing to participate and bear some of the high costs. Barzilai, A., "A Force-Multiplier."

[96] It should be noted that for security reasons, Israeli satellites are launched westward instead of eastward.

tangible good. Nonetheless, the mission was approved. In 2003, Israel's first astronaut, Colonel Ilan Ramon, was lost on NASA's Columbia mission.

Over the past several years, Israel's space community has undergone a long and comprehensive process, re-evaluating its goals, objectives, and policies. This process reached its zenith in November 2009, when Israel's President Shimon Peres and Prime Minister Benjamin Netanyahu appointed a task force to examine Israel's space program and recommend a framework for a new national space program.[97] The task force's main objective was to focus on civil applications and scientific activity that would allow Israel greater industrial scale and competitiveness in the growing global space market. In June 2010, the task force submitted its report and recommendations.[98]

In the report, the task force outlined Israel's strengths, weaknesses, opportunities, and challenges for achieving its goals in space, recommending that the government invest NIS 300 million (US$83 million) a year for a period of five years in space research and activity, in addition to defense-related investments in space activity. The task force also emphasized that international collaborations with other spacefaring nations, as well as with developing nations, would be a priority. The recommendations were adopted by both President Peres and Prime Minister Netanyahu.[99]

The new focus in Israel on civil and commercial space activities is a major step. Nevertheless, Israel's space policy remains pragmatic and focused on specific fields of expertise, especially remote sensing and communications. The primary difference is that instead of focusing its national efforts only on security considerations and military applications, Israel's national activity expands to develop civil services and applications in order to preserve and leverage the existing infrastructure, which was established for various security reasons.

---

[97] The task force was headed by Mr. Menachem Greenblum, Director General, Ministry of Science and Technology; and Professor Isaac Ben-Israel, then Chairman of the Israeli Space Agency.
[98] Paikowsky, D., and Levi, R. "Space as a National Project – An Israeli Space Program for a Sustainable Israeli Space Industry, Presidential Task-Force for Space Activity Final Report," (Jerusalem: Israel Ministry of Science and Technology, June 2010), in Hebrew.
[99] Coren, O. "Reaching for the Stars – A New Space Race, Fueled More by Profit Than by National Pride, has Begun, and Israel Wants In," *Haaretz*, August 5, 2010, available at: www.haaretz.com/print-edition/business/reaching-for-the-stars-1.306093, accessed on August 10, 2010.

Israel's Logic and the Motivation of (In)security[100]

"Israel is a small state with the security challenges of a major power," once said Rear Admiral Ophir Shoham.[101] In this statement, Shoham describes the high level of intensity and complexity of the regional environment in which Israel needs to operate and which shapes its priorities and policies. The statement also reflects the atmosphere of Israel's decision-making, which is influenced by a profound sense of insecurity. Israel's space program is an outcome of pragmatic security thinking aimed at the fulfillment of tangible needs for early-warning intelligence, deterrence, and self-reliance in cutting-edge technologies.

The deep sense of insecurity in Israel is an outcome of a combination of a hostile strategic environment and factors of its national history. The long history of existential threat, powerlessness, insecurity, and isolation of the Jewish people, the national experience of the Zionist enterprise, and of the State of Israel since its establishment in 1948, conceptualize Israel's perception of threat and magnifies the sense of Israeli insecurity. In short, the Jewish-Israeli collective memory shapes the setting in which Israel's security is discussed and its strategy is formulated.[102]

Of the facts of its strategic environment is that Israel is a very small state surrounded by many hostile Arab states. Israel has long borders and no strategic depth, and is therefore vulnerable to surprise attacks and military actions. Its neighbors enjoy numerical superiority in population, territorial size, and scales of military force (if the forces are combined). The fact that by the time the space program was initiated in 1981 (only thirty-three years after Israel was established), Israel had already fought five full-scale wars and suffered many acts of terrorism against Israeli targets both in Israel and abroad is significant.[103] On top of that, Israel also faces threats

---

[100] In the term (in)security, I refer to the deep sense of insecurity of Israel, which is the result of objective challenges and threats faced by Israel in its strategic environment, coupled with a subjective sense of threat developed by a long history of atrocities, which together form strong incentives of Israel to achieve a high level of security and defense.

[101] Rear Admiral Ophir Shoham, in his position as assistant head of the Planning Branch, described the State of Israel at a conference held in March 2004 at Tel Aviv University: Shoham, O. *"Kalkala uvitahon,"* (Economy and Security) Tel Aviv Workshop for Science, Technology and Security, Tel Aviv University, (in Hebrew).

[102] Handel, M., "The Evolution of Israeli," 542; Kleiman, A., "Israeli Negotiating Culture," in Cofman, T., (ed.), *How Israelis and Palestinians Negotiate – A Cross-Cultural Analysis of the Oslo Peace Process*, (Washington, DC: United States Institute of Peace Press, 2005), 85–86.

[103] The War of Independence (1947–1949), the Sinai Campaign (Operation Kadesh, November 1956), the Six-Day War (June 1967), the War of Attrition (1968–1970), the Yom Kippur War (October 1973).

from second- and third-tier states far beyond its geographic borders.[104] Iraq, Libya, and now Iran have made clear strategic WMD threats.

In addition to Israel's significant security problems, the loss and destruction experienced by the Jewish people throughout history, and especially the memory of the Holocaust as a personal and national tragedy, has had a monumental impact on Israel's perception of threat and vulnerability.[105] The fears of the Holocaust play a pivotal role in the public sphere of Israel, which is home to many survivors and their descendants. It defines and shapes perceptions, politics, and international relations, and it serves as an agent of culture and national identity building.[106] In this context, Cohen (1990) described Israel as a post-disaster community that fears the repetition of the trauma and views ongoing events, this time inflicted by the Arabs on Israel, through the prism of its tragedy. This is true even for those who did not suffer the disaster personally.[107] Repeated wars and frequent terror acts in Israel reinforced this perception. In dealing with Israel's security, Israeli leaders want to ensure that such a tragedy will never be repeated. In their perception, a strong and independent Israel is the answer to the agony and pain of genocide and to fears about the future.[108]

The perception of insecurity imbued the ethos of self-reliance. The isolation of the state of Israel in the international community reinforced it. For example, Arab control over oil and strategically important areas enhanced the influence of Arab states, isolating Israel at the UN. After the war of 1967, Israel also suffered a variety of unilateral and multilateral arms embargos.[109] Consequently, Israeli leaders share the premise that Israelis alone should determine their own future and that they should not rely on others when it comes to their security.

---

[104] Israel divides threatening countries into three tiers, according to their geographic distance from Israel.
[105] Cohen, R., *Culture and Conflict in Egyptian-Israeli Relations*, (Bloomington: Indiana University Press, 1990), 112.
[106] For further discussion of the impact of the Holocaust on Israeli culture, see Zertal, I. *Israel's Holocaust and the Politics of Nationhood*, (Cambridge: Cambridge Press, 2005), 3–4; Almog, O. *The Sabra – A Profile*, in Hebrew (Tel Aviv: Am Oved, 2004), 298–299, in English: (Berkeley, CA: University of California Press, 2000); Gal, R., *A Portrait of the Israeli Soldier*, (New York: Greenwood Press, 1986).
[107] Cohen stated that several studies have found that the Holocaust is deeply embedded in the consciousness of young people, irrespective of ethnic background. Cohen, R., (1990), *Culture and Conflict*, 38–39.
[108] Gal, R., (1986), *A Portrait of the Israeli Soldier*, 70.
[109] After the war, France imposed an arms embargo against Israel. Two years later, Britain suspended a sale of Main Battle Tanks to Israel during the War of Attrition. From time to time, the United States also refused transfers or restricted the time and scale of deliveries as a form of political pressure. Meanwhile, the Arab countries acquired advanced weapon systems either from the West or the Soviet Union.

David Ben-Gurion declared early on that the threat posed to the State of Israel from its neighbors and enemies was a fact of life with which Israeli society had to contend.[110] Ben-Gurion based his strategic premise on the fact that Israel suffers from an asymmetric disadvantage in all quantitative parameters when compared to its hostile environment. This fundamental assumption defined the country's domestic and foreign policy from the beginning.[111] Ben-Gurion's awareness of the asymmetry and his assumption that Israel was in existential danger convinced him that Israel had to acquire a level of power that would exceed that of its enemies, would serve as a deterrent against their aspiration to destroy the small state, and would allow Israel to defend itself independently. These underlying premises led Ben-Gurion to develop and infuse in Israeli society the concept that national security should be based on quality rather than on quantity. In his words, "because we are quantitatively inferior, we must be superior in quality."[112] "Quality" was to be achieved by the development of science and technology and their transformation into central components of Israel's power.[113]

The concept of qualitative superiority,[114] in particular in science and technology, has thus been perceived from the time of the state's infancy as a central factor in the power equation between Israel and its neighbors, and paved the way to the development of Israel's defense industries.[115] A strong defense industry dedicated to producing materiel for the IDF became a national priority.[116] Today, Israel's defense industry is one of

[110] Ben-Gurion is considered to be the spiritual father of Israel in strategic as well as political terms.
[111] Ben-Israel, I., *Israel's Defense Doctrine*, (Ben-Shemen: Modan Publishing House and Maarachot, 2013), 15–16.
[112] Ben-Gurion explained this concept in a report (originally forty-six pages long) submitted to the government on October 18, 1953. In the report, he evaluated and analyzed the threats faced by Israel, along with basic factors differentiating Israel from neighboring Arab states. It was published almost word for word, albeit with a number of abridgments and editorial modifications under the heading "Army and State" in *Maarachot* 280:2–9 (May 1981), 2–11. A detailed overview of Ben Gurion's report is in Ben-Israel, I. "Security, Technology and the Future Battlefield," in Golan, H. (ed.), *Israel's Security Net – Core Issues of Israel's National Security in its Sixth Decade*, (Tel Aviv: Maarachot Ministry of Defense Press, 2001), 269–327 (in Hebrew).
[113] Ben-Israel, I., *Israel's Defense Doctrine*.
[114] Quality has three components: Human quality, quality of arms and weapons, and quality in applying force ("For by wise guidance you will wage war," Proverbs, 24:6). For an excellent and detailed discussion on the principle of quality over quantity in the Israeli perspective, see Offer, Z., and Kober, A., *Quality and Quantity in Military Buildup*, (Tel Aviv: Maarachot Ministry of Defense Press 1992); Ben-Israel, I., *Israel's Defense Doctrine*,; Rodman, D., *Defense and Diplomacy in Israel's National Security Experience* (Brighton: Sussex Academic Press, 2005).
[115] Peres, S., *David's Sling* (London: George Weidenfeld and Nicholson Ltd., 1970), 113.
[116] For a detailed discussion, see Cohen, E., Eisenstadt, M., and Bacevich, A., *Knives, Tanks and Missiles: Israel's Security Revolution* (Washington, DC: Washington Institute

the most sophisticated in the world, providing technological proficiency and products that were tested in combat.

Another facet of sustaining qualitative superiority is through large-scale national projects. As discussed above, national decisions to develop large-scale projects such as space programs or nuclear programs are not trivial. Usually, the development of such projects requires massive investments of resources and large-scale national efforts. Despite the difficulties, risks, and high costs, or because of them, nations that aspire to power and high standing often invest valuable resources and efforts in acquiring expertise in these areas. They do so because proving indigenous expertise is perceived as an important mark of strong national capabilities, which reflect on the nation's overall strength and sovereignty.

Israel's nuclear image and policy of ambiguity as well as its space program serve this goal. Cohen (1998) explained that Ben-Gurion believed that Israel needed nuclear weapons as a last resort insurance in the event of an extreme emergency, in which it would not be in its power to compete with its adversaries. Perhaps more importantly, it was thought that nuclear weapons would serve to persuade Israel's adversaries to accept its existence and achieve peace in the Middle East.[117] The state of Israel has never confirmed nor denied foreign reports about its nuclear capabilities. Therefore, the reference to Israel's nuclear project focuses not on its nature, but on the way it is perceived by Israel's adversaries, which believe that Israel has had nuclear weapons for decades.[118]

While not a party to the decision to develop Israel's space program, which was taken almost ten years after his death in 1973, Ben-Gurion nevertheless played a significant role in it. By creating the intellectual security environment and the necessary technological infrastructure, he helped lay the groundwork for the development of the Israeli space program. Through the space program, especially Israel's capability to indigenously launch satellites into space, Israel projects power and a clear message of deterrence to its neighbors, which complements their image of Israel as a nuclear-capable state.[119]

Prime Minister Menachem Begin approved the initiative to develop national space expertise in Israel. He was motivated by a clear

for Near East Policy, 1998); Handel, M., "The Evolution," 534–578; Gal, R., *A Portrait of the Israeli Soldier*, 146.

[117] Cohen, A., *Israel and the Bomb*, (New York: Columbia University Press, 1998).

[118] Ben-Israel, I., *Israel's Defense Doctrine*, 60–63. For a detailed analysis of Israel's nuclear image in the eyes of its neighbors, see Levite A., Landau, E., *Israel's Nuclear Image – Arab Perceptions of Israel's Nuclear Posture*, (Tel Aviv: Papyrus Tel Aviv University Press, 1994).

[119] Paikowsky, D., and Ben-Israel, I., "Space and the 'Iron Wall': What is the Strategic Logic Behind Israel's Space Program?" (Under review).

understanding of the acute intelligence needs enhanced by a profound sense of (in)security and by a strong faith in Israeli scientific and technological community to pull this off. As a leader, Begin saw himself as the embodiment of the Jewish people. The Holocaust, in which he had lost his parents and most of his family, shaped his world-view and personal philosophy.[120] He deeply believed that the lesson of the Holocaust for the Jewish people was to defend themselves in their homeland, in order to prevent a repetition of existential threats.[121] This is what motivated him to sign the peace agreement with Egypt and to order the destruction of the nuclear installation in Iraq in June 1981. Arye Naor, Secretary of the Cabinet at the time, recalls that he heard Begin saying "I have no intention of leaving this problem (Iraq's nuclear program – D.P.) to our children." Begin later revealed that during this operation he thought of his parents and relatives murdered by the Nazis.[122]

Three weeks later, Begin approved the establishment of the space program. We can assume that Begin saw a connection between these two events. The successful operation of destroying Iraq's nuclear installation encouraged him to believe that there was a need for a satellite to serve Israel's security concerns and that Israel was capable of developing and launching one. According to Chaim Eshed, who was present at the meeting in which Menachem Begin approved the program, Begin justified his decision to approve such a risky and ambitious program by arguing that it was important for the national security of Israel and that Jewish genius would overcome all challenges and obstacles.[123] Yehoshu Saguy, who was also present at this meeting, does not recall this exact statement by Begin. However, he agrees that the belief in Jewish genius did play a role in Begin's perspective. "By this statement, Begin means that if the state of Israel decides to pursue something, it will not be stopped technologically. [Begin] was extraordinarily sensitive to Jewish culture and history."[124] The use of space assets to assure early warning and boost Israel's deterrence capabilities fits well with Begin's agenda. He saw the need for early warning intelligence and accepted the solution provided by DMI officials.

Begin was also aware of the power implications of such capability, and was concerned that Israel was gaining "too much" power in the eyes of the

---

[120] Grosbard, O., *Menachem Begin – A Portrait of a Leader – A Biography*, (Tel Aviv: Resling Publishing, 2006), 188 (Hebrew).
[121] Karniel, M., *Menachem Begin – A Portrait of a Leader*, (Jerusalem: Reuvan Mas publication, 1998), 35, (Hebrew).
[122] The interview with Naor is in Grosbard, O., *Menachem Begin*, 252–253.
[123] Interview with Brig. Gen. (Ret). Prof. Chaim Eshed, Head of the Space Program, Ministry of Defense, Israel, November 11, 2007, Tel Aviv, Israel.
[124] Interview with Gen. (Ret.) Yehoshua Saguy, Head of Directorate Military Intelligence, IDF 1979–1983, Israel, October 17, 2007, Beit Chanan, Israel.

international community, as no other small state had done something like this before. In the preliminary discussions, says Saguy, Begin wondered who would be intimidated by this and was concerned with the possibility of overdoing it. "He definitely saw it as a major element of strength, and feared it."[125] Saguy adds that Begin was also concerned with the high risk involved in a large-scale project like this. "It was a huge technological gamble and leapfrog for the whole nation, and we knew it. He did not express it in words, but it was obvious there was a possibility that we would not be able to pull this off, and it was also clear that we could not purchase such a satellite at that time."[126]

Membership in the Space Club as "Peaceful Deterrence"

In 1986, foreign reports began to appear suggesting that

Further development of the Jericho-2[127] missile had succeeded in extending its range. It appears that in May 1987, a modified version of the missile, the Jericho-2B, was tested over a range of 800 kilometers (500 miles) into the Mediterranean. This led to speculation that Israel was developing a further variant of the missile, Jericho-3, capable of ranges of up to 1,450 kilometers (900 miles).[128]

These tests prompted the Soviet Union to issue a stern warning to Israel about its activities because it appeared that the range of this new version of the missile could make it a direct military threat to the Soviet Union.[129] At the same time, the development of the space program progressed and the day of the first launch approached; clearly, it would be impossible to hide the launching of Ofeq 1 from the 12-meter (39 feet) Shavit launcher.[130]

This was the main impetus behind the establishment of an ad-hoc committee, known as the Yotam Committee, by the Ministry of Defense. The committee, composed of experts from various disciplines was given a mandate to conduct the release strategy and public exposure of the expected launch.[131]

---

[125] Ibid.
[126] Ibid.
[127] The Jericho is believed to be a medium-range missile. For further reading, see Missile Threat Project by the George C. Marshall and Claremont Institute, available at: missilethreat.com/missiles/Jericho-123/, accessed on December 2, 2015.
[128] Simpson, J., Acton, P., and Crowe, S., "The Israeli Satellite Launch," *Space Policy*, (May 1989), 117–118.
[129] Freidman, T. L., "Soviet Cautions Israel Against a New Missile," *New York Times*, July 29, 1987, cited in Simpson, J., Acton, P., and Crowe, S., "The Israeli Satellite Launch," 119.
[130] Barzilai, A., "A Force-Multiplier."
[131] Ibid.

In order to meet this target, the committee prepared a detailed manual to be used by Israeli officials who were to appear in the media or in other international forums.[132] The purpose of the manual was to present this event as an international scientific and technological achievement, which placed Israel among other spacefaring nations (i.e. the space club) and not focus on the achievement itself. For example, one of the questions was "What characterizes Ofeq-1 as opposed to other satellites?" The answer provided by the manual was that "Ofeq-1's main characteristic is that it is "Blue and White," a technological product of Israeli industry.[133] As such, it serves as Israel's industrial calling card, introducing it to the exclusive club of satellite manufacturers."[134] The committee was also responsible for drafting the official joint announcement and press release by IAI and the Israeli Space Agency (ISA) immediately after the launch. The press release provided technical data on the satellite, its development process and expected activity, as well as highlighting the space research goals of IAI and ISA. The first goal (out of three) was to place Israel in the community of nations engaged in space research for peaceful purposes and technological advancement.[135]

Simpson, Acton, and Crowe (1989) asserted that

> the Ofeq-1 launch allowed analysts all over the world to calculate the range and payload characteristics of the Shavit booster, and thus to verify that Israel had the ability to threaten some of its regional neighbors with offensive missiles. For its part, Israel could expose the technical credibility of this deterrent in a manner which was internationally acceptable, while sustaining its traditional policies of enhancing security through ambiguity by denying that Ofeq-1 had any military significance.[136]

The message of membership in the space club was used to achieve "peaceful deterrence," to win legitimacy and to shift the focus of the international community away from possible military implications. The latter was achieved by creating a link between Israel's achievement in space and those of other spacefaring nations. The Israeli leadership's objective was to project a message of empowerment to its allies and rivals,

---

[132] Suslik, D., and Meyuchas, J. *Israel's Entry into the Space Age – Briefing Manual in Preparation for the Ofeq-1 Launch*, (IAI and ISA, September 1988) (Hebrew); Suslik, D., and Haiman, L., *Briefing on the Launch of Ofeq-1*, (IAI and ISA, September 1988) (Hebrew), (IAI archives, Israel).

[133] Blue and white are the colors of the Israeli flag; the expression refers to products "made in Israel."

[134] Suslik, D., and Meyuchas, J. *Israel's Entry*; Suslik, D., and Haiman, L., *Briefing on the Launch*.

[135] IAI and ISA Press Release: "Experimental Satellite was Successfully Launched from Israel,") (IAI and ISA archives, Israel September 19, 1988).

[136] Simpson, J., Acton, P., and Crowe, S., "The Israeli Satellite Launch", 117–118.

which in this context would not force them to address Israel's new reality directly. Nevertheless, the strategic message was clear: if Israel is capable of what other launching states are capable of, it must be similarly powerful. Consequently, Israel improved its security while avoiding an exacerbation of its security dilemma. Shimon Peres, as president of Israel, explained this by asserting that it may be understood as "illumination with strategic logic" because it projects the image of a state or its regime.[137]

In the domestic sphere, this message was made to intensify national esteem. Israeli leaders, media, and the public emphasized the international prestige and national pride provided by Israel's first launch into space and featured an extensive use of club rhetoric. Prime Minister Yitzhak Shamir said in an interview on national radio that:

there are very few countries that are capable of such a move, and all the citizens of Israel should be proud of their country, which is capable of displaying such an achievement ... It has no connection with the arms race. If we were speaking about races it is more a race over technological and scientific capabilities ... This is a technical experiment, which introduces us into an era, making Israel a partner in the top ranks of the modern technological era ... We should mainly consider the technological importance, and in that realm there is no doubt that Israel's international prestige has increased tremendously.[138]

In another radio interview, Shamir was challenged regarding the priority and urgency of this event, and he replied:

This is not one of the essential goods, such as bread, clothing, or health services. This is, however, one of the things which bring the State a lot of prestige and that can sometimes result in economic and other advantages ... In our world, (prestige) means a lot of consideration in the international arena. That special consideration has a positive strategic significance.[139]

On a TV news broadcast, Shimon Peres, the then Minister of Foreign Affairs, adhered to this terminology as well by saying that "not many nations have an industry capable of developing a satellite. It shows that

---

[137] Interview with Shimon Peres, the President of Israel, January 18, 2008, Jerusalem, Israel.
[138] Radio Interview with Prime Minister Shamir by Shalom Qital and Oded Ben Ami (live), on Jerusalem Domestic Service in Hebrew, September 19, 1988, FBIS-NES 88-182 (September 20, 1988), (Washington, DC: NASA HQ, History Office, Historical Reference Collection, International Files: Israel).
[139] Radio Interview with Prime Minister Shamir by Dan Shilon and Goni Savir (live), on Tel Aviv IDF radio station in Hebrew, September 19, 1988, FBIS-NES-88-182 (September 20, 1988), (Washington, DC: NASA HQ, History Office, Historical Reference Collection, International Files: Israel).

Israel is one of the most advanced countries in the world, despite its size and limitations ... A small country can be a great country, this is the fundamental conclusion."[140]

In general, according to statements by foreign officials and international media coverage, which expressed admiration and appreciation of Israel's success, many in the international community accepted the interpretation Israel provided regarding its achievement.[141] For the United States and the rest of the international community, this was a much more convenient way to perceive and accept the change in the balance of power created by Israel. Even Israel's neighboring Arab states, which expressed their concerns over Israel's new demonstrated capability, did not undertake operative actions to counterbalance Israel's achievement. Numerous examples in the Israeli and world press in recent years reflect the reaction of Arab countries to Israel's proven ability in space.[142]

In the following years, Israel's space program expanded. More than a dozen satellites for remote sensing and communications were developed. Each launch of a satellite into space was followed by statements by Israeli leaders on the significance of the space program and the capabilities it provided for the overall power and image of Israel as a member of the club. For example, after the launch of Ofeq 2 in 1990, Shimon Peres, as the Labor Party leader, was quoted as saying that the launching should help deter Hussein: "If he wants to deal with Israel, he should look for other means than the military one."[143] In 2003, Minister of Science and Technology Eliezer Sandberg said that the responsibility of the Ministry

---

[140] *Mabat* news show, Channel 1, Israel 9:00 p.m., September 19, 1988, (Hebrew), (IAI, Archives, Israel).

[141] For example, the Chairman of COPUOS (the UN Committee on Peaceful Use of Outer Space), Peter Jankowitsch, conveyed his congratulations and admiration in a telegram to the president of Israel two days after the launch: "By this extraordinary event, that provides testimony once again of the high level reached by Israeli technology, your country, as the first one in the Middle East, joins a small number of others that have begun to engage in the conquest of space for peaceful uses." Source: Telegraph by COPUOS Chairman Peter Jankowitsch to the Israeli President after the first launch of an Israeli satellite (September 21, 1988).

[142] See for example: Rosenblatt, Y., Gabai, S. "Saudi Arabia: Arabs are Checking Into How to Jam Ofek 1's Activity," *Maariv*, (September 29, 1988) (Hebrew); Gabai, Sh., Cohen, A. "Israeli Spy Satellite – Comments," *Maariv* (April 6, 1995), (Hebrew); Granott, O. "Arab States Secretly Concluded: Will Act Against Israeli Satellites," *Maariv*, (April 8, 1998), (Hebrew); Peri, S., Egozi, A. "Arab League is Afraid of Ofek 5," *Yediot Aharonot*, (August 25, 2002), (Hebrew); Blanche, E. "Israel Seeks New High Ground with Drive to Develop Spy Satellites," *The Daily Star*, (Beirut), (August 9, 2003).

[143] Williams, D., "Israel Launches Satellite; Spy Role Rumored: Middle East: The Government Says Ofek 2 Is a Research Craft. The Space Shot Comes Amid a Regional Missile Race," *Los Angeles Times*, April 4, 1990, available at: articles.latimes.com/1990-04-04/news/mn-704_1_israel-launches-satellite, accessed February 28, 2016.

of Science and Technology is to preserve Israel's position among space powers.[144] Two years later, in 2005, shortly after the successful launch of Ofeq 5, a remote sensing satellite, Prime Minister Ariel Sharon and other senior government officials explained that the launch was not aimed only at intelligence gathering, but also to project Israel's power.[145] In 2008, at the President's Convention celebrating Israel's 60th Anniversary of Independence, a short movie of Israel's achievements was screened in which it was declared that the Ofeq 1 launch was Israel's entrance ticket to the space club.[146]

Conclusions

India and Israel share definite needs for the use of space application services. Nonetheless, the different policies and programs each has pursued on its path to space raise important issues regarding the underlying motivation in each case. An examination of the differences and similarities of the Indian and Israeli space programs and national perspectives on the use of space for national and international needs highlights these differences and similarities. To address each country's problems, interests, and objectives, the leadership of each country reached the same conclusion: self-reliance in science and technology is one of the primary keys to meet these challenges. Based on the worldwide premise that having a national space capability is a means and a symbol of power, each nation wanted to acquire, at least partially, the capability to access and utilize space using its own launchers and satellites independently. Thus, they avoided reliance on other nations and bypassed potential pressure.

In the early days of their space programs, Indian and Israeli decision-makers had to make conscious choices of where to focus attention and in which technological areas to invest. In both India and Israel, the decisions were to concentrate on developing independent capabilities in the areas of remote sensing and communications; and to develop launch capability to low Earth orbit. In general, Israel still adheres to this policy in relation to outer space, in which it moves on a very pragmatic vector. India's space policy, on the other hand, has shifted; it now includes a larger variety of ambitious capabilities. The reason for this is that India is moving on two vectors that may seem to be contradictory, but in India's case, these vectors complement each other. In the first one, India's goal is to use

---

[144] Blizovsky, A., (2003), "Space Opens Wide," *Galileo*, Vol. 57, pp. 18–25.
[145] Ben, A. "Shihab-3 Versus Ofeq-5," *Haaretz*, (June 6, 2002), (Hebrew).
[146] The Convention took place on June 13–15, 2008, in Jerusalem.

the space program for national development, which will provide tangible goods and bring prosperity to the Indian people. Along the second vector, which builds on the achievements of the first, the goal is to position India in a high place in the international community as a power whose influence on world affairs is significant and therefore cannot be ignored.

For this reason, India attributes great value to becoming and being acknowledged as a spacefaring nation.[147] In the 1960s, Indian leadership realized that if India could be widely recognized as a power, it would have a better chance to leapfrog into a high level of development. However, in order to be widely recognized as a power, India needed to prove to the world that it is rapidly developing. Therefore, many Indian leaders concluded that an indigenous space program was a prerequisite for India to be counted as a world power.

In their eyes, India's history as an ancient powerful nation, and the fact that the Indian people are one of the world's largest peoples, demands that India be a world power. Therefore, India must develop national expertise in space. Through the prism of club politics, it is therefore clear why India's space policy is an integral part of the state's foreign policy. As Von-Welck (1987) has argued, "the motivation for India's quest in space is both functional and symbolic."[148] For Indian policymakers, the space program was, and still is, a message that it had a great deal to offer the world. The space program plays an important diplomatic role in contributing to India's dominant position in South Asia, in establishing its military and political superiority over Pakistan, and in being a credible competitor with China. Domestically, India's space program is a symbol of its success as a people and as a modern state, able to compete with the world's great powers in one of the most visible areas of high technology. The space program for the Indians is a visible symbol of national achievement and self-reliance.[149]

Israel, by contrast, was, and still is, motivated by much more pragmatic considerations. Israel sees special significance in providing national expertise that is sufficient to keep Israel safe and secure at modest costs. For Israel, membership in the space club is a significant strategy to deal with Israel's challenges, and construct a reality that maximizes Israel's benefits and minimizes its risks by projecting power in a non-aggressive

---

[147] For a comprehensive overview of the Indian approach to space for national empowerment, see: Abdul Kalam A. P. J., and Pillai, A. S., *Envisioning an Empowered Nation – Technology for Societal Transformation*, (New Delhi: Tata McGraw-Hill Publishing Company, 2004).

[148] Von-Welck, S. F., "India's Space Policy – a Developing Country in the Space Club," *Space Policy*, November 1987, 332.

[149] Sheehan, M. J., *The International Politics of Space*, (London: Routledge, 2007), 156–157.

way. In this respect, club membership provided Israel an added value of distinction: creating a clear delineation between itself and the other states in the region, none of which had this capability, while belonging to a superior group.[150] The implication is clear: if Israel is capable of what other launching states are capable of, it must be similarly powerful. Furthermore, perceiving itself as isolated politically, geographically, religiously, and even culturally makes Israel search for recognition, legitimacy, and belonging. Membership in the space club, which is determined by capability and not by geographic, political, or cultural factors, is thus very appealing to Israel, internationally and domestically, and provides a unique sense of belonging.

Domestically, Israel's leadership communicated the achievement as an act of joining the space club in order to vindicate the tremendous national efforts and resources invested in it. The program and its achievements were used to increase a sense of security, national pride, and self-esteem among the Israeli population, reinforcing its faith in the state's ability to stand up to the threats posed to it. This was done primarily by focusing on the indigenous effort and on the success of joining the exclusive club. The affiliation with the "space club" glorified the achievement and sent a message to the public that the success was an outcome of wise policies, which improved Israel's overall position among the nations of the world.

In summary, the differences between India and Israel regarding space are not in technical expertise and knowhow, or in the actual needs. The difference between them lies in the role they perceive to be playing in world politics. In India, membership in the space club serves as a source of political power for international standing and national esteem. It allows India to project a powerful image and to link itself with strong and developed countries in order to restore its heroic past and create a promising future. Israel, on the other hand, pursues its space program for much more security-oriented and pragmatic reasons.

---

[150] This somewhat changed when, in February 2009, Iran demonstrated national capability to launch a small satellite into space. However, Iran still has a long way to go in order to catch up in this field.

8   The Space Club in the Post–Cold War Era

The end of the Cold War with the collapse of the Soviet Union induced dramatic changes in the security environment of the international system. The elimination of the immediate threat of global war brought about positive changes in the development of space technology and exploration. Some of the restrictions imposed on the transfer of sensitive technology and knowledge were removed. More technologies, knowledge, and resources went to civil and commercial activities in space, a process which launched the space economy.

During the Cold War, the ability to use civil space applications for military purposes, even if disguised, led to the imposition of severe restrictions on the transfer of knowledge and technology. The restrictions reinforced the inherent tension between competition and cooperation, creating a boundary between the haves and have-nots. That, in turn, led to the emergence of the space club.

The removal of many of the restrictions in the aftermath of the Cold War triggered a shift in favor of dual-use activity. The change in the security environment and the expansion of the space market made possible the entrance of two new types of players into the space domain: small and developing countries and private sector players.

The dual-use potential of space technology had a great impact on this process. This time, the shift to dual-use technology came in the context of public-private partnerships (PPP).

Under the guiding principle of PPP, civil and defense government agencies cooperate with commercial entities to develop and operate advanced space technologies. These provide tangible goods and benefits to the public as well as to the commercial market, while reducing costs for both sides. Gradually, due to all these changes, space capabilities became more accessible, new technologies were introduced, the cost of access to space declined, and the space market expanded. At the beginning of the 1980s, the space market accounted for a few billion dollars of the world's economy. In 2014, the space market, including ancillary services, was estimated at US$330 billion.[1] The number of countries active in space and the number of worldwide individual users grew quickly, leading to fast commercialization of applications, services, and infrastructures; space technology became a commodity.

These trends challenge the current structure of the space club and will shape its future. The increase in the number of states that are active in space blurs the threshold for entry into the space club. Importantly, the growing involvement of private players in space, especially in launchings, previously the exclusive domain of states, undermines the hegemony of states, eroding the status of the space club and raising questions about its future. The leading spacefaring nations may redesign a clear distinction between the role of the private sector and that of the governmental sector. The outcome of this process may contribute to the renewal of the club.

This chapter is designed to outline these developments and analyze their effects on international activity in space and the status of the space club.[2]

Dual-Use and the Development of Space Activity after the Cold War

As discussed in earlier chapters of this book, space technology is significantly affected by its potential to be used for civil activities in addition to military and defense activities. This duality imposes challenges and constraints on the market, but also contributes to its advancement. Throughout the Cold War, the dual-use nature of space technology for civil-military purposes turned it into a state-only playground, with minor exceptions. The end of the Cold War made possible the removal of some of the limitations and constraints on space activity. The 1991 Gulf War demonstrated the potential of public-private partnerships, when the military utilized commercial sensors to help plan and carry out operations.[3]

---

[1] *The Space Report 2015*, (Arlington, VA: The Space Foundation, July 2015), p. 1.
[2] This chapter builds on the following articles and reports, co-authored by the author of this book: Paikowsky, D., Reichard, A., Baram, G., and Ben-Israel, I., "Space 2015: A Year in Review," Report by Yuval Neeman Workshop for Science, Technology and Security at Tel Aviv University, available at: www.gwu.edu/~spi/2015%20A%20year%20in%20revi ew.pdf, accessed on April 2, 2016; Paikowsky, D., Baram, G., and Ben-Israel, I., "Trends in Space Activities in 2014: The Significance of Space Activities of Governments," *Acta Astronautica*, (January 2016), 187–198; Paikowsky, D., Baram, G., and Ben-Israel, I., "Trends in Government Space Activity and Policy in 2013." *Astropolitics*, 12, (October 2014), 107–126.
[3] Regarding the commercial use of remote sensing during the Gulf War, see Baker, J., and Johnson, D., "Security Implications of Commercial Satellite Imagery," in Baker, J.,

The dual-use nature of space technology was not only a challenge, but an opportunity.

In the 1991 Gulf War, satellite communication, navigation, and guidance systems, including commercial devices, were employed for the first time in combat; space technology contributed a great deal to the coalition's military success. Using a relatively small quantity of weapons, the crushing victory was achieved with few American and allied losses. Those results reinforced the desire among the political and military echelons to try to recreate the conditions and pace of the Gulf War military actions in any future conflicts in which the Americans were required to use force.

Two years later, in 1993, Vice President Dan Quayle submitted a report to the president of the United States in which he included lessons drawn from the conflict. The American superiority in the war, Quayle wrote, was a direct consequence of its space capabilities in the fields of communications, navigation, weather forecasting, intelligence, remote sensing, and early warning. These capabilities were critical to the success of American versus Iraqi forces in 1991, and he argued, should be viewed as a "force multiplier."[4] The systems he mentioned shortened the duration of combat, rendered the armed forces more efficient, and permitted a smaller number of troops to be deployed. The message from the Gulf War was clear. Space constitutes a central component of America's strength as a superpower from a civilian and certainly from a military perspective. Nevertheless, the high price of development, maintenance, and operation of space systems required new concepts of resource management and utilization. The successful use of commercial space services in the Gulf War was a significant catalyst for policy changes in favor of public/private dual-use partnerships in space.

The conditions under which such a partnership succeeds are threefold. First, it must fulfill tangible public (military or civil) needs. Second, the private sector must have an interest in such partnerships as well as the capacity to pull them off. Finally, a significant portion of the project's costs must come from private sources. For the private sector, this method has several benefits:

- Government funds the development of new technologies.
- It contributes to joint ventures with other R&D installations of other industries, government labs, universities, etc.
- Enhanced access to advanced technologies and knowhow.
- The potential market expands.

O'Connell, K., and Williamson, R., (eds.), *Commercial Observation Satellites at the Leading Edge of Global Transparency*, (Santa Monica, CA: RAND, 2001), 104.

[4] National Space Council, *Final Report to the President*, (Washington, DC: January 7, 1993), 8.

For the government, public-private partnerships offer the opportunity to reduce costs, increase efficiency, develop a greater variety of products, provide jobs, and preserve knowledge.[5]

On the other hand, there are also drawbacks to be considered by the public sector. For example, in the past and to a lesser extent today, some of the commercial systems are more vulnerable to both intentional interference and unintentional interference, which is a result of the space environment. Commercial systems are also more sensitive to market fluctuations. The danger also exists that technology and knowledge might be leaked to irresponsible and hostile players.[6] Also, commercial enterprises run the risk of relinquishing a degree of independence. On top of that, when the government becomes a client, the commercial company faces a real dilemma in the case of an emergency: Should the government get priority over other clients?[7]

Despite these challenges, in the absence of a clear enemy and during a period in which many governments had to face necessary budget cuts, justifying the high costs required to develop space capabilities became even more difficult. As a result, the model of public-private dual-use partnerships gained ascendancy in the development of many fields of space activity in the United States and elsewhere. Space industries also found it difficult to finance ambitious technological projects, which require very expensive initial investments in research and development and in building infrastructure, all necessary though unprofitable stages. Thus, during the past two decades, we have witnessed a dramatic change in the politics and economics of space. Taking advantage of the civil-military nature of space technology, the public sector continues to enter into cooperation with and rely on the private sector. Of course, that does not extend to military activity and development, such as space weapons, SIGINT intelligence and so forth.

At present, public space activities, whether for military or civil purposes, are intertwined with commercial space activity; they contribute to the growth of the commercial space market and benefit from it. This

---

[5] Pace, S., "Emerging Challenges: National Security Requirements and Economic/Commercial Interests," in D. Johnson and E. Levite, (eds.), *Toward Fusion of Air and Space*, (Washington, DC: RAND & Fisher Institute, 2003), 45.

[6] Baker, J., and Johnson, D., "Security Implications of Commercial Satellite Imagery," in J. Baker, K. O'Connell, and R. Williamson, (eds.), *Commercial Observation Satellites At the Leading Edge of Global Transparency*, (Santa Monica, CA RAND Corporation, 2001), 101; Baker, J. "Case Studies in Using Commercial Satellite Imagery for Regional Conflict Resolution," in D. Johnson, and E. Levite, (eds.), *Toward Fusion of Air and Space*, (Washington, DC: RAND & Fisher Institute, 2003), 98.

[7] Williamson, R., and Baker, J., "Satellite Technologies and US Policymaking," in R. Williamson, (ed) *Dual-Purpose Space Technologies*, (Washington, DC: Space Policy Institute, 2001), 6–7.

trend was further intensified by the information revolution, with its development of computers and the Internet, which increased the use of satellites to create and transmit information and data. New options for transferring and using information, originally designated for military or national purposes, were now used for various civilian and commercial purposes, further reinforcing the trend of dual-use cooperation between the private sector and the public sector.[8]

This trend blurred the lines between military applications and services on the one hand, and civil or commercial ones on the other. During the Cold War, differentiating between military and civil space applications was easy. In the 1960s and 1970s, the defense sector in the United States developed high-resolution reconnaissance satellites for its needs, while the resolution of NASA's early LANDSAT Earth observation satellites was low.[9] In the 1970s and 1980s, Global Positioning System (GPS) in the United States and GLONASS in the Soviet Union were developed for the benefit of the defense sectors of these countries. The two systems provided better accuracy to military users than to civilian users. During the 1990s, using a feature called Selective Availability, the United States enabled the degradation of GPS accuracy for civilian use, while correcting for such degradation for military use.[10]

Today, advancements in technological development, greater accessibility to technology and the fast-growing market of applications and services based on the new advances, make it very difficult, and in some cases impossible, to differentiate between military and civil space technology, other than at the level of the end user. High-resolution satellite imagery is used for various civil and commercial applications and services. Satellite navigation systems are crucial for global aviation and maritime and ground transportation; one can no longer imagine efficient and sustainable transportation without it. In the early 2000s, recognition grew concerning the fact that civil and commercial benefits accruing from the improvement in the quality and accuracy of civilian GPS signals would be greater than the military advantage of continuing to allow the degraded accuracy of public signals. Denial of systems to correct for

---

[8] Williamson, R. "Remote Sensing Policy and the Development of Commercial Remote Sensing," in J. Baker, K. O'Connell, and R. Williamson, (eds.), *Commercial Observation Satellites*, 37–52.
[9] The resolution of the first LANDSAT was of approximately 60 m (pixel size). For further information on the development of satellite imagery, see Norris, P., *Watching Earth from Space*, (Chichester, UK: Springer, 2010).
[10] For more information, see www.gps.gov/systems/gps/performance/accuracy/, accessed on June 28, 2015.

degradation of GPS public signals was cancelled. Now civilian and military services similarly enjoy high accuracy.[11]

The Tension between Nationalism and Globalism in the Space Market

The increasing worldwide use of communications satellites and navigation satellites make them extremely important for the global economy. It is not an exaggeration to assert that these sectors of the space market are significant drivers behind modern globalization. For this reason, they are strategically valuable to the global economy as well as to the national economy of the countries that master them. At the same time, the significance of space technology for military and defense activity makes the defense sectors highly sensitive about transferring this technology to others.

During the Cold War, the politics of space development and space economy were usually formulated around the principles of techno-nationalism, which use technological development to achieve national objectives. For this reason, techno-nationalism often favors indigenous technological development and controls on transferring sensitive technologies. In the aftermath of the Cold War, and especially under the overarching theme of globalization, the politics of space became more oriented toward techno-globalism, in which technological development is used to leverage the advantages of globalization to enrich the national system of innovation. Techno-globalism thus favors removing barriers and restrictions on international cooperation and commercialization.

The strategic significance of space technology to the sustainability of national economies, and even more so to national security, prevents governments from reshaping their space policies to be fully compatible with techno-globalism. Many countries are concerned by the potential that others will be able to use commercial products for military purposes. They are also concerned about losing their autonomy and flexibility by relying on the private sector too much. Therefore, the development and transfer of space technology and knowhow are still subject to techno-nationalist policies and regulations – utilizing export controls,

---

[11] Today, civilian GPS service broadcasts on one frequency, while the military GPS service broadcasts on two frequencies. This enables military users to utilize a technique that reduces radio degradation caused by the Earth's atmosphere, and provides better accuracy. However, users of civilian GPS service can enhance the basic signal with local or regional augmentation systems, which boosts the accuracy of civilian GPS. For more information, see www.gps.gov/systems/gps/performance/accuracy/, accessed on June 28, 2015.

withholding or distributing resources, etc. – to maintain self-reliance and limit cooperation. It should be noted that these policies and regulations are often the result of national economic considerations as well. Preserving sensitive and strategic knowledge as a national asset helps local industry to sustain commercial scale and be competitive.

The politics of space in the last two decades has been affected by the tensions between techno-nationalism and techno-globalism. Yamada (2000) refers to such an environment or market as driven by a combination of principles from the two approaches, which he calls neo-techno-nationalism. Under the principles of neo-techno-nationalism, technological development is used to attain national interests by leveraging globalization. Innovation is led by private initiative and public-private partnerships and is available to foreign partners under certain conditions. Accordingly, technological development is likely to produce cooperative ventures as well as conflicts.[12]

The American policy regarding commercialization of remote-sensing satellites and imagery in the early 1990s is an example of the tension between techno-nationalism and techno-globalism. During the Cold War, the clear strategic benefits of remote sensing led the superpowers to invest great efforts in controlling the spread of high-resolution remote-sensing technology and prevent others from acquiring it.[13] In the mid-1980s, and especially after the Cold War ended, the Russians and the French commercialized their remote sensing programs.[14] By the early 1990s, Russia was offering satellite imagery of about 2-meter resolution.[15] The United States perceived this development as a threat to its strategic superiority and industrial competitiveness. In an attempt to maintain its leading position, the United States reformed its policy and initiated the Land Remote Sensing Policy Act of 1992. Two years later, the United States issued PDD-23 (Presidential Decision Directive 23–Foreign Access to Remote Sensing Data and Technology).[16] This directive allowed commercialization of remote sensing data and technology produced by American commercial companies. Although the reform loosened

---

[12] Yamada, A., "Neo-Techno-Nationalism: How and Why It Grows," paper presented at the International Studies Association Convention, Los Angeles, CA, 2000.

[13] Deibert, R., "Unfettered Observation," in H. W. Lambright, (ed.), *Space Policy in the Twenty-First Century*, (Baltimore, MD: Johns Hopkins University Press, 2003), 89.

[14] For more information on emerging spacefaring states in the post–Cold War, see Steinberg, G., "Satellite Capabilities of Emerging Space-Competent States," in *Evolving Trends in the Dual Use of Satellites*, (UNIDIR, 1996), 31–56; and J. Baker, K. O'Connell, and R. Williamson, *Commercial Observation Satellites – At The Leading Edge of Global Transparency*, (Santa Monica, CA: RAND, 2001).

[15] Norris, P. *Watching Earth From Space*, (Heidelberg, Germany: Springer, 2010), 197.

[16] The text of PDD-23 is available at: clinton6.nara.gov/1994/03/1994-03-10-statement-on-export-of-satellite-imagery-and-imaging-systems.html, accessed on June 2, 2009.

restrictions on remote sensing services, it did not allow the export of satellites or the transfer of critical technological knowhow, which remained subject to the restrictive export control applied to munitions in the International Traffic in Arms Regulations (ITAR).[17]

One of the primary reasons that the Americans created PDD-23 was to discourage other states from developing their own capabilities by providing them with commercial data services. The fundamental goal was "to support and to enhance US industrial competitiveness in the field of remote sensing space capabilities, while at the same time protecting US national security and foreign policy interests."[18] Instead, the United States discovered that nations are interested in developing national expertise in space. Kevin O'Connell, who took part in creating this policy, claims this assumption failed: "Governments and other actors in the international system are interested in developing their own capabilities. The motives vary from national security to national pride or economic interests."[19] In an interview, O'Connell further emphasized this point. "The premise of PDD-23 was that opening the market will dampen the appetite for other countries to have [space] systems. That was exactly wrong."[20]

In the early 2000s, the Department of Commerce issued licenses to sell imagery at 60 cm. resolution. Nevertheless, for security reasons, this was subject to holding back the imagery for 24 hours. In addition, the National Geospatial-Intelligence Agency (NGA) decided to use commercial high-resolution imagery produced by Geo-Eye and DigitalGlobe under a PPP model. After 9/11, in order to ensure that America's enemies would not get access to satellite images, and to avoid the dilemma of whether to prohibit the sale of imagery to others during a time of war, the NGA bought up all available imagery of Afghanistan.[21]

During the last decade, satellite imagery for commercial use has expanded and improved significantly. Nevertheless, countries became more interested in developing their own capabilities. For example, up until 2009, China acquired most of its satellite imagery from Europe and the United States. In the past several years, China has made efforts to develop independent capability in this field, initially with low resolution,

---

[17] Johnson, D. J., Pace, S., and Gabbard, B. C., (1998), *Space Emerging*, 31.
[18] The White House, Office of the Press Secretary, "Foreign Access To Remote Sensing Space Capabilities," Fact Sheet, March, 10, 1994, available at: www.fas.org/irp/offdocs/pdd23-2.htm, accessed on June 14, 2009.
[19] O'Connell, K. "Commercial Applications of Payloads and Services: Remote Sensing," in D. Johnson and E. Levite, (eds.), *Toward Fusion of Air and Space*, (Washington, DC: RAND Press, 2003), 32.
[20] Interview with Mr. Kevin O'Connell, December 8, 2006, Washington, DC.
[21] Norris, P. *Watching Earth*, 199–200.

but later with higher-resolution satellites, which considerably reduced its dependence on other countries.[22] Japan, too, has gradually become more independent in these fields. During the past several years, Japan reinforced its indigenous capabilities, primarily for national security activities in space.[23] To this end, Japan launched another intelligence satellite in 2013 and announced that it was interested in accelerating its launch program and reinforcing its overall capabilities.[24] In 2014, in order to preserve its leading role in the global market, the American government approved DigitalGlobe's request to sell higher resolution satellite imagery, with features smaller than 50 cm. (20 inches) visible.[25]

In recent years, in addition to this change, pressure from American space industries to ease export controls led to loosening the restrictions on exporting space technology. The decision to reform the export control policy was taken in December 2012.[26] The process of removing a number of items from the US Munitions List was completed in 2014.[27] The changes affected the category of Spacecraft and Satellites, permitting most commercial, scientific and civil satellites and components to be removed from the US Munitions List (USML) and instead be placed on the Department of Commerce's Commerce Control List (CCL).[28] In any event, the easing of export restrictions did not include exports to China; instead, exports to China were to be restricted even more.[29]

---

[22] de Selding, P. B. "China Launches High-resolution Commercial Imaging Satellite," *Space News*, October 7, 2015, available at: spacenews.com/china-launches-high-resolution-commercial-imaging-satellite/, accessed on February 8, 2016. Staff Writers, "China Launches A Jilin-1 Foursome," *Satnews Daily*, October 7, 2015, available at: www.satnews.com/story.php?number=1980596976, accessed on February 8, 2016.

[23] Defense of Japan (Annual White Papers) available at: www.mod.go.jp/e/publ/w_paper.

[24] Mukai, A., and Hasegawa, T., "Japan Launches Two Intelligence Satellites for National Security," *Bloomberg News*, January 27, 2013, available at: www.bloomberg.com/news/2013-01-27/japan-launches-two-intelligence-satellites-for-national-security.html, accessed on January 31, 2013.

[25] "US Lifts Restrictions on More Detailed Satellite Images," *BBC News*, June 16, 2014, available at: www.bbc.com/news/technology-27868703, accessed on June 18, 2014.

[26] Staff Writers, "Space Export Control Reform Passes House and Senate," *Space Mart*, December 27, 2012, available at: www.spacemart.com/reports/Space_Export_Control_Reform_Passes_House_and_Senate_999.htm, accessed on December 31, 2012.

[27] Gruss, M. "US Finalizes Rules Easing Export Restrictions." *Space News*, May 14, 2014, available at: spacenews.com/40563us-finalizes-rules-easing-export-restrictions/, accessed on May 16, 2014.

[28] Blount, P. J., "US Publishes New Satellite Export Regulations." *Res Communis*, May 19, 2014, available at: rescommunis.olemiss.edu/2014/05/19/us-publishes-new-satellite-export-regulations/?utm_source=feedly&utm_reader=feedly&utm_medium=rss&utm_campaign=us-publishes-new-satellite-export-regulations, accessed on May 21, 2014.

[29] Gruss, M. "Government Shutdown Delayed New Satellite Export Regulations," *Space News*, November 19, 2013, available at: www.spacenews.com/article/military-space/38245government-shutdown-delayed-new-satellite-export-regulations, accessed on November 22, 2013.

Another example of neo-techno-nationalism in space politics is the approach to Global Navigation Satellite Systems (GNSS) systems that provide free global services, but because they are considered critical national infrastructures, are nationally developed and operated. Defense funds continue to be allocated for technological development and operation of these systems, even though they are also used for civil and commercial purposes. For instance, even today, the GPS is sponsored, maintained, and controlled by the American Airforce, even though it provides free services to everyone around the world; similarly, GLONASS is operated by the Russian Aerospace Defense Forces.

For this reason, in the last decade, other leading spacefaring nations have aspired to establish national and international alternatives to the American GPS, developing indigenous global or regional space navigation systems. Russia is reinforcing and improving its GLONASS satellite navigation system, expanding its network of ground stations beyond its national borders and establishing stations in more than 35 countries.[30] Russia is also heading toward greater self-reliance in constructing electronic components for its navigation system. Within several years, Russia's domestic industry is supposed to be able to produce electronic components for its GLONASS navigation system, and thus will no longer have to depend on foreign components.[31] Not to be outdone, China is developing its Beidou satellite navigation system. In 2013, the system became operational at the regional level. China continues to develop the system and increase its geographic coverage with plans to make it global.

The desire to establish an alternative to the American navigation system has also encouraged China and Russia to seek cooperation with each other.[32] In July 2014, they signed a Memorandum of Understanding (MOU) to this effect. The two countries are planning to build navigation satellites and "monitoring stations in each other's territory, which will promote the integration of the two satellite

---

[30] Staff Writers, "Russia Eyes Building Glonass Stations in 36 countries," *GPS Daily*, April 25, 2014, available at: www.gpsdaily.com/reports/Russia_eyes_building_Glonass_statio ns_in_36_countries_999.html, accessed on April 26, 2014.

[31] Staff Writers, "Glonass System Can Fully Switch to Domestic Electronics in 2 Years," *GPS Daily*, October 6, 2015, available at: www.gpsdaily.com/reports/Russias_Glonass_ System_Can_Fully_Switch_to_Domestic_Electronics_in_2_Years_999.html,, accessed on February 8, 2016.

[32] Staff Writers, "Russia May Join Forces with China to Compete with US, European Satnavs," *GPS Daily*, June 10, 2014, available at: www.gpsdaily.com/reports/Russia_m ay_join_forces_with_China_to_compete_with_US_European_satnavs_999.html, accessed on June 12, 2014.

navigation systems and improve their performance."[33] Both Russia and China cooperate with other nations around the world to establish local monitoring stations. For example, to expand the satellite navigation system, China and Thailand signed a cooperative space agreement in July 2014. This is the first step in the process that China has undertaken to broaden the system's activities to the Association of Southeast Asian Nations (ASEAN) market.[34]

The European Union, through the European Space Agency, is developing the Galileo satellite navigation system. In 2014, Europe addressed the question of whether to make use of the Galileo system mandatory for European Union citizens. The concern was that such a move would cause protest from other countries, like Russia, China, and perhaps even the United States, who would object to this clear protectionism and stifling of competition.[35] A year later, it was reported that producers of terminals are pushing for terminals that will simultaneously receive signals from a range of systems, among them the Chinese navigation system. Such technology will improve the reliability of navigation devices and contribute to their resistance to disturbances. On the other hand, the process will interfere with the efforts of national industries and governments to promote one system over others.[36] India has also been working on satellite navigation and by 2016 has developed and deployed the seven satellite Indian Regional Navigation Satellite System (IRNSS).

The tension between techno-nationalism and techno-globalism also exists in the global commercial launch industry. In the 1980s, the United States, Europe, the Soviet Union, and China took initial steps toward being competitors in the commercial launch market.[37] In the

---

[33] Staff Writers, "China, Russia to Cooperate in Satellite Navigation," *GPS Daily*, July 7, 2014, available at: www.gpsdaily.com/reports/China_Russia_to_cooperate_in_satellite_navigation_999.html, accessed on July 09, 2014,

[34] Staff Writers, "China's Domestic Navigation System Accesses ASEAN Market," *GPS Daily*, July 3, 2014, available at: www.gpsdaily.com/reports/Chinas_domestic_navigation_system_accesses_ASEAN_market_999.html, accessed on July 5, 2014.

[35] de Selding, P. B., "Wary of Protectionist Backlash Abroad, Europe Divided over Making Galileo Mandatory at Home," *Space News*, June 13, 2014, available at: spacenews.com/40896wary-of-protectionist-backlash-abroad-europe-divided-over-making-galileo/?_wcsid=F74CC0BF4C22D3FF83FC59B6FB3D476433FDA26192541BE01AE4B369EFE25BE4, accessed on June 15, 2014.

[36] de Selding, P. B. "China Official: Beidou Gear Will Receive GPS, Glonass, Galileo Signals." *Space News*, February 6, 2015, available at: spacenews.com/china-official-beidou-gear-will-receive-u-s-russian-and-european-gnss-signals/#sthash.VZTXpjZz.dpuf, accessed on February 12, 2015.

[37] Logsdon, J., and Reed, C., "Commercializing Space Transportation" In J. Logsdon, R. Williamson and R. D., Launius, (eds.), *Exploring the Unknown-Selected Documents in the History of the US Civil Space Program*, (Washington, DC: NASA History Division, 1999), 405.

United States, the Space Shuttle, designed to serve as a reusable vehicle to place satellites in orbit, was added to the array of expendable launch vehicles already used. In Europe, a quasi-private organization, Arianespace, was established to perform commercial launches using the European ELV Ariane, which was successfully launched into space for the first time in December 1979. A year later, Arianespace conducted its first commercial launch, initiating a competition between the United States and Europe over commercial launch services.[38]

In the early 1990s, the commercial launch market experienced a boost. The collapse of the Soviet Union left Russia in serious economic difficulties. The scope of the Russian space activity was drastically decreased and government budgets allocated to aerospace were substantially reduced. The search for external funding sources was thus stimulated; the funding came by expanding commercial launch services. Today, commercial financing enables Russia to continue its activities in space and serves as an important factor in the Russian economy in general. Russia, left with a great deal of military equipment, including a stockpile of ballistic missiles, reduced costs by converting its missiles to space launch vehicles.[39] Russia and China, and later Ukraine, increased the number of commercial launches they conducted; they were followed by the ESA and later by India.

In order to sustain the leading role of American industries in the expanding market, the United States had to adapt to the commercializing trend in space launchers and technologies. Pace (2003) explained the dynamic of the 1990s: "The main competitor to the United States in space is no longer the Soviet Union, but other market economies. The Cold War fault lines have given way to the forces of economic globalization, leading to both new risks and new opportunities from the proliferation of advanced technologies and information."[40] To this end, in 1998, the United States passed the 1998 Space Launch Act. Among other things, the new law allowed American companies to provide commercial launch services. One of its primary objectives was to persuade other countries to refrain from developing their own capabilities.[41]

The American step also had strategic logic and motivation. The United States was concerned by the possibility that the severe economic crisis in

---

[38] Logsdon, J., and Reed, C., "Commercializing Space Transportation" In J. Logsdon, R. Williamson R. D., Launius, (eds.), *Exploring the Unknown*, 407.
[39] For example, the Dneper space launch vehicle is based on the R-36M missile.
[40] Pace, S. "The Future of Space Commerce," in H. W. Lambright, (ed.). *Space Policy in the Twenty-First Century*, 55.
[41] Button, K. "Introduction to Defining Aerospace Policy," in K. Button, J. Lammersen-Baum, and R. Stough, (eds.). *Defining Aerospace Policy*, (Burlington, VT: Ashgate Publishing. 2004), 5–12.

Russia, which lacked appropriate employment opportunities, would lead to dangerous leaks of strategic technology and knowhow, including missile technology, to irresponsible actors.[42] In an historical twist, it was in the interest of the United States to rebuild Russia and strengthen its economy. The United States supported the emerging space economy in Russia by launching American commercial space satellites from Russia, paying Russia for the launches and all the technology and services entailed. In addition, the International Space Station project was reignited, this time with the participation of Russia as a major player.

Launching American satellites from Russia and cooperating on the International Space Station were designed to help stabilize the Russian economy, provide jobs for Russian space engineers and technicians and build a new relationship between the two countries. The US initiative was also motivated by strategy: to improve the relationship and strengthen Russia's commitment to the United States; to loosen Russia's ties to irresponsible countries, and thereby reduce the risk of proliferation of technology and knowhow in these strategic spheres of expertise.[43]

During the past two decades, Russian and American programs of human spaceflight have become intertwined. Astronauts and cosmonauts from both countries train and work side by side, communicating in both English and Russian. Since NASA ended its shuttle program in 2011, the United States now relies on Russia to fly its astronauts into space. Russia even contributed to American military space missions: the American company ULA uses Russian-made propulsion engines (RD-180) for its space launchers, which launch American military missions. In 2014, the United States imposed economic sanctions on Russia over the Crimean and Ukrainian crises, which included purchase of the Russian RD-180 engines. Congress demanded rapid development of American-made alternatives, but the process is estimated to take several years. In December 2015, after successful lobbying by the company and pressure from the Air Force, the Senate gave ULA special dispensation to purchase 20 more RD-180 engines.[44] Nevertheless, the issue of finding a replacement to the reliance on Russian remains unsolved.

---

[42] Throughout the Cold War, the United States and the Soviet Union acted independently but cooperated in order to limit the spread of sensitive knowledge and technology in these areas of expertise. In general, they refused to share such technology even with close allies. Only a very few cases exist in which there was strategic cooperation, which included the transfer of such knowledge and technology in these fields.
[43] In 1995, Russia joined the Missile Technology Control Regime (MTCR), which was established in 1987.
[44] Shalal, A., "ULA Orders 20 More RD-180 Rocket Engines," *Space News*, December 23, 2015, available at: spacenews.com/ula-orders-20-more-rd-180-rocket-engines/, accessed on February 8, 2016

In the last two decades, the commercial launch industry saw vigorous growth. One of the outstanding examples of the change in this field was the establishment of SpaceX in 2002 and rapid growth since then. In June 2015, it was certified to launch NASA Category 2 missions and US Air Force missions.[45] SpaceX is currently developing capabilities to launch astronauts into low Earth orbit, as part of NASA's Commercial Crew Initiative. During 2015, NASA signed agreements with SpaceX and with Boeing to launch astronauts into space on commercial flights.[46]

SpaceX is considered to be the main competitor to the European Arianspace, but both have become the leaders in supplying launchers. The crisis in Russia's space industry, primarily in the field of launches, contributes to their leadership in this field. In fact, there are those who claim that they are gradually becoming a duopoly.[47]

Another field in which SpaceX is gathering momentum is the development of reusable launchers and rocket engines. In December 2015, SpaceX successfully landed the first stage of its Falcon 9.[48] In 2016, Space X began to land the Falcon 9 also at sea. In early December 2015, the Blue Origin company, which is owned by Amazon's Jeff Bezos, successfully launched and re-landed a rocket it had produced.[49] According to estimates by SpaceX, reusable launchers could cut 30 percent of launch cost.[50]

---

[45] Clark, S., "SpaceX Get Certified to Launch NASA Science Missions," *Spaceflight Now*, May 15, 2015, available at: spaceflightnow.com/2015/05/15/spacex-gets-certified-to-la unch-nasa-science-missions/, accessed on May 20, 2015; Gruss, M., "SpaceX Falcon-9 Certified for Military Launchers," *Space News*, May 26, 2015, available at: spacenews .com/u-s-air-force-certifies-falcon-9-for-military-launches-2/, accessed on May 30, 2015.
[46] NASA Press Release, "NASA Orders SpaceX Crew Mission to International Space Station," NASA.gov, November 20, 2015, available at: www.nasa.gov/press-release/na sa-orders-spacex-crew-mission-to-international-space-station, accessed on March 12, 2015.
[47] de Selding, P. B., "SES, Eutelsat CEOs Vow To Do What it Takes to Avoid SpaceX, Arianespace Duopoly," *Space News*, June 12, 2015, available at: spacenews.com/ses-eu telsat-ceos-vow-to-do-what-it-takes-to-avoid-spacex-arianespace-duopoly/#sthash.2R CKvy8Y.dpuf, accessed on June 13, 2015.
[48] Weaver, M., "'Welcome Back, Baby': Elon Musk Celebrates SpaceX Rocket Launch – and Landing," *The Guardian*, December 22, 2015, available at: www.theguardian.com/ science/2015/dec/22/welcome-back-baby-elon-musk-celebrates-spacex-rocket-launch-a nd-landing, accessed on June 6, 2016.
[49] Launch Space Staff Writers, "Bezos Takes Big Step Towards Reusable Commercial Space Flight," *Space Daily*, available at: www.spacedaily.com/reports/Jeff_Bezos_Take s_Another_Step_Toward_Realizing_Reusable_Commercial_Space_Flight_999.html, accessed on December 20, 2015.
[50] de Selding, P. B., "SpaceX Says Reusable Stage Could Cut Prices 30 Percent, Plans November Falcon Heavy Debut," *Space News*, March 10, 2016, available at: spacenews .com/spacex-says-reusable-stage-could-cut-prices-by-30-plans-first-falcon-heavy-in-no vember/, accessed March 21, 2016.

The Challenge of the New Space Economy

The extensive commercialization of the space market induced the trend of New Space. The designation "New Space" means many things, including the introduction of a range of new entrepreneurs into space activities, challenging the hegemony of states by conducting a new commercial space race. As part of this trend, new companies and well-established industries are working to develop low-cost access to space and affordable space technologies and services, some of which were already mentioned above. These industrial and technological developments affect the structure of the space market, leading to greater reliance of governments on the private sector.

Most New Space undertakings are private, commercial ones, offering various developmental and business models for their innovative initiatives, which are very different from the traditional approaches to space activities. The miniaturization of satellites, which lowers the costs of developing and launching a satellite, enables diverse new players to be active in space, greatly contributing to the trend. The participants range from universities and even high school groups,[51] through small companies, developed countries, up to commercial enterprises planning to put large constellations of satellites in orbit.

In 2014, Google Inc. (now Alphabet Inc.) announced that it was expanding its activities to space. As part of this expansion, it acquired Skybox Imaging (in 2016, the company was renamed Terra Bella).[52] Google also showed interest in providing Internet access for people living in remote areas of the world, through the establishment of a space-based wireless network.[53] A year later, Google decided to

---

[51] In June 2014, a Nano-satellite developed by a high school group from Israel was launched into space.

[52] Skybox or Terra Bella is a company created with the idea of launching cheap satellites, using off-the-shelf components. de La Merced, M. J., "Google to Buy Skybox Imaging for $500 Million," *New York Times*, June 10, 2014, available at: nytimes.com/blogs/dealbook/2014/06/10/google-to-buy-skybox-imaging-for-500-million/?emc=edit_th_20140611&nl=todaysheadlines&nlid=67703388, accessed on June 12, 2014.

[53] Kabir, O., "Google Will Launch a Fleet of 180 Micro-satellites," *Calcalist*, June 2, 2014, available at: www.calcalist.co.il/internet/articles/0,7340,L-3632706,00.html?dcRef=ynet, accessed on June 4, 2014; Zolfagharifard, E., "Now Google is Going to Dominate Space: Search Giant to Launch 180 Satellites to Provide Internet Access for the ENTIRE Planet, Sources Claim," *Daily Mail.com*, June 2, 2014, available at: www.dailymail.co.uk/sciencetech/article-2646039/Googles-plans-world-domination-Search-giant-launch-180-satellites-bring-internet-access-ENTIRE-planet.html, accessed on June 4, 2014; Vincent, J., "Google Planning to Launch $1bn Constellation of 180 Satellites, Say Reports," *The Independent*, June 2, 2014, available at: www.sometechnews.com/news/google-planning-to-launch-1bn-constellation-of-180-satellites-say-reports, accessed on June 4, 2014.

abandon this ambitious initiative.[54] In 2015, it was reported that OneWeb had raised US$500 million from a group of global investors to support its plans to provide broadband service via a constellation of 648 satellites.[55] OneWeb awarded the contract to produce the satellites to Airbus.[56] The Arianespace company was chosen to launch the system.[57] SpaceX also announced its intention to develop a giant network of some 4,000 satellites to provide broadband internet access to remote areas that are cut off from the Internet today.[58] Google Inc. and Fidelity Investments invested a billion dollars in the SpaceX initiative, with Google investing 90 percent of the total.[59] Other examples of New Space entrepreneurial companies are Black Sky Global, GeoOptics Inc., OmniEarth Inc., Satllogic Inc., Spire Global Inc., Effective Space Solutions, Sky, and Space Global. These and similar initiatives can dramatically change the traditional structure of space activities.

In the past several years, the number of small satellites (up to 50 kg.) launched has increased dramatically; they constitute a significant portion of the satellites launched annually. In 2014, 158 such satellites were

[54] Fernholz, T., "Facebook and Google Are Out of the Space Race," *Quartz*, June 8, 2015, available at: qz.com/422775/facebook-and-google-are-out-of-the-space-race/, accessed June 10, 2015.
[55] Griffiths, S., and Prigg, M., "Blast Off for World's Biggest Satellite Constellation as OneWeb Signs Deal to Launch 600 Craft to Bring the Internet to Everyone on Earth," *Daily Mail*, June 26, 2015, available at: www.dailymail.co.uk/sciencetech/article-31409 44/Blast-world-s-biggest-satellite-constellation-OneWeb-signs-deal-launch-600-craft-b ring-internet-Earth.html, accessed on June 28, 2015.
[56] "France's President + CEOs Celebrate As OneWeb Selects Airbus Defense + Space To Connect The World w/ Microsatellites," *Satnews Daily*, June 15, 2015, available at: www .satnews.com/story.php?number=1735784868, accessed on June 19, 2015. Staff Writers, "Airbus DS to Build OneWeb Satellite Constellation," *Space Daily*, June 16, 2015, available at: www.spacedaily.com/reports/Airbus_Defence_and_Space_Selected_ to_Partner_in_Production_of_OneWeb_Satellite_Constellation_999.html, accessed on June 19, 2015.
[57] de Selding, P. B., "Launch Options were Key to Arianespace's OneWeb Win," *Space News*, June 26, 2015, available at: spacenews.com/launch-options-were-key-to-arianespa ces-oneweb-win/#sthash.ogIyvEJm.dpuf, accessed on June 29, 2015. Foust, J., "OneWeb Contract A Milestone For Virgin Galactic's Smallsat Launch Effort," *Space News*, June 25, 2015, available at: spacenews.com/oneweb-contract-a-milestone-for-vir gin-galactics-smallsat-launch-effort/#sthash.RouNgYyP.dpuf, accessed on June 29, 2015. Virgin Galactic Press Release, "Virgin Galactic Signs Contract with OneWeb to Perform 39 Satellite Launches, " *SpaceRef*, June 25, 2015, available at: spaceref.com/n ews/viewpr.html?pid=46183, accessed on June 29, 2015.
[58] Petersen, M., "Elon Musk and Richard Branson Invest in Satellite-Internet Ventures," *Los Angeles Times*, January 16, 2015, available at: www.latimes.com/business/la-fi-satel lite-entrepreneurs-20150117-story.html, accessed on January 18, 2014.
[59] Associated Press, "SpaceX Gets $1B US Investment from Google, Fidelity," *CBC News*, January 21, 2015, available at: www.cbc.ca/news/business/spacex-gets-1b-us-invest ment-from-google-fidelity-1.2921335, accessed on January 29, 2015.

launched.[60] This trend already raises serious concerns about the sustainability and safety of the space environment, the implications of crowded orbits and regulation issues, as well as their possible effects on the economics of space.[61] One of the most urgent issues is the impact on the quantity of space debris, which is constantly increasing and poses a real threat to every active satellite in orbit. The increased number of small satellites will further exacerbate the problem; due to their small size and low weight, small satellites do not have deorbiting capabilities. Therefore, once their mission is completed, they become dangerous debris. If their altitude is high, they are likely to remain in orbit for dozens of years. In response to these concerns, OneWeb reported that it is working to prevent the proliferation of space debris it generates. The company even promised that its satellites will deorbit five years after the end of their service rather than in twenty-five years, which current international guidelines require.[62] In 2016, Planet Labs Inc., a cubesat manufacturer and operator, reported that it adopted NASA's guidelines for limiting orbital debris as its policy.[63]

Another important field of growth is commercial human spaceflight. Several initiatives are underway, including Xcor Lynx and Virgin Galactic Spaceship.[64] At the beginning of 2014, after the successful test flight of Virgin Galatic's sub-orbital spacecraft in which it reached a height of 71,000 feet above Earth, expectations for progress in this field were high.[65] At the end of October, 2014, doubts intensified when SpaceShipTwo crashed and the co-pilot was killed. Investment in human spaceflights by the private market is still not a foregone conclusion. The accident renewed interest and discussion about the technological feasibility and economic profitability of space endeavors for the private market. Headlines proclaimed the end of the dream of space

---

[60] Buchen, E., and DePasquale, D., "2015 Nano/Microsatellite Market Assessment." *SpaceWorks*, available at: www.spaceworksforecast.com/docs/SpaceWorks_Small_Satellite_Market_Observations_2015.pdf, accessed on June 17, 2015.

[61] de Selding, P. B., "Signs of a Satellite Internet Gold Rush in Burst of ITU Filings," *Space News*, January 23, 2015, available at: spacenews.com/signs-of-satellite-internet-gold-rush/?_wcsid=F74CC0BF4C22D3FF83FC59B6FB3D476433FDA26192541BE0B26D1F549ADA3DE0, accessed on January 25, 2015.

[62] de Selding, P. B., "OneWeb Pledges Vigilance on Orbital Debris Issue." *Space News*, October 15, 2015, available at: spacenews.com/oneweb-pledges-vigilance-on-orbital-debris-issue/, accessed on October 19, 2015.

[63] Planetlabs, available at: medium.com/@planetlabs/keeping-space-clean-cubesat-constellations-space-debris-f30fcf9ca85b#.j4chaezbo, accessed on January 15, 2016.

[64] For further information on these projects and their status, see www.xcor.com/ and www.virgingalactic.com/, accessed on January 17, 2016.

[65] Staff Writer, "SpaceShipTwo Soars to 71,000 Feet above Earth During Test," *Space Travel*, January 10, 2014, available at: www.space-travel.com/reports/SpaceShipTwo_soars_to_71000_feet_above_Earth_during_test_999.html, accessed on January 12, 2014.

tourism and even hinted that space tourism might be over, because of the high risks involved.[66] Nonetheless, in all likelihood these and new challenges will be faced and overcome as efforts to provide human commercial spaceflights continue.

Finally, there is the issue of harmful space capabilities. Intuitively, one would not think that the commercial actors can play an active role in this sphere; however, the dual-use technology and some of its applications challenge this premise. As mentioned above, one of the major issues with which all space players have to deal with is space debris. A major threat to government and commercial satellites, any piece of floating debris can potentially hit any orbiting satellite. Currently, efforts are underway to develop techniques for "cleaning up" space. Some of these techniques are commercial initiatives. Concern exists that such systems would also "clean up" functioning satellites, and not only the debris. The same concerns apply to technologies being developed to pull an asteroid into an orbit around the Earth to perform space mining. Such a technology could be used to send the asteroid to hit the surface of the Earth. With this in mind, will it be possible for a private company to possess space weapons?

This overall trend of commercialization introduces a new spirit to the economics of space. More energetic, creative, and dynamic than the governmental race, commercial activity in space is likely to effect dramatic changes in space activities, which in turn will be very significant for governmental space activities. Governments can no longer ignore commercial space activities, and instead need to address the questions they raise. Among the relevant issues to be addressed are the current and future role of countries in the space economy; regulating space activity, specifically space traffic, increasing congestion in the electromagnetic spectrum, space debris, export controls and international cooperation; and allocation of funds. All of these subjects and new ones that will arise will affect the future of the space club.

Governmental Activities in Space

The technological developments that produced widespread use of satellites in the last two decades have enabled a large array of medium-sized and small countries to develop and deploy their own satellites, most using foreign launch services. In the years of the Cold War (1957–1990),

[66] For example: Vergano, D., "Will Virgin Galactic's Crash End Space Tourism?" *National Geographic*, November 2, 2014, available at: news.nationalgeographic.com/news/2014/10/141031-virgin-galactic-space-tourism-impacts/, accessed November 4, 2014.

twenty-five countries had a satellite in space. Since then, the number of countries with satellites in space has steadily increased, in what some refer to as a multi-national space race.[67] By 2015, sixty-eight states had sent satellites to space, whether they developed them indigenously or purchased them commercially.

Increasing space budgets reflect the increase in governmental activity as well. In the decade from 2000 to 2009, government budgets for space programs almost doubled, going from US$36 billion to some US$70 billion. According to Euroconsult, the principal contributory factors include defense procurement; increasing interest in space technology in a large number of countries; and increases in research and development investments in space exploration, human spaceflights, launchers and satellite applications.[68] Despite these large allocations, the total governmental budget for space activities is only about a quarter of the market, down from about a third just a few short years ago.[69] Increased private, commercial investment in space accounts for the difference. Nevertheless, the government market is a large source of revenue and remains vital to the industry.

In Asia, space activities have increased considerably. Competition is high and some analysts characterize it as a space race.[70] China, India, Japan, and even South Korea are involved in this space race; all of them invest a great deal of resources in their space programs in a broad spectrum of fields. They do so to enhance their capabilities and display power, so as to improve their standing and status both regionally and globally. Other Asian nations – Vietnam, Malaysia, Indonesia, and Singapore – are promoting space activities as well, although at lower levels. Latin America, too, is experiencing an awakening in everything associated with space activities. Many countries are interested in enhancing their capabilities, among them Mexico, Bolivia, Ecuador, Venezuela, and others.

Space has also become a focus of interest in the Middle East and Africa. The nations of those regions have shown a growing interest in space, and

---

[67] Johnson, D. J., Pace, S., and Gabbard, B. C., *Space – Emerging Options for National Power*, (Washington, DC: RAND, 1998); D. Johnson and E. Levite, (eds.), *Toward Fusion of Air and Space*, (Washington, DC: RAND, 2003); Moltz, J. C., *Asia's Space Race: National Motivations, Regional Rivalries, and International Risks*, (New York: Columbia University Press, 2012).

[68] Bochinger, S., (ed)., Profiles of Government Space Activities 2012, Euroconsult, (Paris, Euroconsult, March 2012), p.1.

[69] According to the 2015 Space Report of the Space Foundation, in 2014, government budgets for space totaled US$79.17 billion, which constituted 24 percent of the global space market of US$330 billion that year.

[70] For a comprehensive examination of Asia's space diplomacy and politics, see Moltz, J. C., *Asia's Space Race*.

Governmental Activities in Space 197

want to affect the type of space activity taking place. Among these countries are Turkey, Algeria, Nigeria, South Africa, Saudi Arabia, Egypt, and of course Iran. In 2015, Turkey stated that developing an independent capability to build its own satellites is of strategic importance to the country, and over time will contribute to the Turkish economy as well.[71] In 2014, Iran announced that it is developing a spacecraft that will be capable of carrying three astronauts.[72] Despite the difficult situation in Syria and the civil war that has been raging there, the Syrian government announced the establishment of a space agency.[73] In June 2014, Iraq launched a small student satellite via a Russian launcher.[74] Algeria is expanding its space activities by signing an agreement with Surrey Satellite Technology Ltd. (SSTL) to develop an observation satellite, the Alsat 1B, and train Algerians in satellite work.[75] One of the more interesting developments is that of the United Arab Emirates (UAE), which announced its intentions to launch its first locally built satellite, the Khalifa-Sat, in 2017. As part of its growing interest in space activities, the UAE also established a space agency, to engage in cooperation with other agencies.[76] In 2015, the UAE signed Memoranda of Understanding with China,[77] Russia, the UK, Kazakhstan, and CNES, the French space agency. The MOU with CNES includes joint work on a probe to Mars. The probe is planned to reach Mars in 2021 as part of the nation's celebration marking fifty years of independence.[78] In addition, the UAE has begun talks with Russia, to acquire maritime launch

---

[71] de Selding, P. B., "Construction of Turksat's 1st Domestic Satellite Now Underway," *Space News*, April 21, 2–15, available at: spacenews.com/construction-of-turksats-1st-domestic-satellite-now-underway/, accessed on April 30, 2015.

[72] Staff Writers, "Towards Manned Orbital Mission: Iran to Build its Own Spacecraft," *Space Travel*, June 10, 2014, available at: www.space-travel.com/reports/Towards_manned_orbital_mission_Iran_to_build_its_own_spacecraft_999.html, accessed on June 15, 2014.

[73] Rupar, T., "Syria Has Set Up a Space Agency," *Washington Post*, March 18, 2014, available at: www.washingtonpost.com/blogs/worldviews/wp/2014/03/18/syria-has-set-up-a-space-agency/, accessed on March 19, 2014.

[74] Lee, J., "Iraq to Launch Satellite this Month." *Iraq Business News*, June 3, 2014, available at: www.iraq-businessnews.com/tag/tigrisat/, accessed on June 5, 2014.

[75] de Selding, P. B., "SSTL to Build Alsat 1B Imaging Satellite in Algeria," *Space News*, July 10, 2014, available at: spacenews.com/41202sstl-to-build-alsat-1b-imaging-satellite-in-algeria/#sthash.3cQVutsD.dpuf, accessed on July 12, 2014.

[76] "UAE It's A First Arab-Built Satellite To Launch," *Satnews Daily*, January 2, 2014, available at: bit.ly/1Svrw4i, accessed on January 5, 2014.

[77] Press Release, UAE Space Agency, "UAE Signs an Mou with People's Republic of China for Cooperation in Space Science," *Thomson Reuters Zawya*, December 28, 2015, available at: spacenews.com/france-uae-sign-cooperative-space-accord/, accessed on January 3, 2016.

[78] de Selding, P. B. "France, UAE Sign Cooperative Space Accord," *Space News*, April 9, 2015, available at: www.spacedaily.com/reports/UAE_Moves_to_Purchase_Russian_Spacecraft_Launch_Platform_999.html, accessed on April 13, 2015.

platforms which would be capable of launching commercial satellites on Zenith-3SL rockets.[79]

Despite the profusion of emerging spacefaring nations and the rapid commercialization of space, the United States is still the main actor and the most advanced spacefaring nation. The United States is followed and challenged by Russia, China, Europe, and India.

The global economic crisis of the past several years has brought about reductions in the space budgets of many countries, especially in the United States, Russia, Europe, and Canada. The need to tighten budgetary belts challenged these countries to re-examine their priorities, choose the most important things in which they wish to invest, and explore the best methods to do so. One could assume that the budgetary difficulties and technological obstacles would result in them narrowing their space activities and focusing on applications which fulfill direct needs, instead of investing in less tangible goals, such as scientific missions. However, interest in scientific research in space and in human spaceflight has not diminished.[80] Most of this activity is generated by the United States and Europe. Even Russia, which has been suffering from severe economic constraints, has a substantial space science program.

Immediately after the collapse of the Soviet Union, Russia's economy suffered a fast decline, which also affected its space program. Nevertheless, in the eyes of the Russian political echelon, the Russian space program is a very important tool for reinforcing Russia's global status and strengthening its economy. Despite technical failures and funding constraints, the government is very attentive to the space sector, aspiring to restore Russia's capacity and increase its market share of space activities.[81] At the end of 2015, Deputy Prime Minister for Defense Dimitry Rogozin, in speaking on the subject, reiterated Russia's pledge

---

[79] Staff Writers, "UAE Moves to Purchase Russian Spacecraft Launch Platform," March 26, 2015, available at: www.spacedaily.com/reports/UAE_Moves_to_Purchase_Russian_Spacecraft_Launch_Platform_999.html, accessed on March 27, 2015.

[80] According to the 2012 Euroconsult report, US$10.9 million were invested in human spaceflights throughout the world in 2011, which constitutes 18 percent of the total government investment in space. That number has been declining. Investment in space science and exploration was ten percent of the total investment in space, i.e., some US$6 billion. Bochinger, S., (ed), *Profile of Government Space Programs*, (Euroconsult, March 2012), 3–8.

[81] The Russian government announced its decision to increase its space budget. The budget is expected to reach seven billion dollars annually, a figure almost equaling Europe's investment in space activities. de Selding, P. B., "Russia Boosting Space Budget To Surpass China, Equal Europe," *Space News*, June 5, 2013, available at: www.spacenews.com/article/civil-space/35638russia-boosting-space-budget-to-surpass-china-equal-europe, accessed on June 7, 2013; "Russia to Aim for 15 Percent of Global Space Market – Medvedev," *SputnikNews*, February 23, 2013, available at: en.ria.ru/science/20130223/179638875/Russia-to-Aim-for-15-of-Global-Space-Market–Medvedev.html, accessed on February 25, 2013.

to continue working toward its space goals.[82] In order to place Russia in the forefront of space activities worldwide and close the gaps in its space program compared to those of other countries, Russia's government initiated several reforms and adopted a plan focused on deep space exploration, with the moon as its principal objective.[83]

A major development in governmental space activity in the aftermath of the Cold War is the rise of China as a prominent member of the space club. During the last two decades, China undertook an ambitious space program for military and political empowerment and to benefit economically. In the 1990s, after several launch failures, China worked to strengthen its capabilities and credibility as a reliable space launch provider. It also focused considerable energy on its ties with other spacefaring nations, including the United States.[84] Nevertheless, at the end of the decade, the United States was concerned with the growing Chinese capabilities and the proliferation of knowhow, which could benefit China's nuclear delivery system. Therefore, the United States increased its controls over cooperation with China, imposed export controls, blocked China's inclusion in the International Space Station initiative, and in general tried to exclude China from full membership in the space club.[85] These efforts were further intensified in 2007, after China performed an experiment in anti-satellite capability (ASAT).

Despite American efforts to rein in China, or because of them, China adopted strategies that are similar to the strategies used by the United States and the Soviet Union during the Cold War space race. China's civilian space program became a significant element in its foreign policy, aimed at gaining soft power through visible high-profile projects. Another objective was to attract other countries to its side. China's visionary goals

---

[82] Staff writers, "Death Rumors of Russian Lunar Program 'Greatly Exaggerated' – Deputy PM," *Moon Daily*, December 31, 2015, available at: www.moondaily.com/reports/Deat h_rumors_of_Russian_lunar_program_greatly_exaggerated___Deputy_PM_999.html, accessed on January 3, 2016; Staff writers, "Russia Postpones Plans on Extensive Moon Exploration Until 2025," *Moon Daily*, December 30, 2015, available at: www.moonda ily.com/reports/Russia_Postpones_Plans_on_Extensive_Moon_Exploration_Unti l_2025_999.html, accessed on January 3, 2016.

[83] Staff Writers, "Russian Deputy PM Attacks Space Industry with Reform Bill," *Space Daily*, May 20, 2015, available at: www.spacedaily.com/reports/Russian_deputy_PM_a ttacks_space_industry_with_reform_bill_999.html, accessed on May 22, 2015; Staff Writers, "Russia Plans to Start Moon Exploration Jointly With Partners," *Moon Daily*, May 15, 2015, available at: www.moondaily.com/reports/Russia_Plans_to_Start_Moo n_Exploration_Jointly_With_Partners_999.html, accessed on May 17, 2015.

[84] For a detailed overview and analysis of China's space program, see Moltz, J. C., *Asia's Space Race*, 70–109.

[85] Yardley, J., "Snubbed by US, China Finds New Space Partners," *New York Times*, May 24, 2007, available at: www.nytimes.com/2007/05/24/world/asia/24satellite.html?_r=0, accessed on May 26, 2007.

were backed by heavy investments in widely diverse fields and spectacular projects, such as human spaceflights and Moon missions. In October 2003, China successfully launched its first Chinese Taikonaut and became the third nation to launch its own citizens into space. Ten years later, in December 2013, China successfully launched the Chang'e 3 to the Moon. This accomplishment made China the third nation in the world, and the first from Asia, to land on the Moon. China's investment in human spaceflight, as well as in robots sent to the Moon, are designed to build up China's image as a strong, leading world power, and project a message of advanced technology and national capability. That message is meant for the ears of three communities: its rivals, the Chinese people, and other nations with which China is interested in strengthening ties.

To meet this objective, China put great effort into establishing and sustaining cooperation with other countries. These cooperative ventures encompass: the development and launch of satellites; training of space scientists and engineers from other countries; and sometimes even providing economic assistance to other nations for their own space programs. In 2013, China announced that it would allow foreign astronauts to fly to the space station it planned to build in the future.[86] China has focused these efforts on countries in Asia, Africa, and South America.

In 2005, China promoted the establishment of the Asia-Pacific Space Cooperation Organization (APSCO). Based in Beijing, APSCO operates as an intergovernmental non-profit organization to promote collaborative space projects among its members.[87] APSCO was formally inaugurated at the end of 2008. Through the establishment and leadership of this organization, China is attempting to position itself as a global spacefaring nation and as a significant space hub for developing countries. As part of these attempts, China offered to train scientists and engineers from developing nations, like Pakistan, Nigeria, and Bolivia.[88] Another example of such cooperative ventures is China's partnership with Thailand to develop an observation satellite to improve early identification and warning of natural disasters.[89] These cooperative ventures enable China to

---

[86] David, L., "China Invites Foreign Astronauts to Fly On Future Space Station," *Space.com*, September 28, 2013, available at: www.space.com/22984-china-space-station-foreign-astronauts.html, accessed on September 29, 2013.

[87] For further details, see APSCO, www.apsco.int.

[88] Qian, W., "China Providing Space Training," *China Daily*, October 29, 2013, available at: usa.chinadaily.com.cn/world/2013–10/29/content_17064723.htm, accessed on October 30, 2013; de Selding, P. B., "China Launches Bolivia's First Telecom Satellite," *Space News*, December 23, 2013, available at: www.spacenews.com/article/launch-report/38800china-launches-bolivia%E2%80%99s-first-telecom-satellite, accessed on December 24, 2013.

[89] Staff Writers, "China's Satellite Navigation System to Start Oversea [sic] Operation Next Year," *GPS Daily*, November 1, 2013, available at: www.gpsdaily.com/reports/Chinas_

augment its ties to a variety of developing countries, increase their dependency on China and position itself as a gatekeeper of the club.

In order to position itself as a significant global actor in space, China has also been working to reinforce its ties to Russia as well as to European countries. In recent years, Russia and China have continually grown closer in their space activities. The two have established a dialogue on various subjects, among them navigation and the establishment of a joint station on the moon.[90] In December 2013, Britain and China signed an MOU on space exploration. Several months after that, they held a joint workshop in Shanghai on space science and technology.[91] In March 2014, a cooperative agreement was signed between China and France. The first tangible manifestation of this agreement is the joint development of an astronomical Space-based Variable Object Monitor (SVOM), to examine gamma ray bursts. The project, announced in August, will mount the Gamma-Ray-Burst Astronomy Satellite on a Chinese Long March rocket, to be launched in 2021.[92] In January 2015, it was reported that the ESA and China are exploring the possibility of sending one of ESA's astronauts to China's future space station.[93]

Judging by these mammoth efforts, China is clearly working its way to legitimately position itself as an important member of the space club. In general, these efforts have proven to be successful. The many cooperative ventures that China has woven with the space agencies of other leading countries and its growing space capacity have reinforced China's status. Consequently, it has become more difficult for the United States to push China out of the club. To further emphasize this point, Russia and Europe have been outspoken in criticizing the United States for

---

satellite_navigation_system_to_start_oversea_operation_next_year_999.html, accessed on November 2, 2013.

[90] Staff Writers, "Russia, China Agree on Joint Exploitation of Glonass Navigation Systems," *Space Daily*, May 14, 2015, available at: www.gpsdaily.com/reports/Russia_China_Agree_on_Joint_Exploitation_of_Glonass_Navigation_Systems_999.html, accessed on May 15, 2015. Staff Writers, "Russia Invites China to Join in Creating Lunar Station," *Moon Daily*, April 29, 2015, available at: www.moondaily.com/reports/Russia_Invites_China_to_Join_in_Creating_Lunar_Station_999.html, accessed on May 3, 2015.

[91] British Consulate General Shanghai, "UK and China's Biggest Yet Joint Workshop on Space Science and Technology," May 28, 2014, available at: www.gov.uk/government/world-location-news/uk-and-chinas-biggest-yet-joint-workshop-on-space-science-and-technology, accessed on June 11, 2015.

[92] de Selding, P. B., "China, France Join Forces on Astronomy Mission," *Space News*, August 4, 2014, available at: spacenews.com/41479china-france-join-forces-on-astronomy-mission/, accessed on August 6, 2014.

[93] Clark, S., "Europe, China Issue Call for Joint Science Mission," *Spaceflight Now*, January 24, 2015, available at: spaceflightnow.com/2015/01/24/europe-china-issue-call-for-joint-science-mission/, accessed on June 11, 2015.

attempting to exclude China from the club. For example, in June 2015, upon retiring from his position, Jean-Jacques Dordain, the Director General of the European Space Agency, sharply criticized the United States for its efforts to exclude China from international space exploration. Dordain stated that the United States cannot continue its attempts to isolate China from space research. Rather, China should be guaranteed a place in the international array of countries working in this field.[94]

While attending the annual International Aeronautics Congress (IAC), which was held in Beijing in 2013, NASA Administrator Charles Bolden said that it was unlikely that the United States and China would enter into large-scale cooperation in the near future. Two years later, in October 2015, at the same venue of the IAC, this time in Jerusalem, Bolden said that the prohibition on cooperation with China in space activities is temporary and will end, at least in the field of space exploration. The head of China's space agency, Xu Dazhe, responded that his country would be happy to cooperate with the United States.[95]

China and the United States, as two leading members of the club, have no alternative but to seek interaction. For this reason, they are active in forums on international space activity, like the Inter-Agency Space Debris Coordination Committee (IADC), in which they are both members. In December 2014 on a visit to China, Frank A. Rose, Deputy Assistant Secretary of the Bureau of Arms Control, Verification and Compliance at the State Department, said that "As two of the principal space-faring nations that derive significant benefits from the use of space, the United States and China have a mutual interest in protecting and preserving the long-term safety, security, stability, and sustainability of the space domain for all nations." According to Rose, one of the areas in which the two countries can cooperate is preventing an increase in orbital debris in space. He stated that at the US-China Strategic and Economic Dialogue held in July 2014, the United States and China reaffirmed the fact that orbital collision avoidance serves their common interest in exploring and utilizing outer space for peaceful purposes. They therefore agreed to take practical steps to improve coordination in this area. Both sides also

---

[94] de Selding P. B., "Dordain Says ESA Cannot Go it Alone in Debris Mitigation." *Space News*, May 21, 2005, available at: spacenews.com/dordain-says-esa-cannot-go-it-alone-in-debris-mitigation/, accessed on October 2, 2016.

[95] de Selding, P. B., "China and the Moon Loom Large Yet Distant for Bolden, Woerner," *Space News*, October 16, 2015, available at: spacenews.com/china-and-the-moon-loom-large-yet-distant-for-bolden-woerner/, accessed on August 2, 2016. Klotz, I., "NASA Chief Says Ban on Chinese Partnerships is Temporary," *Reuters*, October 12, 2015, available at: www.reuters.com/article/us-space-usa-china-idUSKCN0S61S U20151012, accessed on August 2, 2016.

committed to establishing bilateral government-to-government consultation mechanisms and holding regular meetings on outer space activities.[96]

At the end of June 2015, Chinese and American officials agreed to establish a "US-China Civil Space Cooperation Dialogue."[97] The first meeting between the United States and China as part of this official dialogue on space took place in Beijing in October 2015. Both sides agreed on the importance of the meeting and on the need to strengthen the ties between the two countries vis-à-vis space.[98] Another meeting was held in Washington, DC, in May 2016. Similar discussions between the two have also taken place regarding meteorology. At the end of August 2015, the second meeting between high-ranking meteorologists from the United States' NOAA and their Chinese counterparts took place. Agreement was reached regarding the importance of continuing cooperation between the two countries. They also discussed possible cooperative projects.[99]

The above examples show that the growing trend of cooperation does not nullify the strong element of competition that drives international space activity. The field of space exploration enjoys a growing interest on the part of many countries, which are motivated by the desire to both compete in the international space arena and to cooperate with other countries. Their interest is expressed in new national exploration programs, in allocation of resources, and in the statements of decision-makers and senior government and space agency officials in these nations. Human and robotic exploratory flights to areas far from the Earth, to the Moon and Mars, and to asteroids, comets, and other celestial bodies are all examples of missions that the world experiences as synonymous with criteria for technological advancement and competition. For example, in his speech after the ESA's successful landing of the Philae probe on Comet 67P, Jean-Jacques Dordain, Director General of the ESA, said,

---

[96] These remarks were made by Rose at The Johns Hopkins-Nanjing Center for Chinese and American Studies, Nanjing, China, on December 8, 2014, available at: www.state.gov/t/avc/rls/2014/235384.htm, accessed on June 10, 2015.

[97] Smith, M., "US, China Agree to Bilateral Civil Space Cooperation Dialogue," *Space Policy Online*, June 26, 2015, available at: www.spacepolicyonline.com/news/u-s-china-agree-to-bilateral-civil-space-cooperation-dialogue?utm_content=buffer360b0&utm_medium=social&utm_source=facebook.com&utm_campaign=buffer, accessed on June 29, 2015.

[98] Staff Writers, "The First Meeting of the US-China Space Dialogue," *Space Daily*, October 1, 2015, available at: www.spacedaily.com/reports/The_First_Meeting_of_the_U_S__China_Space_Dialogue_999.html, accessed on February 8, 2016.

[99] Staff Writers, "The Second China-US High-level Meeting on Satellite Matters was Held," *Terra Daily*, September 2, 2015, available at: www.terradaily.com/reports/The_second_China_US_high_level_meeting_on_satellite_matters_was_held_999.html, accessed on February 8, 2016.

"We are the first to do this, and that will stay forever."[100] Dordain's message was a clear indication that this achievement was not solely scientific and technological. Rather, this successful mission also has political and strategic significance for the ESA and for all of Europe.

Another example of the political and strategic significance of space exploration in world politics is India's important achievement in space exploration, which was attained when its Mars mission, the Mangalyaan (launched in December 2013) successfully entered Mars orbit in September 2014. The success of the mission proved that even with a modest budget, significant achievements are possible.[101] Later, in December 2014, India succeeded in launching a capsule and it returned to earth, an important step in attaining human flights.[102] These events and the way in which they were treated point to the importance of these achievements, and are evidence of the developing trend amongst the leading spacefaring nations to go further away from Earth and deeper into space.

The growing interest in space activity and the persistence with which traditional spacefaring nations act in space, especially by embarking on missions of space exploration, science and human spaceflight, even in times of global economic crisis, indicates that space technology and exploration continues to be valuable in world politics. This trend should be seen as an attempt by leading spacefaring nations to set the direction for future governmental space activity in contrast to private sector activity. Governments' funds are usually allocated to the areas in which the private sector does not invest. Therefore, the progress made by private sector players, especially in commercial launch services and space tourism, pushes national activity further and deeper into space.

An analysis of government space activities and their effect on the space club cannot ignore the actions taken by North Korea and Iran, and the reaction of members of the club to their activities. During the Cold War, eight states demonstrated their capability to launch satellites into space and were accepted into the club, meaning that their efforts and

---

[100] Sample, I., and Clark, S., "Comet 67P Becomes Landing Site for Philae in Historic Touchdown," *The Guardian*, November 13, 2014, available at: www.theguardian.com/science/2014/nov/12/rosetta-mission-philae-historic-landing-comet, accessed on November 20, 2014.

[101] Choudhury, S., and Sugden, J., "How India Mounted the World's Cheapest Mission to Mars," *India Real Time*, September 23, 2014, available at: blogs.wsj.com/indiarealtime/2014/09/23/how-india-mounted-the-worlds-cheapest-mission-to-mars/, accessed on September 30, 2014.

[102] Staff Writers, "India Launches Biggest Ever Rocket into Space," *Space Daily*, December 18, 2014, available at: www.spacedaily.com/reports/India_launches_biggest_ever_rocket_into_space_999.html, accessed on December 24, 2014.

achievements were internationally recognized as legitimate, enabling them to benefit from cooperation between them. In the post–Cold War era, three more countries achieved this feat. In 2009, Iran successfully launched a satellite into space. In late 2012, North Korea launched a satellite, and in January 2013, South Korea placed a satellite in orbit.[103]

In 2009, after the first Iranian launch of a satellite, the Iranian president declared that Iran had turned into a true and genuine superpower. He also stressed that having a national capacity to explore and use space serves Iran's overall struggle with the "imperialist powers," because the "Iranian nuclear issue and the launch of the Omid satellite ended their [the West and non-Islamic states'] monopoly of science."[104] Hojjat al-Islam Gholam-Hussein Mohseni-Eje'i, Iran's Intelligence Minister, expressed a similar approach by saying that "despite the wishes of the enemies of Islam, we have made outstanding achievements in the field of technology, and we are now the eighth member of the space club, thanks to the efforts of local scientists."[105] Such a statement by an Iranian defense official highlights the military implications of the Iranian launch, which was formally conducted for peaceful purposes. The launch was timed to coincide with the thirtieth anniversary of Iran's Islamic Revolution and to emphasize the fact that Iran became the first Islamic country to launch a satellite into space. The timing of this launch was certainly scheduled to maximize attention to this message, glorify Iran and its Islamic regime.

In North Korea, the failed attempt to launch a satellite in April 2009 was similarly exploited to challenge the leading powers as well as to reinforce domestic support of the regime and its leadership. A political report published in North Korea shortly after the launch took place and failed is a good example:

There are many countries in the world that have launched a satellite. Why, then, does such a great sensation shake the planet each time a satellite is launched from the Democratic People's Republic of Korea? ... What an overwhelming event it is

---

[103] Ukraine did not launch independently, but it manufactures the Zenit rockets launched by Sea Launch and therefore has an orbital launch capability. About twenty countries have sub-orbital capability, which is required for a rocket to enter space; see *Space Security Index 2006*, http://spacesecurityindex.org/2006/10/. 62.

[104] National Technical Information Service, (NTIS). "Iranian President Gives Revolution Anniversary Speech, Vision of the Islamic Republic of Iran Network-1." *World News Connection*, Tuesday, February 10, 2009.

[105] Iran was the ninth country to indigenously launch a satellite into orbit, while Israel was the eighth to do so in 1988. It is no coincidence that both Iranian speakers miscounted and ranked Iran as the eighth member of the club. NTIS, "Iranian Intelligence Minister: Bomb Defused on Revolution's Anniversary," *World News Connection*, Tabnak Online, Tuesday, February 10, 2009.

that the satellite of our country made by its hands and launched with its own efforts is flying in outer space, when even the countries boasting of their economic power as ranking among the highest in the world in terms of national income have to launch by relying on others' means of launch ... We have proudly stepped above the world. The Kim II Sung nation has shown that not only its spiritual strength is incomparably strong, but is also as wise as can be.[106]

Clearly, Iran and North Korea use their capability to launch into space to project their power and transmit a message of deterrence. Their capability to launch satellites testifies to their potential capability to launch missiles and in the future to develop ASATs. Their leaders swaggeringly use the terminology of the space club and take advantage of the peaceful image of the club in order to legitimize their activities. By framing their actions this way, they oppose the club and challenge its members.

Despite their statements that they have joined the space club, other members of the club did not accept them as members and do not treat them as such. In general, North Korea, and to a lesser extent, Iran, get criticized for their actions. They are usually not invited to take part in international ventures and do not enjoy international cooperation in space, except for very limited cooperation with China, and in the case of Iran, Russia. By contrast, South Korea is considered a legitimate member and its achievements enjoy the recognition of the other club members.

The difference in the attitude toward South Korea stems from the overall perception that its space activities are peaceful. To that should be added the fact that South Korea signed the Non-Proliferation Treaty (NPT)) in 1975 and as of 2001 it is a partner to the Missile Technology Control Regime (MTCR). Iran's space program, and to a greater extent, North Korea's program, are viewed in the context of their nuclear and ballistic missiles programs, which are under UN Security Council sanctions. Thus, their space programs are often treated as covers for the development of military capabilities and conducting ballistic missiles tests, which they are prohibited from doing. Both North Korea and Iran are prohibited from conducting any kind of launches, including the launch of satellites into space.

In December 2012, after North Korea launched its first satellite into space, it was seriously criticized and condemned by the Security Council for violating its resolutions. The United States referred to it as "a highly

---

[106] NTIS, "DPRK Party Organ Hails Satellite Launch," *World News Connection*, April 9, 2009; Song, Mi-ran: Political Essay "Knocked on the Gate to a Powerful State," Pyongyang Korean Central Broadcasting Station in Korean, 6:14 GMT, April 7, 2009.

provocative act that threatens regional security."[107] Even China expressed deep concerns and did not publicly congratulate North Korea for its achievement.[108] A few days after the launch, it was reported that the satellite was tumbling and not broadcasting.[109] This assessment gave credence to the theory that the launch was in fact a cover for a ballistic missile test. In April 2013, the United States reported that it had recovered the front section of North Korea's rocket from the ocean. Thus, it was able to learn about North Korea's warhead design, advancing knowledge of the progress of North Korea's nuclear program.[110] In January 2016, North Korea claimed it successfully detonated a hydrogen bomb in a test. A few weeks later, on February 7, 2016, North Korea conducted another launch into space. Prior to the launch, several neighboring countries condemned and warned North Korea, trying to prevent it from taking this action.[111] In this case too, the satellite apparently failed to function.[112]

Until July 2015, when the major powers reached an agreement with Iran over its nuclear program, reactions toward Iran were similar. As part of the nuclear arms agreement, some of the sanctions on Iran were eased. For example, Resolution 1929 of the UN Security Council, adopted in 2010, prohibited Iran from conducting launches.[113] In July 15, 2015, this resolution was replaced with Resolution 2231, the language of which is considered less restrictive:

Iran is called upon not to undertake any activity related to ballistic missiles designed to be capable of delivering nuclear weapons, including launches using

---

[107] Space.com staff, "North Korea Successfully Launches a Satellite: Reports," December 12, 2012, available at: www.space.com/18867-north-korea-rocket-launch-satellite.html, accessed on December 20, 2012.

[108] Associated Press, "North Korean Satellite 'Orbiting Normally' after Rocket Launch," *The Guardian*, December 13, 2012, available at: www.theguardian.com/world/2012/dec/13/north-korea-satellite-rocket-launch, accessed on December 20, 2012.

[109] Staff Writers, "North Korea Satellite Appears Dead: Scientist," *Space War*, December 12, 2012, available at: www.spacewar.com/reports/N_Korea_satellite_appears_dead_scientist_999.html, accessed on December 13, 2012.

[110] Lake, E., "US Recovery of North Korean Satellite Exposed Nuclear Progress," *The Telegraph*, April 15, 2013, available at: www.telegraph.co.uk/journalists/the-daily-beast/9995514/US-recovery-of-North Korean-satellite-exposed-nuclear-progress.html, accessed on June 14, 2015.

[111] Ryall, J., and Connor, N., "Japan Says It Will Shoot Down North Korean Rocket If It Threatens Its Territory," *The Telegraph*, February 3, 2016, available at: www.telegraph.co.uk/news/worldnews/asia/northkorea/12137377/North Korea-announces-plan-to-launch-rocket-into-space.html, accessed on: February 5, 2016.

[112] Williams, M., "The Slow Search for Kwangmyongsong 4," *North Korea Tech*, February 11, 2016, available at: www.northkoreatech.org/2016/02/15/the-slow-search-for-kwangmyongsong-4/, accessed February 25, 2016.

[113] For more information, see www.un.org/press/en/2010/sc9948.doc.htm, accessed on June 20, 2012.

such ballistic missile technology, until the date eight years after the Joint Comprehensive Plan of Action (JCPOA) Adoption Day or until the date on which the IAEA submits a report confirming the Broader Conclusion, whichever is earlier.[114]

A month later, in August 2015, Russia and Iran signed a cooperative agreement on space activities. The agreement between them calls for joint development of a satellite system to monitor the earth's surface, atmosphere and oceans. The launch of the first satellite in the system is expected to take place in 2018.[115]

The efforts made by North Korea and Iran to develop space capabilities, especially capabilities to launch satellites into space, highlight two important aspects regarding the nature and dynamics of the space club. First, the space club is a technological club. Nevertheless, when it comes to technological development, over time, if a country is dedicated to acquiring a technology and is willing to devote sufficient resources, it is impossible to prevent that country from acquiring the technology. Evidence shows that the efforts to prevent Iran and North Korea from getting access to space technology, missile technology, and nuclear technology and knowhow eventually failed. Both Iran and North Korea made efforts to collaborate with each other, as well as with other countries in the Middle East and South Asia, in order to share information on rocketry and gain experience in space development.[116]

Second, acquiring the capability to develop satellites and launch them into space is a condition, but insufficient by itself, to join the space club. Space capable countries are awarded membership in the club through recognition of their achievements, legitimacy of their capabilities, and expressions of interest in cooperation made by the leading members of the club. North Korea does not enjoy this recognition. In Iran's case, as indicated above, things began to change in the second half of 2015, when both China and Russia initiated limited cooperation with Iran.

---

[114] Nuclear Agreement with Iran: Joint Comprehensive Plan of Action (JCPOA) concluded on July 14, 2015, see UN Resolution 2231, Annex B, article 3, dated July 20, 2015, 99. For more information, see www.securitycouncilreport.org/atf/cf/%7B65BFCF9B-6D27-4E9C-8CD3-CF6E4FF96FF9%7D/s_res_2231.pdf, accessed on February 28, 2016.

[115] Staff Writers, "Russia to Help Iran Build own Satellite Observation Systems," *RT*, August 25, 2015, available at: www.rt.com/news/313410-Russia-Iran-space-cooperation/, accessed on February 11, 2016. Staff Writers, "Russia to Develop Earth Remote-Sensing Satellite System for Iran," *Sputnik News*, August 25, 2015, available at: sputniknews.com/science/20150825/1026180063.html, accessed on February 11, 2016

[116] Moltz, J. C., *Asia's Space Race*, 172.

These activities should be carefully reviewed and analyzed as they may indicate a slow change in the dynamic of the space club in favor of Iran.

To conclude this chapter, the space club is a product of the Cold War. Nevertheless, in the post–Cold War era, its conceptual foundation is still evident and its underlying value still appeals to many countries. Space technology and exploration still serve as means and as symbols of power, high standing, and esteem.

9 Conclusions and Future Directions

This book sought to explain and explore the phenomena of nation-state clubs in world politics, using the case study of the space club. The primary argument is that nation-state clubs have a significant role in the organization of the social structure of the international system and the perceived stratification of power and status. Clubs are prime venues for national competition over power, high standing, and governance. They are expressions of and reflect an era's means of power; they are symbols of high standing and national esteem. As such, clubs play a role in the socialization of states about what is expected of them. In addition, nation-state clubs serve as an arena in which states interact and negotiate over the distribution of power, status, and influence in global politics. That said, states join clubs because of what they perceive to be the expectations of others and their own aspirations to achieve power, standing, influence over global governance and national esteem due to geo-strategic considerations and intrastate needs.

Membership in clubs is a criterion by which states compete, compare, and evaluate other states. Therefore, it is one of the tools used by states to claim and project power, standing, influence and national esteem. For these states, joining clubs is a rational consideration because it provides tangible goods and intangible benefits reserved only for members.

In a world in which it is generally believed that countries act rationally to maximize their national interests under clear, tangible cost/benefit considerations, undertaking a large-scale national project like a space program merely out of a motivation to "join a club" may seem arbitrary and irrational. But power is not measured and achieved only by instrumental capability. Power is measured and achieved by symbols as well. Technological capability in space grants power not only because of the instrumental power it entails, but also because of its symbolic power. Therefore, states are rationally motivated to develop space capability by its symbolic power as much as they are motivated to do so by its instrumental power; symbolic power may even be a greater motivation.

Investigating international space activity using the framework of nation-state clubs, this study (a) traced the evolution of the club since the early days of the space age and (b) provided insight regarding the motivations and reasons that caused states to embark on large-scale national space programs. The evidence provided in this study supports the argument that global governmental space activity is explainable with the framework of nation-state clubs. Furthermore, international activity in the area of space technology and exploration clearly paralleled the five-stage process of nation-state club formation.

Traditionally, the politics of space exploration in the Cold War focused on the superpowers' space race. Nevertheless, analysis of this period using the conceptual framework of the space club extends the prism, showing that the superpowers promoted space accomplishments as a means of power and competence, a symbol of high standing and national pride. In this process, states were socialized to perceive expertise in space as one of the significant indicators for being a great power. As a result, nations that were perceived as great powers and those that aspired to achieve this status were expected to master space technology in order to get a seat at the table of global governance.

For the superpowers, space became an arena in which they could exercise their leadership, interact, and compete with one another without risking escalation to nuclear conflict. Using spectacular events, each of the superpowers demonstrated to the world its stellar qualities, justifying claims for world leadership and proficiency, and demanding support in a non-aggressive way. As part of this process, each superpower offered friendly and non-aligned states the opportunity to cooperate on its space program or invited them to participate in it. This strategy, which combined public competition and cooperative initiatives, created an understanding that expertise in space was a first-rate symbol of superiority and an overall measure of power. National expertise in space became a symbol of statehood and an important mark of strong capabilities to develop state of the art technologies and manage large-scale national projects – important qualities for great powers. The superpowers used coercion or attraction or verbal fighting[1] as strategies in order to convince others to accept their interpretation of space capability, to wit, that it was a symbol and means of power. Less powerful countries accepted the superpowers' interpretation of power and followed in this path.

---

[1] Bially Mattern, J., "Why Soft Power Isn't So Soft: Representational Force and the Sociolinguistic Construction of Attraction in World Politics," *Millennium – Journal of International Studies*, 33, (2005), 602.

As a result, the race to space, usually referred to as a bilateral competition, was in practice a multilateral race. However, in order to preserve their relative strategic and economic advantages and because of the strategic characteristics of space technology, particularly the means of launching objects into space, the superpowers feared its proliferation. Therefore, both the United States and the Soviet Union closely monitored the spread of space technology and knowhow by imposing severe restrictions on the transfer of technology and knowhow. In doing so, the superpowers turned space activity into a very exclusive field in which only a handful of dedicated states were involved; these states were acknowledged as an elite group – the space club.

Although no formal organization or association called "space club" existed, nor were there club rules or regulations, admissions committees, or any central management, the politics of space were characterized by an inherent tension between competition and cooperation that have produced the components of what has been termed in political jargon the "space club". The superpowers, monitoring its activities, served as the club's leaders and gatekeepers. The space race and the space club, as its institutionalized form, were intended to construct a reality of American and Soviet attractiveness and so help to cultivate each of the superpower's soft power. The fact that states aspired to emulate the deeds of the superpowers by developing their own space capabilities testifies to the fact that nations accepted this interpretation of space as a symbol of power offered by the superpowers. This highlights the important aspect of public and visible projection of power in club politics.

This examination teaches us about the great importance of intangible considerations in decision-making and in setting policy priorities. Tangible cost/benefit considerations, although prerequisites, are inadequate in explaining the decision-making processes of states. In the realm of space technology and exploration, the premise that states are social entities that are socialized to perceive power in a certain way and act according to a set of international expectations and national aspirations is strengthened. Furthermore, this study points out that joining nation-state clubs is a rational, legitimate, and significant consideration when states decide to undertake space activities.

In addition to the examination of the roots and essence of the space club, the study shows that from the early 1960s on, club rhetoric regarding space activity became an integral part of the international political discourse over power, governance, status, and national identity. Leaders and state officials use declarations of membership in the space club to communicate a message of power and explain a new technological reality. They do so because they often find that the message of membership in a club is easy to understand and provides the important added value of political power. They use the rhetoric of club membership to linguistically and socially construct a message to an international audience and the domestic population.

By claiming membership in the space club, leaders try to convince others to adopt their social and political interpretation of the achieved capability in terms of power, status, and esteem, and provide them a conceptual tool to evaluate the achievement. Membership in the space club serves as a benchmark, signaling a state's worth and power. Thus, the act of joining the club is a means rather than an end for states in their strategy to socially construct a reality of desired power, status, and influence. In general, the instrument of such clubs is utilized to fulfill international expectations and domestic needs, much in the same way that clubs fulfill these functions for its human members in society. The use of club rhetoric by leaders and officials of medium-sized and small nations is a reinforcing cycle to this narrative, socially constructing it as a reality.

Analysis of the case studies of France, Britain, Canada, Australia, India, and Israel demonstrates that these states were socialized to acknowledge space expertise as a means and as a symbol of power. Nevertheless, it shows that differences existed in the way each state transformed this understanding into actual preferences and priorities regarding its level of space activity and involvement in the club. The analysis shows that in all cases, instrumental tangible needs were important initial factors, but they were insufficient by themselves to convince decision-makers to embark on ambitious national space programs. Geo-strategic conditions; domestic needs and considerations; the national narrative, history, and culture unique to each of these states shaped national aspirations to achieve power, status, and esteem, as well as national perceptions of what is expected of the state. These factors, in different combinations, affected the way each state perceived the values of space technology and national space activity, and consequently shaped its preferences and policies.

Comparison of these case studies reveals that France, Canada, India, and Israel were more ambitious about their space activity and membership in the club than were Britain and Australia. In general, as a result of geo-strategic conditions and domestic factors, the more ambitious states suffered from an intense perception of threat or political instability. Israel was threatened by its hostile environment. The country's perception of threat was reinforced by its collective memory and historical experience. Canada was concerned about its geographical position as a bridge between the Soviet Union and the United States, and about being overshadowed by its giant American neighbor. Furthermore, at the time, societal and political turmoil threatened the very existence of the Canadian identity and political stability. France feared a Soviet invasion of Europe during the Cold War. Its perception of threat was reinforced by memories of the world wars, in which it was overrun by Germany. Additionally, France, which suffered political unrest, perceived the American strategic umbrella over Western Europe as a threat to European and French identity and independence in decision-making. As a non-aligned country, India had to project a powerful and independent position. India was challenged by China and was faced with a domestic challenge to achieve fast development.

In each of these cases, having a space program as a means and as a symbol of power fulfilled aspirations and needs for empowerment, lofty status, and high national esteem. Hence, in all of these cases, having a space program was a national priority, and the adopted policies were compatible with the principles of techno-nationalism. In France, Canada, India, Israel, and Britain (before Britain acknowledged its decline), developing space expertise was part of a national process aimed at achieving powerful positions in the hierarchy of nations, and projecting power that would assure their survivability and contribute to their identities. Although each state had its own unique characteristics and reasons, they all aspired to be associated and identified with the spacefaring nations. They wished to be taken seriously in international forums and arenas. Claiming membership in the space club served as a message of intent, capability, and decisiveness aimed at adversaries and even more so at allies, especially the United States, the unofficial leader and gatekeeper of the "club."

The overall British, Australian, and Israeli approaches were pragmatic. The difference between France, Canada, and India, compared to Britain, Australia, and Israel is not in technical expertise and knowhow. Rather, the difference lies in the aspirations of these countries for high status and power and in their perceived expectations of the international community of them by virtue of their status and power. This process affects the degree of political commitment shown by the national leadership. For example, in the 1960s, once the British leadership recognized that Britain could no longer measure up to the superpowers, it lost interest in being a significant player in space. Australian leadership had no aspirations to power and high status in the first place. Israel developed its space program out of a deep sense of threat, not out of an aspiration for the status of a power.

The historian Paul Kennedy remarked that the ambition of Britain, France, and later, China to join the nuclear club was a reflection of weakness rather than strength.[2] Kennedy's observation is applicable to the space club as well. Claiming membership in the space club is a useful tool in the hands of the weak seeking assimilation to the strong, usually at the latters' expense, in order to preserve and upgrade the formers' status or prevent decline. By using club rhetoric, France, Canada, and India (and Britain at the very beginning) tried to link themselves to larger and stronger states. Israel used technological development and club rhetoric to gain proximity to other members, to project a somewhat peaceful deterrence. All of these cases were led by their weakness to seek membership in the space club as a means to prove, improve, and justify their claims of status and power. Kennedy's observation, nevertheless, ignores an important aspect of club politics. That factor is the perspective of the strong nations using club politics to reinforce and justify their power and status as the leaders of an elite group so as to validate their power and supremacy by maximizing their capabilities and influence.

Achieving a national space capability demands a major national effort that is difficult to justify economically or materially. For nation-states that identify themselves as powers or declining powers, developing indigenous space capabilities under a claim of membership in the space club is a means to preserve or restore powerful status. Joining the space club for them is necessary. Therefore, national resources, investments, and all other efforts involved are justified. In these cases, governments explicitly seek to join the club, as in the cases of France and Britain before the latter acknowledged its medium-power status. This was also identified in Brazil and even in Iran, which expressed aspirations to metaphorically "join the club" even before achieving expertise in space technology.

In those situations wherein a state or its leadership want an indigenous space capability for other reasons, and the argument of joining the space club is not primary, it is nevertheless added to the variety of considerations to tip the balance in favor of the decision to develop indigenous space capabilities. In such cases, arguments concerning the significance of joining the space club serve to vindicate the efforts, sometimes when the development comes to fruition and is publicly demonstrated or sometimes in retrospect. In these cases, governments do not explicitly seek to join the club. Instead, they claim membership to vindicate their efforts *ex post facto*, as happened with Canada and Israel.

Another important finding from the analysis of the case studies is the fact that states' actions are not solely directed at their counterparts with the aim of deterring adversaries. Instead, states' actions are often directed

---

[2] Kennedy, P., *The Rise and Fall of The Great Powers*, (New York: Vintage Books, 1987), 370.

toward allies and like-minded states from which they want to gain support and legitimacy, or with which they want to be associated. For that reason, they are willing to carry heavy burdens in order to project power and messages of capability and intent. Their behavior corresponds to the Handicap Principle,[3] in which a reliable signal must be costly to the signaler in order to convince others of his sincere intentions and commitment to achieve his goals.

For example, for both France and Canada, the United States is a major point of reference. The goal of distinguishing their power and position from that of the United States was a significant national consideration, which affected the decision to acquire and project capability in space. By contrast, both Australia and Britain, having strong ties with the United States, are not perceived as a national threat to sovereignty and identity.[4] Both countries thus displayed much more confidence in collaborating with the United States and relying on it, instead of expending significant resources for self-reliance in space. It is worth noting that the initial British decision to embark on a space program had the effect of drawing the United States closer to Britain. Hence, in this case as well, the message was aimed at the United States rather than at Britain's adversaries. By contrast, in India, the fact that it was not aligned with any of the superpowers played a significant role. India needed to project high capability in order to sustain is position as leader of the non-aligned countries. Furthermore, it used the rivalry between the two superpowers in its favor and benefited from cooperation with both of them. In Israel, development of the space program was accelerated because of the United States' refusal to share satellite imagery.

Examination of the case studies also reveals that domestic considerations regarding national development, status, power, and esteem direct space policies. In France, the space effort was aimed at restoring the populace's confidence in the state and its political system by restoring France's seat at the table. In Canada, the space program served important social and political needs, boosting a coherent and unified Canadian identity. In Israel, in addition to acquiring concrete capabilities for its national security, the space program was used by the government to enhance national pride and esteem, as was the case in India, in which the space program was used to restore its heroic past and create

---

[3] Zahavi, A., "Mate Selection – A Selection for a Handicap," *Journal of Theoretical Biology*, 53, (1975), 205–241.

[4] Blaxland, J., *Strategic Cousins – Australian and Canadian Expeditionary Forces and the British and American Empires*, (Montreal and Kingston, Canada: McGill-Queen's University Press, 2006) 272.

a promising future. In these cases, the space programs were also used to encourage the local scientific community and industrial sector.

In sum, countries with strong incentives to project power to enhance international standing, national esteem, and pride are more likely to adopt ambitious strategies about their space activity and prefer the development of indigenous capability. By contrast, low incentives of these kinds result in a more moderate approach to space and even in a decision not to "join the club." These countries are more likely to adopt a strategy of purchasing space services and products from other nations. One way or the other, joining the space club is a legitimate, rational, and significant consideration explaining decision-making and national preferences in the area of space technology and exploration.

Although this research is focused on the space club, it provides a conceptual framework and methodology that can be applied to other political areas, as well as important lessons for understanding world politics and the social construction of power. The concept that nation-state clubs are used and useful in world politics is clearly demonstrated; the study provides a useful model with which to scrutinize and evaluate states' motivations and behavior. Therefore, it warrants attention by International Relations scholars and policy officials.

In general, nation-state clubs are the result of interactions between states about means and symbols of power; such clubs teach states what is expected of them. The framework of clubs is used by superpowers to retain and reflect their world leadership and by medium-sized and small states that aspire to upgrade their status to a level comparable to larger and more powerful states so as to be identified with them and play a role in global politics.

In the process of constructing status and power, membership in a club grants political meaning to technological achievements, and maximizes the gains of political and diplomatic power. Club membership provides a context in which material or tangible capability may evolve into power. By promoting and glorifying achievements, perhaps more than the achievements really warrant, the smaller states aim to broadcast a credible message of power and decisiveness.[5] By placing a state in a higher category of capability and power than the one to which it actually belongs, claims of club membership are often no more than pretenses of power, creating the illusion of power. One way or another, membership in clubs is a means by which members or candidates can claim and generate

---

[5] Jervis, R., *The Logic of Images in International Relations*, (New York: Columbia University Press, 1989), 14, 55.

support for their actions and obtain compliance from other members regarding their status, as well as project a message of deterrence.

In his comprehensive investigation of war, Lebow (2010), regarding the future of warfare, observed that "the possible decline in the traditional military-economic basis for standing, points to a growing interest in the intangible criteria ... to award standing ... by means of unrelated to military muscle."[6] In this context, a club like the space club serves as an arena for contests over power and standing in somewhat peaceful and non-aggressive ways. Nations can thereby gain power, status, and esteem without becoming major military powers. Membership in clubs is one of the criteria by which states can claim standing and national esteem in a world system that no longer admires the use of military force. Therefore, the rhetoric of joining clubs is a means to linguistically define and socially display states' capabilities and identities, shaping and reflecting on their power and images in a way that peacefully but competitively upgrades their status and national esteem (and is less likely to trigger a security issue).

The exploration of nation-state clubs in general and the presented study of the space club in particular, contributes to understanding the process and mechanisms that affect states' preferences, priorities, and policies. That is because it brings together and illuminates the connections and interactions among a wide range of causal factors that are normally analyzed in isolation from one another. The concept of clubs does not supersede existing explanations for state behavior, such as the important role played by national security needs in the process of national decision-making, or the incentives of national economic growth and development. Instead, the concept helps to "complete the picture" by positing that claiming membership in clubs is a communicative strategy used to socially construct a reality of desired status and power for various international and domestic considerations. Furthermore, the politics of clubs is not exclusively related to the international sphere. Club politics plays a role in and is deeply affected by the domestic sphere as well.

Finally, observing states' preferences, priorities, and policies regarding national space programs using a methodology of a contrastive comparison of pairs provides better causal explanations. This comparative method of study also demonstrates that the expected behavior of states is explained not only by international factors but also by domestic considerations, internal political discourse, narratives, culture, and history. All of these elements shape national identity and perceptions, and consequently behavior. Using this methodology shines a light on the

---

[6] Lebow, R. N., *Why Nations Fight* (New York: Cambridge University Press, 2010), 185.

complexity of states' behavior and provides a more comprehensive analysis of states' motivations and aspirations, in which geo-strategic and material needs and conditions are important but are inadequate on their own to convince decision-makers to embark on a large-scale project like a national space program.

An artificial theoretical and methodological separation of the motivations of states to be active in space provides a partial picture and does not allow a comprehensive understanding. The theoretical framework of clubs, together with the methodology of contrastive comparison, integrates these motivations into one structure. This structure simplifies the complexity involved in analyzing motivations and provides the necessary analytical foundation for explaining space politics in particular, and patterns of behavior in the international system in general.

In order to preserve the space club's exclusive status and exclusive nature, the greatest challenge faced by the leading members of the space club is to maintain a clear and exclusive boundary between club members and non-members. Analyzing the trends of the space market and those of governmental activities raises the question of whether the space club is still attractive as a benchmark of national power and high status. The answer cannot be intuited either way. Continuous investments by governments of large sums of money in national and international space activity indicate that governmental interest in space still exists. However, the profusion of governmental actors, in addition to the rapidly growing trends of commercialization, do not necessarily attest to a clear future for the space club and may indicate its slow demise.

Potential Future Scenarios for the Space Club

The space club has several possible future scenarios. In light of the profusion of actors and growing trend toward commercialization, one scenario is that the space club would cease to exist. Other scenarios address possible directions in which the space club could go in order to preserve its exclusivity and significance for power and status in world politics. The future of the club depends on the willingness of its leading members to preserve its small size by redesigning a higher barrier between the haves and have-nots, thus providing an alternative stratification to the current pyramid of the space club.

The space club will cease to operate as an exclusive club if it loses its attractiveness in the eyes of the large powers and wannabes as a symbol for defining a great country. This will happen when the number of actors with proven indigenous space capabilities dramatically increases. Such a process would lead to a drop in the added value and intangible benefits that come with having this capability; the result would be the flattening of the space club pyramid. Another option that may lead to the demise of the space club is the rise of a new club, which would replace it as the benchmark for acquiring a seat at the table of the large powers that affect global governance. In such a case, the superpowers and other large powers would lose interest in preserving a clear boundary between the haves and haves-not in the field of space technology and exploration, and shift their efforts to another field that would better serve their interests vis-à-vis power and status.

Several directions in which the leading spacefaring nations are already headed today could, in effect, redesign and raise the bar for access to the space club. In general, these directions involve complex and sophisticated scientific and technological high-risk projects, which demand long-term national commitments and allocation of extensive resources. Only a small number of dedicated countries would be able to pull off such projects. The following activities, together or separately, have the potential to set a clear and visible boundary to the space club, which most countries would be unable, unwilling or uninterested in crossing: Human spaceflight missions to Mars and beyond, including the settlement of humans in space; the development of super-heavy launch capability; longer-distance journeys deep into the solar system and beyond; space mining; the development and deployment of Space Situational Awareness systems and GNSS; and the development and deployment of space weapons including ASATs. Apart from space mining, it is unlikely that commercial actors will pursue similar visions of their own in these directions in the near future.

Space Exploration

In the past several years, the United States, Russia, China, India, Japan, and the ESA have all announced ambitious intentions to send robotic and human missions to the Moon, Mars, and even much more distant places. Two Moon missions were launched in 2013: the American Lunar Atmosphere and Dust Environment Explorer (LADEE) and the Chinese Chang'e 3 lunar probe. In 2014, Russia declared that it was working towards a human mission to the Moon.[7] In January 2015, the Chinese Spacecraft Service Module entered into orbit around the Moon,

---

[7] Staff Writers, "Russia Plans to get a Foothold in [sic] the Moon." *Moon Daily*, April 15, 2014, available at: www.moondaily.com/reports/Russia_plans_to_get_a_foothold_in_th e_Moon_999.html, accessed on April 17, 2014; Staff Writers, "Russia to take Moon Exploration as Core of Space Program." *Moon Daily*, October 14, 2014, available at: www.moondaily.com/reports/Russia_to_take_Moon_exploration_as_core_of_space_progra m_999.html, accessed on October 15, 2014; Staff Writers, "Manned Mission to Moon

to identify appropriate landing sites for the Chinese Change'e 5 mission that is planned for 2017.[8] ESA's new director general, Johann-Dietrich Woerner, has announced that the Moon will be the principal objective of the ESA's space exploration road map. Woerner's vision is to establish a permanent station on the moon, similar to the International Space Station in composition and cooperation with other participants.[9] In October 2015, it was reported that Russia and the ESA were expanding their cooperation on lunar missions, jointly planning the Luna 27 mission. The mission's purpose is to explore the possibility of an extended stay on the moon, by landing on the moon's southern pole. The mission is slated for launch by the end of the decade.[10]

For many of these spacefaring nations, the moon is only the first stage of a larger roadmap for long-distance and deeper space exploration. Many of them are interested in missions to Mars, the exploration of asteroids, and other celestial bodies. For example, Russia and the ESA cooperate on the ExoMars mission.[11] In addition to this program, Russia announced that it expects to participate in every future human space flight to Mars.[12] In 2015, NASA began initial examination of possible landing sites on Mars, although the mission is expected to take place in another 20 years.[13] The vision to embark on human travel to Mars is accompanied by the development of super heavy launchers that would be capable of

---

Scheduled by Roscosmos for 2020–2031." *Moon Daily*, July 21, 2014, available at: www.moondaily.com/reports/Manned_mission_to_Moon_scheduled_by_Roscosmos_for_2020_2031_999.html, accessed on July 22, 2014.

[8] David, L., "Chinese Spacecraft Enters Orbit around the Moon." *Space News*, January 20, 2015, available at: spacenews.com/chinese-spacecraft-enters-orbit-around-the-moon/, accessed on January 25, 2015.

[9] Derla, K., "Moon Village is International Space Station Successor, Stepping Stone to Mars: ESA Head," *Tech Times*, January 16, 2016, www.techtimes.com/articles/124968/20160116/moon-village-is-international-space-station-successor-stepping-stone-to-mars-esa-head.htm, accessed on February 11, 2016.

[10] Ghosh P., "Europe and Russia Mission to Assess Moon Settlement." *BBC*, October 16, 2015, www.bbc.com/news/science-environment-34504067, accessed on February 8, 2016.

[11] Staff Writers, "Europe Helps Russia get Banned US Electronics for ExoMars Project." *TASS*, September 30, 2015, available at: tass.ru/en/science/824976, accessed on February 8, 2016. Staff Writers, "Russia, Europe Agree on Developing ExoMars Project." *TASS*, August 26, 2015, available at: tass.ru/en/non-political/816654, accessed on February 8, 2016.

[12] Staff Writers, "Roscosmos: Manned Flight to Mars Will Be Impossible Without Russia's Help." *Mars News*, March 15, 2015, available at: www.marsdaily.com/reports/Roscosmos_Manned_Flight_to_Mars_Will_Be_Impossible_Without_Russias_Help_999.html, accessed on February 8, 2016.

[13] Foust, J., "NASA Begins Effort To Find Landing Sites for Human Mars." *Space News*, October 30, 2015, available at: spacenews.com/nasa-begins-effort-to-find-landing-sites-for-human-mars-missions/, accessed on February 8, 2016.

putting such a mission on track to Mars. In recent years, both the United States and Russia began developing such heavy launchers.[14]

Research into asteroids, via dedicated missions, has also gathered momentum and interest. In March 2015, NASA chose the concept for its planned Asteroid Redirect Mission (ARM). The plan calls for a robotic vehicle to pick up a boulder up to 4 meters in diameter from the surface of an asteroid and send it into a retrograde lunar orbit. An Orion spacecraft with two astronauts would then fly to this new, smaller asteroid and collect samples for study on earth.[15] The ESA, too, is planning a mission to a pair of asteroids located 6.8 million miles (11 million kilometers) from earth, as part of the Asteroid Impact Mission (AIM), which will integrate with NASA's Double Asteroid Redirection Test (DART) program.[16]

These missions into deeper space, among other things, convey the message that these spacefaring nations are not marching in place nor remaining in low Earth orbit (LEO), where most space activity currently takes place. By embarking on long-distance missions deeper into space, they set a higher standard for space club members and redesign the entry bar. Further support for this analysis came in January 2016, when Bill Gerstenmaier, Associate Administrator for Human Exploration and Operations at NASA, announced that in order to focus its actions on longer distance missions, NASA would gradually decrease its activities and investments in human spaceflight in LEO.[17] Gerstenmaier's statement was aimed at drawing a line between public and private space activities and simultaneously encouraging the private sector to develop independent and separate platforms.

---

[14] Press Release 14–229, "NASA Completes Key Review of World's Most Powerful Rocket in Support of Journey to Mars," *NASA*, August 27, 2014, available at: www.nasa.gov/press/2014/august/nasa-completes-key-review-of-world-s-most-powerful-rocket-in-support-of-journey-to/#.VAyoRsV_uSp, accessed on September 1, 2014; Staff Writers, "Russia Plans Super-heavy Rocket for Lunar, Mars Missions." *Space Travel*, July 1, 2014, available at: www.space-travel.com/reports/Russia_creates_super_heavy_rocket_for_Lunar_Martian_programs_999.html, accessed on July 3, 2014; Staff Writers, "Putin Approves Developing Super-Heavy Rockets With Up to 150-Ton Cargo Capacity." *Space Travel*, September 3, 2014, available at: www.space-travel.com/reports/Putin_Approves_Developing_Super_Heavy_Rockets_With_Up_to_150_Ton_Cargo_Capacity_999.html, accessed on September 5, 2014.

[15] Foust, J., "NASA Selects Boulder Option for Asteroid Redirect Mission." *Space News*, March 25, 2015, spacenews.com/nasa-selects-boulder-option-for-asteroid-redirect-mission/, accessed on February 8, 2016.

[16] ESA, "Cubesats Offered Deep-Space Ride on ESA Asteroid Probe." *ESA*, February 25, 2015, available at: www.esa.int/Our_Activities/Space_Engineering_Technology/CubeSats_offered_deep-space_ride_on_ESA_asteroid_probe, accessed on February 27, 2015.

[17] Berger, E., "NASA Official Warns Private Sector: We're Moving on from Low-Earth Orbit." *ARS Technica*, December 7, 2015, available at: arstechnica.com/science/2015/12/nasa-official-warns-private-sector-were-moving-on-from-low-earth-orbit/, accessed on December 9, 2015.

Nonetheless, interest exists in using public-private partnerships to carry out some of these long-distance programs. For instance, NASA is entertaining the possibility of involving commercial satellites in its missions to the Moon and Mars. In January 2014, NASA announced that it was seeking ways to increase its cooperation with commercial companies, in order to begin flights to the Moon. Specifically, NASA sought proposals from commercial companies to partner with it in developing small lunar landers, capable of delivering cargo to the Moon.[18] In July 2014, NASA issued a request for information (RFI), to examine the possibility of using commercial satellites to provide telecommunications capabilities for future robotic missions to Mars.[19]

Greater Independence in Global Space Systems

Traditional space club members raise the bar and distinguish themselves from other emerging actors by stressing the value of having autonomous access to space, indigenous development, and the use of large space systems and infrastructures. World powers and emerging ones attribute great value to having their own satellite navigation systems, with impressive accomplishments, instead of relying on the American GPS. In recent years, indigenous GPS development has become a means and a symbol of power and high standing. As noted above, Russia invests valuable resources in its GLONASS System, and plans to indigenously develop all parts and components for it in the future.[20] In 2013, China began to operate the Beidou satellite navigation system at the regional level, with the aim of operating it at the global level. The European Galileo system is also expected to be fully operational within several years. India is working on a regional space navigation system, as is Japan.[21]

---

[18] Klotz, I., "NASA Looking for Commercial Lunar Landers," *Space News*, January 17, 2014, available at: spacenews.com/39142nasa-looking-for-commercial-lunar-landers/, accessed on January 20, 2014.

[19] Staff Writers, "NASA Seeks Proposals for Commercial Mars Data Relay Satellites," *Mars Daily*, July 25, 2014, available at: www.marsdaily.com/reports/NASA_Seeks_Proposals_for_Commercial_Mars_Data_Relay_Satellites_999.html, accessed on July 26, 2014.

[20] Staff Writers, "Russia Unable To Reject Foreign Parts in GLONASS Satellites." *GPS Daily*, September 22, 2014, available at: www.gpsdaily.com/reports/Russia_Unprepared_to_Reject_Foreign_Parts_in_GLONASS_Satellites_999.html, accessed on September 24, 2014.

[21] Staff Writers, "ISRO to Launch India's Third Navigation Satellite on October 16." *GPS Daily*, October 14, 2014, available at: www.gpsdaily.com/reports/ISRO_to_Launch_Indias_Third_Navigation_Satellite_on_October_16_999.html, accessed on October 16, 2014.

Another example of developing global space infrastructure that may serve as criteria for differentiating members from non-members is Space Situational Awareness (SSA). In recent years, tracking of satellites and objects in space, which provides warnings about possible dangers of satellite collisions, became highly significant for space security and sustainability. At present, most of the monitoring and tracking activity is conducted by the United States. However, other leading spacefaring nations are showing interest in developing independent SSA capabilities. Russia established an independent system to monitor and follow up on entities in space, to provide better protection for its properties in space.[22] In June 2015, the Russian Ministry of Defense announced an upgrade for its existing system.[23]

Similarly, the European Union has begun to move forward on establishing a space surveillance network via a consortium of five countries: France, Germany, Italy, Spain, and the United Kingdom. The purpose is to coordinate the optical and radar tracking telescopes that they each have in space in order to reduce Europe's dependency on the American space surveillance system and to enhance Europe's autonomy in this field.[24] This program will operate separately from the ESA's space surveillance program.

China established a center for monitoring space debris, jointly managed by the State Administration of Science, Technology and Industry for National Defense (SASTIND) and the Chinese Academy of Sciences (CAS).[25] India is developing sophisticated radar to track ten objects simultaneously from a distance of 620 miles (1,000 kilometers). The Indian Space Agency will be able to track the return of space vehicles to earth's atmosphere, protect its property in space, and monitor space debris with it.[26]

---

[22] Staff Writers, "Guardians of the Galaxy: Russia Creates International Space Patrol." *Space Daily*, April 12, 2015, available at: www.spacedaily.com/reports/Guardians_of_the_Galaxy_Russia_Creates_International_Space_Patrol_999.html, accessed on February 8, 2016; Staff Writers, "Guardians of the Galaxy: Russia Creates International Space Patrol," *Sputnik News*, April 1, 2015, available at: sputniknews.com/military/20150401/1020316462.html, accessed on February 8, 2016.

[23] Staff Writers, "Russia to Build New Generation Space Surveillance Systems" *Space War*, June 22, 2015, available at: www.spacewar.com/reports/Russia_to_Build_New_Generation_Space_Surveillance_Systems_999.html, accessed on February 8, 2016.

[24] de Selding, P. B., "A European Space Surveillance Network Inches Forward," *Space News*, June 17, 2015, available at: spacenews.com/a-european-space-surveillance-network-inches-forward/, accessed on February 8, 2016.

[25] Zhang, T., (ed.), "China Launches Space Junk Monitoring Center." *China Military Online*, August 6, 2015, available at: english.chinamil.com.cn/news-channels/2015-06/08/content_6530203.htm. Accessed on February 8, 2016.

[26] Staff Writers, "ISRO to Launch First Indigenous Multi-object Tracking Radar in Next 3 Months." *Space Daily*, May 21, 2015, available at: www.spacedaily.com/reports/ISRO_

Space Mining

Looking to the future, one can identify space mining as another area of expertise that may be used to set a higher boundary to the space club through strong involvement by the private sector. Celestial bodies like the Moon and asteroids contain materials and precious metals such as platinum, gold, iron, helium-3, and even water, which are all valuable for human activity on Earth and beyond. To many, space mining is mainly science fiction. Nevertheless, many experts in space exploration agree that it is only a matter of time until a breakthrough is achieved. The private sector is already playing a role in this endeavor. In 2013, two companies were created in order to pursue this goal and were able to raise significant funds to realize their ambitions. The year 2015 will be remembered as the year in which the first national legislation to address space mining was adopted. In the United States, the Spurring Private Aerospace Competitiveness and Entrepreneurship Act was signed into law by US President Barack Obama in November 2015. This act stipulates that the United States does not assert sovereignty or exclusive rights or jurisdiction over, or the ownership of, any celestial bodies. Nevertheless, it includes provisions to protect the property rights of private companies that will mine asteroids for minerals.[27]

In 2016, the government of Luxembourg announced it would seek to develop an industrial sector to mine asteroid resources in space through the creation of regulatory and financial incentives.[28] Under this initiative, the government would invest more than $200 million in research, technology, and the direct purchase of equity in companies relocating to Luxembourg.[29] In November 2016, it has adopted a draft law to create

---

to_launch_first_indigenous_multi_object_tracking_radar_in_next_3_months_999.html, accessed on February 8, 2016.

[27] Foust, J., "House Approves Commercial Space Bill," *Space News*, May 21, 2015, available at: http://spacenews.com/house-approves-commercial-space-bill/, accessed on February 8, 2106. Koebler, J., "The US Mulls Breaking an International Treaty So Americans Can Mine Asteroids," *MotherBoard*, May 14, 2015, available at: http://motherboard.vice.com/read/the-us-mulls-breaking-an-international-treaty-so-americans-can-mine-asteroids?utm_source=mbfb, accessed on February 8, 2016; Foust, J., "U.S. Senate Passes Compromise Commercial Space Bill," *Space News*, November 11, 2015, available at: http://spacenews.com/u-s-senate-passes-compromise-commercial-space-bill/, accessed on February 8, 2016; de-Selding, P. B., "New U.S. Space Mining Law's Treaty Compliance May Depend on Implementation", *Space News*, December 9, 2015. available at: http://spacenews.com/u-s-commercial-space-acts-treaty-compliance-may-depend-on-implementation/, accessed on October 18, 2016.

[28] de-Selding, P. B., "Luxembourg to Invest in Space-based Asteroid Mining," *Space News*, February 3, 2016, available at: http://spacenews.com/luxembourg-to-invest-in-space-based-asteroid-mining/, accessed on February 6, 2016,

[29] de-Selding, P. B., "Luxembourg Invests to Become the 'Silicon Valley of Space Resource Mining', *Space News*, June 3, 2016, available at: http://spacenews.com/luxembourg-

the legal framework for such companies to operate in Luxembourg.[30] Other governments are following suit by developing legislation and other mechanisms to support such initiatives.

Once space mining becomes technologically and economically feasible, it could dramatically change the global economy and world politics. Such a development will have significant consequences for the space club.

Formalizing the Club

Another potential option to preserve the small size of the club and its exclusive role in world politics is by transforming it into a formal club. A process of formalization may be driven by two different sets of considerations or actors: commercial considerations and national security considerations.

The rapidly growing space market and commercialization of space activity enhances the demand for a secure and sustainable space environment and responsible activity by all space actors. In recent years, a number of international efforts have been undertaken with the purpose of drawing up rules of operation and agreements, so as to ensure sustainability in the space environment. The strategic tensions between the United States, Russia, China, and other less powerful countries have affected these processes, making an international agreement on this issue only a distant possibility. Progress at the multilateral diplomatic level suffers from deceleration and even stagnation. A change toward greater regulation and standardization may be driven by the private sector.

The need to coordinate and organize global space activity, especially in light of the growing threat to the sustainability and safety of the space environment posed by crowded orbits and space debris induces improvements in monitoring and coordination of activities in space. Moltz (2007) argues that commercial actors, non-military actors, and other entities are expected to constitute a larger proportion of the international system in the coming decades. As the nascent commercial participants do now, they would pressure their governments to coordinate space activity, especially with regards to their military activity. Thus, they are expected to affect the

---

invests-to-become-the-silicon-valley-of-space-resource-mining/, accessed on October 18, 2016; de-Selding, P. B., "Luxembourg Taking Major Stake in Planetary Resources' European Business," June 13, 2016, available at: http://spacenews.com/luxembourg-government-to-buy-up-to-49-of-planetary-resources-european-business/, accessed on October 18, 2016.

[30] "Luxembourg Gets Serious About Space Mining," *Deutsche Welle*, November 11, 2016, available at: http://www.dw.com/en/luxembourg-gets-serious-about-space-mining/a-36 363959, accessed on November 13, 2016.

development of future guidelines and definitions of legitimate uses of space assets in the space environment.[31] In this context, it is logical to assume that a bottom-up demand would be made by the commercial sector to set explicit guidelines at either the national or international levels, in order to ensure greater responsibility by all actors in space.

Although almost all countries of the world benefit from space technology and many have an asset in space, only a handful of countries have the capacity to commercially launch objects into space. Instead of reaching worldwide consent about acceptable and unacceptable behavior in the global commons of space for all nations to follow, this small number of countries with commercial capabilities could draw up the guidelines. They could do this by international arrangement between them, or through separate domestic legislation that each of them would pursue. In this case, regardless of their consent with this legislation, satellite producers and operators would have to adapt their practices and technicalities to the guidelines, which would ensure responsible activity and safe de-orbiting once missions are completed. Such a process may lead to the formation of a launch supplier regime, i.e. the formalization of the space club around the countries that have commercial capability to launch satellites into space.

In the event that an arrangement of this kind may be reached among countries with commercial launch capacity, countries which have the capability to launch objects into space but lack commercial scale may adhere to the regime by incorporating its principles into their practices.

Further development of this regime may include an arrangement with non-launching countries to motivate them to accept it and abide by its rules. For example, these countries could be provided with space technology, knowhow, and science by an international space technology and research (I-STAR) agency envisioned to be similar to the International Atomic Energy Agency (IAEA).[32] The agency would work with its partners to promote safe, secure, and peaceful space programs. In addition, the I-STAR agency would be responsible for regulating the use of space technology and traffic management in order to mitigate and minimize the quantity of space debris. Efficient tools to verify and enforce compliance would be required to do so. This arrangement could also include the licensing of space mining, in which case the I-STAR agency would be

---

[31] Moltz, J. C., "Next Steps Towards Space Security," in J. M. Logsdon, J. C. Moltz, E. Hinds, (eds.), *Collective Security in Space: European Perspectives* (Washington, DC: Space Policy Institute, 2007), 110–111.

[32] This idea was first introduced in Paikowsky, D., and Ben-Israel, I., "India's Space Program – An Israeli Perspective on Regional Security," *India Review*, 10:4, (October–December, 2011), 394–405.

awarded the mandate to impose a mechanism of taxation on the countries and privately owned companies that would benefit directly from this activity. Revenues from the taxation would be used for the benefit of all. Of course, in the current state of the international system, the development of an international agency of this kind, in addition to or as part of a space regime, seems unlikely to materialize. Nevertheless, the concept described above may serve as a tantalizing prospect and inspire future thinking on the subject rather than function as a proposal for concrete action.

Anti-Satellite Capabilities

Another feasible direction for a future barrier to entry into the space club, which may also lead to the formalization of the club, is the development of military and defense space capabilities, in particular anti-satellite capabilities (ASATs). The development of ASATs requires a variety of capabilities and therefore is considered to be a force multiplier. Thus, ASAT capability could replace space capability itself as a means of power and a symbol of world power status. The military capabilities offered by ASATs and the intangible benefits conferred by developing or acquiring them has led to a growing interest among world powers in their development. In recent years, the United States, China, and Russia have demonstrated abilities in this field.

ASATs produce space debris that may damage functioning space systems. Consequently, the world has recognized that the use of ASATs may cause significant damage to the global economy, to the security of individual countries, and to global security. Therefore, despite the growing interest by many in attaining ASATs, the likelihood of actual using them has decreased.

For this reason, one can assume that world politics is likely to adopt an approach toward anti-satellite capabilities that would be similar to the approach developed during the Cold War regarding military nuclear capabilities. That is, they would be independently developed for deterrence, greater influence, and a higher status achieved through the projection of power rather than actual use.

Possessing anti-satellite capabilities would become a criterion for power and superpower. A country that acquired this capability would get a seat at the global governance table. Under this approach, countries that see themselves as leading players in global politics, and countries that aspire to such a status, would seek to develop independent ASAT capabilities. It is also logical to assume that at some point in the future, in an attempt to prevent irresponsible actors from acquiring such capabilities and using them, a regime similar to the NPT would develop. The result would be a formal space club.

The fact that India, which aspires to be a leading member of the space club, is interested in developing ASATs is significant in this context. India's interest in independent ASAT capabilities stems from its bad experience with the nuclear club from which it was left out. India is working to ensure that this time, if possession of ASATs becomes formalized and limited, as was the case with nuclear weapons, it won't be left out of the club.

To conclude, the history of the space club is an expression of well-known international exclusionary politics on Earth. Motivated by considerations of national security, economics, international status, and national honor, space politics is highly competitive and nationalistic. It is centered on setting boundaries and highlighting the concept of "us" versus "them." Looking far away into the future with a twist of science fiction, will the future journey deeper into space allow humans to leave behind them the existing boundaries between groups on the Earth in favor of more inclusive politics? Will the future search after other forms of life in the universe redesign the concept of "us" versus "them"?

Bibliography

Books

Adler, E., *Communitarian International Relations: The Epistemic Foundation of International Relations*, (London: Routledge, 2004).

Adler, E., and Barnett, M., (eds.), *Security Communities*, (Cambridge: Cambridge University Press, 1981).

Albinski, H. S., *Politics and Foreign Policy in Australia*, (Durham, NC: Duke University Press, 1970).

Almog, O., *The Sabra – A Profile*, (Berkeley, CA: University of California Press, 2000).

Arnold, L., *Britain and the H-Bomb*, (Hampshire: Palgrave, 2001).

Baker J., O'Connell K., and Williamson, R., *Commercial Observation Satellites: At the Leading Edge of Global Transparency*, (Santa Monica, CA: RAND, 2001).

Bell, P. M. H., *France and Britain 1940–1994: The Long Separation*, (New York: Longman, 1997).

Ben-Israel, I., *Israel's Defense Doctrine*, (Ben-Shemen: Modan Publishing House and Maarachot, 2013).

Best, G., *Churchill and War*, (London and New York: Palgrave, Hambledon, and London, 2005).

Blaxland, J., *Strategic Cousins – Australian and Canadian Expeditionary Forces and the British and American Empires*, (Montreal and Kingston, Canada: McGill-Queen's University Press, 2006).

Boyd, L., *Britain's Search for a Role*, (Westmead, Farnborough, Hants: Saxon House and Lexington Books, 1975).

Brodie, B., and Brodie, F. M., *From Crossbow to H-Bomb*, (Bloomington: Indiana University Press, 1973).

Brzezinski, M., *Red Moon Rising*, (New York: Times Books, 2007).

Burleson, D., *Space Programs Outside the United States*, (Jefferson, NC: McFarland & Company Publishers, 2005).

Caidin, M., *Red Star in Space*, (New York: Crowell-Collier Publishing Company, 1963).

Capet, A., (ed.), *Britain, France and the Entente Cordiale since 1904*, (Hampshire: Palgrave Macmillan, 2006).

Cerny, P., *The Politics of Grandeur*, (Cambridge: Cambridge University Press, 1980).

Clark, I., *Nuclear Diplomacy and the Special Relationship*, (Oxford: Clarendon Press, 1994).
Clausewitz, C., *On War*, (Princeton University Press: Princeton New Jersey, 1976).
Cohen, A., *Israel and the Bomb*, (New York: Columbia University Press, 1998).
Cohen, A., *The Worst Kept Secret: Israel's Bargain with the Bomb*, (New York: Columbia University Press, 2010).
Cohen, E., Eisenstadt, M., and Bacevich, A., *Knives, Tanks and Missiles: Israel's Security Revolution*, (Washington, DC: The Washington Institute for Near East Policy, 1998).
Cohen, R., *Culture and Conflict in Egyptian-Israeli Relations*, (Bloomington: Indian University Press, 1990).
Day, D. A., Logsdon, J. M., and Latell, B., *Eye In the Sky: The History of the CORONA Spy Satellites*, (Washington, DC: Smithsonian Institution Press, 1998).
DeGroot, G., *The Bomb – A Life*, (Cambridge: Harvard University Press, 2004).
Deng, Y., *China's Struggle for Status*, (Cambridge: Cambridge University Press, 2008).
Deutsch, K., *The Analysis of International Relations*, Second Edition, (Englewood Cliffs, NJ: Prentice Hall, 1978).
Deutsch, K., Burrell, S., Kann, R., Jr., and Lee, M., *Political Community and the North Atlantic Area; International Organization in the Light of Historical Experience*, (Princeton, NJ: Princeton University Press, 1957).
DeVorkin, D., *Race to the Stratosphere – Manned Scientific Ballooning in America*, (New York: Springer-Verlag, 1989).
DeWitt, D., and Kirton, J., *Canada as a Principal Power*, (Toronto: John Wiley & Sons, 1983).
Dick, S. J., and Launius, R. D., (eds.), *Societal Impact of Spaceflight*, (Washington, DC: NASA History Division, 2007).
Dotto, L., *Canada in Space*, (Toronto: Irwin Publishing Inc., 1987).
Dotto, L., *Canada and the European Space Agency Three Decades of Cooperation*, (Noordwijk, the Netherlands: European Space Agency, 2002).
Finnemore, M., *National Interests in International Society*, (Ithaca, NY: Cornell University Press, 1996).
Flyvbjerg, B., Brizelius, N., and Rothengatter, W., *Megaprojects and Risk: An Anatomy of Ambition*, (Cambridge: Cambridge University Press, 2003).
Fruhling, S., *A History of Australian Strategic Policy since 1945*, (Canberra: Defense Publishing Service, Department of Defense, 2009).
Frutkin, A., *International Cooperation in Space*, (Englewood Cliffs, NJ: Prentice-Hall, Inc., 1965).
Gaddis, J. L., *The Long Peace – Inquiries into the History of the Cold War*, (New York: Oxford University Press, 1987).
Gainor, C., *Arrows to the Moon – Avro's Engineers and the Space Race*, (Burlington, Ottawa: Apogee Books, 2001).
Gainor, C., *Canada in Space – The People and Stories behind Canada's Role in the Exploration of Space*, (Edmonton, Canada: Folklore Publishing, 2006).
Gal, R., *A Portrait of the Israeli Soldier*, (New York: Greenwood Press, 1986).

Gat, A., *War in Human Civilization*, (Oxford: Oxford University Press, 2006).

Gelber, H. G., *The Australian-American Alliance – Costs and Benefits*, (Baltimore: Penguin Books, 1968).

George, A., and Bennett, A., *Case Study and Theory Development in the Social Sciences*, (Cambridge, MA: Harvard University Press, 2005).

Gerth, H. H., and Mills, C. W., (eds.), *From Max Weber: Essays in Sociology*, (London: Routledge & Kegan Paul, 1948).

Gilpin, R., *France in the Age of the Scientific State*, (Princeton, NJ: Princeton University Press, 1968).

Greenfield, L., *Nationalism: Five Roads to Modernity*, (Cambridge, MA: Harvard University Press, 1992).

Grosbard, O., *Menachem Begin – A Portrait of a Leader – A Biography*, (Tel Aviv: Resling Publishing, 2006).

Gyngell, A., and Wesley, M., *Making Australian Foreign Policy*, Second Edition, (Cambridge: Cambridge University Press, 2007).

Hajnal, P., *The G8 System and the G20 – Evolution, Role and Documentation*, (Aldershot: Ashgate, 2007).

Hall, R. B., *National Collective Identity: Social Constructs and International System*, (New York: Columbia University Press, 1999).

Hannesey, P., *The Secret State*, (London: Penguin, 2003).

Hardesty, V., and Eisman, G., *Epic Rivalry – The Inside Story of the Soviet and American Space Race*, (Washington, DC: National Geographic Society, 2007).

Harvey, B. *The Japanese and Indian Space Programs: Two Roads into Space*, (London: Springer Praxis, 2000).

Harvey, B., *China's Space Program – From Conception to Manned Spaceflight*, (Chichester, UK: Springer Praxis, 2004).

Harvey, B., Smid, H., and Pirad, T., *Emerging Space Powers: The New Space Programs of Asia, the Middle East and South America*, (Chichester, UK: Springer Praxis, 2010).

Hays, Peter L., *United States Military Space: Into the Twenty-First Century*, USAF Institute for National Security Studies Occasional Paper 42, (USAF Academy, CO, and Maxwell AFB, AL: Air University Press September 2002).

Hecht, G., *The Radiance of France – Nuclear Power and National Identity after World War II*, (Cambridge: MIT Press, 1998).

Hirschman, A., *Development Projects Observed*, (Washington, DC: Brookings Institution, 1967).

Howard, M., *War and the Nation State*, (Oxford: Clarendon Press, 1978).

Hymans, J., *The Psychology of Nuclear Proliferation*, (Cambridge: Cambridge University Press, 2006).

Jervis, R., *Perception and Misperception in International Politics*, (Princeton, NJ: Princeton University Press, 1978).

Jervis, R., *The Meaning of the Nuclear Revolution*, (Ithaca, NY, Cornell University Press, 1989).

Jervis, R., *The Logic of Images in International Relations*, (New York: Columbia University Press, 1989).

Johnson, D. J., Pace, S., and Gabbard, B. C., *Space Emerging Options for National Power*, (Washington, DC: RAND, 1998).

Johnson-Freese, J., *The Chinese Space Program: A Mystery within a Maze*, (Malabar, FL: Krieger Publishing, 1998).
Johnson-Freese, J., *Space as a Strategic Asset*, (New York: Columbia University Press, 2007).
Johnson-Freese, J., *Heavenly Ambitions: America's Quest to Dominate Space*, (Philadelphia, PA: University of Pennsylvania Press, 2009).
Kalam, A. P. J., *Wings of Fire*, (Hyderabad: Universities Press, 30th impression, 1999).
Kalam, A. P. J., and Pillai, S., *Envisioning an Empowered Nation – Technology for Societal Transformation*, (New Delhi: Tata MacGraw-Hill Publishing, 2004).
Karash, Y., *The Superpower Odyssey – A Russian Perspective on Space Cooperation*, (Reston, VA: American Institute of Aeronautics and Astronautics, 1999).
Karniel, M., *Menachem Begin – A Portrait of a Leader*, (Jerusalem: Reuvan Mas publication, 1998), (Hebrew).
Kash, D. E., *The Politics of Space Cooperation*, (West Lafayette, IN: Purdue University Studies, 1967).
Katzenstein, P., *The Culture of National Security*, (New York: Columbia University Press, 1996).
Kegely, C., and Wittkopf, E. R., *World Politics: Trends and Transformation*, (Belmont: Thomson/Wadsworth, 1999).
Kennedy, P., *The Rise and Fall of the Great Powers*, (New York: Vintage Books, 1987).
Keohane, R., (ed.), *Neo-Realism and Its Critics*, (New York: Columbia University Press, 1986).
Keohane, R., *International Institutions and State Power*, (Boulder, CO: Harvard University, Westview Press, 1989).
Keohane, R., and Nye, J., *Power and Interdependence: World Power in Transition*, (Boston: Little, Brown, 1977).
Kirton, J., (ed.), *Canada, the United States, and Space*, (Toronto: Canadian Institute of International Affairs, 1985).
Klotz, A., and Lynch, C., *Strategies for Research in Constructivist International Relations – International Relations in a Constructed World*, (Armonk, NY: M. E. Sharpe Publishers, Inc., 2007).
Kolodziej, E., *French International Policy under De Gaulle and Pompidou – The Politics of Grandeur*, (Ithaca: Cornell University Press, 1974).
Krasner, S., (ed.), *International Regimes*, (Ithaca: Cornell University Press, 1983).
Krige, J., *American Hegemony and the Postwar Reconstruction of Science in Europe*, (Cambridge, MA and London: The MIT Press, 2006).
Krige, J., Callahan, A. L., and Maharaj, A., *NASA in the World*, (New York: Palgrave Macmillan, 2013).
Krige, J., and Russo, A., *A History of the European Space Agency 1958–1987*, (Noordwijk, the Netherlands: European Space Agency, 2000).
Kulacki, G., and Lewis, J. G., *A Place for One's Mat: China's Space Program 1956–2003*, (Cambridge, MA: American Academy of Arts and Science, 2009).
Lake, D. A., *Hierarchy in International Relations*, (Ithaca, NY: Cornell University Press, 2009).

Lambright, H. W., (ed.), *Space Policy in the Twenty-First Century*, (Baltimore, MD: Johns Hopkins University Press, 2003).

Launius, R. D., Logsodn, J. M., and Smith, R. W., (eds.), *Reconsidering Sputnik – Forty Years since the Soviet Satellite*, (Amsterdam, the Netherlands: Harwood Academic Publishers, 2000).

Lebow, R. N., *A Cultural Theory of International Relations*, (New York: Cambridge, 2008).

Lebow, R. N., *Why Nations Fight*, (New York: Cambridge, 2010).

Levite, A., and Landau, E., *Israel's Nuclear Image – Arab Perceptions of Israel's Nuclear Posture*, (Tel Aviv: Papyrus Tel Aviv University Press, 1994).

Logsdon, J., *The Decision to Go to the Moon: Project Apollo and the National Interest*, (Chicago, IL: University of Chicago Press, 1970).

Logsdon, J., Day, D., and Launius, R. D., (eds.), *Exploring the Unknown – Selected Documents in The History of the US Civilian Space Program Volume II: External Relationships*, (Washington, DC: The NASA History Series, NASA History Office, 1996).

Lupton, D., *On Space Warfare – A Space Power Doctrine*, (Maxwell Air Force Base, AL: Air University Press 1998).

Mandler, P., *The English National Character*, (New Haven, CT, and London: Yale University Press, 2006).

Mardor, M., *Rafael – On the Path of R&D for the Security of Israel*, (Tel Aviv: Maarachot Ministry of Defense Press, 1981).

McCurdy, H., *Space and the American Imagination*, (Washington, DC, and London: Smithsonian Institution Press, 1997).

McDougall, W., *The Heavens and the Earth: A Political History of the Space Age*, (New York: Basic Books, 1985).

Migdal, J. S., *Boundaries and Belongings: States and Societies in the Struggle to Shape Identities and Local Practices*, (Cambridge: Cambridge University Press, 2004).

Millard, D., *An Overview of United Kingdom Space Activity 1957–1987*, (ESA Publications, April 2005).

Mineiro, M. C., *Space Technology Export Controls and International Cooperation in Outer Space*, (New York: Springer Press, 2012).

Moltz, J. C., *The Politics of Space Security*, (Stanford, CA: Stanford University Press, 2008).

Moltz, J. C., *Asia's Space Race*, (New York: Columbia University Press, 2012).

Moltz, J. C., *Crowded Orbits – Conflict and Cooperation in Space*, (New York: Columbia University Press, 2014).

Morgan, K. O., *The People's Peace – British History, 1945–1990*, (Oxford: Oxford University Press, 1992).

Morgenthau, H., *Politics among Nations*, Fourth Edition, (New York: Alfred Knopf, 1967).

Morse, E., *Foreign Policy and Interdependence in Gaullist France*, (Princeton: Princeton University Press, 1973).

Morton, P., *Fire across the Desert: Woomera and the Anglo-Australian Joint Project 1946–1980*, (Canberra: Australian Government Publishing Service, 1989).

Nair, K. K., *Space – The Frontiers of Modern Defence*, (New Delhi: Knowledge World: 2006).

Neufeld, M., *Dreamer of Space – Engineer of War*, (New York: A. A. Knopf, 2007).
Norris, P., *Watching Earth from Space*, (Chichester, England: Springer, 2010).
Nye, J. S., *Bound to Lead: The Changing Nature of American Power*, (New York: Basic Books, 1991).
Oberg, J., *Red Star in Orbit*, (New York: Random House 1981).
Offer, Z., and Kober, A., *Quality and Quantity in Military Buildup*, (Tel Aviv: Maarachot Ministry of Defense Press 1992).
Oye, K. A., *Cooperation under Anarchy*, (Princeton University Press, 1986).
Pacey, A., *Technology in World Civilization*, (Cambridge, MA: MIT Press, 1991).
Papp, D., and McIntyre, R., (eds.), *International Space Policy*, (New York: Quorum Books, 1987).
Paul, T. V., Larson, D., and Wohlforth, W., (eds.), *Status in World Politics*, (Cambridge: Cambridge University Press, 2014).
Peres, S., *David's Sling*, (London: George Weidenfeld and Nicholson Ltd., 1970).
Perkovich, G., *India's Nuclear Bomb*, (Berkley, CA: University of California Press, 1999).
Peter, N., *Space Policies Issues and Trends, 2007–2008, Report 15*, (Vienna: European Space Policy Institute, 2008).
Portree, D., (ed.), *NASA's Origins and the Dawn of the Space Age, Monographs in Aerospace History #10*, (Washington, DC: NASA History Division, September 1998).
Rabinowotz, O., *Bargaining on Nuclear Tests: Washington and Its Cold War Deals*, (Oxford: Oxford University Press, 2014).
Rodman, D., *Defense and Diplomacy in Israel's National Security Experience*, (Brighton: Sussex Academic Press, 2005).
Roland, A., (ed.), *A Space-Faring People: Perspectives on Early Spaceflight*, (Washington, DC: The NASA History Series, 1985).
Roth, G., and Wittich, C., (eds.), *Economy and Society: An Outline of Interpretive Sociology, by Max Weber*, (Berkley: University of California Press, 1978).
Sarabhai, V., *Science Policy and National Development*, (New Delhi: Macmillan, 1974).
Serfaty, S., *France, De Gaulle, and Europe*, (Baltimore, Johns Hopkins Press, 1968).
Shalom, D., *Beyond the Horizon*, (Private printing, 2004).
Shashi, T., *Reasons of State: Political Development and India's Foreign Policy under Indira Gandhi, 1966–1977*, (New Delhi: Vikras, 1982).
Sheehan, M., *The International Politics of Space*, (London, England: Routledge, 2007).
Shepherd, G., and Kruchio, A., *Canada's Fifty Years in Space*, (Burlington, Ontario: Apogee Books Publication, 2008).
Siddiqi, A., *Challenge to Apollo: The Soviet Union and the Space Race, 1945–1974*, (Washington, DC: National Aeronautics and Space Administration, 2000).
Smolders, P., *Soviets in Space*, (Guildford and London, England: Lutterworth Press, 1970).
Solingen, E., *Nuclear Logics*, (Princeton: Princeton University Press, 2007).
Spaey, J., Defay, J., Ladriere, J., Stenmans, A., and Wautrequin, J., *Science for Development*, (Paris: UNESCO, 1971).

Stein, A., *Why Nations Cooperate?* (Ithaca: Cornell University Press, 1990).

Suzuki, K., *Policy Logics and Institutions of European Space Collaboration*, (Burlington, VT: Ashgate Publishing, 2003).

Tellis, A. J., *India's Emerging Nuclear Posture: Between Recessed Deterrence and Ready Arsenal*, (Arlington, VA: RAND, 2001).

Tilford, E. H., *The Revolution in Military Affairs: Prospects and Cautions*, (Carlisle, PA: Strategic Studies Institute, US Army War College, 1995).

Tint, H., *French Foreign Policy since the Second World War*, (London: Wiedenfeld and Nicolson, 1972).

Toffler, A., *The Third Wave*, (New York: W. Morrow, 1980).

Toffler, A., and Toffler, H., *War and Anti-War – Survival at the Dawn of the 21st Century*, (Boston, MA: Little, Brown, 1993).

Van Creveled, M., *Technology and War: From 2000 B.C. to the Present*, (New York: The Free Press, 1989).

Van Dyke, V., *Pride and Power*, (London: Pall Mall Press, 1965).

Vital, D., *The Making of British Foreign Policy*, Second Edition, (London: George Allen and Unwin Ltd., 1971).

Volgy, T., Corbetta, R., Grant, K., and Baird, R., (eds.), *Major Powers and the Quest for Status in World Politics*, (New York: Palgrave Macmillan, 2011).

Wahl, N., *The Fifth Republic – France's New Political System*, (New York: Random House, 1959).

Wallace, W., *The Foreign Policy Process in Britain*, (London: The Royal Institute of International Affairs, 1975).

Watt, A., *The Evolution of Australian Foreign Policy 1938–1965*, (London: Cambridge University Press, 1968).

Watts, B. D., *The Military Use of Space: A Diagnostic Assessment*, (Washington, DC: Center for Strategic and Budgetary Assessments, 2001).

Wendt, A., *Social Theory of International Politics*, (Cambridge, England: Cambridge University Press, 1999).

Zahavi, A., and Zahavi, A., *The Handicap Principle: A Missing Piece of Darwin's Puzzle*, (New York: Oxford University Press, 1997).

Zertal, I., *Israel's Holocaust and the Politics of Nationhood*, (Cambridge: Cambridge Press, 2005).

Journal Articles

Adler, P., and Adler, P., "Dynamics of Inclusion and Exclusion in Preadolescent Cliques," *Social Psychological Quarterly*, 58:3, (1995), 145–162.

Adler, E., and Hass, P. M., "Conclusion: Epistemic Communities, World Order, and the Creation of International Policy Coordination," *International Organization*, 46:1, (Winter 1992), 367–390.

Art, R., "To What Ends Military Power?" *International Security*, 4:4, (Spring 1980), 3–35.

Ashton, N., "Harold Macmillan and the 'Golden Days' of Anglo-American Relations Revisited, 1957–1963," *Diplomatic History*, 29:4, (September 2005), 691–723.

Bailes, K. E., "Technology and Legitimacy: Soviet Aviation and Stalinism in the 1930s," *Technology and Culture*, 17:1, (January 1976), 55–81.

Barnett, M., and Finnemore, M., "The Politics, Power and Pathologies of International Organizations," *International Organizations*, 53:4, (Autumn 1999), 699–732.

Bennett, A., "Case Study Methods in the International Relations Subfield," *Comparative Political Studies*, 40:2, (2007), 170–195.

Bergals, E., "On the Theory of Clubs," *American Economic Review*, 66, 2, (1976), 116–121.

Bially Mattern, J., "Why Soft Power Isn't So Soft: Representational Force and the Sociolinguistic Construction of Attraction in World Politics," *Millennium – Journal of International Studies*, 33, (2005), 583–612.

Buchanan, J. M., "An Economic Theory of Clubs," *Economica*, 32:125, (1965), 1–14.

Burt, R., "Models of Network Structure," *Annual Review of Sociology*, 6, (1980), 79–141.

Clark, P., "Australian Space Looking for a Direction," *Space*, (April–May 1992), 6–12.

Cheng, D., "China's Military Role in Space," *Strategic Studies Quarterly*, 6:1, (Spring 2012), 55–77.

Cohen, E., "A Revolution in Warfare," *Foreign Affairs*, 75: 2, (March/April 1996), 37–54.

Davis, Z., "The Realist Nuclear Regime," *Security Studies*, (Spring/Summer 1993), 79–99.

Day, D., "Taking the 'Special Relationship' to New Heights," *JBIS*, 52, 1999, 417–418.

DeSerpa, A. C., "A Theory of Discriminatory Clubs," *Scottish Journal of Political Economy*, 24:1, (1977), 33–41.

Doetsch, K., "Canada's Role on Space Station," *Acta Astronautica*, 57, (2005), 661–675.

Dougherty, K., "Upper Atmospheric Research at Woomera: The Australian-Built Sounding Rockets," *Acta Astronautica*, 59, (May 2006), 54–67.

Edgerton, D. E. H., "The Contradictions of Techno-Nationalism and Techno-Globalism: A Historical Perspective," *New Global Studies*, 1:1, (2007), 1–32.

Evans, W. M., "The Canadian Space Program – Past, Present, and Future (A History of The Development of Space Policy in Canada)," *Canadian Aeronautics and Space Journal*, 50, (2004), 19–32.

Finnemore, M., "International Organizations as Teachers of Norms: The United Nations Educational, Scientific, and Cultural Organization and Science Policy," *International Organization*, 47:4, (Autumn 1993), 565–597.

Florini, A., "The Evolution of International Norms," *International Studies Quarterly*, 40: 3, (September 1996), 363–389.

France, M., "Back to the Future: Space Power Theory and A.T. Mahan," *Space Policy*, 16, (2000), 237–241.

Gainor, C., "The Chapman Report and the Development of Canada's Space Program," *Quest*, 10:4, (2003), 3–18.

Gire, B., and Schibler, J., "The French National Space Programme, 1950–1975," *JBIS*, 40, (1987), 51–66.

Glaser, C. L., "The Security Dilemma Revisited," *World Politics*, 50:1, (1997), 171–201.

Godefroy, A., "Canada's Early Space Policy Development 1958–1974," *Space Policy*, 19, (2003), 137–141.

Grant, R., "French Defense Policy and European Security," *Political Science Quarterly*, 100:3, (Fall 1985), 411–426.

Gray, C., "Space Power and the Revolution in Military Affairs A Glass Half Full?" *Aerospace Power Journal*, 13:3, (Fall 1999), 23–38.

Greasley, D., and Oxley, L., "A Tale of Two Dominions: Comparing the Macroeconomic Records of Australia and Canada since 1870," *Economic History Review*, 2, (1998), 294–318.

Grynaviski, E., "Contrasts, Counterfactuals, and Causes," *European Journal of International Relations*, 19:4, (December 2013), 823–846.

Haggard, S., and Simmons, B., "Theories of International Regimes," *International Organization*, 41:3, (Summer 1987), 491–517.

Handberg, R., "Outer Space as a Shared Frontier – Canada and the US, Cooperation between Unequal Partners," *American Behavioral Scientist*, 47:10, (June 2004), 1241–1262.

Hansmann, H., "A Theory of Status Organization," *Journal of Law, Economics and Organization*, 2:1, (Spring 1986), 119–130.

Hass, E. R., "Why Collaborate? Issue-Linkage and International Regimes," *World Politics*, 32:3, (April 1980), 357–405.

Hass, E. R., "Words Can Hurt You, or Who Said What to Whom about Regimes," *International Organization*, 36:2, (Spring 1982), 207–243.

Heimann, G., "What Does It Take to Be a Great Power? The Story of France Joining the Big Five," *Review of International Studies*, 41:1, January 2015, 185–206.

Heyman, J., "The Ups and Downs of Australia in Space," *Space Times*, (May–June 2001), 11–14.

Hogg, M., Hohman, Z., and Rivera, J., "Why Do People Join Groups? Three Motivational Accounts from Social Psychology," *Social and Personality Psychology Compass*, 2, (2008), 1269–1280.

Holt, L., "Integrating Space Efforts into Australia's Joint Operations," *Australian Defense Force Journal*, 175, (2008), 51–65.

Hornsey, M. J., "The Individual within the Group: Balancing the Need to Belong with the Need to Be Different," *Personality and Social Psychology Review*, 8:3, (2004), 248–264.

Hughes, C. W., "The Slow Death of Japanese Techno-Nationalism? Emerging Comparative Lessons for China's Defense Production," *Journal of Strategic Studies*, 34:3, (2011), 451–479.

Huntley, W. L., "Smaller State Perspectives on the Future of Space Governance," *Astropolitics*, 5:3, (2007), 237–271.

Jackson, J. M., "A Space for Conceptualizing Person-Group Relationships," *Human Relations*, 12:1, (1959), 3–15.

Jervis, R., "Cooperation under the Security Dilemma," *World Politics* 30:2, (January 1978), 167–214.
Jervis, R., "Security Regimes," *International Organization*, 36:2, (1982), 357–378.
Johnson-Freese, J., "The Geostrategic, Techno-Nationalist Push into Space," *OASIS*, (2014), 9–22.
Katzenstein, P., Keohane, R., and Krasner, S., "International Organization and the Study of World Politics," *International Organization*, 52:4, (Autumn 1998), 645–685.
Kinsella, D., and Chima, J., "Symbols of Statehood: Military Industrialization and Public Discourse in India," *Review of International Studies*, 27, (2001), 353–373.
Knorr, K., "On the International Implications of Outer Space," *World Politics*, 12:4, (July 1960), 564–584.
Kolodziej, E. A., "Revolt and Revisionism in the Gaullist Global Vision: An Analysis of French Strategic Policy," *The Journal of Politics*, 3:2, (May 1971), 448–477.
Kulacki, G., "Chinese Intentions in Space – A Historical Perspective for Future Cooperation" *Space and Defense*, 4:1, (Winter 2010), 101–113.
Larson, D., and Shevchenko, A., "Status Seekers: Chinese and Russian Responses to U.S. Primacy," *International Security*, 34:4, (2010), 63–95.
Levi, J., "The Offensive/Defensive Balance of Military Technology: A Theoretical and Historical Analysis," *International Studies Quarterly*, 28:2, (1984), 219–238.
Logsdon, J. M., "A Sustainable Rationale for Human Spaceflight," *Issues in Science and Technology*, (Winter 2004), 31–34.
Logsdon, J. M., "Human Space Flight and National Power," *High Frontier*, (March 2007), 11–13.
MacLean, A., and Sheehan, M., "A Hare Turned Tortoise: 40 Years of UK Space Policy," *Quest*, 6:4, (Winter 1998), 15–24.
Mahoney, J., "Qualitative Methodology and Comparative Politics," *Comparative Political Studies*, 40:2, (2007), 122–144.
Mallett, J., "Canada's Space Programs," *Space Policy Journal*, 6:1, (February 1990), 53–59.
Marriott, J., "Britain's Space Program – A Respectable Past and a Future Yet Uncharted," *Air Force Magazine*, (August 1970), 58–63.
Marwah, O., "India's Nuclear and Space Programs: Intent and Policy," *International Security*, 2:2, (Fall 1977), 96–121.
Maslow, A., "A Theory of Human Motivation," *Psychological Review*, 50:4, (1943), 370–396.
McGuire, M., "Private Good Clubs and Public Good Clubs: Economic Models of Group Formation," *Swedish Journal of Economics* 74:1, (1972), 84–99.
Merrett, N., "New Directions for the Heavens from National Security Statements," *Australian Defense-Business Review*, (January–February 2009), 43–47.

Middleton, B., "Australia's Space Development at the End of the 20th Century," *News Bulletin*, 20:8, (May 1995), 81–90.

Middleton, B. S., and Cory, E. F., "Australian Space Policy," *Space Policy Journal*, (February 1989), 41–46.

Mistry, D., "The Geo-Strategic Implications of India's Space Program," *Asian Survey*, 41:6, (2001), 1023–1043.

Moll., K., "Politics, Power, and Panic: Britain's 1900 Dreadnoughts 'Gap'," *Military Affairs*, 29:3, (Autumn 1965), 133–144.

Mowthorpe, M., "The Soviet/Russian Approach to Military Space," *The Journal of Slavic Military Studies*, 15:3, (September 2002), 24–48.

Nakayama, S., "Techno-Nationalism versus Techno-Globalism," *East Asian Science, Technology and Society: An International Journal*, 6:1, (2012), 9–15.

Nye, J., and Owens, W., "America's Information Edge," *Foreign Affairs*, 75: 2, (March/April 1996), 20–36.

Ocampo, A., Friedman, L., and Logsdon, J., "Why Space Science and Exploration Benefit Everyone," *Space Policy*, 14, (1998), 137–143.

Onea, A. T., "Between Dominance and Decline: Status Anxiety and Great Power Rivalry," *Review of International Studies*, 40:1, (January 2014), 125–152.

Owens, W., "The Once and Future Revolution in Military Affairs," *Joint Force Quarterly*, 31:3, (Summer 2002), 55–61.

Paikowsky, D., "From the Shavit-2 to Ofeq-1– A History of the Israeli Space Effort," *Quest*, 18:4, (Fall 2011), 4–12.

Paikowsky, D., and Ben-Israel, I., "India's Space Program – An Israeli Perspective on Regional Security," *India Review*, 10:4, (October–December, 2011), 394–405.

Paikowsky, D., Baram, G., and Ben-Israel, I., "Trends in Government Space Activity and Policy in 2013," *Astropolitics*, 12, (October 2014), 107–126.

Paikowsky, D., Baram, G., and Ben-Israel, I., "Trends in Space Activities in 2014: The Significance of Space Activities of Governments," *Acta Astronautica*, (January 2016), 187–198.

Pant, H. V., "India-Israel Partnership: Convergence and Constraints," *Middle East Review of International Affairs [MERIA]*, 4, (December 2004), 60–73.

Parkinson, R. C., "Review of Rationales for Space Activity," *Journal of The British Interplanetary Society*, 51, (1998), 275–280.

Quandt, W., "Soviet Policy in the October Middle East War-II," *International Affairs*, 53:4, (October, 1977), 587–603.

Rao, U. R., "India's Space Program – Past, Present and Future," *Harvard Asian Pacific Review*, 9:2, (Spring 2008), 24–27.

Rochester, J. M. The Rise and Fall of International Organizations. *International Organizations*, 40:4, (Autumn 1986), 777–813.

Rumsfeld, D., "Transforming the Military," *Foreign Affairs*, 81:3, (May/June 2002), 20–32.

Sagan, S., "Why Do Nations Build Nuclear Weapons? Three Models in Search of a Bomb," *International Security*, 21:3, (Winter 1996–1997), 54–86.

Sanders, B., "The French Diamant Rockets," *Quest*, 7:1, (Spring 1999), 18–22.

Sandler, T., and Tschirhart, J., "Club Theory: Thirty Years Later," *Public Choice*, 93, (1997), 335–355.

Sato, Y., "A Contested Gift of Power: American Assistance to Japan's Space Launch Vehicle Technology, 1965–1975," *Historical Scientiarum*, 11:2, (2001), 176–204.
Savant, S. S., and Seelan, S. K., "India's Remote-Sensing Program – A Historical Perspective," *Quest*, 24:4, 2005, 26–33.
Scott, W., "Strategic Space," *Aviation Week & Space Technology*, 161:16, (October 25, 2004), 83–86.
Serale, T. R., "The Air Force of the Future," *Air and Space Power Journal*. 18:2, (Summer 2004), 19–26.
Sheldon, K. M., and Bettencourt, B. A., "Psychological Need-Satisfaction and Subjective Well-Bring within Social Groups," *British Journal of Social Psychology*, 41, (2002), 25–38.
Shelton, W., "The United States and the Soviet Union: Fourteen Years in Space," *Russian Review*, 30:4, (1971), 322–334.
Sherwood, R., "Britain in Space," *Spaceflight*, 33, (May 1991), 174–176.
Simmons, N., "The British National Space Program," *Spaceflight*, (January 1971), 6–11.
Simpson, J., Acton, P., and Crowe, S., "The Israeli Satellite Launch," *Space Policy*, (May 1989), 117–128.
Smucker, O., "The Campus Clique as an Agency of Socialization," *Journal of Educational Sociology*, 21:3, (November 1947), 163–168.
Sokolsky, J., "A Seat at the Table: Canada and Its Alliances," *Armed Forces and Society*, 16:1, (Fall 1989), 11–35.
Sorenson, J., Tschirhart, J., and Whinston, A., "Private Good Clubs and the Core," *Journal of Public Economics*, 10:1, (1978), 77–95.
Spufford, F., "Operation Backfire," *London Review of Books*, (October 28, 1999), 21–27.
Steinberg, G., "Large Scale National Projects as Political Symbols," *Comparative Politics*, 19:3, (April, 1987), 331–346.
St-Hilaire, A., "North America and the Francophonie: Local and Transnational Movements for the Survival of French-Speaking North America," *Language Science*, 19:4, (1997), 369–380.
Sulfikar, A., "Nationalist Rhetoric and Technology Development: The Indonesian Aircraft Industry in the New Order Regime," *Technology in Society*, 29:3, (2007), 283–293.
Suzuki, K., "Administrative Reforms and the Policy Logics of Japanese Space Policy," *Space Policy*, 21, (2005), 11–19.
Thomson, D., "General de-Gaulle and the Anglo-Saxons," *International Affairs*, 41:1, (January, 1965), 11–21.
Tiebout, C., "A Pure Theory of Local Expenditures," *Journal of Political Economy*, 65:5, (1956), 416–424.
Von-Welck, S. F., "India's Space Policy – A Developing Country in the Space Club," *Space Policy*, (November 1987), 326–334.
Wallace, W., "Foreign Policy and National Identity in the United Kingdom," *International Affairs*, 67:1, (1991), 65–80.
Wendt, A., "Collective Identity Formation and the International State," *American Political Science Review*, 88:2, (1994), 384–396.

Whyte, N., and Gummett, P., "Far beyond the Bounds of Science: The Making of the United Kingdom's First Space Policy," *Minerva*, 35, (1997), 139–169.

Wright, D., "What Went Wrong with Dan Dare? The Failure of England's Space Program," *History Today*, 47:7, (July 1999). Available at: http://www.historytoday.com/dave-wright/what-went-wrong-dan-dare. Accessed on June 1, 2016.

Zahavi, A., "Mate Selection – A Selection for a Handicap," *Journal of Theoretical Biology*, (1975), 53, 205–241.

Zhuk, E. I., "Astronautics: The Military-Political Aspect," *Military Thought*, (March–April 2003). Available at: https://www.highbeam.com/doc/1G1-107201419.html. Accessed on June 6, 2016.

Zorn, E. L., "Israel's Quest for Satellite Intelligence," *Studies in Intelligence*, 10, (Winter–Spring 2001), 33–38.

Chapters in Edited Books

Baker, J., "Case Studies in Using Commercial Satellite Imagery for Regional Conflict Resolution," in D. Johnson, and E. Levite, (eds.), *Toward Fusion of Air and Space*, (Washington, DC: RAND & Fisher Institute, 2003), 98–106.

Baker, J., and Johnson, D., "Security Implications of Commercial Satellite Imagery," in J. Baker, K. O'Connell, and R. Williamson, (eds.), *Commercial Observation Satellites: At the Leading Edge of Global Transparency*, (Santa Monica, CA: RAND Corporation, 2001), 101–138.

Ben-Israel, I., "Security, Technology and the Future Battlefield," in H. Golan, (ed.), *Israel's Security Net – Core Issues of Israel's National Security in Its Sixth Decade*, (Tel Aviv: Maarachot Ministry of Defense Press, 2001), 269–327, (Hebrew).

Ben-Israel, I., "The Revolution in Military Affairs in the War in Iraq," in S. Feldman and M. Grundman, (eds.), *After the War in Iraq*, (Tel Aviv: Jaffe Center for Strategic Studies, Tel Aviv University Press, 2004), 55–74.

Brown, B., "The Role of Peer Groups in Adolescent Adjustment to Secondary School," in T. J. Berndt and G. W. Ladd, (eds.), *Peer Relationships in Child Development*, (New York: Wiley & Sons, 1989), 188–215.

Button, K., "Introduction to Defining Aerospace Policy," in K. Button, J. Lammersen-Baum, and R. Stough, (eds.), *Defining Aerospace Policy*, (Burlington, VT: Ashgate Publishing, 2004), 5–12.

Collin, A., "The Canadian Space Program," in J. Kirton, (ed.), *Canada, the United States, and Space*, (Toronto: Canadian Institute of International Affairs, 1985), 55–64.

Day, D., "Cover Stories and Hidden Agendas: Early American Space and National Security Policy" in R. D. Launius, J. M. Logsdon, and R. W. Smith, (eds.), *Reconsidering Sputnik – Forty Years since the Soviet Satellite*, (Amsterdam: Harwood Academic Publishers, 2000), 161–195.

Deibert, R., "Unfettered Observation," in H. W. Lambright, (ed.), *Space Policy in the Twenty-First Century*, (Baltimore, MD: Johns Hopkins University Press, 2003), 89–114.

Eyre, D., and Suchman, M., "Status, Norms and the Proliferation of Conventional Weapons: An Institutional Theory Approach," in P. Katzenstein, (ed.), *The Culture of National Security*, (New York: Columbia University Press, 1966), 79–113.

Ezell, E. C., "Space Activities in the Soviet Union, Japan, and the People's Republic of China," in A. Roland, (ed.), *A Space-Faring People: Perspectives on Early Spaceflight*, (Washington, DC: The NASA History Series, 1985), 118–130.

Franklin, C., "Industrial Opportunities in Space," in B. MacDonald, (ed.), *Canada's Strategy for Space*, (Toronto: The Canadian Institute of Strategic Studies, Spring 1983), 53–66.

Galloway, E., "Sputnik and the Creation of NASA: A Personal Perspective," *NASA – 50 Years of Exploration and Discovery*, (Tampa, FL: Faircount LLC, 2008), 48–49.

Handel, M., "The Evolution of Israeli Strategy: The Psychology of Insecurity and the Quest for Absolute Security," in W. Murray, M. Knox, and A. Bernstein, (eds.), *The Making of Strategy: Rulers, States, and War*, (Cambridge: Cambridge University Press, 1994), 534–578.

Harford, J., "Korolev's Triple Play: Sputniks 1, 2 and 3," in R. D. Launius, J. M. Logsdon, and R. W. Smith, (eds.), *Reconsidering Sputnik – Forty Years since the Soviet Satellite*, (Amsterdam: Harwood Academic Publishers, 2000), 73–94.

Kacowitz, A., "Case Study Methods in International Security Studies," in D. F. Sprinz and Y. Wolinsky-Nahmias, (eds.), *Models, Numbers, and Cases: Methods for Studying International Relations*, (Ann Arbor, MI: University of Michigan Press, 2004), 107–128.

Kennedy, D. E., "The Debate on Distinctive Australian Foreign Policy," in M. Teichman, (ed.), *New Directions in Australian Foreign Policy – Ally, Satellite or Neutral?*, (Victoria: Penguin Books, 1969), 65–78.

Khrushchev, S., "The First Earth Satellite," in R. D. Launius, J. M. Logsdon, and R. W. Smith, (eds.), *Reconsidering Sputnik – Forty Years since the Soviet Satellite*, (Amsterdam: Harwood Academic Publishers, 2000), 267–287.

Khrushchev, S., "How Rockets Learned to Fly" in V. Hardesty, and G. Eisman, *Epic Rivalry – The Inside Story of the Soviet and American Space Race*, (Washington, DC: National Geographic Society, 2007), xi–xiii.

Kirton, J., "Canada-United States Space Co-operation; Current Choices," in J., Kirton, (ed.), *Canada, the United States, and Space*, (Toronto: Canadian Institute of International Affairs, 1985), 79–98.

Kleiman, A., "Israeli Negotiating Culture," in T. Cofman, (ed.), *How Israelis and Palestinians Negotiate – A Cross-Cultural Analysis of the Oslo Peace Process*, (Washington, DC: United States Institute of Peace Press, 2005), 81–132.

Knottnerus, J. D., "Social Structure Analysis and Status Generalization: The Contributions and Potential of Expectation State Theory," in J. Szmatka, J. Skvoretz, and J. Berger, (eds.), *Status, Network, and Structure – Theory Development in Group Processes*, (Stanford: Stanford University Press, 1997), 119–136.

Krige, J., "Building a Third Space Power," in R. D. Launius, J. M. Logsdon, and R. W. Smith, (eds.), *Reconsidering Sputnik – Forty Years since the Soviet Satellite*, (Amsterdam: Harwood Academic Publishers, 2000), 289–307.

Krige, J., "NASA as an Instrument of US Foreign Policy," in S. J. Dick, and R. D. Launius, (eds.), *Societal Impact of Spaceflight*, (Washington, DC: NASA History Division, 2007), 210–211.

Krige, J., "Building Space Capability through European Regional Collaboration," in S. Dick, (ed.), *Remembering the Space Age*, (Washington, DC: NASA History Office, 2008), 37–53.

Laidet, L., "The French Space Program," in W. Thompson and S. Guerrier, (eds.), *Space: National Programs and International Cooperation*, (Boulder, CO: Westview Press, 1989), 63–78.

Lakoof, S., "Scientists, Technologists and Political Power," in I. Spiegel-Rosing and D. de Solla-Price, (eds.), *Science, Technology and Society*, (London: Sage Publications, 1977), 355–392.

Launius, R. D., "What Are Turning Points in History and What Were They in the Space Age?," in S. J., Dick and R. D. Launius, (eds.), *Societal Impact of Spaceflight*, (Washington, DC: NASA History Division, 2007), 19–40.

Logsdon, J., "Opportunities for Policy Historians: The Evolution of the US Civilian Space Program," in A. Roland, (ed.), *A Space-Faring People: Perspectives on Early Spaceflight*, (Washington, DC: The NASA History Series, 1985), 81–107.

Logsdon, J., "Outer Space and International Space Policy: The Rapidly Changing Issues," in D. Papp and R., McIntyre, (eds.), *International Space Policy*, (New York: Quorum Books, 1987), 31–41.

Logsdon, J., "The Development of International Space Cooperation," in J. Logsdon, D. Day and R. D. Launius, (eds.), *Exploring the Unknown – Selected Documents in the History of the US Civilian Space Program Volume II: External Relationships*, (Washington, DC: The NASA History Series, NASA History Office, 1996), 1–15.

Logsdon, J., "Space in the Post-Cold War Environment," S. J. Dick and R. D. Launius, (eds.), *Societal Impact of Spaceflight*, (Washington, DC: NASA History Division, 2007), 89–102

Logsdon, J., "Ten Presidents and NASA," in *NASA – 50 Years of Exploration and Discovery*, (Tampa, FL: Faircount LLC, 2008), 226–239.

Logsdon, J., and Reed, C., "Commercializing Space Transportation" in J. Logsdon, R. Williamson, R. D. Launius, (eds.), *Exploring the Unknown, Selected Documents in the History of the US Civil Space Program*, (Washington, DC: NASA History Division, 1999), 405–422.

Mitchell, R., and Bernauer, T., "Beyond Story-Telling: Designing Case Study Research in International Environmental Policy," in D. F. Sprinz,. and Y. Wolinsky-Nahmias, (eds.), *Models, Numbers, and Cases: Methods for Studying International Relations*, (Ann Arbor: University of Michigan Press, 2004), 81–106.

Moltz, J. C., "Next Steps towards Space Security," in J. M. Logsdon, J. C. Moltz, and E. Hinds, *Collective Security in Space: European Perspectives*, (Washington, DC: Space Policy Institute, 2007), 109–130.

Neufeld, M., "Orbiter, Overflight and the First Satellite: New Light on the Vanguard Decision," in R. D. Launius, J. M. Logsdon, and R. W. Smith, (eds.), *Reconsidering Sputnik – Forty Years since the Soviet Satellite*, (Amsterdam: Harwood Academic Publishers, 2000), 231–258.

O'Connell, K., "Commercial Applications of Payloads and Services: Remote Sensing," in D. Johnson and E. Levite, (eds.), *Toward Fusion of Air and Space*, (Washington, DC: RAND & Fisher Institute, 2003), 29–34.

Pace, S., "Emerging Challenges: National Security Requirements and Economic/Commercial Interests," in D. Johnson and E. Levite, (eds.), *Toward Fusion of Air and Space: Surveying Developments and Assessing Choices for Small and Middle Powers*, (Santa Monica, CA: RAND Corporation, 2003), 39–50.

Pace, S., "The Future of Space Commerce," in H. W. Lambright, (ed.), *Space Policy in the Twenty-First Century*, (Baltimore, MD: Johns Hopkins University Press, 2003), 55–81.

Rao, P. V. M., "No Ambiguity of Purpose – The Indian Space Programme," in P. V. M. Rao, (ed.), *50 Years of Space– A Global Perspective*, (Hyderabad: Universities Press, 2007), 203–244.

Ridgeway, C., "Where Do Status Value Beliefs Come From? New Developments," in J. Szmatka, J. Skvoretz, and J. Berger, (eds.), *Status, Network, and Structure – Theory Development in Group Processes*, (Stanford: Stanford University Press, 1997), 137–158.

Siddiqi, A., "Korolev, Sputnik, and the International Geophysical Year," in R. D. Launius, J. M. Logsdon, and R. W. Smith, (eds.), *Reconsidering Sputnik – Forty Years since the Soviet Satellite*, (Amsterdam: Harwood Academic Publishers, 2000), 43–72.

Siddiqi, A., "Spaceflight in the National Imagination," in S. Dick, (ed.), *Remembering the Space Age*, (Washington, DC: NASA History Office, 2008), 17–36.

Smith, M., "Selling the Moon," in W. Fox and J. Lears, (eds.), *The Culture of Consumption*, (New York: Pantheon Books, 1983), 175–210.

Steinberg, G., "Satellite Capabilities of Emerging Space-Competent States," in *Evolving Trends in the Dual Use of Satellites*, (UNIDIR, 1996), 31–56.

Stone, L., "Britain and the World," in D. Mackie and C. Cook, (eds.), *The Decade of Disillusion: British Politics in the Sixties*, (Bristol: Macmillan St. Martin's Press, 1972), 122–136.

White, H., "Four Decades of the Defense of Australia: Reflections on Australian Defense Policy over the Past 40 Years," in R., Huisken, and M., Thatcher, (eds.), *History as Policy – Framing the Debate on the Future of Australia's Defense Policy*, (Canberra: Australian National University Press, 2007), 163–188.

Williamson, R., "International Cooperation and Competition in Space," in D. Papp and R. McIntyre, (eds.), *International Space Policy*, (New York: Quorum Books, 1987), 105–118.

Williamson, R., "Remote Sensing Policy and the Development of Commercial Remote Sensing," in J. Baker, K. O'Connell, and R. Williamson, (eds.), *Commercial Observation Satellites: At the Leading Edge of Global Transparency*, (Santa Monica, CA: RAND Corporation, 2001), 37–52.

Williamson, R., and Baker, J., "Satellite Technologies and US Policymaking," in R. Williamson, (ed.), *Dual-Purpose Space Technologies*, (Washington, DC: Space Policy Institute, 2001), 6–7.

Reports and Unpublished Material

Biddington, B., "Skin in The Game: Realizing Australia's National Interests in Space to 2025," The Kokoda Foundation, paper no. 7, (May 2008).

Chen, Y., *China's Space Activities, Policy and Organizations, 1956–1986*, unpublished Ph.D. dissertation, George Washington University, (1999).

Drobik, I., "The Role of Defense Science in Achieving Australian Self-Reliance, Australian Defense College," *Monograph Series*, 3, (2003). Available at: http://www.defence.gov.au/adc/hqadc_mono.htm. Accessed on May 20, 2009.

Franklin, C. A., "Alouette/ISIS: How It All Began," IEEE International Milestone in Engineering Ceremony, Shirley Bay, Ottawa, (May 13, 1993). Available at: http://www.ieee.ca/millennium/alouette/alouette_franklin.html. Accessed on January 8, 2009.

Freeland, S., "Australia National Space Law and Space Policy" presentation at the United Nations Workshop on Space Law, Beijing, (November 17–20, 2014). Available at: http://www.unoosa.org/pdf/spacelaw/activities/2014/pres09E.pdf. Accessed on June 21, 2015.

Gibson, R., "Britain and Space," The Eighteenth J.D. Bernal Lecture, delivered at Birkbeck College, London, (May 7, 1987).

Godefroy, A. B., *Defense and Discovery Science, National Security, and the Origins of the Canadian Rocket and Space Program 1954–1974*, Ph.D. dissertation, Royal Military College of Canada, (March 2004).

Logsdon, J., *Learning From the Leader – The Early Years of US-Japanese Cooperation in Space*, unpublished paper, (Washington, DC: Space Policy Institute, George Washington University, 2002).

Moody, J. B., *The Importance of Complex Product Systems to the Space Industry in Australia: A Small Satellite Case Study*, unpublished Ph.D. dissertation, The Australian National University, Canberra, (2004).

Morton, P., *Testing Blue Streak at Woomera: An Episode in Anglo-Australian Collaboration and Conflict*, Working Paper No. 32 (Sir Robert Menzies Center for Australian Studies, Institute of Commonwealth Studies, University of London, 1998). Available at: http://www.kcl.ac.uk/content/1/c6/01/51/32/WP32Morton.pdf. Accessed on December 4, 2008.

Moulin, H., "D-1 French Satellite Program (1962–1967)," paper presented at the 47th International Astronautical Congress, Beijing, China, (IAA-96-IAA.2.3.06), (October, 7–11, 1996).

Paikowsky, D., *The Impact of Space Technologies on Warfare and Force Build-Up in the USA Military Forces and the IDF*, M.A. thesis, Tel Aviv University, (2005).

Paikowsky, D., Reichard, A., Baram, G., and Ben-Israel, I., "Space 2015: A Year in Review," report by Yuval Neeman Workshop for Science, Technology and Security at Tel Aviv University. Available at: https://www.gwu.edu/~spi/2015%20A%20year%20in%20review.pdf Accessed on April 2, 2016.

Siemon, N., *Public Policy Planning and Global Technology Dependence: Strategic Factors for a National Space-Related Innovation System*, unpublished Ph.D. dissertation, University of Western Sydney, (2003).

Tegger, J. A., "The French Space Program: Political and Social Implications," AIAA Paper no. 68–898, presented at the Impact of Aerospace Science and Technology on Law and Government Conference, Washington, DC, (August 28–30, 1968) (NASA Head Quarters, History Office, Reference Collection, Country Files: France).

Tonkin, R. and Mace, O., "Australia – A History of the Development of the Australian Student Built Satellite," presented at the IAA 1998 Convention, (September 1998).

Wells, D., *France and Japan in Space: Niche Market Players with Evolving Assets and Roles*, unpublished M.A. dissertation, MIT, (1991).

Yamada, A., "New Techno-Nationalism: How and Why It Grows," paper presented at the International Studies Association Convention, Los Angeles, (2000).

Index

Algeria, 86, 102, 103, 106, 197
Arianspace, 191
ASAT, 10, 25, 34, 46, 154, 199, 206, 220, 228, 229
Asia-Pacific Space Cooperation Organization, 200
Association of Southeast Asian Nations, 188
Australia, 26, 27, 66, 75, 104, 115, 116, 117, 132, 133, 134, 135, 136, 137, 138, 139, 140, 141, 142, 143, 144, 213, 214, 216
   AUSSAT, 136
   FedSat, 137
   Madigan Report, 136, 137
   Sparta, 135
   Woomera, 132, 133, 134, 135
   WRESAT, 135

Ballistic missiles, 8, 9, 10, 12, 14, 49, 51, 52, 59, 70, 98, 134, 153, 189, 206, 207, 208
Begin Menachem, 162, 164, 169, 170
Ben-Gurion David, 89, 145, 160, 168
Bhabha Homi, 149, 151, 152, 156
Blue Origin, 191
Bolden Charles, 202
Bolivia, 196, 200
Brazil, 22, 68, 75, 81, 85, 215
Britain, 22, 26, 27, 43, 44, 55, 66, 68, 78, 79, 92, 93, 94, 95, 96, 97, 98, 99, 100, 102, 103, 104, 105, 108, 109, 110, 111, 112, 113, 114, 115, 116, 126, 132, 133, 134, 135, 136, 142, 143, 145, 167, 201, 213, 214, 215, 216, 234
   Ariel-1, 66, 98, 116
   Black-Arrow, 99, 132
   Black-Knight, 94, 103
   Blue-Streak, 94, 98, 103, 104, 134

   Hurricane, 95
   Prospero, 99, 110, 132

Canada, 12, 26, 27, 66, 75, 95, 104, 115, 116, 117, 118, 119, 120, 121, 122, 123, 124, 125, 126, 127, 128, 129, 130, 131, 132, 135, 139, 140, 141, 142, 143, 144, 198, 213, 214, 215, 216, 237
   Alouette, 66, 116, 118, 139
   Anik, 120, 128
   Avro Arrow, 124
   Canadarm, 116, 120, 121, 122, 124, 125, 130, 131, 132
   Canada's Space Agency, 121, 122, 127, 129, 131, 132, 140
   Chapman Report, 118, 119, 124, 126, 127
   Quebec, 4, 121, 122, 124, 126, 127, 128, 129, 143
   RADARSAT, 122
Chifley Ben, 132
China, 15, 16, 19, 21, 22, 26, 32, 34, 36, 55, 65, 68, 71, 72, 75, 76, 80, 87, 89, 106, 133, 149, 150, 151, 152, 153, 154, 155, 176, 185, 186, 187, 188, 189, 196, 197, 198, 199, 200, 201, 202, 203, 206, 207, 208, 214, 220, 223, 224, 226, 228
   Beidou Satellite Navigation System, 187, 223
   Chang'e-3, 15, 200, 220
Churchill Winston, 79, 94, 95
CIA, 71, 72, 85, 93, 145
CNES, 101, 103, 105, 108, 197
Cold War, 2, 3, 8, 11, 18, 20, 21, 22, 23, 24, 25, 36, 45, 49, 52, 53, 58, 67, 74, 78, 90, 92, 106, 130, 131, 141, 142, 146, 157, 178, 179, 182, 183, 184, 189, 190, 195, 199, 204, 209, 211, 214, 228

248

Index

Cold War Space Race, 19, 199
Czechoslovakia, 58, 63, 64, 88

De Gaulle Charles, 63, 89, 96, 101, 102, 104, 106, 107, 112, 113
Deep Space, 31, 199
Deterrence, 10, 13, 43, 46, 50, 52, 55, 83, 159, 160, 161, 166, 169, 170, 172, 206, 215, 218, 228
Diefenbaker John, 118, 124
Dordain Jean-Jacques, 202, 203
Dreadnoughts, 1, 42, 43
Dual-use, 9, 11, 12, 33, 46, 49, 70, 178, 179, 180, 181, 182, 195

Ecuador, 196
Egypt, 71, 81, 160, 161, 163, 170, 197
Eisenhower Dwight, 53, 54, 55, 56, 57, 69, 96, 112
Eitan Rafael, 163
ELDO, 98, 104, 105, 134
ESRO, 98, 104, 105, 134
Europe, 19, 61, 68, 70, 71, 78, 92, 97, 99, 103, 104, 105, 106, 107, 109, 110, 112, 113, 134, 135, 148, 185, 188, 198, 201, 204, 214, 221, 224
European Space Agency, 22, 64, 75, 77, 92, 99, 100, 103, 104, 106, 114, 120, 125, 188, 189, 198, 201, 202, 203, 204, 220, 221, 222, 224
  Ariane, 103, 105, 189
  Philae, 203, 204
  Spacelab, 64
European Union, 56, 108, 188, 224
Export controls, 7, 20, 35, 183, 186, 195, 199

France, 12, 22, 26, 27, 32, 42, 44, 57, 63, 66, 67, 68, 71, 72, 75, 78, 79, 92, 93, 94, 95, 98, 99, 100, 101, 102, 103, 104, 105, 106, 107, 108, 110, 111, 112, 113, 114, 127, 128, 131, 149, 167, 193, 197, 201, 213, 214, 215, 216, 224
  Diamant, 67, 102, 103, 104, 240
  FR-1, 67, 102
  Veronique, 94
Frutkin Arnold, 4, 62, 67, 68, 70, 84, 150

G7, 131
Gagarin Yuri, 58, 60
Gandhi Indira, 87, 152, 158, 160
Garneau Marc, 121, 129, 140
Germany, 12, 44, 49, 53, 63, 66, 94, 98, 107, 160, 214, 224

Global Navigation Satellite Systems, 187, 220
Gulf War, 179, 180

Handicap Principle, 85, 216
HCOC, 12
Holocaust, 167, 170
Humphrey Hubert, 69

India, 4, 5, 15, 26, 27, 34, 66, 67, 68, 81, 84, 85, 87, 104, 145, 146, 147, 148, 149, 150, 151, 152, 153, 154, 155, 156, 157, 158, 159, 160, 164, 175, 176, 177, 188, 189, 196, 198, 204, 213, 214, 215, 216, 220, 223, 224, 227, 229
  Aryabhata, 153, 159
  Bhaskhara-1, 154
  Chandrayaan-1, 155
  Department of Atomic Energy, 149, 151, 153
  GSLV, 154, 155
  INCOSPAR, 67, 68, 149, 153
  Indian Regional Navigation Satellite System, 188
  ISRO, 153, 224
  Mangalyaan, 4, 155, 204
  Nike-Apache, 150
  PSLV, 81, 154
  SITE, 152
  Thumba, 67, 68, 149, 150
Indonesia, 196
Intelsat, 63, 71, 105
Inter-Agency Space Debris Coordination Committee, 202
International Geophysical Year, 52, 55, 100, 133, 148
International Organizations, 34, 35, 36, 37, 38, 115
International regimes, 36, 37, 38, 39, 88
International Space Station, 116, 121, 129, 131, 132, 144, 190, 191, 199, 221
Iran, 21, 55, 59, 75, 87, 90, 167, 177, 197, 204, 205, 206, 207, 208, 215
  Omid, 205
Iraq, 164, 167, 170, 197
Israel, 22, 26, 27, 34, 71, 75, 82, 87, 89, 145, 146, 147, 154, 160, 161, 162, 163, 164, 165, 166, 167, 168, 169, 170, 171, 172, 173, 174, 175, 176, 177, 192, 205, 213, 214, 215, 216, 227
  Amos series, 100, 164
  Egyptian-Israeli Peace Treaty, 163
  EROS series, 164

Index

Israel Defense Forces, 3, 161, 162, 163, 164, 168, 173
Israel Space Agency, 165, 172
Jericho-2, 171
Ofeq, 82, 87, 90, 162, 164, 171, 172, 174, 175
Shavit-2, 22, 89, 90, 160, 161
TecSAR, 154, 164
Yom Kippur War, 161, 163, 166
Italy, 12, 66, 98, 224

Japan, 12, 16, 22, 66, 68, 71, 72, 75, 79, 80, 103, 113, 135, 137, 186, 196, 207, 220, 223
Johnson Lyndon, 60, 79

Kalam A. P. J., 84, 149, 150, 153, 156, 157, 158, 176
Kazakhstan, 164, 197
Kennedy John, 1, 10, 58, 59, 60, 61, 69, 150
Khrushchev Nikita, 51, 52, 60, 89
Killian James, 56
Korolev Sergey, 51

MacLean Steve, 104, 129, 140
Macmillan Harold, 96, 97, 98, 104, 110
Malaysia, 86, 88, 196
Mars, 4, 5, 15, 155, 197, 203, 204, 220, 221, 222, 223
McNamara Robert, 60, 69
Menzies Robert Gordon, 133, 134
Mexico, 196
Moon, 10, 15, 48, 59, 60, 61, 75, 155, 157, 199, 200, 201, 202, 203, 220, 221, 223, 225
MTCR, 11, 12, 147, 190, 206

NASA, 4, 49, 57, 60, 61, 62, 66, 67, 68, 69, 70, 71, 86, 98, 99, 101, 105, 120, 121, 124, 129, 132, 135, 149, 150, 151, 152, 164, 182, 190, 191, 194, 202, 221, 222, 223, 244
Nation-state club, 1, 2, 5, 6, 7, 14, 17, 18, 27, 28, 33, 34, 35, 39, 210, 211, 212, 217, 218
NATO, 106, 112, 134
Neeman Yuval, 82, 162
Nehru Jawaharlal, 145, 148, 156, 157
Netanyahu Benjamin, 165
New Space, 192, 193
Nigeria, 86, 197, 200
Nixon Richard, 80
NOAA, 203

Non-aligned states, 52, 81, 211
Non-Proliferation Treaty, 1, 38, 146, 206, 229
NORAD, 123, 142
North Korea, 21, 133, 146, 204, 205, 206, 207, 208
Nuclear capability, 10, 38, 69, 80, 95, 96, 133
Nuclear club, 1, 6, 21, 34, 38, 42, 69, 95, 96, 214, 229
Nuclear energy, 6, 8, 31, 38, 54, 81, 108, 157
Nuclear program, 11, 32, 90, 142, 169
Nuclear weapons, 1, 2, 8, 11, 21, 38, 69, 70, 79, 80, 92, 93, 94, 147, 150, 151, 152, 153, 169, 207, 229

OECD, 34, 141

Pakistan, 66, 146, 151, 153, 176, 200
Pearson Lester, 127
Peres Shimon, 160, 165, 173, 174
Portugal, 86
Post-Cold War, 22, 27, 37, 178, 184, 205, 209

Quayle Dan, 180

Rabin Yitzhak, 90, 161, 162
Ramon Ilan, 165
Revolution in Military Affairs, 3, 242
Rogozin Dimitry, 198
Russia, 19, 44, 115, 130, 141, 184, 187, 188, 189, 190, 191, 197, 198, 199, 201, 206, 208, 220, 221, 222, 223, 224, 226, 228
  GLONASS, 182, 187, 223

Sarabhai Vikram, 148, 149, 150, 151, 152, 153, 156, 157, 160
Sato Eisaku, 79
Saudi Arabia, 174, 197
Security community, 36, 37, 38
Security dilemma, 44, 45, 46, 76, 173
Shamir Yitzhak, 87, 173
Sharon Ariel, 82, 164, 175
Shastri Lal Bahadur, 151
Shepard Alan, 4, 58
Singapore, 86, 196
South Africa, 83, 197
South Korea, 21, 75, 82, 88, 133, 196, 205, 206
Soviet Union, 4, 11, 19, 25, 36, 49, 50, 51, 52, 54, 55, 57, 58, 61, 63, 64, 65, 68, 71, 72, 73, 82, 87, 95, 101, 102, 108,

Index 251

112, 118, 142, 149, 150, 153, 154, 162, 167, 171, 178, 182, 188, 189, 190, 198, 199, 212, 213
Interkosmos, 63, 64
Sputnik, 48, 51, 52, 53, 55, 58, 65, 87, 96, 118, 148, 208, 224
Space club, 2, 3, 4, 6, 8, 11, 13, 14, 15, 16, 17, 18, 20, 21, 22, 23, 25, 27, 34, 35, 42, 46, 48, 49, 68, 73, 74, 76, 77, 78, 90, 91, 111, 112, 113, 125, 126, 131, 134, 135, 136, 139, 140, 147, 156, 172, 175, 176, 177, 178, 179, 195, 199, 201, 204, 205, 206, 208, 209, 210, 211, 212, 213, 214, 215, 217, 218, 219, 220, 222, 223, 225, 227, 228, 229
Space Launch Vehicles, 9
Space mining, 225
Space race, 2, 25
Space Situational Awareness, 220, 224
SpaceX, 191, 193
Spain, 224
Superpowers, 5, 7, 8, 10, 11, 13, 14, 27, 39, 40, 41, 42, 48, 49, 50, 51, 58, 61, 62, 70, 72, 73, 74, 78, 83, 88, 91, 103, 105, 106, 109, 111, 112, 146, 151, 157, 171, 184, 211, 212, 214, 215, 216, 217, 220
Surrey Satellite Technology Ltd., 85, 197
Sweeting Martin, 85
Syria, 161, 197

Techno-globalism, 183, 184, 188
Techno-nationalism, 16, 17, 18, 27, 47, 48, 51, 74, 78, 82, 183, 184, 187, 188, 214
Thailand, 86, 188, 200
Trudeau Pierre Elliott, 119, 120, 125, 128
Tse-tung Mao, 89
Turkey, 197

U.N. COPUOS, 57, 58, 77, 86, 174
U.N. COSPAR, 66
U.N. Security Council, 34, 92, 206, 207

Ukraine, 82, 189, 205
United Arab Emirates, 197, 198
United States, 4, 11, 12, 19, 21, 25, 34, 49, 50, 51, 52, 54, 55, 56, 57, 58, 59, 60, 61, 64, 65, 66, 67, 68, 69, 70, 71, 72, 73, 79, 80, 93, 94, 95, 96, 97, 98, 99, 101, 102, 103, 104, 105, 106, 107, 108, 109, 110, 112, 113, 115, 117, 118, 120, 123, 124, 125, 126, 130, 131, 132, 133, 134, 135, 141, 142, 143, 149, 150, 151, 154, 155, 162, 180, 182, 184, 185, 188, 189, 190, 198, 199, 201, 202, 203, 206, 212, 213, 214, 216, 220, 222, 224, 225, 226, 228
Apollo program, 10, 48, 61, 62, 135
CORONA, 111
Explorer-1, 53, 56, 58, 76
Global Positioning System, 182, 183, 187, 223
ITAR, 185
LADEE, 220
LANDSAT, 182
National Aeronautics and Space Council, 69, 152
Redstone, 135
The Shuttle Program, 64, 121, 189
Vanguard satellite, 56

V-2 rockets, 49, 53
Venezuela, 196
Virgin Galactic, 193, 194, 195
Von Braun, Wernher, 53

Webb James, 49, 60, 61, 69, 70, 152
Weitzman Ezer, 163
Wiesner Jerome, 59
Wilson James Harold, 98
WWI, 1, 42, 107, 214
WWII, 1, 42, 49, 70, 79, 94, 95, 97, 106, 108, 111, 112, 115, 118, 132, 133, 142, 214

For EU product safety concerns, contact us at Calle de José Abascal, 56–1°,
28003 Madrid, Spain or eugpsr@cambridge.org.

www.ingramcontent.com/pod-product-compliance
Lightning Source LLC
LaVergne TN
LVHW021657060526
838200LV00050B/2387